The Composer-Piar

Hamelin and The Eight

by Robert Rimm

Foreword by Stephen Hough

AMADEUS PRESS
Portland, Oregon

Photographs are from the author's collection unless otherwise noted.

The author acknowledges permission to publish quotations from

Antony Beaumont, *Busoni the Composer*, 1985. Courtesy of Indiana University Press.
David Charlton, ed., *E. T. A. Hoffmann's Musical Writings*, Trans. Martyn Clarke, 1989.
    Reprinted with the permission of Cambridge University Press.
Edward J. Dent, *Ferruccio Busoni*, 1933. Used by permission of Oxford University Press.
The Etude. Used by permission of the Theodore Presser Company.
Barrie Martyn, *Rachmaninoff: Composer, Pianist, Conductor*, Scolar Press, 1990; and Paul
    Rapoport, *Sorabji: A Critical Celebration*, Ashgate Publishing Company, 1992. Used by
    permission from Ashgate Publishing Limited.
Musical America. Courtesy Musical America Archives.
Musical Quarterly. Used by permission of Oxford University Press.
Bernard Shaw, *Music in London*, vol. 1. Constable and Company, 1949. Used by permission
    from England's Society of Authors, on behalf of the Bernard Shaw estate.
The Sorabji Archive. As owner of the materials written by Kaikhosru Sorabji quoted herein, the
    archive has given permission for their use.

Published in 2002 by
Amadeus Press (an imprint of Timber Press, Inc.)
The Haseltine Building
133 S.W. Second Avenue, Suite 450
Portland, Oregon 97204 U.S.A.

Printed in Hong Kong

Library of Congress Cataloging-in-Publication Data

Rimm, Robert.
    The composer-pianists : Hamelin and The Eight / by Robert Rimm; foreword by
    Stephen Hough.
        p.   cm.
    "Composer-pianists . . . collectively referred to Alkan, Sorabji, Busoni, Godowsky,
    Feinberg, Scriabin, Medtner, and Rachmaninov as The Eight"—Pref.
    Includes bibliographical references, discographies, and indexes.
    ISBN 1-57467-072-7
    1. Hamelin, Marc-André, 1961—Criticism and interpretation. 2. Alkan, Charles Henri
    Valentin, 1813–1888—Criticism and interpretation. 3. Sorabji, Kaikhosru Shapurji, 1892—
    Criticism and interpretation. 4. Busoni, Ferruccio, 1866–1924—Criticism and
    interpretation. 5. Godowsky, Leopold, 1870–1938—Criticism and interpretation.
    6. Feinberg, Samuil Evgenyevich, 1890–1962—Criticism and interpretation. 7. Scriabin,
    Aleksandr Nikolayevich, 1872–1915—Criticism and interpretation. 8. Medtner, Nikolay
    Karlovich, 1880–1951—Criticism and interpretation. 9. Rachmaninoff, Sergei,
    1873–1943—Criticism and interpretation. 10. Pianists—Biography. 11. Composers—
    Biography. I. Title.

ML397 .R56 2002
786.2′092′2—dc21
[B]
                                                                    2001046425

Justinian II

For Nana and Papa

THE COMPOSER-PIANISTS

To my parents,
Betty and Jerry Rimm

CONTENTS

FOREWORD

There was a time, until roughly the 1920s, when composer-pianists did not exist, at least not as a separate group. It was as expected for a pianist to compose as it was for a chef to create his own recipe. To place one's hands on the keyboard was a creative act in more than one sense, and the path from playing works by other composers to writing one's own was natural and organic, whether through cadenzas, transcriptions, or original pieces. These may have been as modest as a Blumenfeld prelude or as ambitious as Busoni's *Fantasia contrappuntistica,* but the same creative impulse was at work.

Composers often have a greater understanding of the works they play than do those who have never written music. However much one may question Busoni's Bach transcriptions or Godowsky's studies on Chopin's études, there is no denying the deep respect and love for the two masters that the two transcribers had. Indeed, both possessed profound intellectual gifts in their own right, and their acts of arranging were done not only with great skill, but with humility and reverence as well.

In an age when recognizable personality in performance was treasured, and before the advent of recordings, a concert pianist's published "album leaves," however insubstantial, were a way for keen concertgoers to preserve the image of a favorite artist after the event. Many of these souvenir scores were even published with the pianist's photograph on the cover, and hundreds of them were reprinted in simplified versions for the enormous amateur market. But things changed after the First World War. The fashion for nineteenth-century musical sweetmeats declined, leaving only serious classical composers, who might or might not play their own works—it did not seem to matter. They generally took paths that led them away from the concertgoing public and, thus, away from instrumental performance. Many of them formed an intellectual elite, aloof and apart from popular taste. Yet in this same postwar period, jazz—that performer-creative art par excellence—burst into bloom, taking us back in a circle of history to the age of improvisation and, for pianists, back to the pivotal figure of Liszt.

Although he was the personification of the composer-pianist, Liszt's career actually marked the beginning of the end of the category, for he introduced the idea of playing solo piano recitals and with them the necessity to perform substantial amounts of other composers' works. Very few of the great composer-pianists primarily played their own music (the notable exceptions being Scriabin and Medtner). As the piano repertoire expanded, a new category of artist was created: the concert pianist, a middleman to whom the composer delegated the role of interpreter. Piano playing thus became not just a way to reproduce great music, but a craft in itself requiring ever-greater numbers of hours to perfect its particular skills.

Robert Rimm's book serves both as a fascinating, exhaustive study of the riches of the past and as a stimulating inspiration for the future. May it encourage composers to become better acquainted with the instrument for which they are writing, and may it encourage concert pianists to sharpen their pencils and try their hand at writing music themselves.

Stephen Hough
New York

PREFACE
Related Keys

This book took shape over many years. It was written and published to assemble, for the first time in one volume, a portrait of eight legendary, enigmatic, and inter-related composer-pianists. Recalling France's Les Six and Russia's Mighty Handful, I have collectively referred to Alkan, Sorabji, Busoni, Godowsky, Feinberg, Scriabin, Medtner, and Rachmaninov as The Eight.[1] (Hamelin, who is still living, is considered separately.) This sobriquet was inspired by the similarity of their lives, which transcended diverse eras and disparate backgrounds, cultures, nationalities, and personalities. "Related keys" refers to the close tonal and harmonic relationships both within and between pieces of music. For the most part, The Eight knew one another personally, published articles about each other, or played one another's music.

This book reaches beyond biography to explore broader themes common to The Eight. Criticism, virtuosity, eroticism, and transcription are topics integral to our fuller understanding of their creative processes. The Eight represent a remarkable lineage of great pianists. Their enriching music, heard with increasing frequency on the world's concert stages, often approaches the limits of the piano's possibilities. With the exception of Alkan, all were born during the last thirty-five years of the nineteenth century, inaugurating the so-called Golden Age of the Piano, which lingered until Rachmaninov's death in 1943.

The Eight contributed significantly to my own development as a pianist. While still a boy, I found a collection of Alkan's sheet music and played several of his shorter pieces. When I read that an Italian composer named Busoni placed Alkan among the greatest writers for the piano, I was curious to know who Busoni was. I learned that his life in many ways paralleled that of Godowsky, a great friend of Rachmaninov, whose solo piano works and concertos I had aspired to play. The Rachmaninov connection led me to Medtner and Scriabin, each of whom graduated from the famed Moscow Conservatory in Russia—the music, language, and culture of which I have always loved. In my freshman year at the University of Pennsylvania, I came across Sorabji's two books, in which Alkan, Busoni, Godowsky, Medtner, and Rachmaninov featured prominently. By my late teens, I was playing much of Scriabin's music and especially loved the Fourth Sonata. It was then that I learned Feinberg was Scriabin's favorite interpreter of that piece.

While working for an artists management agency in the late 1980s, I was assigned to hear a violinist we were considering for our roster. All I remember about that concert was the dynamic, fluid playing of her accompanist, one Marc-André Hamelin, who was then a student at Philadelphia's Temple University. We ended up speaking at length after the performance. Hamelin was engaging and utterly without the pretense so common among exceptional young virtuosos. He shared with me his doubts about the possibility of making a career as a soloist in today's increasingly competitive world, then left for Canada that evening to perform an all-Alkan recital the next day.

Hamelin's series of three New York recitals in 1996 led me to the idea of including him in this book. He played, among other composers featured at those concerts, Alkan, Bach-Busoni, Godowsky, Chopin-Godowsky, Medtner, Rachmaninov, and several of his own works. Here was a top-flight pianist and fine composer whose credentials were unmatched in performing and recording the composer-pianists I was researching.

As it turned out, Hamelin and I lived just a mile away from one another, and he agreed to meet me for a long series of interviews in Philadelphia, conducted from 1996 through 1998. During this process, we planned a compact disc devoted to the works of the composer-pianists profiled in my book. I arranged the details with Ted Perry, founder of Hyperion Records, and the resulting disc—*Marc-André Hamelin Plays the Composer-Pianists*—has become a bestseller. At the beginning of the twenty-first century, Hamelin is widely considered the preeminent interpreter of works by many of The Eight. His vital Alkan, Busoni, and Godowsky recordings, as well as those of the complete Scriabin and Medtner sonatas, have set the standard by which others are judged. To the piano's Golden Age, Hamelin represents an alter ego of contemporary pianism, an artist whose sovereign command has caused the inscrutable to become indispensable.

Each of The Eight created music of unprecedented ingenuity, often complex and lengthy, with the technique at their fingertips to perform such works publicly. Each was a genuine virtuoso. Each developed intricate musical vocabularies within the bounds of classical tradition. Each composed primarily for the piano. And Busoni, Feinberg, Godowsky, Medtner, and Sorabji became accomplished essayists. The specific pieces treated in this book comprise representative, if subjective, samples from their collective oeuvre, chosen to illuminate a particular thought or to highlight a mode of creativity, not to provide exhaustive musical analysis. I defer to the example of the eloquent critic Sorabji, who rarely wrote of technical matters, believing they were more suited to professionals than to the wider audience of music lovers. In high banter, he wrote:

All that infantilistic babble about "form," "subjects," "development" and all
the rest of the classroom claptrap, tells us less than nothing about the music.
. . . If it did, and it were possible to verify, we should be in the realm not of
archeology but psychometry. It is high time to declare roundly that all that
pseudo-anatomical nonsense of the text-books and the analytical programme
is so much pernicious and noxious rubbish, confusing the issues and
darkening counsel. It distracts attention from what matters—the music—to
subordinate and subsidiary matters that, in the totality of the music, are as
germane thereto as a man's skeleton to the whole of him.[2]

Much has been made of the fact that Busoni and his student Egon Petri regularly
played Alkan's music, and Ronald Smith and Raymond Lewenthal revived his works
in the 1960s. But music survives beyond the advocacy of the few only if prevailing
sentiment supports it. The current era, in a backlash against frequently astringent
mid-twentieth-century music, is highly receptive to the brand of musical romanticism put forth by The Eight. With ever-increasing numbers of pianists presenting
their music, they have risen above the repertorial backwaters to which they had previously (for the most part) been relegated. Among them, Rachmaninov remains
the most mainstream figure.

The Eight were lauded and esteemed by some of the greatest musicians and critics of their day, yet performances and recordings of their major works could be
found only sporadically, at least until well after their deaths. Sorabji provided a
ready explanation:

It is a lugubrious and dreary task making an inventory of the piles of fine
and often great works, old and new, ignored or neglected, because of the
atrophy and refrigeration that appears to attack the brains of most executive
musicians so early in life who are, now as always, with a few rare and shining
exceptions, the greatest curse and hindrance to the progress and spread of
music, repeating all their lives the few handfuls of works at which they
drudged in their student days, incarnated automata, without anything like
the resources of a first-class pianola or gramophone.[3]

Much of the music composed by The Eight breaches traditional conventions.
We are sometimes captive, when the radical confronts the norm, to preconceived
notions of musical rights and wrongs; but accepted wisdom often boasts the freshness of faded flowers. Readers are invited to enter a world both rapturous and
refined, within which a group of ingenious composer-pianists communed daily
with the piano and made it the center of their creative lives.

Acknowledgments

To Betty Rimm, a most exacting editor, who introduced me to both words and music.

To Eve Goodman at Amadeus Press, for her encouragement and expert guidance as this book progressed from manuscript to publication; and to Barbara Norton, musicologist and copyeditor, whose care and thoroughness with the manuscript in its final stages are deeply appreciated.

To Jay Reise, composer and professor, long familiar with The Eight, who offered many insightful comments on the book. Twenty years before completing it, I attended his inspiring classes as a freshman at the University of Pennsylvania.

To Stephen Zerby, for his integrity and professionalism, and for his important contributions to this book's completion.

To Mark N. Grant, composer and author (*Maestros of the Pen*), who in reviewing the manuscript shared his perceptive knowledge of music and related subjects.

To Carole Verona, devoted student of the piano, for her unwavering support and considerable assistance with innumerable detail-oriented tasks.

To Ray Lewis, whose avocations neatly dovetail with this book's subjects, for his editing suggestions and commentary on the manuscript.

To Anzhela Reno, for her multilingual translating and research contributions. Her dependability and persistence also facilitated my obtaining critical books and photographs.

To Alistair Hinton, composer and curator of the Sorabji Archive in Bath, England, for sharing his personal recollections of Sorabji and for providing research materials and photographs.

To François Luguenot, secretary of the Société Alkan in Saint-Maur-des-Fossés, France, for the Alkan photograph and pencil drawing; and to Cyril Ray of Australia for granting permission to reproduce the pastel portrait of the composer.

To Tamara Rybakova, director of the Scriabin Museum in Moscow, for Scriabin's photographs and for a modern book about the composer.

To Pia Segerstam, director of the Association Internationale Feinberg-Skalkottas in Paris, for Feinberg's photographs.

To my research assistant Raphael Fenton-Spaid, for his selfless dedication to this project over several years.

To Susan Fenton, photographic artist, for her assistance in reproducing a number of this book's photographs.

To Lexicomm International, Ltd., for their translation of excerpts from Piero Rattalino's book, *Da Clementi a Pollini*.

To the many publishers who have kindly granted permission to reproduce excerpts from their source materials.

To Leah Rimm—grandmother, mentor, confidante—whose words and encouragement will be with me always.

To Jill Patton, whose delightful company in many late-night working sessions provided companionship and laughter in the often solitary pursuit of writing.

To Suzanne Erb and Marc Dickstein, for their meaningful, steadfast friendship over the course of this book's gestation, and many years prior to it.

And finally, to those who graciously shared their time and insights in interviews and who made important contributions to the quality and depth of this book: Lazar Berman, Norman Gentieu, Alistair Hinton, Stephen Hough, Zoltán Kocsis, Boris Lvov, Radu Lupu, András Schiff, Harold C. Schonberg, Jane Swan, Earl Wild, Krystian Zimerman, and Marc-André Hamelin.

Robert Rimm
Philadelphia

I ALKAN AND SORABJI
Hermetic Genius

"Few remarkable and outstanding figures in music have been the subject of such persistent misunderstanding, denigration, and belittlement as C. V. Alkan."[1] So wrote Sorabji in 1932 in his book *Around Music,* with which he reintroduced Alkan to the world, forever joining their names in the written and musical literature.

The hermetic composers Charles-Valentin Alkan (1813–1888) and Kaikhosru Shapurji Sorabji (1892–1988) were widely read, erudite scholars. Both men were religious; Sorabji developed a profound interest in Christianity, Hinduism, and Buddhism, while Alkan devoted a great deal of time to the Talmud and to his Jewish faith. Some of their daring and ingenious music fairly rips the lines from manuscript paper in a fantastic display of length, originality, and complexity. Perhaps their most bewildering similarity is that although they were serious and dedicated composers, they did next to nothing to promote or propagate the products of their intense, sustained work. Later in life, Alkan rarely accepted opportunities to showcase his own works; the public consequently failed to register him as a viable composer. As for Sorabji, from his thirties he was not to be seen on the concert stage. Neither envisioned much likelihood of public performances. Did they really devote so much of their lives to what amounted to a private calling? At one point Sorabji even went so far as to disdain concerts of his own music, in a manifesto that exceeded even Alkan's reticence and has no precedent among serious composers:

> Taking the dimmest view of public performances, and an even dimmer one of performers, I not only don't seek but actively discourage them; and so that there may be no doubt about it at all, in what the performers are pleased, but rarely anyone else, to call their minds, I have latterly gone to the length of categorically forbidding public performance.[2]

Alkan's and Sorabji's personalities provoked much misunderstanding. Private, reserved, and modest, they went to extraordinary lengths to distance themselves from the general public (although this behavior was occasioned by personal reticence rather than a disdain for society; their awareness of and interest in public affairs, for instance, increased as their reclusiveness became more pronounced). Alkan once rented two floors in a Paris apartment building; his official residence was on the first floor, but he actually lived on the second. In this way, he could be, technically, never at home, and the concierge had standing instructions to relay that information to all visitors. For his part, Sorabji placed several signs outside his property, one of which read, "All calls and visits Strictly Barred unless previously arranged."[3]

It took the advocacy of a persistent group of devotees to spread the names of Alkan and Sorabji further than the composers themselves ever imagined. New York radio was among the sources of a significant revival of their works. In 1963 Raymond Lewenthal's Alkan broadcasts created widespread public interest. Six years later Donald Garvelmann presented tapes of Sorabji's playing, with commentary by the composer's friend Erik Chisholm.

An examination of their lives offers fascinating similarities, although one important difference forever shaped their personalities. Sorabji was no child prodigy, nor did his ambitions ever extend beyond personal aspiration into a desire for public acceptance and popularity. Conversely, because of Alkan's prodigious talent, his fame was widespread, and he was expected to live up to his powerful early promise.

Youth, Fame, and Reclusiveness

The first of The Eight, Alkan was born in 1813 into a wealthy, education-oriented family. Accepted as a student at the Paris Conservatory when only six years old, he emerged as an extraordinary prodigy, reminiscent of Mozart. Alkan excelled in the vocal art of solfège (for the purpose of ear training rather than singing) and within two years made his public debut playing the violin. He joined the class of the most sought-after and influential piano teacher at the conservatory, Pierre Zimmermann, teacher of Georges Bizet and César Franck and admired by Beethoven. Alkan became Zimmermann's favorite student. Beginning at age eleven, the boy won a series of prizes, including those for piano, harmony, and organ. He soon came to the attention of Gioacchino Rossini and Franz Liszt. From his family as well as from Zimmermann, Alkan absorbed a lavish cultural background, influences that fed his knowledge and stoked an expansion of his compositional ideas. His forum became the piano, for him the indomitable force of music.

As he grew older and his musical stature increased, Alkan became actively involved with an intellectual and artistic clique that included Eugène Delacroix, Victor Hugo, Alexandre Dumas, Frédéric Chopin, and George Sand. In mid-nineteenth-century Paris, then the musical capital of Europe, Alkan was viewed as being on a par with Chopin, Liszt, Mendelssohn, and Schumann. A brilliant man, he was widely celebrated in the best Parisian salons. His name was made before he was twenty; his ascendancy was commented on by all the influential papers and periodicals of the day. Among his many admirers was Anton Rubinstein, founder of the Russian school of pianism.

Alkan taught part-time at the conservatory until 1836. Several years later, not quite twenty-five, he largely withdrew from society. His initial fame was replaced by an oblivion unimaginable in his early years, a situation that was to be redressed only in the latter part of the twentieth century. By his thirties, Alkan had begun to experience a series of severe disappointments. After a few sporadic concerts over the next fifteen years, Alkan retired for a further two decades (until roughly 1853), during which time he composed a great deal and immersed himself in the Talmud. His musical and religious interests often directly coincided. For example, several lines of the Old Testament preface the slow movement of his Cello Sonata, Op. 47.

Although he taught privately, Alkan never worked steadily, nor did he hold any official position. He longed to be recognized and decorated, but his reclusiveness often intervened. The story has been told that when an unannounced delegation came to his door to provide a long-sought appointment to the Légion d'Honneur, they were turned away under the pretext that Monsieur Alkan was busy digesting his dinner.

When Chopin's biographer Frederick Niecks attempted to call on Alkan, he received the usual rebuff. When told that he might try to see Alkan at one of his regular appearances at the Salle Érard (a small hall seating fewer than 250 people), Niecks feared the worst, but Alkan proved to be quite gracious. He had not wanted to see Niecks at his home simply because he was concerned about not being able to provide enough meaningful information. (Potential visitors to Sorabji were also put off, yet one found him similarly receptive in stimulating company.) The Alkan scholar Ronald Smith describes the composer's contradictory character as "that dangerous compound of authority and humility, conviction and doubt, fervent enthusiasm and basic caution."[4]

Alkan resumed an annual series of concerts at the age of sixty, but he played very little of his own music. This would have been the perfect opportunity for him to assert his position as one of France's leading composers, but a combination of modesty and bitterness prevented self-promotion. His contemporary Liszt (they were born and died within two years of each other) demonstrated no such reticence, which is part of the reason he dwarfs Alkan in the public consciousness. Liszt's fame rests not only with his compositions, which embraced genres beyond piano music, but also upon his reputation as one of history's greatest pianists. Had Alkan also been a flamboyant lover, bon vivant, and headline seeker, his reputation as both a composer and a virtuoso would be far greater than it is today.

Although he was not a public figure, Alkan had friends and influence. When Liszt was in Paris, he usually made a point of visiting him. Chopin and Alkan were by all accounts close, both personally and professionally; they were neighbors at the Square d'Orléans in Paris and also shared a distaste for Liszt's lifestyle and brand of

Charles-Valentin Alkan. Pastel by Edouard-Louis Dubuffe. Collection of Cyril Ray.

public display. The young Alkan felt threatened by Liszt's virtuosity when they met at a salon as teenagers, a feeling Liszt himself was later to reciprocate. Liszt studied and used a number of Alkan's ingenious pianistic innovations and later called Alkan's technique the greatest in his experience. Although Paganini is most often cited as the prime influence upon Liszt the virtuoso, Alkan's gifts as a composer-pianist also stirred Liszt. His B Minor Sonata may well have been a different creation had he not known Alkan's *Grande sonate*, written six years earlier. Always generous toward colleagues, Liszt did what he could to help Alkan. In 1836, when a teaching position opened at the Geneva Conservatory, he proposed (unsuccessfully) that Alkan be considered for the position.

Much of Alkan's output was a by-product of his reclusiveness; he knew none of Liszt's difficulties in balancing the schedule of a celebrity with the seclusion of a creator. Alkan and Sorabji were alone among The Eight in their decisions not to make this sacrifice. Whatever his personal reticence, Alkan was supremely confident in the vitality and necessity of his life's work. Bernard van Dieren observed in his 1935 book *Down among the Dead Men*: "His personality . . . was like his music, strangely varied and consistent; the 'texture' of the gnarled oak-bark next to the silkiness of a lily-petal."[5]

Alkan the recluse had at least some companionship: he fathered Elie Delaborde, who became known as a pianist, painter, lover, and eccentric. (It is ironic that Alkan's child was so outgoing, in the manner of Liszt.) Alkan's first withdrawal from the stellar concert career expected from him occurred shortly before Delaborde's birth. That he had a son outside marriage may well have contributed to his desire for privacy. Alkan's reemergence six years later, in 1844, came at a concert attended by Chopin, Sand, Liszt, and other notables. Featured on this program were Alkan's Opp. 22–25. One work, *Saltarelle*, became a sensation. *La France musicale*, a leading French music journal, rhapsodized over the brilliance and success of Alkan's compositions. Along with Chopin, he was the rage of Paris.

Energized, Alkan gave two more concerts the following year at the Salle Érard, at which other musicians joined him. Many of his own works were performed, along with pieces by Mozart, Beethoven, Schubert, and Mendelssohn. This time he received a few negative reviews. Just when his career might have been sustained, Alkan, ever sensitive to the vicissitudes of critical opinion, withdrew further. Public reaction to the avant-garde harmonic and textural originality of Alkan's later music left him feeling misunderstood and somewhat outcast. Yet whatever the shifting musical fashions of the moment, he believed that one of his missions was to lead music in new directions, rather than to perpetuate the status quo. Alkan was also among the first to recognize the dangers of a worldly career. He felt that money, fame, and success contradicted the life of a true artist devoted quietly and steadfastly to his craft. (In his opinion, Liszt had sold out.) Léon Kreutzer wrote in the *Revue et Gazette* of Alkan's campaign against "the false, the convulsive, the affected,

Alkan. Photograph courtesy of the Société Alkan, Saint-Maur-des-Fossés, France.

and the portentous,"[6] and gave us a timeless truism about artists such as Alkan who, "having spent too much time on their work to spend any part of it on publicity and canvassing, become a little disgusted with a public which does not come and seek them out."[7]

Despite his increasing disaffection, Alkan dreamed of a permanent position at the Paris Conservatory, which would have given him financial security as well as ongoing confirmation of his worth beyond the vagaries of the concert world. Zimmermann had decided to retire as head of the piano department, and everyone assumed that his favorite student—who had both an established reputation and teaching experience—would assume the post. Alkan wrote pleading letters seeking the influence of his famous friends, but to no avail. He had little taste for the social graces that served Liszt so well, nor could he bring himself to embrace the hypocrisy of fawning over people in positions of power and influence. This one attempt to play that game ended in humiliation: another former student of Zimmermann, Antoine Marmontel, through defter political agility, was named instead. (Ironically, Marmontel became not only a distinguished professor, but also one of Alkan's most steadfast supporters.) One can only wonder what would have become of the vast, exciting compositions that Alkan produced during this time had he won his conservatory post. Would the music of Alkan (and Sorabji) have reached such lengths and heights had he been a more public figure? Although he was still considered a celebrated pianist in his day, Alkan's latest compositions were overlooked amidst the turmoil of the 1848 revolutions that jolted France and the rest of Europe.

Chopin's death in 1849, a year after Alkan's decisive career disappointment, further isolated him. His friend, supporter, and confidant was no longer there. Thanks to the respect he commanded, Alkan inherited many of Chopin's students, although his teaching diminished as he became more reclusive. He had difficulty making ends meet. The extravagant nature of his larger works from this period fairly ruled out any meaningful royalties. Not for Alkan the compensation of fast-selling nocturnes and mazurkas.

Alkan well knew the direction his life was taking, yet he felt powerless to alter it. Admitting his desperation, he wrote in 1861: "I'm becoming daily more and more misanthropic and misogynous . . . nothing worthwhile, good, or useful to do . . . no one to devote myself to. My situation makes me horribly sad and wretched. Even musical production has lost its attraction for me for I can't see the point or goal."[8] Alkan had made his choice, but remnants of the ambitious young student of the piano remained. He longed for acceptance and an audience for which to write. Instead, he found marginal consolation primarily through a private life of composing music and studying the Talmud.

Alkan finally reemerged in 1873, beginning with six concerts at the Salle Érard, covering an exceptionally wide range of classical and romantic works. Once again, however, he chose to forgo the opportunity to fully espouse his own music, and he offered none of the major works in his later annual series, titled "Six petits concerts." The only other living pianist capable of playing Alkan's signature works persuasively was Liszt, who, having retired from public concertizing in 1847, did not propagate the compositions of his only real rival.

Perhaps, at the age of sixty, Alkan felt that his technique and stamina were not up to the task. Also, his fragile sense of self could not withstand the possibility that the public would reject or misunderstand his mammoth works, thus further invalidating his life. Alkan's last concerts did include a number of his shorter pieces, several late Beethoven sonatas, much Bach and other baroque music, as well as Mozart, Chopin, and Mendelssohn. Although he received generally positive reviews, Alkan was in poor physical health, and his concertizing tapered off. His bizarre legend continued with an oft-told story—now largely discredited—that he died while trying to reach a copy of the Talmud on the top shelf of a bookcase, which fell and crushed the seventy-five year-old composer to death. The actual circumstances, while not entirely known, were undoubtedly less colorful.

Alkan remained true to himself until the end, refusing to alter his style or way of life for public acceptance. This streak of fierce independence is a prime characteristic that the other members of The Eight would later display, with widely varying consequences.

Visual Music

Alkan's manuscripts are filled with bold strokes, carefully laid out and beautiful to the eye, although interpreters must be careful with his sometimes complex notation. Describing one performance of the symphony comprising Études 4 through 7 from Op. 39, Lewenthal wrote that the pianist played an entire passage in the wrong clef, "thereby adding a choking dollop of futuristic cayenne to Alkan's already spicy repast. The result was so patently absurd that anyone with any ear at all would have realized that Alkan, even in the wildest transports of Nostradamic trance, would never have materialized such nonsense."[9] Writing in the prefatory notes to an Alkan volume that he edited, Hamelin cautioned:

> The unwary reader should approach Alkan's notation with the greatest care. It is all too easy to misread his often-bewildering accidentals, and come to the most astonishing (and incorrect) conclusions! The watchword for the uninitiated is most definitely "Eyes open!"[10]

Alkan shone as a miniaturist, yet this important aspect of his music is largely unknown, overwhelmed by larger compositions not suitable for inclusion in anthologies of piano music. One way a composer may gain wider acceptance is to write relatively easy pieces that are accessible to young or amateur pianists. Mendelssohn's *Songs without Words*, Grieg's *Lyric Pieces*, Schumann's *Album for the*

Alkan. Pencil sketch by A. Osborne Campbell. Courtesy of the Société Alkan.

Young, and many of Chopin's shorter works fit comfortably into this category. With the exceptions of Rachmaninov and Sorabji, each of The Eight produced this type of music. Alkan wrote many pieces—including a number of the forty-eight *Esquisses* [Sketches], Op. 63, and the thirty *Chants*—that are quite approachable and of a far higher quality than much of the music typically assigned to students. That he nonetheless fell through the cracks of public awareness is inexplicable.

From Op. 63, works such as "Le premier billet doux," "En songe," and "Les cloches" are technically easy, yet they convey a wide range of emotion. Alkan's *Chants,* generally more involved and longer than his *Esquisses,* are modeled closely after the *Songs without Words* and surely belong in the repertoires of those who play Mendelssohn's ubiquitous pieces. An additional sketch, the impressionistic *Le tambour bat aux champs,* is well worth knowing. Bernard van Dieren compared it, by dint of its imagery, sentiment, and meaning, to the most intense lines of Poe or Blake.

Alkan's *Trois grandes études,* Op. 76, were published in 1846, when he was twenty-three. They represent a landmark in romantic piano writing. The first study is written for the left hand alone. Alkan was the first major composer to accomplish this feat, well before Scriabin's Prelude and Nocturne, Godowsky's famous expansions on the left-hand concept, or the commissions of necessity from Paul Wittgenstein, the Austrian pianist who lost his right arm in World War I. (One of those was the celebrated D Major Concerto by Maurice Ravel, among whose papers Alkan's left-hand study was discovered.) Alkan's work reflects his sense of dark irony. The French term for the left hand is *main gauche,* the latter word also meaning awkward or tactless. At that time left-handed people were ridiculed and ostracized for being abnormal and sinister. How it must have delighted Alkan—the recluse, the perpetual outsider, the deserving figure denied the respectability of a prestigious teaching position at the Paris Conservatory—to produce a work of real substance and craft for this hand. Pieces written for the right hand alone—the second of Op. 76—are even scarcer, given that in most two-hand music the right hand usually gets the bulk of the work and generally does not require special pleading. Ronald Smith notes that although Busoni had played the left-hand piece and Rudolf Ganz presented the perpetual-motion finale, as of 1976 no public performance of the "appallingly difficult" right-hand work had been documented. Smith later played the complete set, as did Hamelin in 1994 at London's Wigmore Hall. The finale of Op. 76, marked "presto, in unison," in which the hands are reunited, was written a year before Chopin's similar and much-celebrated finale of the B-flat Minor Sonata. Given the close friendship between the two composers, it is quite possible that they compared notes on their respective pieces.

Creatively, Alkan resolved to stretch all limits of his imagination without regard to a public he grew to see as increasingly closed-minded. In 1847, he produced the twelve études, Op. 35, and later that year the *Grande sonate,* Op. 33, dedicated to his father. The work's complex cross-rhythms and inner voices foreshadow much music by The Eight. Sorabji considered this sonata beautiful and original, if uneven. It reminded him of Berlioz's *Symphonie fantastique,* and he called it a "clever piece of musico-psychological characterization."[11] In high romantic style, the four movements of Alkan's sonata describe four stages in a man's life, at ages twenty, thirty, forty, and fifty. Tellingly, his sonata does not include the ages of sixty or seventy. Alkan perceived his fifties as his old age. In homage to his friend, Alkan quoted all four of Chopin's scherzos in the first movement. In the second, marked "quasi Faust," a complicated fugue arrives, predating the fugato section in Liszt's B Minor Sonata. Beethoven had written a concluding fugue for his "Hammerklavier" Sonata, also intricate and difficult to convey at the proper speed. Alkan's sonata ends with an inward and thoroughly remarkable adagio, stark and austere after the preceding movements. He appears to have aspired to the otherworldly states of the psyche that Beethoven—whom Alkan idolized and idealized—evoked in his late works. Whereas Beethoven moved into elysian realms, however, Alkan's response was more earthbound and resigned.

Beethoven's romantic temperament and mastery of large-scale forms greatly inspired Alkan. Similarities can be found between the two composers. Both men's metronome markings appear to be extreme—Beethoven's breakneck tempos in the "Hammerklavier" Sonata and those in Alkan's own sonata are prime examples. Context, however, proves the metronome markings to be the result of deliberate consideration. Alkan had a very strict rhythmic sense; his was not an art based on the rubato of Chopin. Alkan also shared with Beethoven an innate contrapuntal understanding. The successful use of counterpoint—simply defined as two or more distinct musical lines appearing simultaneously—indicates a level of craftsmanship attained by the best piano writers.

The "Hammerklavier" Sonata is often cited as one of the longest works in the literature, yet the first movement of Alkan's Concerto for Solo Piano contains more measures than Beethoven's entire work. Alkan's cadenza to Beethoven's Third Concerto is a striking free association of homage and humor. When Alkan resumed his limited concertizing, he programmed late Beethoven and discussed that composer's music at length with Chopin. Alkan also adopted Beethoven's device of using the coda as a dramatic conclusion.

Another feature Alkan's longer works have in common with Beethoven's is their cumulative effect upon audiences. Alkan's sonata is much more than a collection of its parts. When the final note sounds, the listener has shared a rich journey with the pianist. Many of Alkan's daunting conceptions in the hands of the right interpreter reveal the imagination of a virile, true romantic.

Schumann called Alkan the "Berlioz of the piano." Berlioz's flamboyant attempts to extend harmonic and orchestral possibilities were echoed in Alkan's expansive keyboard works. When listening to Alkan's piano symphony (an intentional misnomer), one almost subconsciously starts to score the work in terms of instrumental sonorities. Its funeral march could well have come from Berlioz. Alkan's Sonatine (Op. 61), noted Sorabji, "makes one feel as if Berlioz had written a Beethoven Sonata."[12] The title itself is misleading, for its nearly forty pages could hardly be called a diminutive sonata (though it may seem so next to his concerto or symphony). Alkan took an obstinate satisfaction in confounding accepted norms. It suited his sense of irony and mischief to title one of his most ambitious works with an epithet more often given to miniatures of the minor classical repertory.

Not everything that Alkan wrote rose to the level of his greatest works. Even a committed Alkan supporter such as Raymond Lewenthal—whose teacher, Olga Samaroff Stokowski, studied under Alkan's son at the Paris Conservatory—acknowledged some variability in Alkan's oeuvre. In 1964 he characterized the few generally known Alkan works as

> very long, very dull, and totally uncharacteristic pieces. Each is a difficult technical tour de force, excellent for finger wiggling, but soul-killing for player and listener alike. One of these is "Le Vent." . . . The second piece is a "Perpetual Motion" [*Comme le vent*], which Mme. Samaroff used to assign to every unsuspecting new pupil, 20 treacherous pages of unremitting sewing-machine 16th-note unisons.[13]

For his part, Schumann wrote, "one is startled by such false, unnatural art."[14] Sorabji considered it unfortunate that Alkan's name was associated with such inferior works. However, although Lewenthal also recommended avoiding *Le chemin de fer*, the first known musical depiction of the newly invented locomotive, Sorabji felt differently about it. He compared it to another, more famous piece written to evoke this icon of the industrial age, calling Alkan's work "an amazingly powerful piece of evocative suggestion which makes the feeble fatuities of Arthur Honegger and his 'Pacific 231' appear even more feeble and ineffective by comparison with Alkan's brilliant and masterly composition so many decades earlier."[15]

Another piece, *Mort,* dedicated to Liszt, is an elegy that makes use of the ancient Dies Irae theme, a rhymed sequence essential to the Requiem Mass for centuries (and also taken up by Mozart, Berlioz, Liszt, Rachmaninov, and many other composers). Schumann called it "a crabbed waste, overgrown with brushwood and weeds."[16] His later judgments were more generous. Writing of Alkan's Six Characteristic Pieces (later incorporated into *Les mois,* Op. 74), Schumann felt they were "of a far gentler morality and please us infinitely more."[17]

The twenty-five preludes of Op. 31 (one work per key, with an additional piece in C major) are Alkan's response to Chopin's famous preludes. In 1859 appeared one of the oddest works from any composer: the *Funeral March for a Dead Parrot,* written for three oboes, bassoon, and mixed voices. Other parodic works abound, such as the *Capriccio alla soldatesca,* Op. 50. Sorabji called it "a remarkable piece of brilliant grotesque, caricatural and mocking, with an extraordinary cadence."[18]

The twenty-four études of Opp. 35 and 39 are among the peaks of Alkan's creative genius. Liszt's biographer Sacheverell Sitwell called Alkan an extravagance of nature and noted that "the elaborate processes by which he perfected his transcendental études make him comparable to such slaves to craftsmanship as the Japanese lacquerers, whose passion for technique produced the most elaborate and technically finished productions in all the history of the arts."[19] Sorabji would later compose his own *Transcendental Études*—one hundred altogether.

Of the Op. 35 works, all in major keys, the fifth is an *Allegro barbaro*, an amazing study of pianistic force and dissonance, anticipating by seventy-five years Bartók's well-known work of the same name. This feral octave study for the white keys alone may have been composed as a response to Chopin's black-key étude. The tenth piece of the set, *Chant d'amour—Chant de mort,* recalls Berlioz in melodic form and colorful expression. A cunning play on words, the two parts of the title sound nearly identical in French, but one means "Song of Love," the other, "Song of Death."

The twelve minor-key études that form Op. 39 comprise three introductory works, plus a concerto (which Sorabji compared to Busoni's as one of the most original examples of the form), a symphony sans orchestra, an overture, and a final set of brilliant variations titled "Le festin d'Ésope." These études form a freakish display of unbridled creativity, requiring intelligence, humor, stamina, and consistent virtuosity from the pianist.

Mysticism

Sorabji, writing of "Le festin d'Ésope," said it brought forth "the same suggestions of Black Magic—devilry, sardonic, leering gargoyles that may come to life at any moment, masks of satyrs that may suddenly burst into cackling laughter as soon as your back is turned—the face that may grin grizzly-wise over your shoulder from the other side of the looking-glass."[20] Alkan played on the Mephisto and Faust themes, and although he was an Orthodox Jew, it would appear that the devil was never very far away. His faith did seep into his music: the theme of "Le festin d'Ésope," for example, is tinted with elements of Hasidic dance. Alkan studied Cabala, a branch of Jewish theosophy and mysticism as well as a guide to interpreting the Scriptures. The Jewish people's history of suffering repression and isolation further reinforced Alkan's perception of his status as an outsider. His mysticism and asceticism drove him to produce works—most prominently the études of Opp. 39 and 76, and the sonata—that he felt induced a tantric state of euphoria by means of mental and physical endurance.

In describing the attributes and depth required to interpret Chopin, the critic James Huneker wrote words that could be applied equally to Alkan:

A capricious, even morbid, temperament is demanded, and there must be the fire that kindles and the power that menaces; a fluctuating, wavering rhythm yet a rhythmic sense of excessive rectitude; a sensuous touch, yet a touch that contains an infinity of colorings; supreme musicianship—Chopin was a musician first, poet afterwards; a big nature overflowing with milk and honey; and, last of all, you must have suffered the tribulations of life and love, until the nerves are whittled away to a thin, sensitive edge and the soul is aflame with the joy of death.[21]

Critical Response to Alkan

Because of the extreme yet ambiguous nature of his music, Alkan fell outside the critical duels of the Brahms and Wagner acolytes that raged during the last part of the nineteenth century; most observers and practitioners simply did not know what to make of Alkan. He was much easier to ignore than to explore. A sentence from Alkan's obituary perfectly summarizes his reluctant obscurity: "Charles-Valentin Alkan has just died. It was necessary for him to die in order to suspect his existence."[22] With his personality and the demands of his sardonic music, it is not surprising that response to Alkan and his works has ranged from denigration to deification. Some praised him as a visionary, while others saw him as a base fraud. About one of Lewenthal's London concerts, Peter Brown wrote in *Music and Musicians* that "the music itself emerged like an outsize slag heap."[23]

It is often claimed that Alkan's music is not better known because much of it is too difficult to play, and therefore inaccessible. True, Alkan's eccentric, gargantuan works are beyond the capacities of many professional pianists, but some have always sought out Alkan's music and played it with great conviction and ability. Claudio Arrau did so early in his career. Hans von Bülow (who gave the world premiere of Tchaikovsky's First Piano Concerto) performed many of Alkan's works, and Busoni was a major advocate. Alkan's supporters have encountered resistance when trying to reverse his reputation for intractable difficulty, and critics have not generally helped matters. In describing the Concerto for Solo Piano, Henry Bellamann, though finding it one of the more interesting monuments of piano literature, wrote that it would have to remain a private pleasure for the pianist, as its public performance was self-evidently impracticable. "All of the flood of his imaginings was turned into decoration and design," Bellamann observed. "Absorbed in technical efflorescence, he worked over and over again the same slight material."[24] He called this Alkan's fatal defect as composer, yet acknowledged that the primary reason he wrote about Alkan's music in the first place was its unexpected musical quality. Rather than stimulate interest, Bellamann's assessment (he also believed that no one would ever play the sonata) only increased the distance between Alkan and the public. However, the efforts of Busoni and his student Egon Petri, as well as Lewenthal, Smith, Hamelin, and others, have emphatically brought the "impracticable" to life. Even Bellamann ultimately conceded that "the neglect and obscurity into which he has fallen is one of the most puzzling things in the history of modern music."[25]

From Alkan to Sorabji via Busoni

A generation after Alkan's death, Busoni became the first of the world's major pianists to champion the French composer. Writing of Liszt's music, he placed Alkan in exalted company: "These . . . pieces alone would place Liszt in the rank of the greatest pianoforte composers since Beethoven, Chopin, Schumann, Alkan, Brahms."[26] Busoni wrote to his publisher specifically about Alkan's études: "They are the most significant after Chopin and Liszt."[27]

Busoni defiantly programmed Alkan on his first and a number of his subsequent Berlin recitals, knowing full well that the traditional German public and press would be as willing to bear Alkan's deep romanticism as they would a French takeover of their country. Busoni included several of the études in these fin-de-siècle concerts. He was harshly denounced for bringing such "preposterous French rubbish" to their fair city, especially after his earlier espousal of Liszt left them cold. He later returned to Berlin armed with Alkan's outlandish cadenza to Beethoven's Third Concerto in performances of that classical mainstay and was repaid with venomous criticism. Busoni adopted Alkan's peculiar use of the title "Sonatina" for six of his own major works. Sorabji's later pastiche on themes from Bizet's opera *Carmen* was a result of his study of Busoni's Sonatina No. 6 (subtitled "Chamber-Fantasy on Bizet's *Carmen*").

That Alkan remained a scholar and intellectual his entire life was not lost on Busoni, whose own powerful intellect often left him at odds with those around him. Such qualities in turn inspired Sorabji, Busoni's ardent, lifelong champion. The scathing criticism that Busoni received only enhanced his status in the eyes of Sorabji, who doggedly pursued redress when he perceived a musical injustice. Sorabji came to view audiences in much the same way as did Busoni, who wrote of the virtuoso's place among listeners: "The public to whom he will address himself in his imagination will always be a small circle of intimate and chosen people, with whom he has mutual intellectual interests, whose capacity, culture, and inclinations are in sympathy with his own intentions and aspirations."[28] Not wishing to subject himself to the public life of a virtuoso pianist, Sorabji chose the pen as his theater and forum.

Busoni, describing a creator's need for solitude, once wrote: "The artist should . . . receive money to be able to avoid popularity," he wrote, "since it is only in a relative isolation that he can continue to aim at higher things."[29] Such withdrawal appears to have come to Alkan reluctantly and to Sorabji willingly. In any case, both were free to aim for those "higher things." They wrote for themselves.

Sorabji: Youth and Sexuality

Born in 1892, four years after Alkan's death, Leon Dudley Sorabji eventually adopted his given Parsi names, Kaikhosru Shapurji. He was not a prodigy on the order of Alkan, neither in composition nor in piano performance. Sorabji began serious self-directed study in his twenties. He gave relatively few concerts, enough to demonstrate superior abilities. Unlike Alkan, who continued to play sporadically even after retreating from public view, Sorabji found the glare of the concert stage too intrusive and gave up performing entirely. Although a private person, he developed an extroverted aesthetic and remained courageously true to himself in his music, his writing, and his sexuality.

From his early years, Sorabji spoke out against the injustice displayed by those who saw homosexuality as being against nature, just as he did with respect to commonly held prejudices against certain composers. This innate sense of right and wrong would later incite his critical sparring and encourage him to believe he was upholding basic rights and truths, whether in music or against ignorant attitudes toward human sexuality. In 1921, twenty-eight years after Tchaikovsky apparently killed himself over inner conflicts about his own homosexuality, during an era in which homosexual acts between men were illegal and homosexuality was still largely viewed as a perversion, the twenty-nine-year-old musician wrote a rational and fearless article titled "Sexual Inversion," published in the *Medical Times*. With the logic and lucidity of a sharp lawyer, he presents a compelling argument to live and let live:

> Although one does not expect manufacturers of laws to have much knowledge of the results of modern scientific and psychological research into the subject of sex, such ignorance as this should not go without strong protest from all interested in the progress of enlightenment and humanity. The time is more than overdue for a wholesale reconsideration of the question referred to above. None but the very ignorant can now . . . regard the invert merely as a moral monster, a "degenerate," or a perverted vicious sensualist. It is recognized that the inverted instinct, comprising the emotional and psychological as well as the specifically sexual aspects of the matter, is congenital. . . . The unreasoning cruelty and absurdity of punishing a man or a woman for feelings which he or she can no more help nor is no more responsible than for the color of eyes and hair, is manifest. No invert was ever or could ever be cured by imprisonment any more than a boiler could be cured of excessive steam pressure by getting someone to sit on the safety valve.

Sorabji was widely read and unusually self-aware as a young man, qualities that lent substance to his convictions. He continued: "Modern psychology has shown what physical and mental havoc repression can work in a human being. In addition,

Kaikhosru Sorabji. Courtesy of the Sorabji Archive, Bath, England.

Society demands of the invert, under pain of severest legal and social penalties, an asceticism it asks of no normal individual." He realized that the law would not be eradicated in the foreseeable future, but he offered an intermediate solution geared toward instituting a semblance of rationality in procedures devoid of reason:

> Pending the bringing of the law into line with the results of modern science and research, it should be demanded that all such cases as come into the purview of the courts should be tried by experienced medical men and medical psychologists only. Germany and Austria have a very excellent court procedure in such cases. Medical evidence is always called and, if the court is satisfied that the accused has acted from innate impulses and not from acquired viciousness, he is invariably acquitted. Here, it is a foregone conclusion that the accused is just a vicious pervert.

Sorabji concludes by addressing several of the most widely used arguments against homosexuality and offers a direct response:

> The supreme moral objections to inversion in the eyes of most people are that it is "against nature" and that it "defeats the logical end of sex relations," i.e., "the production of offspring." To say that inversion is "against nature" is one of those vague muddle-headed pieces of sentimentality so beloved of the unthinking. The invert receives the gifts of his feelings and desires from nature, i.e. they are something over which he has no control and which are to him from birth. How then "against nature?" The second objection is singularly hypocritical and ridiculous from a society that practices birth control and prostitution. Moreover, it is very questionable indeed whether production of offspring is the sole end of normal intercourse. A final word may be said on the cumbersome and unsatisfactory nature of the laws dealing with sexual offences. A short, one-paragraph statute could accomplish all and more than the present, while omitting all their objectionable features. It might run somewhat as follows: "Any adult person who commits a sexual act with any other person, without the consent of that person, by force, fraud, or intimidation, or with any person under the age of seventeen years, shall be guilty of an offence."[30]

The brilliant wit and critic Oscar Wilde also inspired the young Sorabji. In 1895 Wilde had been convicted of the crime of homosexuality in a widely publicized trial in England and sentenced to two years at hard labor. This case, with its attendant publicity, served to strengthen the resolve of Sorabji and many others who were appalled at the trial's outcome. Sorabji's article shows his humanity at work, which extended to his championing of great, misunderstood composers such as Alkan, Busoni, Godowsky, Medtner, and Rachmaninov.

Recluse as Critic

Sorabji's sense of self was also shaped by his Sicilian-Spanish mother, an accomplished singer who possessed a strong, perceptive, no-nonsense personality. He acknowledged how much he had learned from her. Sorabji's Indian (Parsi) father was away on business much of the time; the composer's home life could not be called stable. Because of his foreign-sounding name, dark skin, and the prevailing prejudices in England at the time, especially during his youth, Sorabji was treated as an outsider. In addition, his music was mostly greeted with incomprehension and bewilderment. These factors stoked his reclusive tendencies and conferred upon him the proud status of an independent thinker—the ideal foil for his musical and verbal creativity.

The thought that anyone would peer into his own life was for him the ultimate hubris, yet as a critic he thought nothing of mordantly dismissing any musician—creative or recreative—who failed to meet his high standards. He was not above arguing for argument's sake to prove a larger point. If an unqualified critic insisted that an ebony piano was black, Sorabji might well have shot back a multipage diatribe explaining why it was not so, and, furthermore, how such a judgment revealed the critic's abject ignorance.

Such a personality was bound to draw ridicule. One commentator asserted that Sorabji

> creates much the same impression as a child throwing everything within reach in order to draw attention to himself. Sorabji, entirely convinced of his own greatness and necessity, is the *reductio ad absurdum* of all this self-centered bombast, which cloaks, ineffectively, strong symptoms of withdrawal from all responsibility, social and artistic.[31]

Sorabji, in fact, took his writing quite seriously. He reveled in language at once witty and outrageous, colorful and vigorous. Would Sorabji have us believe that Alkan's "Le festin d'Ésope" is truly comparable to Beethoven's *Diabelli Variations*? Of course not; but he convincingly argued that Alkan's was an extraordinary set of variations containing both craft and humor. Sorabji the critic often felt it necessary to go beyond staid reporting into realms of hyperbole to convey the essence of his thoughts, and his readers came to cherish the crisp, exhilarating breezes he blew their way. To read Sorabji as a literalist is to see Vincent van Gogh as a model of photorealism. His extremes alienated more than a few people, many of whom wrote of their undisguised disgust in letters to editors of the various magazines where his words found their home. One reader railed against Sorabji's indiscriminate "distribution of ecstatics and abuse" and complained that his "personal idiosyncrasies, masquerading as criticism, are not sufficiently interesting to carry the weight of the riot of words in which they are set down."[32] Despite such protests, Sorabji developed a large and devoted readership, drawn by his conviction and vehemence, and by the sheer entertainment his prose provided. Although his reputation as a curmudgeonly recluse is unwarranted, he let people think of him what they wished, often finding their conjectures ironic and amusing.

He was much more concerned about those composers whom he felt were unfairly slighted. Not only did Sorabji fight for others of The Eight (of them, only Feinberg fell outside Sorabji's radar), but he was also among the first to advocate and write persuasively about the then little-known Gustav Mahler, decades before Leonard Bernstein made him a household name. In fact, the longest chapter in Sorabji's *Around Music* is devoted to Mahler. This cannot have been coincidental. The sheer scope of Mahler's music—emotionally, technically, in length, and in meaning—finds parallels in Sorabji's creativity. After hearing Mahler's Eighth Symphony, Sorabji wrote that it "is one of the authentic marvels and glories of all music of all time."[33] He was similarly effusive about the Ninth. Romantic works conceived on a grand scale were for Sorabji the sine qua non of compositional worth. This value remained a consistent thread throughout his own compositions and critical writing.

Many of Sorabji's thoughts on his favored composers may be read in his two books, *Mi Contra Fa* and *Around Music*. (The Scottish composer Alistair Hinton, who became curator of the Sorabji Archive, while reading *Mi Contra Fa* on a train journey became so immersed in the book's style and humor that he could not put it down, finding himself traveling 250 miles farther than he had intended.) "Mi contra fa" refers to the specific tonal combinations that represented, in medieval times, "the devil in music"—the name for the tritone, classical music's most dissonant interval. Sorabji delighted in his own dissonance, and many of those on the receiving end of his quick-witted criticism considered him the devil in words.

Sorabji felt fulfilled if, through his words and advocacy, people discovered something that they otherwise might have missed. Without becoming pedagogical, he considered the process a sharing of musical loves. However, when it came to his own music, he was anything but friend and advocate. Just as he would not assert himself in social situations, Sorabji's personality did not permit him to push his music upon others. His credo was music over musician, creation over performance.

Sorabji's Music

Sorabji has tended to be passed over as a composer, for several reasons. Like others of The Eight, his triple activities as pianist, composer, and critic have led to the assessment that he could not possibly excel in more than one of these pursuits. His scores are generally available only through the Sorabji Archive, and there are few recordings. Finally, the wide scope of his intricate music makes it difficult to interpret well. Sorabji has given us a legacy of compositional tours de force, many of which remain elusive.

Sorabji wrote for the piano as Berlioz or Mahler might have, transporting their grand design and universality—stretched over fabulously ornamented lattice-work—to his instrument's eighty-eight keys. While Sorabji's music is less formally constructed than works by the rest of The Eight, its contrapuntal and rhythmic complexity nonetheless demonstrates a profound knowledge of the keyboard's possibilities. His admiration for Berlioz was unqualified. That composer's way with chromaticism, orchestration, and form found a home in Sorabji's own work. The impressionism and delicacy of Debussy and Ravel are also reflected in much of his music. By contrast, Sorabji intensely disliked the heaviness and clashing harmonies of Stravinsky. Nor did he respond to Bartók, wondering if "such a bluntness tending often to an uncouthness, is really compatible with musical expression at its highest."[34] Schoenberg's atonality and serialism remained foreign to Sorabji. He could also be harsh toward composers from the classical period, writing of the "click-clack symmetries of Haydn and Mozart," the "square-toed flat-footed pomposities" of Brahms, or the "drubbings, growlings, [and] gruntings" of Beethoven.[35]

Whereas Alkan's music requires less obvious use of the pedal and employs a great deal of staccato, Sorabji's imparts more lushness, akin to the indefinite, blended tones of a Renoir. Clarity is still crucial in Sorabji, however, lest the music become mired in inchoate sound. Notwithstanding the substance and effort that went into his music, its effect must remain one of transparency and beauty. Sorabji's description of the "intricate ornamentation" of Rachmaninov's Third Concerto, "which, complex and elaborated to the utmost as it is, never obscures nor distracts attention irritatingly or disquietingly from the splendid lines of the great work," points to his own philosophy.[36] Such complexity, and the general inability of most pianists to cope with it ably, has so far resulted in relatively few opportunities for the public to appreciate Sorabji as a composer.

The subtle virtuosity and highly decorative nature of Sorabji's music stresses its impressionistic and polyphonic aspects. The writing is contrapuntally forbidding, with constant filigree; interpreted by inadequate hands, its beauty can easily be obscured. This relentless ornamentation, however, is an essential part of the music's fabric. Sorabji insisted that this characteristic met the highest musical tests, as opposed to the "'trimmings and fripperies' of lesser mortals."[37]

Busoni was moved to write a letter of recommendation for Sorabji after hearing him play his First Sonata at their first and only known meeting in 1919. That Sorabji played for his idol, one of the most famous pianists of the day, shows the young composer-pianist's confidence under pressure in his ability to perform music of bewitching difficulty. Although he was extremely nervous, it was obvious that this was no dilettante pianist. Busoni's reaction was generally favorable, if qualified:

Here is a realm of liberty, even if still disordered and exuberant. The music is written conscientiously and is unaware of its irregularities—chiefly of proportion—but it departs . . . from 'traditions' and breaks through to a zenith which is no longer purely *European* and is capable of producing exotic vegetation. . . . Above all: a budding talent of an altogether novel variety, which gives us cause to think and hope.[38]

After Sorabji dedicated his Second Sonata to Busoni—"in profound venera-tion"—the Italian wrote, "I became the dedicatee of a piano sonata (from the pen of a 20-year-old [*sic*] Indian, Kaikhosru Sorabji) with tropical ornamentation, luxuri-ant foliage, absorbing."[39] He had previously written to his wife: "A fine, unusual person, in spite of his ugly music. A primeval forest with many weeds and briars, but strange and voluptuous."[40] Given Busoni's imposing intellect, it is not surprising that the music's heady ornamentation and ostensible lack of form held mixed appeal to his sense of musical grounding.

Until his mid-twenties, Sorabji admired Scriabin more than any other composer. Sorabji heard both of Scriabin's London concerts a year before the Russian died; these performances made lifelong impressions on the twenty-two-year-old. He began composing shortly after Scriabin's death in 1915. Sorabji evidently shared Scriabin's conception of tone quality, preferring a suggestive rather than a harsh sound "clean through to the wood."[41] His First Sonata was modeled on Scriabin's Fourth. Both composers also felt a strong streak of mysticism and reported psychic experiences. Sorabji started, but never finished, a Black Mass for Chorus, Large Orchestra, and Organ in a nod to Scriabin's "Black Mass" Sonata. Sorabji under-lined a maxim of medieval theologians when he wrote of some music, "in its higher, its transcendental regions, *omnia exeunt in mysterium*."[42]

Sorabji's letters, filled with underscorings, exclamation points, and capital letters, reveal his intensity: "No composer living or dead has written or could write music so transcendental as this: Scriabin stands absolutely alone, but <u>what</u> an isolation! <u>what</u> an eminence!!"[43] Sorabji's approach to composing mirrored his conversa-tional style; Hinton called his speech "bursts of high-velocity verbal athletics."[44] Sorabji kept much in his head but feared that it would not stay there long. His mind racing, he set down music with tremendous speed and demonstrated little patience for editing, the results of which were sloppy manuscripts, mistakes in notation, and a lack of careful directions to the performer.

Comparisons between Sorabji's compositions and his prose are illuminating. It is no surprise that Sorabji's music reflects those qualities he admired and reviewed favorably. Curiously, however, the delicate and suggestive aspects of Sorabji's music —its sensuousness and insinuation—are rare in his music criticism. He was an uncompromising critic, his opinions formed and rendered in black and white. On the other hand, his baroque and highly ornamented style with the written word, as well as a seemingly endless fount of ideas, are evident in his music.

His scores have very few expression marks. Sorabji's music needs a performer who understands its implications, as he did not indicate every detail. Sorabji also understood that composers in the end cannot control what performers do, and he was open to the possibility that his music could be interpreted in any number of ways, as long as it was taken up by the best artists.

Although he found public performances a trial, he was persuaded by his friend Frank Holliday to make a series of recordings at his home, the only documents we have of Sorabji playing his own music. He was sixty-nine years old and had stopped practicing, and these few private recordings provide only a rough approximation of the actual notation in his manuscripts. But to have heard Sorabji in person or through recordings lends an understanding not entirely possible through visual exposure to the sheet music or manuscript alone.

Because Sorabji's music is so difficult to read, let alone play well, it is inevitable that most pianists could provide only approximations. A glance at the scores may be enough to discourage critic and pianist alike, filled as they are with—as Schumann described Alkan's music—"black on black." The pianist Stephen Hough observes that music of extreme difficulty can become an obsession: "One has to weigh these things very carefully in choosing to program music such as Sorabji's. There comes a point when one must question if the time isn't better spent going for a walk in the park, talking with a good friend, or reading. Being cloistered for endless hours in front of the piano working on one of Sorabji's immense scores may not always seem attractive."[45]

Sorabji's innate disinclination toward self-promotion always led him to downplay his accomplishments as a pianist. This attitude was colored by his admiration for the others of The Eight, all great keyboard interpreters. Sorabji had the stamina and ability, thanks to his exceptionally flexible wrists, to play repeated, fluttered chords very fast and quietly; his music is filled with such figures. When he chose to perform, the same critics who questioned the length or validity of his music were overwhelmingly positive about the quality of his playing. A review in the *Musical Times* is typical: "Sorabji seems to have bemused the good Viennese with his music, and amazed them by the astounding skill of his performance."[46]

Sorabji's four-hour *Opus clavicembalisticum*, inspired by Busoni's *Fantasia contrappuntistica*, found its way into the *Guinness Book of World Records* as the longest piano piece ever composed (although later, unpublished works are longer). Sorabji gave the premiere performance in 1930. Its twelve movements—with four fugues—took a little more than two hours to play (he made substantial cuts and revisions from the original score). It seemed to bewilder the audience and critics, who found the pianist's technique remarkable but thought the music lacked variety for a work of such length. Scotland's Active Society for the Propagation of Contemporary Music hosted Sorabji a number of times. Regarding one of those concerts, devoted entirely to the Fourth Sonata, a critic wrote that "despite its length and complexity one felt that the extraordinary technical command was not merely a diabolical cleverness but the inevitable means in the expression of a rare and significant poetic mirage."[47]

Sorabji once actually reviewed a concert in which he participated. In fun and with irony, he wrote that it included "the present writer's own Second Piano Sonata played by himself."[48] To be sure, he included the candid review by the critic Herbert Antcliffe: "It is so full of notes, of chords complicated for the sake of complication, of scales put in for the sake of brilliance and elaboration, of accents and stresses for the sake of sensation and surprise, and is so lacking in any control or balance."[49] By contrast, Clinton Gray-Fiske wrote a decade later in the *New Age*: "The music of Sorabji is characterized by a force, originality, breadth, and nobility of conception that simply transcends everything else that is now being written."[50] Eric Blom wrote of a Sorabji nocturne that it was "constructed on an unaccustomed plan and profusely ornamented by lavish detail . . . Mr. Sorabji's works have been called unplayable, an assertion he refuted triumphantly."[51]

Sorabji was influenced by a number of Alkan's works, including the Symphony for Piano, which he viewed as "one of the most important single works ever written for the instrument. Every bar, every harmony is instinct with original feeling and vitally compelling expression, and the mechanical treatment of the instrument is breathtaking."[52]

Admirers and Critics

Sorabji considered his Third Sonata a piano symphony, in view of its orchestral scope. Others described it differently. Reviewing Yonty Solomon's London performance of this work, Bryce Morrison (after mentioning that the huge score must have required a furniture van to bring it into Wigmore Hall), wrote:

> At the risk of a ballistic missile from Corfe (the Dorset village where Sorabji lives in rancorous seclusion), the mystery would have been better left undisclosed. The writing is surely complicated rather than complex, and despite Yonty Solomon's remarkable advocacy one was left ultimately astonished that someone can write a work lasting approximately one and a half hours without producing a semblance of a genuine idea.[53]

Many musicians, however, admired Sorabji's music, including the great French pianist Alfred Cortot. The English composer Frederick Delius wrote to Sorabji of the sensuous beauty of *Le jardin parfumé*, which he had heard on the radio. In the early 1970s, a few taped home recordings of his music were broadcast and caught the interest of the pianists Michael Habermann and Yonty Solomon, both of whom obtained Sorabji's permission to perform his music in public. The musical reputations of Sorabji and Alkan suffer because of the exclusive nature of their music and the polarization of critics. Listeners, pressed for time and easily distracted, often leave with superficial impressions. Given the commercialism of modern society, where products must sell quickly to remain viable, what hope does a Sorabji have? That his music is generally unknown is ironic, because Sorabji believed that great art must be available to all: "No genius has any right to lock up in one difficult and costly-accessible corner of the world, a work of supreme art—even his own. Great Art is universal. It should not be made the monopoly of a few."[54]

Nor should great literature. The poetry of the philosopher Sa'di made a profound impact upon Sorabji. Sa'di means as much to the Persian culture as Pushkin does to Russia. Persian was an important language in India, home of Sorabji's ancestors. Sorabji was an adherent of the ancient Persian religion Zoroastrianism. He also cherished his English translation of Sa'di's book *The Gulistān*, on which he based his own piece of the same name. Translated as "Rose Garden," it is named for a famous one that has bloomed in Shiraz for centuries. Sa'di's is a legendary work in the history of Persian literature, a combination of prose and poetry, aphorism and allegory. Its wisdom and sensibility are balanced (as written in the English-language foreword) by an air of shrewd amusement.

Le jardin parfumé is another of Sorabji's exquisite tone poems. Played quietly throughout, it is modeled on the mystic, erotic work of Sheikh Nefzawi, again demonstrating the Arabic influence upon Sorabji. The piece's florid, steamy aura recalls Scriabin's music. Sorabji's Nocturne: *Djâmi*, which takes its inspiration from the fifteenth-century Persian poet Jāmī, is a mystical meditation on the redemptive powers of love. Its languidly beautiful mood rises above elaborate ornamentation. These were among Sorabji's favorite works, and he recorded them privately. As with all his music, many levels of very soft dynamic shading are required. They resemble the still atmosphere in parts of Ravel's *Gaspard de la nuit* and also capture the hypnotic effect of the best minimalist music.

Myths and Contradictions

Would that Sorabji's reputation rested upon such music. In many fields of public endeavor, however, critics and the larger society will often seize upon a person's assumed primary trait and build a legend around it, in the same way that a caricaturist depicts a prominent feature of a subject's face and deliberately distorts it. Sorabji gained a reputation, by dint of his words and music, as difficult; in fact, he was stoic, kind, and generous. His sense of humor—a trait that never left him—was at least as stimulating as his writing. Hinton recalls: "He was very ebullient in person, far too positive and forward thinking to get bogged down in his own hard criticism of people. These qualities likely permitted him to live as long as he did."[55] Sorabji preferred the company of individuals over groups. Although reclusive, he kept quite busy by composing, writing, and maintaining a very active correspondence. Often viewed as eccentric and uncompromising, Sorabji demonstrated a warmth and loyalty to his friends that was instantly endearing and long lasting.

Sorabji generally kept his distance from the people he wrote about, even those he admired most. Though he easily could have developed lasting relationships with Busoni, Rachmaninov, and Medtner, for example, he did not want to intrude. In one instance, while having lunch with Egon Petri in a London restaurant, Sorabji noticed Medtner. Petri tried to get Sorabji to introduce himself, but, out of respect, he would not think of imposing. Sorabji felt that people such as Medtner had their work to do and did not need the meddling of others. He also found it easier to write about Medtner if he did not know him personally. Sorabji acted as though other people were somewhat like him, wanting to be left alone. Conversely, given the opportunity to meet with those whom he did not favor, he was too much of a gentleman to vent his spleen in person.

While he possessed little of Alkan's bitterness, Sorabji nonetheless remained concerned about who was going to listen to his music. He realized that it appealed to a specialized audience. Also, Sorabji generally thought very little of performing pianists. In reflecting upon other pianists' approach to Alkan, Sorabji wrote: "Pianists, like other executive musicians, are the most timid and unenterprising of human beings, and . . . the extremely individual and original quality of Alkan's work, its remarkable 'oddness,' which makes it impossible to label it or pigeon-hole it here or there in the customary and conventional groupings, disconcerts and repels them."[56]

However, Sorabji did not dislike the prospect of other people hearing his music, and its limited availability was largely a matter of expedience. The *Opus clavicembalisticum* was the last published work of his younger years, but this landmark creation appeared in print only as a result of funding he received from his father. The common perception that Sorabji was of independent means and could do whatever he pleased is not quite accurate. He did have a modest income through a trust fund set up by his father (about £2000 a year), as well as minimal royalties from his music. But when inflation climbed in the 1970s, his income was barely sufficient for a lower-middle-class lifestyle.

Sorabji gave his last performance in December 1936. He was no longer to be found in front of an audience receiving applause for his own work and later refused to go to any concerts at which his music was played, a position he maintained until the mid-1970s. In early 1971 Sorabji found himself at a low point and wanted to burn everything he had composed, fundamentally questioning whether his time and effort had produced anything of value. A group of friends dissuaded him from destroying his music. Five years later, public performances of many of his works began in earnest. Although these concerts provided him pleasure, Sorabji remained indifferent to the wider acceptance of his music. After Yonty Solomon's Wigmore Hall concert in 1976, he was much more interested to know what the critics and audience thought of the pianist, rather than of his music.

Legend has it that Sorabji took out an injunction against his music's being performed, but it is doubtful that he would have or even could have done so. He simply wanted to exercise some form of control over who performed and listened to his music. Sorabji's concern—that it must not be played at all unless an exemplary performance was possible—hardly lacked precedent. In 1914 Arnold Schoenberg wrote, "Have I the right to forbid a performance of my Second Quartet if the singer isn't adequate or if rehearsals show that the quartet won't do? Must I put up with a failure due to an inferior performance? Is there nothing at all I can do to prevent it?"[57]

Sorabji did not dwell on his legacy, which ultimately did little to further his reputation as a composer. He was not interested in talking about his works, believing that they should speak for themselves. The Sorabji Archive exists thanks only to Hinton's persistence; the composer himself felt extremely reticent about it because of the amount of time, effort, and money involved. In truth, Sorabji loved it when people went to trouble on his behalf, but only after the fact.

Sorabji's longtime friend Norman Gentieu confirms these aspects of the composer's personality. They developed a close correspondence after Gentieu read *Around Music* and sought out its author. After the Second World War, Gentieu sent Sorabji a steady supply of provisions to help him through the postwar shortages. He also offered to microfilm and selectively distribute Sorabji's complete works. He correctly assumed that Sorabji would consider such a project well beyond the means of any one person, so Gentieu created a fictitious "Society of Connoisseurs" (later "The Criterion Club") for the purpose of demonstrating widespread support. This good-natured subterfuge had the added attraction of a letterhead created by the well-known former counterfeiter Baldwin Bredell: an eye-catching depiction of Thoth and Isis from Egyptian mythology.

Like Alkan, Sorabji continued composing well into his old age. Although in full possession of his mental faculties, he stopped creating new music in 1982 at the age of ninety, but only because his vision had deteriorated and he could not easily hold a pen. His practice of yoga helped him come to terms with the loss.

Sorabji was not a pessimist but a realist, personal traits he had in common with his idol Busoni. He could be philosophical and pragmatic when necessary. Nor was he a misanthrope like Alkan. Even when he hurled his full critical arsenal, a sense of fun remained in his writing, which for him was a relief from the rigors of composition. Everything that came from his pen, whether in the written word or in music, demonstrated the potency of a first-class mind.

In the beginning of the twenty-first century, limited evidence exists of a performing tradition for Alkan, and even less for Sorabji. Pianists speak of learning the entire Beethoven or Schubert repertory, for example, as providing essential insights into classical performance practice. Given the number of works in the Alkan and Sorabji canon, their general lack of availability, and the technical and intellectual difficulties most of them present, such an ideal would be nearly impossible with Alkan,

THE SOCIETY OF CONNOISSEURS
Norman P. Gentieu
President

Letterhead for the Society of Connoisseurs.

and literally impossible with Sorabji. At least pianists now have recordings from which they can judge some of their music.

Increasing numbers of critics are educating themselves to the repertoire's more uncommon composers. One sees a glint of recognition when the names Alkan and Sorabji are broached. These two composers may be called frontiersmen of the piano, despite their nineteenth-century births. Their works, much more than those by many better-known composers, require serious investment by pianists. Played exceedingly well, their music arouses and astonishes; played poorly, it bores and baffles. The listener who goes home from a bad Beethoven concert is apt to try the composer again. The Alkan and Sorabji causes may lose potential adherents with subpar concerts or recordings. Both men remain among the piano's last great composers to be fully explored, played, and recorded.

It took more than a hundred years for the major Alkan works—a number of which defy convention in their length and difficulty of execution—to be heard publicly. Many of Sorabji's astronomical creations have yet to receive their premieres. The stinging diablerie found in much of Alkan's music led a bewildered public to

Sorabji. Courtesy of the Sorabji Archive.

perceive him as unfathomable; Sorabji's lavish music has come to be viewed in much the same way. Their radical works, coupled with personal distaste for self-promotion and publicity, have had the effect of separating these composers from their listeners. Thus liberated from the vicissitudes and practicality of writing for public performance, Alkan and Sorabji gave free rein to unbridled inspiration.

2 BUSONI AND GODOWSKY
Revered and Reviled

Peers and colleagues. Self-taught pianists and composers. Teachers, editors, and writers. Restless virtuosos and legendary perfectionists. Musical scientists and researchers. Revered and reviled. Ferruccio Busoni and Leopold Godowsky.

Music history has revealed remarkably similar pictures of these influential men, whose music was at various times either de rigueur or out of fashion. Wary of each other, if admitting mutual respect, Busoni (1866–1924) and Godowsky (1870–1938) maintained their independence at every turn. They came to be recognized worldwide as devoted teachers, yet their status as self-taught musicians—unbeholden to any school—left them with little patience for the rigidities of institutional settings or curricula. They could be counted on to offer honest counsel to their students as well as to the large coterie of artists who sought them out. Each fulfilled teaching stints from one institution to another, and each ended up in Berlin at a crucial point in his career. Their educational and compositional philosophies took root in the counterpoint of Bach, whose music they studied, transcribed, and highly valued. Their primary teachers were Bach and Mozart, whom Busoni considered two of the strongest and most enduring figures in classical music.

Both Busoni and Godowsky were sensitive boys and well-traveled prodigies. They experienced the world at a young age, enhancing their perceptiveness and self-awareness. Neither suffered hypocrisy or incompetence very well, often responding with sharp wit. As a result of difficult family circumstances, both men developed an active distaste for and distrust of commercialism. They were ill inclined to respond to the driving, corrupting influences of blatant careerism.

The Shaping of Busoni

The father of Ferruccio Dante Michelangelo Benvenuto Busoni presciently assigned him three middle names, hoping that some of the greatness of those Italian masters would pass through to his son. Though the adult Busoni used only his first name, he did in fact show more than traces of the three Tuscan masters, becoming one of the

47

great Renaissance men of his era. Busoni's mother, a noted concert pianist of German descent, had played for Franz Liszt at his home, so Busoni came by his early love of Liszt naturally. It was his father, though, a peripatetic clarinet virtuoso, who was Ferruccio's greatest early influence. He gave his eager and receptive son the works of Bach and other great German composers to play and, intending to turn his son into another Mozart—whose C Minor Concerto the boy played in public at age eight—forced him to practice four hours daily. When not quite ten, Busoni accompanied his father to Vienna for an audition with Anton Rubinstein. Soon afterward, the adolescent Busoni's wildly successful Viennese debut brought him the first strong taste of the critical and public notoriety that he was to experience throughout his life.

It has often been noted that Busoni became a synthesis of influences, with his Italian-German heritage shaping a hybrid personality—one both romantic and classical. He did have a clear musical lineage: Beethoven's student, Carl Czerny, had taught Liszt; in his twenties, Busoni absorbed many of Liszt's principles to correct deficiencies in his playing. About Beethoven, whom he came to admire greatly, Busoni wrote:

> The Latin attitude to art, with its cool serenity and its insistence on outward form, is what refreshes me. It was only through Beethoven that music acquired that growling and frowning expression which was natural enough to him, but which perhaps ought to have remained his lonely path alone. "Why are you in such a bad temper?" one would often like to ask.[1]

Busoni also absorbed many of Johannes Brahms's compositional tenets, and he benefited from Brahms's endorsement and close interest, especially in the musical capitals of Leipzig and Vienna. (In Busoni's day, the patronage and recognition of established musical figures played a much greater part in the making of a successful career than critics in the musical press did.) Busoni remained on good terms with the revered German composer and dedicated his Six Études and the *Étude en forme de variations* (Opp. 16 and 17) to him.

In 1890 Busoni began teaching at the Moscow Conservatory. He had already established his credentials as editor and transcriber by editing Bach's two-part inventions and by writing several of his soon-to-be-celebrated piano transcriptions, including that of the chaconne from one of Bach's solo violin partitas. Though productive, his time in Moscow was not happy. Busoni felt frustrated that his huge workload took away from more creative pursuits. He also found himself ill suited to Russian politics and wrote to his father of deceitful colleagues, xenophobia, and the country's unstable financial situation. Barely a year later Busoni left Russia for Boston's New England Conservatory, whereupon he fell into a peripatetic existence. He soon moved to New York and then to Berlin, quickly outgrowing what he saw as the restrictive guidelines of established conservatories. He spent much time touring in a wanderlust reminiscent of Liszt.

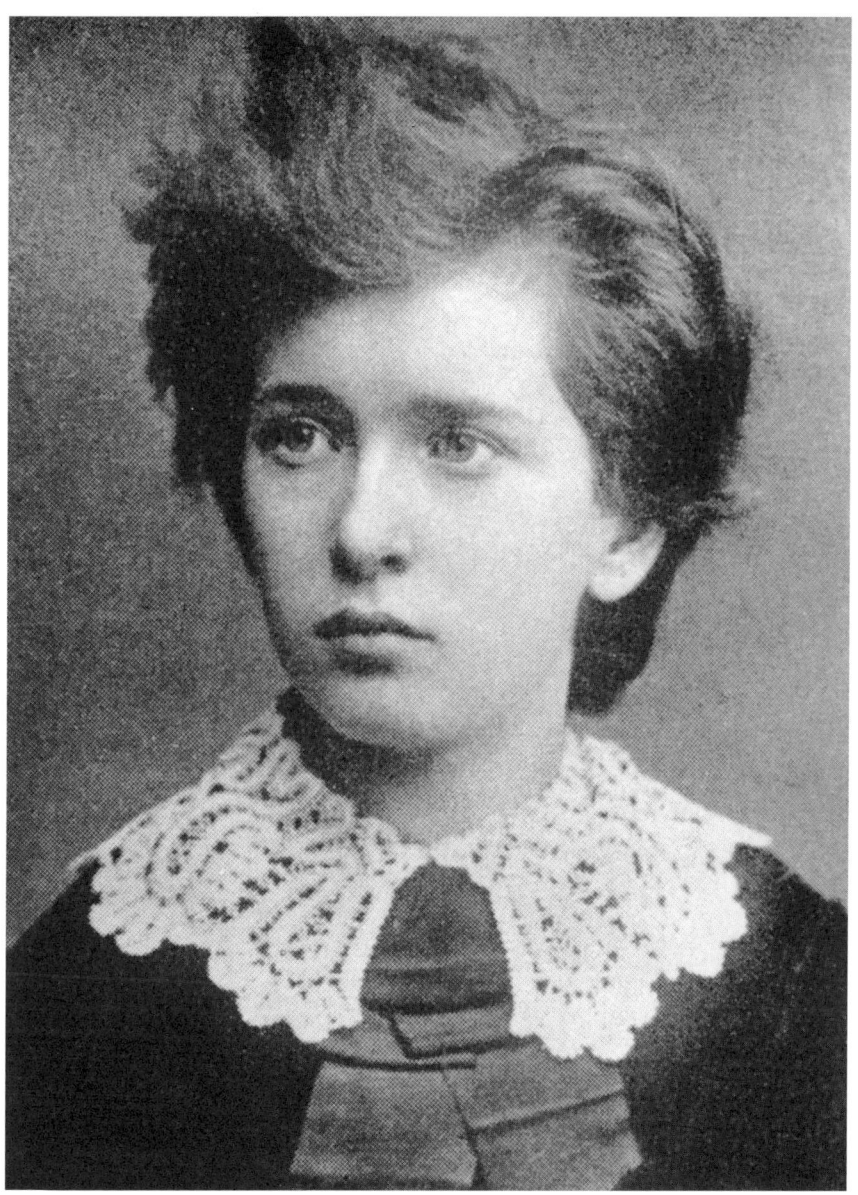

Ferruccio Busoni as a twelve-year-old in Vienna, 1878.

Busoni, c. 1890s.

As his career developed, Busoni insisted that his work be free from the profit motive, a desire that can be traced directly to his childhood and to his father's emphasis on money. The older Busoni extracted loans in the name of his son, took from one to pay another, and frequently claimed poverty despite the considerable sums that passed through his hands. Constantly exposed to such mercenary machinations, as a young boy Busoni came to detest this combination of art and commerce. He continued to feel its effects even into his forties:

> As soon as I make my aim a *profitable* one, as soon as there begins to be a practical advantage in doing a thing, something in me begins to bleed, a kind of disablement overtakes me, and it is only with pain and effort that I can carry through what, otherwise, I could achieve easily, happily, and better. . . . A similar feeling comes over me when I see others behaving and thinking in a purely utilitarian manner in matters connected with art—and outside art too. . . . If I am playing only because of the fee I always play badly, worse than the average pianist; besides this, I am always *ashamed* while I am playing and afterwards too, and that is distressing.[2]

In general, as a matter of principle, Busoni took no fee from his private students. His spiritual aspirations—in both playing and composing—were the farthest thing from materialistic:

> The despotism of money is in no way better than the "terror" of militarism; the latter is confined to a *class* of people, the former is general. . . . The worthiest things, as art and philosophy, love and nature, good taste and inner satisfaction, are independent from it.[3]

Not only did Busoni react against materialism, he avoided realism in his musical philosophy. He believed that all the arts—sculpture, painting, architecture, poetry, and music alike—aimed at "the imitation of nature and the interpretation of human feelings."[4] He disliked Wagner's overt ideals in dramatic music, choosing to focus instead on mystic and spiritual themes along the lines of several composers he admired, including Scriabin and Alkan. Busoni's mystical inclinations included his belief in telepathy as an undeniable, if undeveloped, trait of mankind.

He played many of Alkan's works and may have had in mind that composer's *Grande sonate*—describing the different stages of man's life up to the fiftieth year—when he wrote, "I am dreading my fiftieth birthday, which is something of a funeral."[5] Throughout his career, Busoni placed great value on freedom, and as he approached fifty he felt threatened by world events, which included the burgeoning atrocities of World War I. "When one is no longer master of one's own freedom of movement, life has no further value. No matter whether it is the result of sickness, old age, imprisonment or—the glorious matters of the present time."[6] At the end of the war, the Weimar government appointed him to a special professorship in composition, on his own terms.

Busoni made the strictest demands on himself, yet he insisted on maintaining his personal and creative freedom. His stage manner, as described in a vignette by the writer Alexander Pasternak, reflected his need to feel liberated:

> When he was sitting at the piano—or to be more exact almost lying on it—he became completely lost in the world of music he was interpreting. The hall, the audience, even his own personality, ceased to exist for him. At such moments he behaved with a spontaneous childish naiveté . . . making hoarse, quite audible noises; he would hum loudly, particularly at pathetic moments, neither hearing himself nor noticing anything around him, so that he would infect the audience—who still forgave him everything, charmed by his playing. They forgave him, too, for his apparent lack of interest in the effect of his performance. He would rush off backstage with a single nod, showing merely that he took account of the ovation.[7]

But Busoni also made it clear that real achievement comes from consistent study and discipline:

> If a doctor advises the enjoyment of wine, he does not wish his patient to become a drunkard. The state of freedom must not be confused with anarchy, because in anarchy, every individual is threatened by the other. Magnanimity is not the mania of prodigality and free love is not prostitution. Moreover, a good idea is not an artistic creation, someone with talent is not a master; a seed of corn, however strong and fruitful it may be, produces no harvest for a long time.[8]

Busoni drew great strength and support from his wife, Gerda: "I think of you every hour," he wrote, "especially if I see something beautiful or am with good people."[9] She provided Busoni, the constantly striving perfectionist, with love and the deep human connection that prevented him from becoming, as an artist, isolated and emotionally remote.

The Search for Perfection

Busoni was one of the first pianists to go beyond an exclusive reliance on his talent in the pursuit of perfection. He ceaselessly studied the mechanics of technique and saw its limitations as weaknesses. Busoni's credo was that everything was possible on the piano. He performed on a long concert bench for the same reason that Vladimir Horowitz later did: to focus on the upper or lower register by subtly shifting to the right or left on the bench. In touch, pedaling, and awareness of his own physique, Busoni knew precisely how much distance and weight would produce the desired effect. Along with these advanced precepts, he acknowledged the pianist's more mundane tasks: "There is still presence of mind which is also to be desired, control over moods in irritating conditions, the ability to rouse the attention of the public, and finally in 'psychological moments' to forget the public."[10]

Busoni is the father of what is generally called the modern Italian school, exemplified by Arturo Benedetti Michelangeli and Maurizio Pollini. Their clear emphasis on technical perfection, intellectual depth, and structural cohesion came straight from Busoni but in no way precluded the loftier goals of musical expression. Many critics have observed in their music making a too-calculated approach, but music speaks to the widest range of human responses; what is too perfect or intellectual for some may be intensely stimulating to others. Busoni defended his preoccupation with pianistic detail by citing a conversation with a stained-glass artisan, who demonstrated that only a fragment was needed to judge the greatness of a window.

Busoni could afford to focus on details and a deeper awareness of his art. His prodigious memory and capacity for knowledge allowed him to master a huge amount of repertoire, and he performed many lengthy, neglected works along with his own grand compositions. He took particular pleasure in introducing audiences to Alkan and other then-unfamiliar music. Busoni also publicly played Bach long before it was fashionable. His Bach editions are probing, highly personal guides to points of interpretation, musical analysis, and technique. Although never a historical-music purist, Busoni could be counted upon for the highest level of scholarship and research. He intended his edition of Book 2 of Bach's *Well-Tempered Clavier* to "concern itself with the profundities of polyphony, the roots of melody, and the innermost workings of compositional mechanisms."[11]

Busoni also carefully studied the piano's pedals. He stated poetically that "the pianoforte has one possession wholly peculiar to itself, an inimitable device, a photograph of the sky, a ray of moonlight—the Pedal."[12] The perfection of his pedal technique—a result of constant study, application, and experience—was legendary. Here and in the larger quest for elemental musical truths, Busoni relentlessly pursued supremacy:

> I never neglect an opportunity to improve, no matter how perfect a previous interpretation may have seemed to me. In fact, I often go directly home from the concert and practice for hours upon the very pieces I have been playing, because during the concert certain new ideas have come to me. Those ideas are very precious, and to neglect them or to consider them details to be postponed for future development would be ridiculous in the extreme.[13]

The perfectionist often walks hand in hand with the workaholic. "It is the old story," Busoni wrote to his wife. "I can sleep after I have done good work; if I do no work, I become nervous."[14] Busoni called the real artist someone "who has formed the habit of stopping at nothing short of his highest ideal of perfection."[15]

A Musical Thinker's New Aesthetic

Busoni codified many of his ideals in *Outline of a New Aesthetic of Music*, first published in German in 1907. This short book is the product of a first-rate intellect, but the fascinating material suffers from a convoluted and stilted presentation. Though his ideas are often groundbreaking and even profound, for the most part the work remains impenetrable by all but specialists and musicologists. Busoni himself realized this but seemed unable to express his insights any more clearly. He described criticism of the work as "well-meant and full of peace."[16] But given Busoni's views about music, one can discover his aims for the book: "Music is the most aloof and secret of the arts. An atmosphere of solemnity and sanctity should surround it."[17]

One of those secrets involves finding new ways of musical expression. "The function of the creative artist," Busoni wrote, "consists in making laws, not in following laws already made. He who follows such laws, ceases to be a creator."[18] But throughout history, creative artists have borrowed from the past while expanding upon the limits it has set. Musically speaking, Busoni insisted:

> Never, never, can one set up a rule when it is a question of art. Every stroke of the pen demands its own conditions. . . . In new works one avoids the old mistakes but makes new ones again, because the problem is always changing. . . . With the beginning of every new thing one is timid and awkward again.[19]

Busoni saw himself as a musical reformer who

> in any given period, excites irritation for the reason that his changes find men unprepared and, above all, because these changes are appreciable. The Reformer, in comparison with Nature, is undiplomatic; and, as a wholly logical consequence, his changes do not win general acceptance until Time, with subtle, imperceptible advance, has bridged over the leap of the self-assured leader.[20]

Such qualities made Busoni one of the most sought-after teachers of his time; however, because he never felt completely happy in academic settings, he failed to establish a base from which he could cement his artistic legacy. Although he felt that his work with students kept his piano playing fresh, Busoni became increasingly disenchanted with teaching, repeatedly covering the same paths he himself had crossed so often and usually with greater results.

As an educator, Busoni was forward thinking and held no deep ideological bias against those contemporaries moving in different directions from his own. Though not always in agreement with the latest advancements in music theory, he was fascinated by modern music, if not initiating such codifiable new techniques as Schoenberg's atonality. Upon hearing Stravinsky's *Histoire du soldat* for the first time, Busoni stood up in his box and shouted, "Masterpiece! Masterpiece!" amidst all the laughing and hissing around him.[21] Fully confident in his own aesthetic values, he took an almost perverse satisfaction in publicly proclaiming his views, as he did by performing Alkan, to the Berliners' disgust. Conversely, during the early part of the twentieth century, Berlin enjoyed its reputation as a hotbed of experimentation, which Busoni found enormously stimulating. Through his concerts and writings, he constantly challenged convention.

Busoni empathized with Liszt's outsider status as a composer and sought to redress it in 1904 with a series of Liszt recitals in Berlin. The critics were appalled. (Several years earlier Busoni had attempted Alkan's resurrection by playing eight of that composer's most important works and received even more venomous criticism. The larger public would not show itself to be ready for that French master until half a century later.) Having since contributed to the Liszt critical editions sponsored by the Duke of Weimar, in 1911 Busoni again gave Berlin an abundant selection of Liszt. In six concerts commemorating Liszt's one-hundredth birthday, Busoni performed a virtual catalog of the Hungarian's works.

Busoni's reputation as a penetrating thinker complemented his grand, romantic playing style, one that caused waves of criticism in his adopted country, more used to sober-minded pianists such as the reigning Germans Artur Schnabel and Edwin Fischer. Moreover, Busoni's few recordings betray certain modifications to the scores, which would have aroused additional reservations. However, because he never recorded the monumental works that most engaged him as a performer—Bach's *Goldberg Variations,* Beethoven's "Hammerklavier" Sonata and *Diabelli Variations,* Liszt's Sonata, Brahms's Variations on a Theme of Paganini, and his own *Fantasia contrappuntistica*—it is difficult to compare Busoni's theoretical positions with their practical realization.[22]

Modernism took decisive turns at the beginning of the twentieth century through the pioneering work of Schoenberg, Stravinsky, Scriabin, and Busoni, who understood tradition as "a plaster mask taken from life, which, in the course of many years and after passing through the hands of innumerable artisans, leaves its resemblance to the original largely a matter of imagination."[23] Busoni's respect and love for tradition may be seen in his repertoire, which took in practically the whole Bach keyboard canon, much Mozart and Beethoven, and selected works by Alkan, Chopin, Schumann, Liszt, and many other composers. Busoni spared no effort defending his beliefs. He summarized his creed in an open letter, a response to a polemic by the Belgian critic Marcel Rémy:

> You start from false premises in thinking that it is my *intention* to "modernize" the works [that I play]. On the contrary, by cleaning them of the dust of tradition, I try to restore their youth, to present them as they sounded to people at the moment when they first sprang from the head and pen of the composer. [Beethoven's] *Pathétique* was an almost revolutionary sonata in its day, and ought to sound revolutionary. One could never put enough passion

into the *Appassionata,* which was the culmination of passionate expression of its epoch. When I play Beethoven, I try to approach the liberty, the nervous energy, and the humanity which are the signature of his compositions, in contrast to those of his predecessors. Recalling the character of the man Beethoven and what is related of his own playing, I have built up for myself an ideal which has been wrongly called "modern" and which is really no more than "live." I do the same thing with Liszt; and oddly enough people approve in this case, though they condemn me in the other.[24]

Bach-Busoni and Original Busoni

A prodigy at both piano playing and composition, Busoni wrote his first four opus numbers before he was thirteen years old. Tellingly, his Op. 3 comprises five pieces for piano—Prelude, Minuet, Gavotte, Étude, and Gigue—that represent the young man's homage to Bach, a kind of Italian Suite that in spirit could have fit among Bach's French or English Suites. Elements of dance rhythms and complex contrapuntal styles abound in Busoni's earliest works. He also wrote a set of twenty-four preludes in the manner of Alkan and Chopin and composed seven volumes of études after Bach.

Busoni's initial impetus to transcribe Bach's organ works came from his friend Kathi Petri (the mother of one of his students, the pianist Egon Petri). After they heard an organist play the Prelude and Fugue in D Major at Bach's Thomaskirche, she suggested that Busoni arrange the work for piano. A week later it was finished. This experience opened rich new areas for Busoni to explore: the possibilities of the piano's pedals and touch that were to give his playing such distinction. Alexander Pasternak recalls:

> Busoni was an especially fine interpreter of Bach. The exceptional sounds and the unusual richness of tone he extracted from the instrument gave the impression of an organ performance. When he played Bach he seemed to be in a special mood, as if improvising, playing at a slower tempo than was usual with other pianists.[25]

Busoni believed the genesis of a composer's training to be rigorous grounding in counterpoint and fugue. His years of analyzing and playing Bach permanently influenced his creative efforts, all tempered by an increasingly determined search for new sounds, polytonality, and modern modulations. His editions of Bach's two- and three-part inventions, the *Well-Tempered Clavier,* and other keyboard works stand as models of Bach scholarship applied to modern piano technique. His carefully planned fingerings and suggestions for phrasing and expression, within a framework of rigorous analysis, makes them essential editions for all pianists interested in Bach. The debate continues between musical purists and those less strictly inclined about the viability of playing Bach on the piano rather than on the harpsichord.

Musicians may look to Busoni's example for guidance. In common with Bach, he believed that the musical idea transcended the actual means of expressing it.

It was Mozart, however, who—through his clarity and economy of expression—assumed the role of Busoni's compositional angel. He noted of Mozart's music that "architecture is next of kin to his art" and took his model's precepts to heart in his own structurally sound, finely chiseled works.[26] Ever the independent, Busoni wrote, "Mozart! the seeker and the finder, the great man with the childlike heart—it is he we marvel at, to whom we are devoted; but not his Tonic and Dominant, his Developments and Codas."[27] Not for Busoni the tried and true—his was the spirit of the explorer: "There is no new and old. Only known and not yet known. Of these . . . the known still forms by far the smaller part."[28] After the First World War, Busoni began performing eight of Mozart's mature piano concertos at a time when they were practically unknown (despite Camille Saint-Saëns's concert performances of many of these works in Paris fifty years earlier).

Another important influence upon Busoni's development was Beethoven: "Bach is the foundation of piano playing. Liszt the summit. The two make Beethoven possible."[29] In his capacities as pianist, conductor, and composer, Busoni studied Beethoven's music thoroughly. He felt drawn to its monumental and spiritual qualities. Beethoven's music, however, was continuously performed after his death, unlike that of Bach, Mozart, and Liszt—a situation generally unchanged until Busoni's unflagging efforts on their behalf. The Italian writer Piero Rattalino succinctly observed, "Busoni was the protagonist of three crucial moments in the history of concert music: the discovery of Liszt the musician, the complete rediscovery of Bach, and the recovery of Mozart placed on the same level as Beethoven."[30]

Busoni also met contemporary composers, including Mahler in 1887 and Tchaikovsky soon afterward. Several years later, the twenty-four-year-old Busoni proceeded to win first prize in the inaugural Anton Rubinstein competition, for his *Konzertstück* for piano and orchestra. Dedicated to Rubinstein, the work bears the influence of the D Minor Piano Concerto by Busoni's only mentor, Brahms. Despite his early promise as a composer, Busoni soon recognized the extreme difficulty of maintaining the highest artistic standards as both composer and pianist:

> My development as a composer would already be at quite a different stage if it had not been for the long interruptions and having to gather up the threads again so laboriously. I have only four months in the year in which to produce some better work and then I have to take a little step backwards again.[31]

In the decade between his twenty-fifth and thirty-fifth birthdays, starting with his Moscow period, Busoni generally chose the concert stage. When he returned to serious composition, his works moved away from the chromatic, tonal harmony characteristic of Chopin and into new, experimental realms. He used major and minor chords simultaneously—a technique originally explored by Alkan—and blended different keys within the same measure or beat, resulting in an indefinite haze of sound reminiscent of Scriabin. "Strange, that one should feel major and minor as opposites," Busoni explained.

> They both present the same face, now more joyous, now more serious; and a mere touch of the brush suffices to turn the one into the other. The passage from either to the other is easy and imperceptible; when it occurs frequently and swiftly, the two begin to shimmer and coalesce indistinguishably.[32]

Busoni also explored the intervals of the second and the fourth, finding in them innovative approaches to modulation. His radical use of scales grew well beyond the different modes used in medieval church music, Far Eastern harmonies, and other world influences. In fact, his experiments led to the existence of over a hundred different scales, compared to the traditional scales of Western harmonic theory. Busoni came by his innovations via systematic, intensive study, filtered through one of music history's great intellects. His compositional advances represent what we would today consider technological advances: each new miracle is made possible by what has come before it.

In 1902 Busoni organized and conducted a seven-year series of concerts with the Berlin Philharmonic. (It was also during this time that Busoni first conceived of "a composition in which drama, music, dancing, and magic are combined"—an idea Scriabin, independently, would later develop more fully.[33]) Although he gave more than lip service to the new music of Bartók and Schoenberg, it was to past masters—including Alkan and others he felt were unfairly neglected—that his affinities drew him. During these concerts, Busoni performed a pivotal work in his canon, the epic, late-romantic Concerto for Piano, Orchestra, and Male Chorus. Eight years after its premiere, he wrote:

> I endeavored with this work to gather together the results of my first period of manhood, and it represents the actual conclusion of it. Like every work that falls into such a period of development, it is ripe through experience gained and supported by tradition. It does not know about the future at all, but represents the present at the time of its origin.[34]

In this work, Busoni rejects the idea of putting virtuosity on display, as in the Liszt concertos, though that composer's *Totentanz* and *Faust Symphony* did influence him. The concerto was initially decried as ugly music, barren of invention and senselessly modern: "If only Herr Busoni had not won the Rubinstein Prize for *composition!*" cried one reviewer. "Then he would have stuck to his Bach transcriptions."[35] Busoni took a stoic stance toward the work's early reception and defended it in a letter written just after its premiere: "I have created a work for every note of which I can answer and which will endure, inasmuch as human achievements are at all durable."[36] He referred to it as his "Skyscraper Concerto," while Sorabji called it

Busoni, 1898.

Busoni in London, 1905.

the highest pinnacle ever reached in the piano concerto genre.[37] A decade later it had much success, after the efforts of Scriabin, Schoenberg, and Richard Strauss made the new seem acceptably modern. Busoni originally wanted to write an opera based upon *Aladdin,* by the Danish poet Adam Oehlenschläger, but instead used the text in the finale of the five-movement concerto.

Just over three years after the concerto's premiere, Busoni's compositional style leapt forward with the seven elegies for piano. They brilliantly fuse contrasting and highly distinct musical lines. Using his own scientifically advanced pedal techniques, an ingenious distribution of parts between the hands, and harmonic clashes of unusual beauty, Busoni achieved extraordinary levels of technique and originality. He considered these compositions—each of which is dedicated to a young pianist he admired—his most mature to that point, and wrote that he put his entire personal vision into them. Alternately sensual, vivid, withdrawn, and mystic, they refute the classic Greek meaning of *elegy* as a song of lamentation and instead point to Goethe's passionate work. "A German should at least know his Goethe," Busoni told his colleague José Vianna da Motta, "and are this prodigy's 'Roman elegies' songs of lament? Practically the opposite."[38]

The last of these works is the Berceuse, gentle and expressive, composed several months before his mother died. Upon her death he transcribed its material into the *Berceuse élégiaque* for chamber orchestra, in its way every bit as moving as the *Fantasia after J. S. Bach,* written after his father died and dedicated to him. The cast of both these works is elysian, vulnerable, and consolatory.

The four pieces comprising *An die Jugend* followed the elegies by a year. The second, "Preludio, fuga e fuga figurata," is based on the D Major Prelude and Fugue from Book 1 of Bach's *Well-Tempered Clavier.* Busoni actually combines the prelude and fugue in the *fuga figurata* section, hinting at several of Godowsky's ingenious combinations of Chopin études. The third of Busoni's set combines two works by Mozart. The fourth piece, "Introduzione, capriccio ed epilogo," begins with a free fantasy on a Paganini theme in the manner of Liszt, this time for left hand alone, then gallops through a virtuosic capriccio and a thoroughly original epilogue. The left-hand section is reminiscent of the fascinating works by Alkan, Scriabin, and Godowsky for that hand alone.

Although less obviously massive than that by Alkan, Busoni's sonatinas surely belie their diminutive name. The Second Sonatina, written in 1912, joins the later Scriabin sonatas in its journey outside the bounds of traditional tonality and harmony. It is written without key signature, with sharps and flats written as needed, and its complexity and forward thinking further contributed to Busoni's reputation as a futurist as he grappled with atonality. Busoni had become interested in occult matters and met Scriabin that year in St. Petersburg, where both Mephisophelean composers had the opportunity to exchange ideas. Scriabin's Ninth Sonata, written during this time, became a particular inspiration for Busoni's works of the period.

Busoni in Zurich during World War I.

He wrote to Scriabin: "Let me congratulate you on your last works, and particularly the Ninth Sonata, which I consider a work of *inestimable value!*"[39] In his Sixth Sonatina, Busoni took the genre of operatic fantasy given to the world by Liszt and made his own unique contribution to the form, in this case based upon Georges Bizet's *Carmen*. Toward the end the sonatina's mood darkens, becoming mystic and meditative—far from the expected grand conclusion of Liszt's paraphrases.

Although Busoni the pianist was universally acknowledged to have few peers, judgment of his compositional talent came more slowly and less decisively. He also failed to produce a popular piece to impress his name into the larger musical consciousness, on the order of Rachmaninov's Prelude in C-sharp Minor. Sorabji frequently wrote of Busoni's music in terms of its "hints and suggestions at dangerous forces and powers lurking below the surface of things just without reach, or within it of those who have the courage to put forth their hand and seize them—Black Magic . . . fantastic unreal eerie beauty."[40] Busoni responded strongly and personally to the works of E. T. A. Hoffmann, writing of "the veil of mysticism, the secret harmonies of Nature, the thrill of the supernatural, the twilight vagueness of the borderland of dreams, everything, in fact, which [Hoffmann] so effectively limned with the precision of *words*."[41]

The *Fantasia contrappuntistica* is based upon several fugues from Bach's *Art of Fugue*, which Busoni referred to as Bach's last and greatest work. Busoni wrote that his fantasia "grew out of the attempt to complete J. S. Bach's last unfinished fugue. It is a study. (Every self-portrait of Rembrandt's is a study; every work is a study for the next one; every life's work a study for those who come after.)"[42] In this philosophy we again find Busoni's approach to tradition and the importance of learning from one's forebears. He also reiterated his belief that music is absolute: "The *Fantasia contrappuntistica* is thought for neither for pianoforte nor organ, nor orchestra. It is music. The sound-medium which imparts this music to the listener is of secondary importance."[43] (It is still not entirely clear for which instrument[s] Bach wrote the *Art of Fugue*.) Busoni felt strongly that musicians and audiences should be less concerned with notes, phrases, and instrumentation than with their spiritual essence. Above all, Busoni believed that "form, imagination, and feeling are indispensable to the artist, they are the most precious of all things—those to which he offers sacrifice—the sacrifice of himself."[44]

Further exploring ideas that Busoni had earlier written into the *Indian Fantasy* for piano and orchestra, his *Indianisches Tagebuch* (Red Indian Diary) comprises short rhythmic pieces based upon North American Indian melodies and folk songs. He referred to its "poetic simulations, such as the melancholy of the race; a glimpse of the Mississippi caught in passing; a hint of warlike proceedings; exotic coloring."[45] The idea for the work first came to him in Los Angeles in 1911. While on a United States concert tour the previous year, Busoni saw a former student, the ethnomusicologist Natalie Curtis-Burlin, who gave him her just-published *Indians'*

Book. Busoni was thus introduced to the native spirituality of American Indian melodies, which, to Western ears, have a wistful quality. Further research led him to feel a natural and immediate kinship with Indian culture and its lack of commercialism: "The Red Indians are the only cultured people who will have nothing to do with money and who dress the most everyday things in beautiful words."[46] In these four pieces, Busoni first presents their melodies simply, then colors them with his unique brand of mysticism. Sorabji commented on their Indian themes:

> They are not developed, in the ordinary sense, so much as *haunted* by a strange powerful entity that overshadows them, and so takes possession of them that, without any great physiognomical alteration they assume an appearance totally different, uncannily changed, extraordinary lights play upon them and they take on an aspect, hallucinated and obsessed. It is a spectacle for the ear of boundless fascination for those who are in tune with Busoni's strange genius and who are privileged to enter that peculiar world in which his mind lived and moved. It is a necromantic magical world.[47]

Sorabji's thoughts could well be applied to his own works, or to Scriabin's. And Busoni echoed Scriabin's final aesthetic several years after the Russian's death: "I yearn for change, for a great definitive scheme, for freedom of movement . . . for clarity and finality."[48] One of Busoni's most important goals for his own music was eliminating affectation, believing that "*sincerity* is one of the absolute necessities for the existence and activity of creation."[49] As a composer, he retains into the twenty-first century the austere reputation of an intellectual giant, with great emotional impact, and his music has been widely embraced by artists and audiences.

Colleagues and Competition

Busoni's peers—those in the best position to judge—considered him among the most persuasive of the piano's exponents. Ronald Stevenson, the Scottish composer-pianist, wrote of Busoni as a "twentieth-century master in an age of few masters. He was both consummator and pioneer."[50]

Isidor Philipp, a long-time professor at the Paris Conservatoire, explored several of the same ideas on the piano's potential at the same time Busoni and Godowsky did (often in discussions with them), thus furthering their influence upon France's musical life. Philipp said that Busoni "never played anything twice in the same way. He relied on the inspiration of the moment, and when he was inspired he did amazing things. A conductor would have had a hard time following *him* without score!" He also called Busoni "the most extraordinary of them all—his face, his hands, everything about him spoke of nobility."[51] Sorabji labeled Busoni "an artistic and intellectual titan like those divine men of the Renaissance, da Vinci or Buonarroti."[52] Indeed, Busoni considered himself a Renaissance man, was a great admirer of Leonardo da Vinci, and intended to write an opera on that master's life. The philosopher-scholar in Busoni appeared to know no limits. Sorabji wrote of Busoni's "extraordinary cold white fire of intellectualized emotion . . . a command of variegated tone quality that could leave one gasping breathless at the black magic that could make an indifferent piano an instrument."[53] And Arthur Rubinstein called Busoni "a towering personality, a shining example to all musicians for the noble way in which he pursued his career so uncompromisingly, for the high standard he set for his own compositions, and for his general culture, so rare among artists."[54]

Notwithstanding such praise, Busoni instinctively reacted against anyone who could be considered a rival. Despite a rare level of accomplishment and a healthy ego, Busoni never felt completely secure with his position in life. Is it that lonely at the top? Surely he had every outward reason not to feel threatened, yet he did. The pianist André Watts, after having gone backstage to congratulate a colleague on a great performance, describes a type of pianist who shares this aspect of Busoni's psyche:

> Looking around me I saw some of my colleagues with teeth gritted
> murmuring, "Marvelous concert." It was really killing them that [the artist]
> was so good. I don't get that at all. These murmurers were pianists who
> had nothing to fear. They had their careers. Their names were plastered on
> billboards all over the world. What were they so unhappy about? They should
> have been content and they should have enjoyed it. They had secure positions
> but had no security . . . It's very strange to me, this inability to be convinced
> that someone else can do well.[55]

Vanity appears to be a common theme among those threatened by rivals, but any further speculation would straddle the tightrope of responsibility. These are complicated matters best left to the psychoanalyst. How easy it has become to categorize this composer or that pianist; critical epithets rarely take full measure of lives as enigmatic as they are fascinating.

Coincidences

Busoni's wariness of any competitor was further demonstrated by an unpleasant, very public row. In 1909 Godowsky succeeded Busoni as director of Vienna's prestigious Klaviermeisterschule. Busoni had been disappointed with most of his students, and the hours his teaching required ate into his cherished free time. Godowsky was approached to fill the position, and as soon as his services were secured, the powers-that-be canceled Busoni's contract. The Vienna press had a field day at his expense, claiming that he ignored his responsibilities. That the Jewish Godowsky was granted such a position in the then anti-Semitic country—and took his oath on the Talmud in the presence of Emperor Franz Joseph—appears altogether extraordinary in that milieu. Those circumstances prove the power of music and personality to assuage deeply felt prejudices. (What Alkan would not have given for such recognition by his own country!) Godowsky, the amiable genius, the master teacher beholden to no method, was on the rise and actually secured terms much more favorable for the continuation of his concert career than did Busoni.

Godowsky never seemed to shake the insecurities of his own early life. His circumstances, in the lack of both strong family ties and formal music education, were remarkably similar to Busoni's. Godowsky offered a phrase that could apply equally to Busoni: "The public builds up an illusion about any conspicuous person but sometimes it is most difficult to live within that illusion."[56] Realizing his own position all too well, Godowsky experienced increasing pressures throughout his career; his later public concerts proved less than spontaneous. Busoni, at least as a performer, was better able to deal with such stresses. Both musicians developed tremendous repertoires, demonstrating, in addition to their artistic gifts, an immense capacity for work.

Busoni and Godowsky each cultivated a wide professional and social network. Among their mutual close friends was Philipp, who, it seems, knew everyone. He was one of only four people at Alkan's funeral and was on the best of terms with Tchaikovsky and hundreds of other musical luminaries.

Godowsky sailed to Europe in 1900, settling in Berlin as had his contemporary Busoni six years earlier. In 1901 Busoni was in the audience—along with an array of distinguished pianists—for Godowsky's debut with the London Philharmonic Society. In a pattern that was to follow him for the rest of his life, Godowsky wrote of his London recital debut: "The critics, with a few exceptions, could not tolerate my Chopin audacities. Some of them actually lost their temper."[57] Busoni faced similar critical scorn over his Bach adaptations, but Godowsky greatly admired those transcriptions and had them in mind when he dedicated to Busoni his paraphrase of Weber's *Invitation to the Dance*.

Busoni's Variations and Fugue in C Minor on Chopin's Prelude No. 20, written when he was eighteen, predates Godowsky's Chopin studies by at least a decade. Busoni also wrote variants of a number of Chopin études as exercises to enhance their technical value. Both Godowsky and Busoni played much of Chopin's music, including the twenty-four études. (In turn, all three of these great composer-pianists shared a deep love and respect for Bach and Mozart.) Busoni's most famous and oft-performed transcription is the chaconne from Bach's Solo Violin Partita No. 2; among Godowsky's best transcriptions are those from Bach's solo violin and cello works.

Busoni thought that Godowsky was one of the most significant contributors to the piano's development, but both men lamented the fact that their brand of perfectionism was unappreciated and misunderstood. Their friendship was uneasy, mainly because of Busoni's insecurities toward potential rivals, and he allowed himself the occasional jealous barb: "What is the difference between Godowsky and a pianola [player-piano]?" he would ask. Then, answering his own riddle: "Godowsky can play ten times as fast as a pianola but, to make up for it, a pianola plays with ten times as much feeling as Godowsky."[58] Ironically, Godowsky displayed nothing but contempt for those pianists without what he called the necessary individuality, character, and temperament to make their performances better than those of a player piano. Despite their indisputable importance to the piano's development, Busoni and Godowsky lived during an age when their discoveries did not necessarily endear them to the larger world.

Their perfectionist views about making records were largely the same. Busoni felt, despite his interest in the nascent medium, that the recording process was fraught with compromise and limitations. His few recordings, made in London in 1919 and 1922, reveal enough about Busoni's style to cast him as one of the major pianists of his era; however, their poor sound quality conveys little of the wide timbral variety he cultivated. Though truer to Busoni's reputation than Godowsky's discs were to his, the recordings, while historically engaging, are not overwhelming. Busoni confessed:

> My suffering over the toil of making gramophone records came to an end yesterday, after playing for 3½ hours! . . . Since the first day, I have been as depressed as if I were expecting to have an operation. To do it is stupid and a strain. . . . They wanted the Faust waltz (which lasts a good ten minutes) *but it was only to take four minutes!* That meant quickly cutting, patching, and improvising, so that there should still be some sense left in it; watching the pedal (because it sounds bad); thinking of certain notes which had to be stronger or weaker in order to please this devilish machine: not letting oneself go for fear of inaccuracies and being conscious the whole time that every note was going to be there for eternity; how can there be any question of inspiration, freedom, swing, or poetry?[59]

Godowsky himself wrote of the recording process, "It was a dreadful ordeal, increasingly so the more sensitive the artist. I broke down in my health in London in the Spring of 1930, owing to these nerve-killing tortures. How can one think of emotion!"[60]

A Life in Music

From his earliest years, Godowsky was possessed of a voracious need for music. He studied incessantly. Taught by a family friend up to age six, he then largely went his own way. Nonetheless, such was the strength of his instinct that he was able to take full advantage of his talent.

Godowsky began to reap public and financial success, until a lawyer and music lover put an end to what he saw as exploitation of the prodigy. He arranged for

Leopold Godowsky, c. 1890s. Courtesy of Leopold Godowsky III.

Godowsky's scholarship to the Russian Imperial Conservatory in Petrograd. It was turned down at the insistence of his teacher, who feared losing his young charge. This sequence of events affected the rest of Godowsky's life. Had he become the product of the same training methods as Rachmaninov, Medtner, and Scriabin, Godowsky might have developed into a different type of virtuoso, although the rigors of his contrapuntalist thought would doubtless have been encouraged. He attended Berlin's Hochschule für Musik after a precocious audition in front of several luminaries, including the eminent violinist Joseph Joachim. Godowsky's gifts put him far ahead of his classmates and even his instructors. He lasted twelve weeks there.

Determined to make the most of his talent, the fifteen-year-old Godowsky traveled to Weimar to study with Liszt, but the famous pianist had just died. Godowsky then went to Paris to meet with Saint-Saëns, for whom he played on many subsequent occasions. Without giving him formal lessons, Saint-Saëns offered Godowsky much guidance and advice—one former brilliant prodigy to a prodigious young pianist.

Godowsky spent his late teens in France, broadening his knowledge and education. Saint-Saëns arranged for Godowsky to meet Tchaikovsky, whose encouragement strengthened and inspired the young composer-pianist. Saint-Saëns continued to guide Godowsky through the social and musical circles of Paris, where he quickly found favor with the most influential people of the time.

Godowsky's status as largely self-taught gave him an independence he exhibited throughout life. Back in New York at age twenty, looking to claim his destiny, he managed to get an invitation to play at the Vanderbilt mansion. At that time the influence of society and money was a prerequisite for success. The making of a public virtuoso was then, as it is today, prohibitively expensive and time consuming; with the right introductions (and, of course, the right gifts), the young pianist could count on doors being opened, finances arranged, concerts forthcoming. Subscription and symphony programs were still controlled by wealthy society figures; the stage was largely closed to those unable or unwilling to follow the expected routine. Social skills were of paramount necessity. As the Vanderbilt occasion turned out, Godowsky was treated as a hired hand, akin to, as he saw it, a circus entertainer; after that experience, he swore never to play at social gatherings again. Despite this setback, New York had the chance to hear Godowsky at the first of his many recitals at Carnegie Hall, made possible in April 1891 through the influence of Tchaikovsky, who officially opened Carnegie Hall several weeks later. Shortly after his debut Godowsky married his childhood sweetheart, Frieda Saxe, and he became an American citizen the next day.

Godowsky turned to teaching for income and found in it a second career that fascinated him. He soon took charge of the piano department at the Chicago Conservatory after a brief tenure at a Philadelphia school. In Chicago, Godowsky established his lifelong habit of offering an open and welcoming home. His personality, accessibility, hospitality, and legendary reputation made his residence a way station for artists, painters, writers, and intellectuals. The conductor Theodore Thomas, founder of the Chicago Symphony Orchestra, was a frequent guest and another influential musician on whom Godowsky relied. The Tchaikovsky connection continued to help him, as he had great success playing that composer's First Concerto with Thomas and his orchestra.

Godowsky became increasingly determined to use his newfound fame and stability to further his international performing career. Following Anton Rubinstein's lead and inspiring the composer-pianist Ernő Dohnányi to do likewise, Godowsky presented a comprehensive series of eight concerts devoted to a wide range of the piano's literature. His endurance, technique, and communicative skills were now beyond question or compare.

Godowsky's appearance—stout, with a cherubic face portraying much wisdom and authority—combined with his standing among musicians as an innovator, a seeker of philosophical truths, and a prophetic composer led to his nickname, the "Buddha of the Piano." Those closest to him, who were the beneficiaries of his genial informality, knew him affectionately as "Popsy." Liszt or Paderewski, with their distinctive profiles and flowing hair, fit the public's image of a great pianist; not so Godowsky, who could just as easily have been mistaken for a good-natured baker.

Godowsky's Berlin debut in 1900 proved to be one of those storied affairs that launch lasting careers in brilliant fashion, marking an unusual confluence of talent, opportunity, and the happy coincidence of being in the right place at the right time. On this occasion, the pivotal concert of his nascent career, he played the Brahms D Minor and Tchaikovsky B-flat Minor Concertos with the Berlin Philharmonic, along with a selection of his studies on the Chopin études and his arrangement of Weber's *Invitation to the Dance*. Godowsky's audience—filled with pianists and knowledgeable critics—received everything ecstatically, even the Chopin studies, which were later to receive widely mixed reactions. As encores he performed the Scherzo from his mentor Saint-Saëns's Second Concerto and his arrangement of Chopin's "Black Key" étude for the left hand alone. His wild success, far beyond anything he dared imagine, opened every door to him among society and musical circles, clearing the way for a magnificent career. It was also the proverbial double-edged sword as his natural modesty succumbed to fear. Godowsky admitted after that concert:

> A success like the one I had is embarrassing to the artist. Musicians talk so extravagantly about me that, unless I play better than I did at the first concert, I would disappoint my audience. I never expected a tenth of the success I had. I felt overawed and almost frightened.[61]

Godowsky reached professional, social, and material heights he could not have imagined. But like many young artists who win enormous acclaim, he began to see each concert as a proving ground for him to justify his position. The strain, combined with his embarrassment at the encomia constantly put before him, became difficult to bear. When he was invited to make gramophone recordings—before the age of editing—the same fears came into play: how could he perform perfectly, convey the purest emotions straight through, under the cold stares of posterity, with an unforgiving microphone at his hands? Even in his later concert career, he was held back by the fear of disappointing the high expectations he engendered. Audiences go to concerts not only to hear music, but also to see and applaud celebrated musicians who have given them so much. The listener's perception of the performance is refracted through the lens of the artist's reputation.

Even at the beginning of the twentieth century, word traveled fast in the music world. Despite his increasing fears, when Godowsky toured the United States and

Godowsky in Vienna. Courtesy of International Piano Archives, College Park, Maryland.

Canada after his Berlin conquest, he was already received as a legendary virtuoso. His Russian tour in 1905 left a lasting impression on the many famous musicians with whom he came in contact. Godowsky was the dedicatee of numerous works written around that time. He also took the opportunity to cement his lifelong friendship with Rachmaninov. Each frequently performed the other's music in his recitals, and they publicly praised one another.

Godowsky continued to give first priority to his work and commitments: he insisted on perfection, no matter what the cost. In 1915 he caused a sensation when he left his home to finish contracted work for the Art Publishing Company but told no one. His family reported him missing. The police, after an exhaustive search, determined that no sinister fate had befallen the great pianist, despite his family's concerns. He had apparently left a letter, but it was never found. Godowsky, unaware of the commotion until he read about it in the newspapers—it occasioned a front-page headline in the *New York Times*—called home to assure everyone that he was safe and offered his heartfelt apologies. Nonetheless, he refused to say where he was, repeating only that he needed to work undisturbed. Godowsky had departed with a clear conscience, sure that the letter—left for his wife in their bedroom—would be seen. This kind of obsessive behavior was characteristic, and it grew more pronounced with age. His friend Maurice Aronson observed astutely:

> [He had] a most persistently persuasive way about him, and in dealing with him it was difficult to assert one's will. People the world over had always met him with much genuine willingness to be of service to him and to please him; on that account he grew to believe opposition to his wishes as acts of unfriendliness, of which, because of his rarely generous nature, not anyone wanted to be guilty. To that extent he had become somewhat spoiled.[62]

Godowsky's hospitality, nearly as legendary as his playing, fed his need to be accepted. He and Frieda were beloved hosts to all who came their way. They established the same pattern in Berlin, Vienna, and New York as they had in Chicago. Why was everyone so fond of Godowsky? His colleague Hofmann answered, more generously than Aronson, "Because his character is as true as gold and his art as pure as crystal. Little wonder that everyone who knows him and his art loves him."[63] Artists, writers, actors, and musicians, especially pianists, were recipients of his social generosity. His salon rivaled the great musical gatherings in the nineteenth century, where musicians would gather to play, dine together, gossip, and generally relax, free from the strains of public performance and critics' pens.

Despite his position, Godowsky lacked pretense. He was equally and genuinely gracious to all people, regardless of their position or what they could do for him. His bohemian gatherings included both the celebrated and the not so famous, as well as new music-loving acquaintances. However, his intolerance of injustice, hypocrisy, and commercialism served to stimulate often-abrasive emotional conflicts that

Godowsky. Courtesy of International Piano Archives.

increased as he grew older. He refused to accept any slights of business or advertising, either real or perceived. He canceled a New York concert in 1915 after discovering that the great tenor Enrico Caruso was given preferential advertising in a subscription series, even though his contract stipulated that no artist would be so favored. Conversely, Godowsky would never think of demanding superior billing over his colleagues. He had the highest respect for Caruso, but could not see himself in a subordinate position.

Godowsky's sense of self and his perfectionism, honed without the soothing guidance of a musical mentor, had by then infiltrated his personal life as well as his professional career. His Busoni-like obsession with perfection magnified a series of grueling disappointments late in his life. He lost a very considerable fortune in the stock market crash of 1929, and then, while recording music of Chopin in a London studio, he suffered a series of strokes that ended his performing career at age sixty. His health problems and the Great Depression served to heighten a pessimism he had expressed several years earlier:

> I am constantly in a state of depression. I really think there is no purpose that we, mortals, can find in our being here and having all those terrifying puzzling things around and about us. Why? Wherefore? What do even the sublimest efforts of mortal geniuses amount to in the scheme of Cosmic phenomena?[64]

However, only a month before writing those words, Godowsky had felt empowered by the completion of his Passacaglia:

> It is my most important work since the Sonata (seventeen years ago!), is considerably more mature (no wonder!), and touches depths which only intense suffering can produce—but there is emancipation and defiance in it. The Passacaglia gave me new strength and a feeling of aloofness. I hope you will not interpret this as a gesture of conceit or bravado. I simply believe that my latest work is a great expression of human loftiness. While composing it I felt that I was purifying my soul and looking closer into eternity.[65]

Godowsky apparently hid his depression for many years, but it was only magnified by advancing age:

> I always suffered from "Weltschmerz" and heartaches—from the pain of living and the utter hopelessness of it all, but we must play our little stupid comedy before yielding the stage to some other unfortunate. However, there must be some ultimate reason for everything and therefore we must go on courageously. . . . Art is the greatest consoler because it creates beautiful illusions which can never be realized and therefore cannot be destroyed. The realization of a desire is the death of it.[66]

Godowsky wrote in 1924, "As we grow older . . . we become more awed by the mystery of creation and life but less concerned about our little self. To people that reflect and meditate, life itself is a painful consciousness, a baffling reality."[67] Busoni—who died soon after those words were written—had been trying to come to grips with similar thoughts, though apparently without the very real tinges of desperation Godowsky experienced. Despondency, hopelessness, depression—this kind of sickness knows no economic, social, or career bounds; yet it did not prevent Godowsky, Busoni, and others of The Eight from producing great work.

The Humorist

Toward the end of his life, Godowsky retreated very far from the easy sense of humor that had become part of his legend. Before his heart attacks and despite the latent depression, he possessed a sharp, often devastating wit. In a remark to the pianist Harold Samuel, he observed, "Your last recital shows you've been working very hard. I noticed particularly much more feeling in your right elbow."[68] Once at Carnegie Hall, Godowsky and Hofmann were in the audience for another famous pianist's recital. Hofmann asked, "Isn't it terrible how many notes he missed?" Whereupon Godowsky quickly answered, "Not as terrible as the ones he didn't miss."[69] At Carnegie Hall on another occasion—the debut of the brilliant teenager Jascha Heifetz—he was sitting with the violinist Mischa Elman, who remarked to Godowsky at intermission, "It's awful hot in there." "Not for pianists," came the reply.[70]

His humor clearly had a realistic edge. As movers were installing two new grand pianos for Godowsky, one of them, drenched in perspiration, told Godowsky just how he felt having to do all that heavy lifting. "What are you complaining about?" Godowsky asked with a laugh. "You only have to move pianos. I have to move audiences."[71] But his wit could be generous as well. When told of wrong notes at a Hofmann recital, Godowsky simply replied, "Why look for spots on the sun?"[72]

The Virtuoso

Godowsky's Berlin and London debuts were among the most important of the era. However, he always had an aversion to the idea of a public virtuoso. Importantly, he felt the utmost contempt for virtuosity. In this he was like the others of The Eight: endowed with preternatural musical-athletic abilities, each strove to transcend his physical gifts.

One of Godowsky's most meaningful discoveries came early in his career. In a bid to quickly increase his repertoire, he practiced twelve to fourteen hours a day. This grueling schedule taught him the importance of relaxation. He would play at night just for his own pleasure after working the entire day, and found that his weariness caused his arms to fall at his side under their own weight.[73] Busoni and Godowsky

were the first to take a more intellectual approach to the mechanics of piano playing, delving into and codifying the most complicated issues involved for the virtuoso, including relaxation and efficiency. They both detested showmanship and
worked for the greatest economy of means at the instrument.

H. G. Wells made an observation that both Busoni and Godowsky took to heart:
"Most of the good men we know are not doing the best work of their gifts: nearly all
are a little adapted, most of them shockingly adapted, to some second-best use."[74]
Both these great artists were determined to avoid such a compromise. Godowsky
may have had one of the legendary techniques of all time, but out of respect for his
abilities, he always stressed the necessity for exceptionally hard work, knowing that
perfectionism becomes the baseline from which inspiration develops. "The strain of
such work is so severe," he said, "that only those who have endured it know how
exhausting it may become."[75]

It has been well documented that, owing to a combination of perfectionism and
nerves, Godowsky played at his peak only privately or among a small circle of friends.
One of his colleagues mischievously observed, "Godowsky's aura extends for just
two yards."[76] The pianist, composer, and writer Abram Chasins—present when
Godowsky played his *Java Suite* for the first time at a small gathering—recalled:

> It was sorcery, nothing less. Later, when I was walking Hofmann back to his
> hotel, he said: "Never forget what you heard tonight; never lose the memory
> of that sound. There's nothing like it in this world. It is tragic that the public
> has never heard Popsy as only he can play."[77]

Godowsky was often sad and resigned after a concert, apparently unable to attain
the highest levels he expected of himself despite the esteem he enjoyed among the
greatest pianists of his day. Hofmann called him "the master of us all."[78] Vladimir
de Pachmann, the celebrated pianist, eccentric, and bon vivant, admitted, "We are
all children, all woodchoppers, compared with him!"[79] (Anton Rubinstein had
made the same remark with respect to Liszt.) James Huneker called Godowsky "a
pianist for pianists, as Shelley is a poet for poets." He meant that as a pianist, especially in private surroundings, Godowsky was most appreciated by connoisseurs
who recognized the magic he produced from the instrument. He called Godowsky
a Brahma, explaining, "I can't help picturing him as a sort of impassive Asiatic deity
seated before the keyboard of his instrument calmly surveying the grand spectacle
of music and its many masques."[80] Echoing Huneker, the pianist Clarence Adler
observed:

> Godowsky's hands always reflected the mood of the music he was
> propounding. He was less of the showman than any other artist I ever heard.
> He would never resort to anything theatrical, nor to any external effect in
> order to bring forth applause. . . . His serious attitude, his philosophic
> countenance was like a Brahma.[81]

Godowsky retreated into the security of his technical supremacy. To an unaware public his musicianship became suspect. Contemporary accounts of his stage manner reveal much about his style. Critiquing a London concert, George Bernard Shaw wrote of Godowsky's Schumann: "Though the difficulties of the *Études symphoniques* seemed to give him no trouble, a certain shyness, rather engaging than otherwise, prevented him from standing on his merits emphatically enough to get full credit for his performance."[82] A review by Sorabji, although acknowledging Godowsky as one of the world's greatest pianists, is also representative: "There is the same effect of neutrality about it. . . . The pianist was obviously not at his ease in the early part of his program."[83] After panning Godowsky's Beethoven and praising his Chopin, Sorabji noted:

> The Albéniz *Tango* arrangement is wholly successful and was admirably played, as was also a most diverting and exciting elaboration of an already exceedingly difficult composition, the same composer's *Triana*. Here, in his element and at his best, was Godowsky, the *prestidigitateur* of the prodigious symphonic metamorphoses on Strauss Waltzes. It was magnificently played.[84]

The Teacher

Few performers found themselves on the same pianistic plane with Godowsky. To students, fellow teachers, and other pianists, Godowsky established himself as an irreplaceable fount of wisdom and knowledge. His absolute gifts, geniality, and stimulation in the company of talented, eager young pianists inspired a rare brand of loyalty between student and teacher. Godowsky approached teaching without the rigid didactic precepts common to many others in his position, which left him able to focus to an unusual degree on individual students and their particular musical problems. "I have no use for the conventional type of class teacher, the horn-rimmed type so academically stiff!" he insisted. "Perhaps it was this which caused me to make musicians and artists out of my pupils, rather than pianists."[85] Godowsky the pianist had no mold to break, no years of indoctrination into one particular method. This attitude, combined with a scientist's sense of discovery, led to revelations of the piano's possibilities. It was no coincidence that Godowsky and Albert Einstein developed a deep admiration and friendship. They were both researchers of the highest order.

Godowsky expected disciplined, hard work from his students:

> The fault with many students is the erroneous idea that genius or talent will take the place of work. They minimize the necessity for careful, painstaking consideration of the infinite details of technique. . . . But this is not all. Individuality, character, and temperament are becoming more and more significant in the highly organized art of pianoforte playing. Remove these,

and the playing of the artists again becomes little better than that of a piano-playing machine.[86]

Writing in 1953, James Francis Cooke concurred: "No teacher was ever more insistent upon precision, yet none had a higher regard for the artistic, the emotional, and the spiritual."[87] Godowsky believed in using difficult sections of the best music to develop a virtuoso playing mechanism, rather than turning to the usual drudgery of technical exercises. He advocated Chopin's études as one of the basics of learning technique, in addition to his own works for left hand alone.

Given a desire to impart their unique discoveries—in a way, to produce musical progeny so their hard-won knowledge would survive them—Busoni and Godowsky devoted much of their energies to teaching. The music world would not see other such brilliant, beloved teachers until Feinberg and Godowsky's student Heinrich Neuhaus began their work at the Moscow Conservatory a generation later. Neuhaus took to heart many of Godowsky's precepts and transmitted them to his students, including his three stars: Sviatoslav Richter, Emil Gilels, and Radu Lupu. The vaunted Russian school thus exists in part because of Godowsky's influence, making his musical presence more wide ranging than that of any other pedagogue of the period. Yet, like Busoni, he eventually came to see teaching more as a responsibility than a great love. Initially so eager to share his new discoveries, he had difficulty finding able and receptive students who could fully absorb and then implement his ideas:

> I consider that the years I spent teaching were an unfortunate choice of my early career. Of course teaching is a noble profession, but I have found that the results are not in proportion to the time and effort spent. It is so futile to teach where there is no pure gold—like preaching in the wilderness. Great genius is exceedingly scarce and I have not yet found one supreme talent. It is discouraging to realize that there is not one Chopin or Liszt living today who has created a new art for the piano.[88]

Nonetheless, Godowsky remained devoted to the idea of education throughout life; he saw his role as going far beyond noblesse oblige in transmitting to others the knowledge he had gained through his own hard work. He became editor in chief of a series of progressive educational publications that gained great popularity and were widely quoted in the educational press. Godowsky also produced his brilliant *Miniatures,* forty-six piano duets for beginners and their teachers—an avenue for joint musical exploration. Greatly admired by no less than Rachmaninov, Hofmann, Huneker, the conductor Bruno Walter, and a host of other luminaries, the *Miniatures* remain some of the most stimulating tools for piano pedagogy ever devised. Written for four hands so that the teacher may accompany the student, they rival and even surpass Bartók's *Mikrokosmos* in their graded, detailed approach to the instrument. For many years they were seen as the gold standard of teaching material. Godowsky emphasized in his preface:

My aim is to interest while I instruct; to educate while I entertain. . . . I have given a great deal of thought and loving care to them and though the pieces are smaller and considerably less complicated than anything I have ever written, they represent the best there is in me. The experience and assimilated knowledge, the aims and aspirations, the hopes and ideals, the disappointments and yearnings of a sensitive nature and an artist's soul are all to be found in this series of simple five-finger pieces.[89]

Godowsky's Music

The *Miniatures* represent a brilliant meeting of pedagogue and composer. Godowsky placed great emphasis on their craft, through complicated textures, counterpoint, and structural clarity. In general, his music is laid out so logically that but for the required reflexes, it is accessible to any good pianist-scholar.

As for Godowsky's piano sonata, he was much engaged in its publication during a period when he played Liszt's sonata. Both of these great virtuoso composer-pianists made one attempt at the form. Godowsky's work employs a five-movement structure used earlier by Brahms in his third sonata, to which the German critics favorably compared it. Although it contains some of his finest music, Godowsky performed the piece only once, in Berlin. Its structure and length—well into the Alkan or Sorabji class—has subsequently limited its appeal to pianists and, as a result, to audiences.

The issue of length in piano compositions is richly debatable. Audiences have shown themselves quite capable of sitting entranced through the hour-plus-long Mahler symphonies. Is it the musical material that keeps audiences returning? The timbral variety of the various orchestral instruments? Busoni would aver that good ideas are good ideas, regardless of instrumentation. Beethoven's *Diabelli Variations,* the Brahms concertos, and other works approach an hour, yet have never lost favor. Busoni's seventy-minute piano concerto would be played far more often if it did not require a male chorus.

Godowsky's sonata is one of his few extended works; most of his pieces were composed in smaller dimensions. He drew inspiration from a wide range of folk melodies and shared with Busoni an instinctive love for other cultures. Godowsky was an incessant traveler and became the first pianist of international stature to perform in Japan, China, and Java, Indonesia, where he found the rich material he was later to turn into his picturesque *Java Suite.* Sorabji put these pieces above Albéniz's great *Iberia Suite* in their evocative musical imagery. Godowsky called his journeys in sound "phonoramas." "In order to eliminate the cheap clap-trap endings to programs, sending the audience away with a little melodramatic excitement," he explained, "I am doing a series of travelogues, ranging from 'Java' to 'jazz.'" Here his receptivity to other cultures met his compositional gifts:

A visit to Java is like entering another world or catching a fleeting glimpse of immortality. Musically, it is amazing. . . . The sonority of the "gamelan" is so weird, spectral, fantastic, and bewitching, and the native music is so elusive, vague, shimmering, and singular, that on listening to this new world of sound I lose my sense of reality. It is the ecstasy of such moments, possible only through world travel, that makes life full of meaning and raises art to the pedestal of the Golden Age.[90]

Godowsky's *Triakontameron*, published five years earlier, in 1920, comprises "Thirty Moods and Scenes in Triple Measure" and is among his most effective music. Akin to Alkan's *Esquisses*, Medtner's *Tales*, or Rachmaninov's *Études-Tableaux*, they explore different moods and scenes, in Godowsky's case all in waltz time as their subtitle indicates. Among these pieces is Godowsky's most celebrated work, "Alt Wien" (Old Vienna), his nostalgic look at that city's storied past. The American influence, though, is primary:

I believe that any composer who steeps himself in a new national atmosphere, and comes in contact with new national ideas and trends, cannot help reacting to them in what he writes. . . . In my "Triakontameron," five of the numbers are of direct American inspiration; the "Ethiopian Serenade"— I know the old colored mammy who cooked for me while in Seattle, where I wrote it, seemed to think it was the real thing—and the "Whitecaps"—which I have tried to set down in tone just as they used to cover the waters of Puget Sound on a windy day. Then there is my "American Idyll" which is an essay in American piano romanticism; my "Little Tango Rag," where I think I have secured the real syncopated effects in three-quarter rhythm; and, finally, my "Requiem (1914–1918)," a solemn threnody, with the roll of drum and clarion call climaxing in "The Star-Spangled Banner."[91]

In some respects, this set recalls Godowsky's earlier *Walzermasken* (1912), subtitled *Twenty-Four Tone Fantasies in Three-Quarter Time*, a marvelous collection of melodic insouciance.

Vastly different are the studies on the Chopin études, composed between 1893 and 1914. They had their genesis in tragedy: Godowsky's just-married brother-in-law and his wife were killed in a train crash. The news devastated Godowsky, who had received a letter from them the morning of the day they died. To distract himself from his grief, he began experimenting with one of Chopin's famously difficult works, the étude in thirds, a piece he was practicing at the time. He first developed an entirely new fingering that he found more practical. Then, wanting to see if the fingering would work for his left hand as well, he reversed the piece's pattern and transplanted the difficult double notes to the left hand.

After Godowsky's Berlin success, Robert Lienau (of the well-known German publishing house Schlesinger), recognizing the enormous impact and importance of his Chopin paraphrases, offered the fledgling composer a considerable advance for them, establishing him for the first time as a mainstream published composer. Godowsky explained their rationale:

> The fifty-three studies based upon twenty-six Études of Chopin have manifold purposes. Their aim is to develop the mechanical, technical, and musical possibilities of pianoforte playing, to expand the peculiarly adapted nature of the instrument to polyphonic, polyrhythmic, and polydynamic work, and to widen the range of its possibilities in tone coloring. The unusual mental and physical demands made upon the performer by the above-mentioned work must invariably lead to a much higher proficiency in the command of the instrument, while the composer for the piano will find a number of suggestions regarding the treatment of the instrument, and its musical utterance in general. Owing to innumerable contrapuntal devices, which frequently encompass almost the whole range of the keyboard, the fingering and pedaling are often of a revolutionary character, particularly in the twenty-two studies for the left hand alone.[92]

Godowsky carefully studied Scriabin's Prelude and Nocturne for the left hand, Op. 9 (and may have done likewise with Alkan's ingenious left-hand étude from Op. 76), in developing his own unique contributions to this specialized genre. He frequently included in his concerts the two Scriabin works, published just as Godowsky began to develop his own ideas for the left hand. He considered the eight-part Suite for the Left Hand Alone one of his most mature works. It emerged at the end of the 1920s, shortly before Ravel's famous Concerto for the Left Hand drew fresh attention to that hand's singular possibilities. Of his suite, Godowsky wrote, "It will be a most unique contribution to the piano literature, more so than any other I have made in the past. What pleases me more than any other consideration is the fact that it is real, inspired music."[93] He described one of his works, the *Étude macabre* for the Left Hand Alone, as "an intensely dramatic and gruesome picture."[94] Because that hand usually resides in the lower part of the keyboard, with its deep, resonant tones, Godowsky ascribed to it several benefits, including "the incontestable advantage of enabling the player to produce with less effort and more elasticity a fuller and mellower tone, superior in quantity and quality to that of the right hand."[95]

The piano world took no time in recognizing Godowsky's genius, even if it sometimes disagreed with his efforts. Taking an interest in his compatriot's achievements, the celebrated pianist Ignace Paderewski became absorbed in the younger pianist's studies on the Chopin études and offered his public approval, further solidifying Godowsky's rise in stature.

Godowsky said enigmatically, "Music is music—a definite emotional stimulant, and stimulants, as everyone knows, are possessed of dangerous properties."[96] He based his Passacaglia—technically dangerous and emotionally dark—on the opening theme of Schubert's "Unfinished" Symphony. This huge work comprises forty-four variations, a cadenza, and a fugue, written as an homage to Schubert and commemorating the one-hundredth anniversary of that composer's death. Horowitz, a great admirer of Godowsky, began learning this work, only to give it up, he said, because of its difficulty. A much more likely explanation, however, is that because many of Godowsky's extraordinary challenges are hidden from public view, the intense labor that goes into their mastery often remains unnoticed by nonpianists. The difficulties are not of the type that call attention to themselves; they exist solely to serve Godowsky's musical aims and are consistent with his disdain for virtuosity (a sentiment Horowitz vacillated upon). Chasins described the first time Godowsky performed his Passacaglia, at a private gathering in his home:

> This was sheer enchantment, both the work itself and Godowsky's pianism. It had the cool, colorful clarity of a stained-glass window. Although I was greatly moved and impressed by what I heard, Godowsky's effortless mastery made me unaware of the vastness of his pianistic feat that night.[97]

Godowsky summed up his compositional achievements four years before he died: "I consider my Passacaglia and my Suite, the latter for the left hand alone, my most mature compositions, while I believe that my *Étude macabre* is my most tragic and the *Capriccio patetico* my most humanly touching."[98] Godowsky composed two versions of these last two works, one for left hand alone, another for both hands. It was a pattern he followed for a number of other pieces as well, including the *Meditation,* Impromptu, Intermezzo, and *Elegy.*

Godowsky at first viewed his elaborate cadenza to Mozart's Concerto K. 488 as a stand-alone concert piece; not quite two years later, he decided to rework the entire concerto in keeping with the stylistic nature of his cadenza. Such an enterprise distinctly recalls Alkan's flamboyant concert transcription of (and cadenza to) the first movement of Beethoven's Third Piano Concerto. At this stage in his life, Godowsky anticipated the abuse he knew such tampering with Mozart would provoke, so he took pains to explain his reasoning:

> It is a fallacy to assume that the executant is obliged to imitate the style, construction, or even the idiosyncrasies of the composer, for the cadenza allows the player an opportunity to reveal his musical, intellectual, emotional, and spiritual faculties—to reveal the scope of his knowledge, the caliber of his logic, and the range of his inspiration. It is obvious that an extravagant and disproportionate display of any of these attributes would be in bad form, jeopardizing the harmonious relation of the cadenza to the concerto. But there exists as little authentic reason for a servile imitation of the composer's style as there can be an ethical objection to a free functioning of the performer's imaginative faculties. Finally, in the cadenza, the player is expected to impart his subjective interpretation of the composer's work,

in contrast to the more objective presentation required in the body of the composition.[99]

Godowsky's complicated, involved works are anything but showy or obvious, and he appears to have reached the absolute limits of the piano's technical possibilities. He regretted having started serious composition relatively late: "I am tempted to confess that my greatest wish is that I had begun earlier to realize the tremendous satisfaction derived from this angle of music as an artistic outlet."[100] Only toward the end of his career did Godowsky realize the importance of playing his own music to propagate his legacy.

Guiding Philosophies

Busoni and Godowsky saw themselves as musicians and creative artists above all, not wanting to be seen merely as pianists—the profession that earned them their first fame. However, these perfectionists made an intensive, lifelong study of the piano and its mechanism, techniques, and compositional possibilities. Their bent toward discovery, combined with complete self-discipline toward their craft, led to experiments and breakthroughs that should be required study for all serious students of the piano.

Although professional similarities between Busoni and Godowsky continued throughout their lives, their personal philosophies diverged, especially toward middle age. Despite bouts of pessimism and occasional stresses with people and events surrounding him, Busoni kept moving forward. "There is nothing worse than looking back," he insisted, "or than places, people, and facts that lead one to do so."[101] Busoni provides significant insight into his own personality and his quest to stretch the limits of his potential:

> Scriabin's death—alas!—has been repeatedly confirmed and I have to accept the fact. He was most admirable in regard to the fact that he never felt satisfied with his achievements. It is a rare quality in men and an exception in Russian composers.[102]

Godowsky, on the other hand—especially after his heart troubles—could not stop the constant brooding that collared his muse. Busoni became more stoic and accepting: "I am beginning to understand . . . late, in the twilight of my life—that, as one cannot form the world according to one's own ideas, one has to form oneself—in accordance with the world."[103] It is a very Buddhist thought. Busoni wrote these words before his forty-seventh birthday, a time in his life when he felt an increasing necessity to create. He wrote to Egon Petri: "The composer [in me] has rested too long, here too an urgent inner voice is summoning me to unilateral action and will hear nothing of postponement."[104] Godowsky felt a similar urgency, but his outlook was increasingly intolerant:

Commercialization is the curse of our age; idiotic conventionalism and blatant hypocrisy are the two other curses. I don't say all this in bitterness: I look upon things from an isolated elevation. Am I not the Buddha of the piano, according to Huneker? Why can't I transfer that serene vision to life itself?[105]

During his long final illness, Busoni tried to work as much as he could. After his musical genius, Busoni is often spoken of in terms of his vanity. Although he possessed no false modesty, his hundreds of letters reveal a questing and sensitive artist, alive to his surroundings. He took nothing for granted and sought higher truths through study, emotion, and intellect. He could be aloof—some would say arrogant—but his letters and writings display no such remoteness. He once wrote, "It is embarrassing to speak of oneself and it annoys others."[106]

Godowsky succinctly codified his core creative beliefs, which were clearly at odds with the difficult reputation he was wrongly accorded: "My compositions have such a personal idiom, involved inner voices, complicated contrapuntal and polyrhythmic devices, sonorities of a new kind, that the hoi polloi of pianists keep away from them." With shades of Sorabji, Godowsky continued:

They are too indolent mentally and physically to make the supreme effort. . . . The technical side of music, though it interests me, is not the one to attract me at the expense of the emotional. I am convinced that emotion is the prime requisite of art, though it must be tempered by knowledge and intelligence. I have never written a note that I did not feel. My music is my self divulged through sound.[107]

Both Busoni and Godowsky remained uncompromising toward their craft to the end of their days. Musicians who, they felt, were less than faithful to their art provoked the two composers to anger they scarcely bothered to conceal. Godowsky said in an interview several years before his death:

The objectionable in ultra modern music and art is a natural product of individuals, often sincere and even highly trained technically, who have lost their equilibrium. There are values that are permanent, perhaps eternal. . . . Will the music of the eccentric modernists take the place of the classics? Bach, Beethoven, Mozart, Schumann, Chopin, Liszt, Brahms . . . will be played as long as the piano lasts.[108]

Busoni and Godowsky occupy an elite position in music history. Part musicians, part scientists, part historians, and part intellectuals, they would have risen to the highest levels in any field they wished to pursue. That they chose to devote themselves to the keyboard speaks volumes about the piano's profound possibilities.

3   FEINBERG AND SCRIABIN
Humanity and Mysticism

The Odessa-born Samuel Evgenyevich Feinberg (1890–1962) became, along with Alexander Goldenweiser and Heinrich Neuhaus, one of the founders of the modern Russian school at the Moscow Conservatory, where he enjoyed universal esteem. Feinberg is remembered with warmth and respect; a former student of his recalls, "Feinberg was an extremely cultured, educated, intellectual, honest, and decent person. His great knowledge and respect for people gave him an ability to win favor through his artistic and personal nature."[1] Archives and personal memoirs of the period consistently reveal similar affection and acknowledgment of his stature. While aware of his importance, Feinberg remained modest. Quoting a Russian proverb, he used to say that everything he knew was just a drop in the ocean of all that exists in the world of culture.

A bachelor all his life, Feinberg lived with his brother's family in the House of Composers. His apartment became a lively artistic center: his brother was an artist with a cultured daughter and a son who wrote about the study of art and its criticism. Feinberg always fostered a strong creative climate among those around him and befriended a wide range of prominent artists. His awareness of the importance of leading-edge creativity led him to become an ardent advocate of contemporary music (he was among the first major pianists to include works by Medtner in his active repertoire). Feinberg's energetic membership in the Association of Contemporary Music in the 1920s resulted in material opportunities for a legion of young Russian composers.

A quiet generosity reflected his oft-told concern for peer and student alike. Boris Lvov studied with Feinberg for nearly six years, as both an undergraduate and a postgraduate student at the Aspirantura (for advanced studies, in the hierarchy of the Russian educational system). Lvov was rather poor during the difficult post–World War II years and had to work many hours outside music to support himself. He graduated from the conservatory in 1947 after winning first prize in the Beethoven Competition. Three months before final examinations, Feinberg told Lvov to take time off to study full time for the diploma exam. He then produced a wad of cash and on the spot gave Lvov five thousand rubles—a large sum in those days— remarking that it would last for two or three months. When handing him the money, Feinberg looked more bashful than Lvov did. Another, more humorous instance of Feinberg's generosity took place in a classroom with many students. He entered with a large amount of ice cream, at the time a true luxury. He simply said that he wanted to treat them. The students, feeling that it was impolite to accept such a gift, refused, protesting, "No, Samuel Evgenyevich, we do not want it." This went on until the ice cream started melting in Feinberg's hands, whereupon he implored in mock despair, "Do you have no shame or good breeding? I want to treat you, and now I must run around the classroom with melting ice cream offering it to each of you!" Everyone began to laugh and finally partook of the rare treat.[2]

Feinberg demonstrated directness and goodwill toward everyone with whom he came in contact, regardless of their position in life or what they could do for him. His humor stayed just below the surface—never loud nor flaunted. He spoke in a unique manner as well. Like the romance languages, Russian stresses certain syllables to create an almost musical way of speaking. Feinberg often accented minor words to give a sentence unusual meaning and to cause his students to think in new ways about what he was saying.

He came to be highly respected, even cherished, not only by those in his classes, but by other professors and their students as well. He displayed tact and sensitivity with other faculty members and would shake hands with all students while inquiring about their progress. Among his closest friends at the conservatory was Alexander Goedicke, the noted pianist, organist, and senior professor, who was close to both the Rachmaninov and the Medtner families. Feinberg found another confidant in his teacher, Goldenweiser, whose diaries—in a fascinating running commentary on the musical milieu of the period—describe his chess partner and fellow Muscovite as an engaging and warmhearted person.

Feinberg was an aristocrat in his outward appearance, although he did not like having his photograph taken and avoided all notions of self-publicity. An imposing, impressive man, he also believed in the importance of character, a personal moral center unshakable by external events or other people. His performances reflected this nature, along with an impeccable technique and fully developed emotional projection.

The Pianist

Feinberg garnered the same widespread admiration on stage as in his personal life. His achievements cast him as a musical pioneer; he was the first Russian pianist to play and record Bach's entire *Well-Tempered Clavier,* and he gave the Russian premiere of the complete Beethoven sonatas. There are well-known stories of Rosalyn Tureck and Feinberg's classmate Tatyana Nikolayeva, who at competitions and

Samuel Feinberg. Courtesy of the Feinberg/Skalkottas Society, Paris.

examinations asked the judges which of Bach's forty-eight preludes and fugues they would like to hear, but Feinberg was first to do so. Very few musicians ever have dared such gambits. At his graduation examination, Feinberg exhibited his gifts through a dazzling interpretation of Rachmaninov's Third Concerto. His performances of this masterpiece gave it widespread attention in his country, long before the composer's recording with the Philadelphia Orchestra appeared. A Feinberg student, Viktor Merzhanov, has called him one of Rachmaninov's few legitimate heirs:

> Feinberg completely understood the subtle laws of plasticity of rhythm and dynamics in that composer's works, and developed them so that he was able to approach the furthest possible limits of the interpreter's art, touching on aspects of the human soul and human feelings that are rarely studied. Improvisation, absolute mastery, and rare insight into the possibilities of the piano were elements of his style.[3]

Feinberg made another Third Concerto, the Prokofiev classic, one of his specialties and became famous throughout Europe and Russia for his performances of that masterwork. A German review captures the public's response: "Feinberg found particles of his own soul in this concerto. He is connected with this type of music by inner kinship and the most subtle understanding."[4] He tackled it with such precision and abandon that the composer himself was astonished. Prokofiev's letters often refer to Feinberg in this way. Feinberg and Prokofiev also gave duo recitals in which they played Prokofiev's transcriptions of Schubert waltzes.

Feinberg's first acquaintance with the music of Alexander Scriabin (1872–1915) came at the conservatory; he found it difficult, if highly attractive. In 1913, at age twenty-three, Feinberg finally met Scriabin, and he became one of the very few pianists whom the composer appreciated. Scriabin's main complaint with most pianists was that their styles were too much like Prokofiev's: steely and hard, more concerned with realism than fantasy. Yet Feinberg was Prokofiev's most celebrated interpreter. He was the bridge—the most important link—between the two distinct factions of the celebrated Russian school of pianism, which pitted Scriabin's mystical, sexual, opiate music against Prokofiev's dynamism and percussive approach to composition. Feinberg was the pianist both composers admired above all. This management of such diametrically opposed styles, reflecting his eager absorption of all manner of culture from painters and architects to writers and composers, made him a respected and enduring artist.

Feinberg combined elements of extreme contrast, an extraordinary variety of touch and sound, a sharp rhythmic and agogic sense, and charisma—all considered touchstones of the Russian school. In concert, he paid great attention to sound, derived from his twin passions for Prokofiev and Scriabin—one percussive and finite, the other liquid and evolving. Feinberg's reputation for amazing stamina was enhanced by his recitals of the complete Scriabin sonatas, performed in one evening.

He became associated with large segments of the repertoire of Bach, Beethoven, and Schumann, as well as much contemporary Russian music. Feinberg always took seriously his responsibilities toward the music of his time and did not limit himself to his own works, as Scriabin and Medtner largely did. Typical of his adventurousness with programs was an all-sonata recital in May 1924 in Leningrad, where he played Miaskovsky's Second, Alexandrov's Third, Prokofiev's Fourth, Scriabin's Fifth, and his own Sixth.

Feinberg captivated his listeners. The writer and pianist Jan Holcman heard Feinberg's Russian recitals in 1941 and reported, "He was so emotionally involved with the music that listeners could hear him breathing heavily at every crescendo, modulation, or climax."[5] Pianist and audience became inseparable. Feinberg had definite views about the dynamic on both sides of the stage:

> A fatal mistake of the artist-interpreter is his underestimation of the listener's personal participation in the process of musical perception. Not all of what the performer lives for and what stirs him on stage fully touches the audience. The concert artist may be content with silence and attention. However, that is not enough: accord and like-mindedness are also needed. His playing should carefully avoid that which is . . . excessively personal. A performance for an audience is, at the same time, an act of clearing oneself of everything reserved and subjective, an act of consolidating the individual features that possess universal meaning. The performer who deservedly demands listeners' focused attention gives them not the transient achievements of taste, fashion, or artistic whim, but his special talent for revealing the depths and values inseparably connected with genuine creativity.[6]

Only Feinberg could have written music so perfectly suited to his hands and temperament. Like the others of The Eight, he composed music without considering whether it was playable by anyone but himself. As Feinberg said, "Great composers such as Rachmaninov, Medtner, and Scriabin were wonderful pianists who came to their pianism through their own compositions."[7] In these cases, musical content and its subsequent execution became inviolable partners, a subject persuasively treated in Feinberg's article "Artistry and Mastery Are Inseparable."[8] Above all else, a composer-pianist's creativity perfectly mirrors both soul and psyche. The Russian writer Victor Belaiev observed:

> Feinberg's piano technique is not that of splendor nor of the grandiose; it is rather that of the intimate expression of both composer and executant— nervous, capricious, vehement, an expression sounding the whole diapason of feelings of the contemporary man and artist, from the extreme limits of horror, despair, and pain to those of joy, triumph, and victory.[9]

The Teacher

In the classroom, Feinberg always stressed the pure qualities of sound as part of a global approach to teaching, never discussing details about phrasing or fingering without first placing the conception and meaning of a piece in his students' thoughts. Put another way, the concrete could not be poured until the plans were firmly drawn up. Feinberg then carefully spoke of phrases and their character, and how to make sure that the "little bricks" (as he called separate phrases) could be put together smoothly when the musical text is securely in head and hands. He demonstrated how a phrase could be joined, disjoined, and finally combined into the whole, and he delved passionately into all aspects of a composition's character.

The atmosphere in his classroom was conducive to the search for creative truth. When his students initially came to Feinberg, they invariably betrayed nervousness and occasional strain, but they soon relaxed under the spell of Feinberg's gentle personality. He always sought the most important things to say without speaking very much, wasting few words painting pictures of images or paintings, nor talking about the endless complicated ideas that can be found in the best compositions. If he needed a specific image, he could at any given moment quote a line or two of poetry, of which he had an encyclopedic knowledge. He did not use this gift excessively, however, believing it useless to describe music in words—the sounds themselves were so essential and inspiring. He and the rest of The Eight were the piano's aural sensualists.

Feinberg took the connection between poetry and music seriously, a distinctly Russian conviction supported by a rich literary legacy. Setting Russian poetry to music in song occupied many composers. Feinberg's works for voice and piano—like those of his predecessors Rachmaninov and Medtner—were brilliant settings of words by their poetic idols, especially Lermontov and, above all, Pushkin. Russians regularly speak of Pushkin's poems as being like music. The pianist Lazar Berman explains:

> Each word by Pushkin is a word of gold and every *sound* should be golden to true musicians, both in its quality and as it relates to the composition as a whole. Everything must be completely clear and listened to with ease—the way we easily read Pushkin, knowing of course that these elements cannot be called "easy." Further, Pushkin was extremely theatrical and music based on his words often shares this quality. When we read his *Boris Godunov* and other works for the stage, we are inspired to visualize entire productions.[10]

"A poem," Feinberg wrote,

> also implies performance. Recitation depends on individual interpretation to an even larger extent than music. The reader of a poetic composition with his eyes is, at the same time, its performer. If he does not recite the poem aloud,

then his imagination still beholds the rhythm, euphony, and all the sonic elements of the verse.[11]

Feinberg's legendary memory permitted him at any time not only to recite a vast array of poetry, but also to have much of the piano's repertoire at his fingertips. He bore his intellect lightly and without vanity, inspiring in his students not only great respect, but also the ambition to learn as much as they could themselves—the mark of true greatness in a teacher. In addition, Feinberg's human qualities shone through to his students, who were all known for their receptivity to the highest forms of culture. Feinberg was also gifted with a sense of irony and humor, similar to that of Godowsky or Sorabji, though his remarks were always tempered by compassion.

Among friends, he could be riotously funny. Goldenweiser's diaries describe Feinberg's parodies, such as his variations on "Why Are You Madly in Love?" (a popular Russian love song) played in the style of different composers, or his burlesque of the overture to Wagner's *Tannhäuser*. "We laughed ourselves into fits," wrote Goldenweiser.

On the concert stage, Feinberg displayed inexhaustible technical and musical resources. Backing up his intellect and imagination were clarity, refinement, and perfection, qualities that, combined with his natural self-effacement, made Feinberg a refreshing figure. As for competitions, Feinberg was never caught up in the mania they can produce among teachers and students alike. He witnessed the severe effects of such events upon those who tied their lives and careers to them. Just before the Second World War, however, Feinberg did serve on the jury of the prestigious Ysaÿe Competition in Brussels—along with Arthur Rubinstein and Walter Gieseking, among others—balancing an active European career with duties at home.

Feinberg produced no world-famous names from his student list. This was due in part to his extensive concert activity, which permitted somewhat limited classroom time. Were history to have given him three students who would become among the greatest pianists of the twentieth century—as Heinrich Neuhaus had in Sviatoslav Richter, Emil Gilels, and Radu Lupu—Feinberg's name would be projected far wider today through program notes and reference books. Neuhaus well knew and in fact chose the trade-offs, for he himself never became a top-tier pianist. Lupu recalls his teacher and the milieu in which he studied:

> The Moscow Conservatory was an incredible place to be while I was there. The Russian School is a kind of half-political, half-musical situation. The system was and still is extraordinary in taking young, talented pianists and building them up. Feinberg contributed greatly to this philosophy and on a human and musical level he was every bit as influential as Neuhaus.[12]

Feinberg left his mark on scores of young pianists. He was an unusually gifted and beloved educator, with a deep sense of humanity and humility. His classes came to be seen as a sanctuary for his students, less glamorous perhaps than Neuhaus's, but the more serene. Among the conservatory's pedagogues and professors, there were many rather strict critics; Feinberg alone was noted for his special kindness. He was not a well-wisher who would say that a performance was good if he did not believe it. Rather, during an examination, he always sought out the best in a student's playing, attempting to find the exceptional qualities that did come across (another hallmark of a great teacher). But Feinberg could use guile when appropriate. For example, Lvov could not play a passage anywhere near as well as required in a Beethoven sonata. Feinberg simply said in the kindest way, after they had tried many different ways to find a solution, that it was a matter of talent. If Lvov had it, he could do it. This mild teasing—and the lack of a precise explanation—forced Lvov to worry about the difficulty, provoking him to deep thought and a firm determination, ultimately successful, to do something about it.

At the end of the twentieth century, a number of Feinberg's former students were important figures at the conservatory, and their grandchildren have become teachers there, continuing Feinberg's lasting impact upon the musical history of Russia and the Moscow Conservatory. His legend continues in concrete form through a remarkably insightful and comprehensive book, *Pianism as Art,* which examines the highest ideals—both practical and intangible—of the pianist's art.

Pianism as Art

The language of Feinberg's book is exquisite, its ideas invaluable, its conclusions original. Once again, he demonstrates his concern for both external and internal forms, analogous to a fine meal that not only looks beautiful, but is incredibly satisfying. Berman believes that *Pianism as Art* deserves a much wider airing and advocates publicizing this work, as Feinberg's name is well known not to a wide circle of listeners, but only to an elite group of musicians. He also understands that

> the point of view from which Feinberg's book is read also plays a crucial part. Knowing firsthand what a significant phenomenon its author was, I would read *Pianism as Art* differently than if I did not know what kind of person he was.[13]

Pianism as Art assays the piano's complexities more completely than has ever been attempted in a single volume, perceptively analyzing style, sound, technique, and rhythm. Its detailed section on the pedals should be required reading for pianists unaware of the infinitely varied possibilities of pedal usage. In-depth segments on Beethoven, Chopin, Scriabin, Schumann, and Prokofiev feature their music and development to highlight larger points of interpretation and technique. *Pianism as Art* contains chapters titled "The Composer and Performer," with a section on transcriptions; "Style," including an examination of virtuosity; "Sound," which explains the types of possible sounds and how to achieve them; "Technique" and the proper way to accomplish specific goals and avoid problems; "Pedals," which has a section called "Vocal Pedal" describing how to sing on the piano; "Rhythm and Meter," including an essay on the étude as a musical form—from Bach to Liszt, Rachmaninov, and Scriabin; and other chapters dealing with time, meter, and the strong connection between poetry and music. One reads within its pages a lifetime of wisdom and humanity experienced through the piano's unique voice.

Recordings

Through no less tangible means than his written words, Feinberg's recordings reveal a similar force of spirit, beautifully on display in Bach's *Well-Tempered Clavier*. A contemporary review called Feinberg "an intelligent, impulsive, and independent artist, whose long experience with polyphony is particularly well reflected in his performances of Bach."[14]

Although health problems forced him to retire from the concert stage in the mid-1950s, Feinberg continued to record until the week of his death in 1962. His discs of the *Well-Tempered Clavier* were completed when he was over seventy, but they show an assurance and intuition outside the grasp of many pianists of any age. His complete identification with Bach's idiom is rare in an artist celebrated for his Beethoven, Prokofiev, and Scriabin. Feinberg recorded as very few musicians do: he set down his interpretations from the first attempt, with no retakes. Feinberg's professionalism was widely admired throughout his career. The accuracy of his technique—the product of a perfectionism that only increased with age—was always up to the mark and surprised even those closest to him.

Feinberg's recordings of late Beethoven recall live performances by Rudolf Serkin; every phrase is invested with an unusual combination of humility, power, and conviction. Beethoven was always central to Feinberg's repertoire. He used to repeat the quip that young pianists sat on volume two of the Beethoven sonatas while playing from volume one; the second was simply too difficult for budding musicians.

As for Feinberg's Scriabin discs, they fully justify the composer's admiration; the Fourth Sonata and Piano Concerto are played with unmatched authority. Through their power and poignancy, these recordings suggest the darker sides of life experienced at first hand.

Politics and War

Feinberg, unlike Scriabin, was not spared the horrors of war. After the Second World War, he was denounced and disgraced as a result of the ill-fated decree of 1948, whereby the Communist Party's Central Committee censured Prokofiev,

Dmitri Shostakovich, and so many other Soviet composers. Feinberg's Fourth, Fifth, and Sixth Sonatas were singled out for their "extreme subjectivism," and he was deprived of concert and recording opportunities. The era saw a frightening confluence of atrocity and repression, and afterward many artists were hospitalized with heart attacks and other stress-related ailments. Feinberg suffered greatly. His complicated music, increasingly remote and austere, obviously did not endear him to the authorities.

Similar decrees were enacted in other fields; all technical, scientific, and artistic issues were controlled. Vissarion Shebalin, director of the Moscow Conservatory and a prominent composer, was removed and persecuted for no reason. Perhaps he could not confess as well as others did. There were many such meetings, during which professors alternately confessed and then—kneeling and begging—refused to have anything to do with the charges. Such cruel scenes occurred daily at the conservatory. Lvov likened the situation to the Inquisition, when people, books, and scientific inventions were burned out of hatred and ignorance. Professors and students were starving; everything was distributed through the card system. They would go to the store, begging from salesgirls: "Tonechka, sweetheart, please, give me some butter," and Tonechka would say, "But there is no butter today." More often than not, they went home with nothing. "It was very difficult for us to survive in those years," wrote Feinberg's younger brother Leonid, "but we looked beyond the material hardships." He related the following charming story:

> Once, we managed to exchange one of Samuel Evgenyevich's tailcoats for some potatoes. Not long afterward, the peasant who had brought the potatoes came to us with a new offer. "Do you have any more of such clothes? It is so comfortable to walk behind the plough in such a thing."[15]

Through it all, Feinberg managed to maintain his dignity and nobility of purpose, and somehow the family lived a joyful life with what they had.

The Composer

Well before this repressed, chaotic period, Feinberg absorbed life's bleaker offerings with unusual awareness and perception. Personally, he was sensitive and highly refined in the manner of Scriabin, but without the latter's tendency to consider himself the center of the world. Feinberg's brand of musical poetry does not explore the rarefied, ephemeral, or sensuous, but rather focuses on the deeper psyche and problems of man. As Belaiev observed, Feinberg's art is "founded upon the purely philosophical understanding of the contradiction between humanity and nature, both intellectually and brutally."[16] His refined sense of touch and style allowed him to coax the most ephemeral overtones from the piano and prevented any hint of bombast from entering his compositions.

Feinberg, c. 1905. Courtesy of the Feinberg/Skalkottas Society.

A complicated man, Feinberg generally kept his anxieties and inner demons to himself. However, in a remarkable admission for a twenty-two-year-old of such innate gifts and outward charm, Feinberg wrote to his friend Vera Efron:

> You cannot imagine how terrible it can be to stay lonely. I feel sure that I am often drawn to people only by my desire to seek oblivion and to stop hating myself for at least some time. . . . You are probably surprised by the contrasts between what I have written, and my usual garrulousness and inclination to talk about myself. . . . When I am alone, it seems to me that many thoughts which cross my mind regarding myself could scare you.[17]

Feinberg's mother, Anna, recognized these conflicts in her son, imploring him to "struggle with all your might to find your own way, you owe that to yourself and your talent . . . the whole secret lies in your nervousness that made you a musician but which is killing him in you now."[18]

Deep emotional states—both positive and negative—can elicit musical ideas or recollections, especially in musicians. "Regarding my own creativity," Feinberg explained, "I always feel while composing that a large part of my real emotions and life are involved, and that my creative process is not remote. There can be such vivid artistic impressions reflecting what happens in life."[19]

Feinberg did not formally study composition for very long, relying instead on improvisation and then independent experimentation away from the piano. The composer Anatoly Alexandrov recognized that for Feinberg, "what is inexpressible is most important. His palette includes an aesthetic theory of so-called 'non-existent' shades, the elements of musical realization which can be sensed only by the pianist, not the listener."[20] Feinberg came to these concepts well into his development, although composition became part of his creative life starting with the early teen years. His intensive study of works by Bach, Beethoven, Chopin, Schumann, Prokofiev, Medtner, Rachmaninov, and Scriabin undoubtedly influenced his style, as did other avenues of his life, including performing and teaching.

Feinberg took note of the beneficial interrelationship of his activities, though he also spoke of the conflict they engendered:

> I have moments when I regret that I gave too much to performing. . . . Unfortunately my creative work was very often interrupted by difficult responsibilities such as performance goals and teaching—that I was absolutely knocked out from the compositional world. Creative work needs the same cultivation, even more than performing work. I can tell you the terrible feelings I experienced. When you have a musical thought but it is not fully formed for a final draft, you doubt that you are at a certain edge and are afraid to forget something very important or notate it incorrectly, but at the same time you need to leave this work for other commitments. . . . Yet,

I noticed that along with the appearance of my compositions, my abilities as a pianist were improving. For me it was absolutely clear that my pianism and technical mastery of the instrument owe a lot to my composing. . . . You are writing, seated at the table, and when you get to the piano after, you realize you are playing better. Somehow this moment of activating the sound image influences the kinetic process.[21]

Of course, the technical and theoretical foundation must be present, which it was abundantly in Feinberg's case. As with many of his peers and predecessors, an early fascination with Bach informed his awareness of counterpoint and independence of the fingers. And although his achievements as a composer are underestimated, all of his celebrated contemporaries—including Prokofiev and Shostakovich—noted the great philosophical richness of his compositions as well as a piano technique entirely in service of his ideas. Feinberg's work is distinguished by an originality combining the attributes of his Russian training with modern pianism. His experimentation was never driven by the need to be different; true emotion became an end in itself as opposed to the means required to obtain it. His melodies are too expressive to be merely attractive; they strive for something weightier.

The difficulty of Feinberg's compositions is always an issue. They are heavily contrapuntal, and the entire keyboard takes part in musical dialogues between the hands. Few pianists choose to handle such complicated works; on the concert stage their greatest successes usually emanate from the compositions of the better-known composers. But as difficult as they are, Feinberg's piano works remain no less approachable than music by György Ligeti, Olivier Messiaen, or others who write in their own resonant musical languages.

Feinberg's tonally experimental music is closer in style to that of Nikolai Roslavets and late Scriabin. As in the music of the others of The Eight, technical difficulties must be rendered invisible in order for a given work to succeed. This all but guarantees that some of the labor required of the performer will go unnoticed by audiences. For the selfless pianist, though, tangible rewards await in this expressive, undiscovered repertoire.

Most musicians, however, must cultivate material success simply to continue their careers. If they consistently play compositions like Feinberg's, they will generally not experience the level of acclaim necessary to remain on the concert stage. This reality creates a troubling disproportion. Such magnificent works deserve the best possible airing; on the other hand, their textures and musical impulses can be so subtle that audiences may not appreciate them immediately. Listeners would ultimately benefit if they would give such music a second or third chance—but the demands this kind of programming makes on both audience and performer make the re-presentation of such works unlikely. Furthermore, the opportunity for financial returns through playing Feinberg's music is still limited. Pianists appear each

Feinberg, c. 1950s. Courtesy of the Feinberg/Skalkottas Society.

season at all the major musical centers performing all-Chopin concerts, yet few have the drawing power to give Feinberg equal due, much less play his major pieces individually.

Feinberg's direction as a composer became clear after the pivotal first perform-ances in Moscow of Scriabin's Fifth Sonata and *The Poem of Ecstasy* in 1909. Fein-berg was deeply moved by this music. His ideas were precisely formed in his mind, but he experienced difficulty putting those thoughts down on paper. Curiously, his first attempts at real composition excluded the piano, despite his complete mastery of the instrument. Continuing on his own and initially unable to find the right expression, Feinberg turned to the violin, voice, string quartet, and orchestra. After much soul searching, he finally chose the piano as his preferred compositional medium. He began composing in earnest in 1915, the year of Scriabin's death—an event that sharpened Feinberg's focus.

Scriabin was the greatest influence in Feinberg's earlier creative experiments. Both composers were musical poets, although their works explored vastly different terrain. Scriabin derived much from Chopin in his early works; in Feinberg's early compositions, however, his unique voice, beholden neither to Scriabin nor to any-one else, was already developed. Musically original from the beginning, Feinberg quickly found his own mature style.

As Scriabin grew older, his world turned egocentric and ecstatic. By contrast, Feinberg became, in Victor Belaiev's words, more concerned with "the subordina-tion of chaos to the power of the will."[22] In addition, Feinberg possessed neither the temperament nor the inclination to push his music on others; rather, Russia's embracing musical atmosphere allowed him to quietly become known and per-formed. Which internationally renowned pianist will champion Feinberg's music persuasively in the twenty-first century, as Vladimir Horowitz did with his Scriabin revival in the 1950s and 1960s? In an age when people exceed ever-higher goals in Olympic records, huge technological advances, and worldwide competition, in-creasing numbers of enterprising pianists will likely continue to resurrect Feinberg's and other previously overlooked music.

In 1925 Belaiev, who had his hand on the pulse of musical life in Moscow, called Feinberg Russia's most outstanding modern composer. The legendary pianist Tat-yana Nikolayeva called each one of his sonatas a "poem of life."[23] As a Russian con-tributor to sonata form, Feinberg ranks with Medtner, Scriabin, and Prokofiev in the substance and body of his work. In common with Scriabin's, Feinberg's sonatas are usually monothematic and comprise tightly organized structures. In seeking to distill their ideas even further, both composers came to prefer one-movement forms, to which Scriabin turned in his Fifth Sonata. Feinberg's works are models of the age's spirit, combining Scriabin's highly developed chromaticism with new directions of atonality that follow the experiments of Roslavets. Polyphony (in the principles laid out by Bach) and polyrhythm became Feinberg's watchwords.

The preludes, Humoresque, and Berceuse (Opp. 15, 19, and 19a) may be viewed as fine starting points for Feinberg the miniaturist. His first two piano sonatas, suggesting the differing textures of Bach and Schumann, appeared the year Scriabin died. They speak of a youthful, pastoral lyricism. The lengthy, three-movement Third Sonata displays a completely different tone of tragedy and substance. (Scriabin's First Sonata, with its pessimism and concluding funeral march, explores similar terrain.) Feinberg's Fourth Sonata, written in 1918 during the culmination of World War I, plumbs significant depths of experience, sharing spiritual kinship with Chopin's "Winter Wind" Étude and Medtner's "Night Wind" Sonata. Feinberg's work explores the nightmarish, chaotic mood of its time, with the finest craftsmanship. His Sixth Sonata, which he premiered to great acclaim at the Vienna Festival of Contemporary Music in 1925, comes close to the later works of Scriabin in expressions of the otherworldly or supernatural, although comprising textures more aligned with Rachmaninov. The Sixth is the only sonata for which Feinberg provided an epigraph, an excerpt from *The Dawn of Europe* by the German philosopher Oswald Spengler. In the 1930s, however, Russia's political climate led to Spengler's being branded a fascist. The epigraph could have caused Feinberg serious problems, but he bought the remaining copies in circulation and had the sonata reissued, substituting the offending passage with a quote from Fyodor Tyutchev's poem "Sleeplessness."

Feinberg's Seventh Sonata may be held as a mirror to Scriabin's own Seventh, both playing upon the conflict of spirit and body. Feinberg's work asserts self-control, as if he has willed himself to contain the sensual; Scriabin simply revels in it. The Russian writer Victor Bunin suggested that the rhythmic and melodic fluctuations of Feinberg's sonata "create a mood of anxious indefiniteness resembling a wary wandering in the dark."[24]

Feinberg's remaining five sonatas, written from 1933 to 1960 and uninterrupted by the composition of smaller works, continued his exploration of the human experience through substantial, innovative keyboard writing. With chiseled strokes, both Feinberg and Scriabin forged works undaunted by traditional limitations. Belaiev offered a statement as relevant for the future as it was in 1925:

> The artist must not fear to reach out to the uttermost limits of human emotions, though it is only by desperate experience and full knowledge of all phases of human life and feeling that the artist can give complete play to his intellectual powers and exercise them at the highest tension.[25]

Scriabin: Personality, Character, and Influences

Scriabin surely flexed his own powers. His vanity and ego, coupled with an intense sexual drive, led him decisively past the early Chopin influence; he became known throughout Europe as a leader of the avant-garde and modernist movements. Later in life his outlook narrowed to the point that he lacked any interest in other composers' music. In another reflection of his self-absorption, none of Scriabin's works bears a dedication—a curiosity almost unique among composers. He fully relinquished himself to his muse. Maurice Aronson's unpublished manuscript on Godowsky contains a revealing passage about Scriabin:

> He was a man of modest, retiring disposition, who shunned glaring lights and brilliancy. One evening he disappeared from a dinner party and could not be found anywhere about the house. Godowsky led the search for his colleague from cellar to garret. Suddenly he heard a funny tinkling sound emanate from an attic room that had been discarded from use long ago. Into this little room, in which an old upright piano had been stored, Scriabin had taken flight, overcome by the desire to give immediate expression to what he had conceived.[26]

Another memorable snapshot of Scriabin's personality came from Arthur Rubinstein, who recalled their introduction:

> "Come and have a cup of tea with me," [Scriabin] said amiably, and we went to the nearby Café de la Paix and ordered some tea and cakes. [He] was short and slender, with wavy dark blond hair, a carefully trimmed pointed beard . . . and cold brown eyes which seemed to ignore everything around him. "Who is your favorite composer?" he asked with the condescending smile of the great master who knows the answer. When I answered without hesitation, "Brahms," he banged his fist on the table. "What, what?" he screamed. "How can you like this terrible composer and me at the same time? When I was your age I was a Chopinist, later I became a Wagnerite, but now I can only be a Scriabinist!" And, quite enraged, he took his hat and ran out of the café, leaving me stunned by this scene and with the bill to pay.[27]

Boris de Schloezer, one of the composer's intimate friends, perceptively observed that Scriabin was

> overjoyed when he glimpsed a spark of sympathy in others. But he was bitterly disillusioned when his friendship was not fully reciprocated. He was oversensitive; he was easily disheartened by a lack of understanding. He was not intolerant and was quite willing to engage in discussion with his most determined critics, but the moment he encountered a callous indifference, he would retreat into himself for a very long time.[28]

Scriabin took an active interest in architecture, painting, literature, and other artistic forms only to the extent to which they coincided with his own vision of the world and could help his work. Viewing people in this way as well, he could be welcoming and receptive, but only as far as people either agreed with his concepts or could help to further his aims. If not, his impatience and vanity closed ranks around him. His personal culture stood a world away from Feinberg's.

Alexander Scriabin upon graduation from the Moscow Conservatory, 1892.

Scriabin in Moscow, 1897.

Scriabin saw his birth on Christmas Day as significant and chosen. His mother died barely after his first birthday, and three elderly female relatives raised him—an aunt, a great-aunt, and a grandmother. They spoiled him lavishly, probably contributing to his egomania.

Principally drawn to Nietzsche, Scriabin in his late teens also encountered the theosophists Helena Blavatsky and Annie Besant, and his works began to take on a mystical cast. His study of theosophy led him to the mystic philosophers, including Dmitri Merezhkovsky, whose teaching stressed the equal sanctity of flesh and spirit. For Scriabin, anything less than fastidious control over himself, in mind and body,

Scriabin, Moscow, 1898. Photograph by the well-known Moscow photographer
R. F. Brodovsky, who was affiliated with the Moscow Philharmonic Society.

was intolerable. In matters such as his prophecies and mystical aspirations, he lent more credence to psychology than to logic. "Logically, it may be an impossibility," Scriabin would say, "but . . . one must take a psychological view; logical contradictions abound in spiritual life, and I have more confidence in what I feel intuitively than in any ratiocination."[29]

Scriabin became fanatical about his personal and artistic freedom, relentlessly pursuing narcissistic feelings of ecstasy and mystical love. He separated from his first wife because of her inability to share his philosophical ambitions or his dreams of changing the world through his music. His second wife, Tatyana Schloezer, was much more in sympathy with her husband's vision and had a profound influence upon him.

Scriabin always had his supporters. Among the most important was the wealthy and influential publisher and patron of composers Mitrofan Belaiev, who had met Scriabin at a St. Petersburg recital in 1894. Belaiev was captivated by Scriabin and disagreed with his own chief artistic adviser, Nikolai Rimsky-Korsakov, who disliked Scriabin both personally and musically. After Belaiev's death, Sergei Koussevitzky's publishing firm, Edition Russe de Musique (later nationalized by the Bolshevik government in 1918), gave Scriabin its first contract and agreed to pay the composer a fixed sum of five thousand rubles a year to alleviate his financial stress. (Koussevitzky never missed a chance to promote worthwhile young Russian composers; Rachmaninov and Medtner, among others, were later supported as well.)

Scriabin's was a life of joy, undimmed by the obstacles he encountered. De Schloezer wrote, "He did not know the tranquil repose of a man of wisdom who by an effort of his will places himself above life's turmoil; nor the beatific quietude of a mystic absorbed in contemplation of his object of worship."[30] Scriabin's notebooks are filled with references to God, the universe, consciousness and subconciousness, truth, and his own uniqueness in the world. "I am nothing," the composer insisted. "I am only what I create. The destiny of the universe is clear. I have a will to live. I love life. I am God. I am nothing. I want to be all."[31] If these words appear convoluted and melodramatic, their conviction and sincerity are nonetheless undeniable.

Critical Opinion

Scriabin's strong biases have always polarized listeners. But he simply kept true to his hyper-romantic nature. The erotic and subjective nature of some of Scriabin's music found resistance after his death, as the tides of musical fashion shifted into modernism, atonality, neoclassicism, and, in the mid-twentieth century, a stultifying academicism with largely intellectual appeal. With the return of freedom and romanticism toward the end of the century came a concurrent resurgence in Scriabin's popularity.

As early as 1923, opinion in the Russian musical press started to shift away from Scriabin and toward Prokofiev. Scriabin's self-obsessed music dealt with the intangibles of inwardness, whereas Prokofiev's immediately accessible works reflected the mood of the times. These were the qualities young Russians needed and responded to. Prokofiev was one of them, a young man out to capture the public's attention with his own revolution. Feinberg eloquently summed up the transition:

> At the beginning of this century, near 1911 or 1912, when piano style achieved supreme elegance in Scriabin's late works, when the picturesque and fluid trend called musical impressionism arrived from the West, when Rachmaninov's open and diverse temperament became too direct and emotive against this background, there appeared the figure of a youthful composer who presented his First Piano Concerto. His name was Sergei Sergeyevich Prokofiev, and he totally revolutionized piano style.[32]

Prokofiev's was not the only competitive voice hindering the acceptance of Scriabin's music. Shostakovich, early in his career during Stalin's rule, was decidedly harsh toward Scriabin, calling him a bitter musical enemy in light of his music's unhealthy eroticism, mysticism, passivity, and general flight from the reality of life—all characteristics absent from Shostakovich's own music.

Many composers changed their initially negative impressions of Scriabin. Recalling when he first heard his compatriot's music, Rachmaninov admitted, "I thought Scriabin was simply a swine, but it seems he is a composer after all."[33] Busoni offered a candid response after reading through much of Scriabin's early output: "Une indigestion de Chopin."[34] It was not until the later works that Busoni came to recognize Scriabin's shimmering genius. His reaction was somewhat muted by the Russian's narrow focus:

> Chopin had heroic aspirations too, but on the whole he remained in his own more limited waters. It is not in Scriabin's nature, either, to compose big scores, but he tries to do it. I don't consider that they will live, but I respect Scriabin for striving for such a high ideal.[35]

Scriabin has always attracted fervent acolytes as well as severe critics. Even his first wife, Vera, continued to idolize him; she became the first pianist to perform all-Scriabin recitals. The pianist Hilde Somer authored a curious article in which she apparently saw herself at the center of the Scriabin revival, to which she appended her poem "Ecstasy." Never mind that years earlier Horowitz in the United States, Richter elsewhere, and Feinberg before either of them, were at the forefront of Scriabin performances; many pianists became part of the Scriabin cult and saw themselves as chosen to deliver his message. "Scriabin," wrote Somer, "is like an infusion penetrating one's innermost core: mind—emotion and sexuality expanding." She concluded her article, after two pages of fatally over-the-top prose about Scriabin's greatness, by discussing the Ninth Sonata, which emerges from sulphurous fumes, invoking diabolic incantations. . . . One senses the mysterious tracing of occult symbols in the sand, summoning the spirits of the underworld with snake-like writhing and curling figurations, spiked by trills quivering with venom.

More down-to-earth is her perceptiveness in pointing out the following parallel: "D. H. Lawrence said, 'a whole man is a first-rate thinker and a first-rate animal, for one without the other is nothing.' Such a man is Scriabin."[36] This profound observation perfectly sums up Scriabin's being. Exploratory and highly sexual, he constantly sought bridges from the ethereal to the earthly.

Critics often saw Scriabin as a crazy eccentric, as far removed from the realities of life as a vaporous hallucination. In 1957 Rollo Myers articulated the prevailing opinion of Scriabin's music: "On purely aesthetic grounds Scriabin's hysterical, almost maniacal outpourings offend our twentieth-century canons of taste, and we are right to question the propriety of trying, as he did, to mix music and metaphysics."[37] Offended critics similarly abused Scriabin in his own time. In 1915, just before the composer's death, John Runciman wrote in the fledgling *Musical Quarterly*: "Scriabin puts himself in line with the futurists by giving us a lot of pretentious comment on his work—stuff which, without malice or any wish to pre-judge him, I can only call pompous rubbish." These words appeared *after* Scriabin's magnificent, explosive later works came to light. The critic, in his ignorance, reduced Scriabin's music to

> Chopin diluted with Henselt and water, and slightly flavored at times with Russian folk tune. . . . It is neat, slight music, totally uninspired, but graceful. By the application of a novel harmonic system, [his themes] are somewhat disguised, and incidentally most of the color and all of the expressiveness are bleached out of them.

Runciman called the case of Scriabin, along with those of Stravinsky and Schoenberg, "almost tragic. To have at their command the means of saying a new thing and to have the desire to say it, and yet have nothing new to say—how could any mortal be more unhappily endowed or have a sadder burden of fate laid upon him!" Unfortunately, such a judgment misses the highly disciplined, rigorous, and methodical nature of their compositional habits, developed from the best musical education and pedigree. Such teeming genius always looks for ways to expand the boundaries; this is the essence of creativity. One need not be steeped in extravagant philosophical writings to love and respond to Scriabin's music. He was always true to his heritage and education, while employing a harmonic structure that gave validity and meaning to his racing thoughts.

Runciman wrote of Scriabin, "The desire to be original, startling, and astonishing at all costs is a symptom common to all the arts at the present day."[38] To be sure, he sought fame and glory, but with a firmly grounded craft and true inspiration.

Scriabin, St. Petersburg, 1914. Taken at the Rentz-Schrader photo studio.

Composer and Pianist

Scriabin was not above self-posturing, but even his earlier, Chopin-tinted (some would say Chopin-tainted) music could never be called insincere. It was conceived according to ideals of clarity, logic, and intellect, filtered through increasingly relentless questioning and self-criticism. Scriabin initially wrote only for the piano and had to pay the influential publisher Jurgenson to have his first pieces published. They were given scant attention.

Scriabin's teacher at the Moscow Conservatory, Vasily Safonov, became a devoted supporter and saw to it that Scriabin's Piano Concerto of 1897 was performed often. Safonov gave him a professorship at the conservatory, but the young composer—who perpetually struggled to find periods of isolation in which to compose, and for whom money was always a restraining issue—increasingly viewed this responsibility as hindering his creative life. From 1902 to 1903, after completing his Second Symphony, Scriabin worked diligently at composition to earn enough money to leave Russia. The artistic results were astonishing. As Alfred Swan observed: "At this 'mercenary' objective one can only smile, since that mass of piano music included such utterly unheard-of and perfect inspirations as the fourth sonata, the poems, Op. 32, and the 'Tragic' and 'Satanic' Poems."[39] In the early 1900s, Scriabin was little noticed in Moscow or by the larger musical public, although his earlier works would later find considerable popularity. Despite his repeatedly falling in and out of favor, Scriabin's influence has proven to be lasting and meaningful.

The Russian pioneers of nontonal music developed their own methods of working with the scale independently of Schoenberg's theories. Scriabin first used what he called the "mystic" chord, based upon the interval of a fourth, rather than the traditional triadic harmony of the third and fifth. Scriabin abandoned conventional harmonic thinking in his later works and developed his own unique chordal construction. Had he not died so young, Moscow might very well have become competitive with Vienna as the home of atonality. The triumvirate of Schoenberg, Alban Berg, and Anton Webern could have been supplanted by Scriabin, Roslavets, and Arthur Lourié, likely giving atonalism a more emotional aesthetic.

The essential Scriabin may also be discovered in large measure through use of the pedals. Feinberg put the pedals in a larger context relating to Scriabin's enigmatic art:

> He refined methods of composition to such a degree of perfection and exquisiteness that his creative work touches extreme boundaries, beyond which there is a mystery of sound that has not yet been discovered . . . a creative non-existence. Scriabin approached this border by such devices as complicated polyrhythm, hidden thematicism, and an exquisite use of the pedal—so delicate and subtle that a simple pedal change may appear primitive or even rough. Accuracy in notating pedal marks—already difficult

with Chopin's style—is thus almost inconceivable to achieve Scriabin's sound properly. As a result, he largely refused to enter pedal markings in his manuscripts.[40]

The pedals must be manipulated in the most refined way in order to properly project many simultaneous strands of music. No amount of finger control by itself will compensate for the pedals' finishing sheen. Feinberg devoted considerable space in *Pianism as Art* to Scriabin and the special pedal techniques he used to further his music's sense of quixotic fantasy. One should not be percussive when playing Scriabin. During his years teaching at the Moscow Conservatory, from 1898 to 1903, he admonished his students to play as if in a dream; even their *fortissimo*s had to sound soft. His "dream tones" are thus hazed and suggestive, as one would experience the murmur of distant conversation.

This concept is beautifully illustrated in one of the composer's surviving piano rolls. In the famous Étude, Op. 8, No. 12, modern listeners are used to Horowitz's demonic, hard-edged interpretation, born of his sheer virtuosity. Scriabin's way with the piece was much less public. Soft-grained and subtle, his conception of the work provides invaluable insight into authentic Scriabin style (despite the unreliability of the reproducing piano rolls on which he recorded). According to Safonov, "Scriabin possessed in the highest degree what I always impressed on my students: the less like itself a piano is under the fingers of the player, the better it is."[41]

Scriabin placed great emphasis on the piano's more diaphanous qualities, producing transparent, ethereal, and sensuous sonorities. Alexander Pasternak, upon hearing the composer firsthand in the drawing room of his family's dacha, described Scriabin's style:

> As soon as I heard the first sounds on the piano, even if I was sitting with my eyes shut not looking at Scriabin's hands and fingers, I immediately had the impression that his fingers were producing the sound without touching the keys, that he was (as it were) snatching them away from the keyboard and letting them flutter lightly over it. This created an extraordinary illusion that his fingers in some strange way were drawing the sound *out* of the instrument. . . . His enemies used to say that it was not real piano playing, but a twittering of birds or a mewing of kittens, meaning both his interpretation and the actual sound of the instrument.[42]

"With Scriabin, harmony and timbral coloring are inseparable," wrote Feinberg. "In the sonority of his last-period compositions, the smallest upsetting of balance and accurate distribution of force . . . may be perceived as falsity or excessive nervousness."[43] Scriabin had little tolerance for hammer-virtuosos, as Rachmaninov's biographer Victor Seroff explained:

> Scriabin had an almost magical touch, especially bewitching when he played softly, superbly using his pedal for an ephemeral effect. He hated pianists who

played "as though they were washing laundry or smelling the instrument," and especially when they played his compositions with the same approach and touch as if his piano pieces were Rachmaninov's or Tchaikovsky's.[44]

Scriabin the performer was much like Chopin. Both musicians preferred to play in intimate surroundings. They were slight of build and not muscular, and they rarely played loudly. The compensations were dramatic, however, and Scriabin was a pianist to be taken seriously. A review in the *Russian Musical Gazette* noted Scriabin's great success:

> The impression that lingers is one of ravishment . . . the enchantment of his performance. He is a wizard with the pedal, though his ethereal sounds cannot quite fill the hall. He captivates his audience, too, by giving the impression of improvising. He breaks the rhythmic flow and something new comes out each time. This suffuses the performance with freshness. Never has he played his Fourth Sonata with more mastery or sincerity. . . . What power he put in the theme in the second movement! Yet the *actual* sound was not big. The secret is in the energetic rhythm.[45]

This aspect of the pianistic art is generally stressed in Russia at an early stage of training. Feinberg elaborated: "The most significant difference between post-Beethoven pianism that led—through Chopin and Liszt—to Scriabin's piano style, is in the absolutely new principles of rhythmic interpretation."[46] In tandem with sound and rhythm, a critical attribute of Scriabin's art is the individuality of the left hand. In one of his most serious setbacks, the strain of repetitive practice had caught up with him as he tried to exceed his natural limits: he had injured his right hand trying to imitate the virtuoso Josef Lhévinne, his classmate at the conservatory. His jealousy of Lhévinne cooled their friendship, and Scriabin could barely control his devastation over what he thought would be permanent damage. In one of the private notebooks he kept at the time, he touched on themes that were to have a profound impact upon his art:

> At twenty, an ominous hand ailment, a most decisive event in my life. Fate puts an obstacle, incurable according to the doctors, to the attainment of an ardently desired goal—brilliance, fame. The first serious failure in life. The first earnest attempt at philosophy; the beginning of self-analysis. Reluctance to admit that my ailment is incurable, and yet an obsession with somber moods. First reflections on the value of life, religion, God. Continued strong faith . . . Ardent, long prayers, constant church attendance . . . Reproaches addressed to fate and to God. Composition of the First Piano Sonata with a funeral march.[47]

Scriabin therefore concentrated on perfecting his left hand to extraordinary refinement and independence. His early Prelude and Nocturne, Op. 9—the former defiant, the latter sensuous—appeared after Alkan's Étude, Op. 76, and foreshadowed Godowsky's developments in music for the left hand alone. Traces of the mature Scriabin may be observed in these two pieces through their construction, pedal technique, deceptive transparency, and expressiveness.

These factors coalesced in his Second Sonata. It was conceived in 1892, a decade before Debussy's *La mer* appeared. Both pieces evoke a very personal reaction to the beauty and expanse of the sea. Scriabin's work and Feinberg's own Second Sonata express intense lyricism, as if under the sway of the first blush of nature.

Scriabin's performing directions for his Fourth Sonata's concluding Presto sum up a crucial principle of his later works: "I want it *even faster,* as fast as possible, on the *verge of the possible.* . . . It must be a flight at the speed of light, right towards the sun, into the sun!"[48] Feinberg correlated the overwhelming effect of the Fourth Sonata's conclusion with the slower material that precedes it:

> An impetuous musical torrent may be born within the bounds of a slow tempo. With Scriabin's prestissimo, his fastest textures are built of the elements ripened in the intense expressiveness of slower constructions. The rapidity of Scriabin's tempos grows out of the fabric of an emotional andante. . . . A slow melody with Scriabin is developed smoothly, with neither sharp accents nor a distinct reliance on rhythmic meter. Gradually accelerating its movement can achieve the feeling of alienation from material foundations, precisely that "soaring" which is so necessary for the realization of Scriabin's intentions. The *prestissimo volando* of the fourth sonata is not so much a quick tempo as an andante raised to a new degree.[49]

A year before he died, Scriabin publicly declared Feinberg's interpretation of the Fourth Sonata unsurpassed and unimagined even by himself. Eighteen years older than Feinberg, Scriabin became highly deferential to his young colleague. Their relationship could not be called father and son, nor mentor and protégé; rather, they shared a common heritage and devotion to the best their country had to offer.

Composed immediately after *The Poem of Ecstasy,* Scriabin's Fifth Sonata is fundamentally tonal, chromatic, and sensual. Its composer said that this music existed outside him in images he could not express verbally: "I am but the translator."[50] One of Scriabin's most physical works, it also abundantly displays the languid atmosphere of reverie that is unmistakably his. A barely controlled onrush of sound opens and concludes the work, scaling rapidly up the keyboard with increasing intensity, only to vanish suddenly. At the end, silence resonates, as the work departs with the glorious ambiguity that would only deepen in his later works.

Scriabin subtitled his favorite sonata, the Seventh, "White Mass." Bowers noted that the composer called it "'purest mysticism,' and felt that in it he had at last achieved 'the highest complexity within the highest simplicity,' for finally his system was clear and concentrated, while the message it conveyed was ultimate and absolute." In the Eighth Sonata, which followed a year later, traditional tonality is dissolved. Of it, Scriabin wrote, "There must not be any difference at all between harmony and melody. . . . In form and essence, the inner and outer must be the same and one."[51] Especially in his later works, Scriabin blurred the lines of melody and accompaniment in a constantly shifting play of sound.

Scriabin's music frequently operates at a high emotional or physical pitch: witness the Ninth Sonata, which he often performed. Given the title "Black Mass" by his close friend Alexei Podgaetsky, it is demonic and satanic; Scriabin said he was "practicing sorcery" while playing it.[52] Bowers described this sonata's atmosphere as "perverse. The rite is a spitting at all that is holy or sacred. If the seventh exorcizes demons, the ninth resummons them. Corruption, perversity, diabolism recurs."[53] The *Satanic Poem* (Op. 36) explores similar themes; Bowers called that work "*Faust in miniature.*"[54]

Scriabin referred to his harmonies as "sensations," a provocative concept actively discussed among his followers. His use of trills and birdsong was widely adopted by composers after him, including Messiaen. Scriabin's later music, such as the Op. 74 Preludes, inhabits a spare milieu that presages that of the twenty-first century's religious mystics—Arvo Pärt, Henryk Górecki, and John Tavener. During his lifetime Scriabin's creations were viewed as veering toward physical exhaustion and world-weariness, perhaps even death. But he never thought that he would die so young; he was fascinated, indeed stimulated, by what would exist for him once freed from the earth. He was constantly trying to stretch himself, never satisfied with what he had just accomplished, always looking ahead to the next work. Scriabin said many times about his creative development that he lived only by the hope of the future. Having explored the physically challenging and erotic sides of his muse, Scriabin looked increasingly beyond his earthly being into the unknown world beyond life. The year before he died, Scriabin spoke passionately of "the ultimate divestment of fleshly garments, of dematerialization [a theosophical expression for the transformation of all earthly senses], of a return to a state of pure spirituality."[55]

Yet he remained bound to the wonders of nature. *Vers la flamme* (Toward the Flame) is an extraordinary musical depiction of the elements, akin to Debussy's aquatic *L'isle joyeuse*. The two works move relentlessly toward climactic ecstasy through fire and water, respectively. Of the Tenth Sonata, completed less than two years before his death, Scriabin wrote, "It is a forest! . . . the sounds and moods of the forest. This sonata will be absolutely different. . . . It will be joyously radiant and earthy."[56] Despite these images, the burning nature of his later music is never far away. Scriabin said that during this sonata "the sun comes down and blisters the earth."[57] This image was created partly through trills, which for Scriabin represented "palpitation . . . trembling . . . the vibration in the atmosphere."[58] Little more than a year before Scriabin's death, an inspired Sorabji wrote of the "radiant ecstatic quality that no other [composer] past or present has."[59] Over forty years later, he

Scriabin, Moscow, 1915. One of the last photographs of Scriabin.
On the back is inscribed: "A gift to the Museum from L. A. Skriabina. 7/17/1924."
Lyubov Alexandrovna Scriabina was Scriabin's aunt, who helped to raise him.
She was the first curator of the museum, from 1922 through 1941.

continued to be fascinated with Scriabin, writing, "The sheer *sound* of the later Scriabin is invariably exquisite."[60] By this time Sorabji's music itself had absorbed a number of Scriabin-inspired textures and trills.

Scriabin's ultimate aesthetic, though, was to transcend imagery. In an article published in April 1915, the month he died, he is quoted as saying, "Through music and color, with the aid of perfume, the human mind or soul can be lifted outside or above merely physical sensations into the region of purely abstract ecstasy and purely intellectual speculation."[61] His words highlight the visceral, narcotic quality found throughout his later music. Scriabin intended to follow these precepts with an unfinished mystical monument to art, *Mysterium*, designed to be his ultimate contribution to the world. To further these aims, Scriabin befriended luminaries from Moscow's theatrical life, including Konstantin Stanislavsky and Isadora Duncan, and learned from them much about the possibilities of performance art. Scriabin conceived a weeklong celebration of music, dance, colored lights, and incense, all with philosophical ambitions—a huge event boasting only participants, with no audience. Fifty years later, the words "Woodstock" and "free love" would evoke similar aspirations.

Contrasts

Feinberg, in contrast to Scriabin, was very much a man of this world, with all the qualities to inspire tremendous loyalty among fellow professors, students, composers, and audiences. Busoni's description of Mozart could well be applied to Feinberg: "He is not demoniacal and not supernatural, his realism is of this earth."[62] Not for Feinberg were Scriabin's flights of fantasy and flesh. Cultured, widely read, outwardly serene, and well grounded, Feinberg showed genuine interest in all people around him. His modesty allowed openness to new thoughts and ideas, reflected in a huge repertoire of historic and contemporary works. The self-centered Scriabin rarely played music other than his own, thought that his was the only possible way, and showed scant interest in those around him. He possessed the otherworldly attitude of a dreamer, albeit with the tools and means of a master craftsman. Feinberg's charisma represented the attainment of power to Scriabin's hunger for it, urgency to Scriabin's mania. They did share a central compositional tenet in their desire to go well beyond previously set limits, to express, in Alexandrov's words, "that which has not yet found its voice but is longing to do so."[63] Music by the great humanist and the great mystic remains starkly relevant to our present society, perpetually seeking balance through life's universal, unanswerable questions.

4 MEDTNER AND RACHMANINOV
Romantic Compatriots

Nikolai Medtner (1880–1951) and Sergei Rachmaninov (1873–1943) took traditional harmonic thinking to a new level of depth and sensuousness. History has cast these two Russian-to-the-core friends as twentieth-century throwbacks to an era of romanticism and nostalgia. Their careers and music took sharply disparate turns —one in a perpetual struggle, the other high profile and prosperous. Rachmaninov—well known for his three careers as pianist, composer, and conductor—kept the piano closest to his heart, as did Medtner.

Although their music and legacies are quite different, these friends and classmates—brilliant pianists and composers—were pervasively romantic and nostalgic. While Medtner had a core group of adherents, however, he never managed to accumulate Rachmaninov's wide public audience nor even much critical debate. In commenting on their piano music seven years after Medtner's death, a lone voice proclaimed in *Musical Opinion,* "We see at once that Medtner, so far from being a shadow of Rachmaninov, is, in fact, vastly superior to the latter."[1] This assertion centered on the facile opinion that Rachmaninov was all superficial virtuosity and Medtner the deeper musician. Yet while it is true that Medtner often represented the more subtle and inward craft, he and Rachmaninov should never have engendered a debate of heart-on-sleeve versus heartfelt.

Medtner and Rachmaninov instinctively grew to need each other, developing a lifelong closeness. As Medtner's wife, Anna, affectionately wrote to her brother-in-law, Emil: "When [Rachmaninov] talks with Kolia [Medtner's nickname, following Russian custom], liveliness appears on his tired face, and his look becomes tender and attentive. I love watching them when they are together."[2] A mutual friend, Alfred Swan, spoke of their pure bond that recalled other famous relationships, including Goethe's with Schiller and Haydn's with Mozart. Although it was a source of comfort and joy, their friendship was not entirely without friction. Medtner always firmly asserted that his compatriot was a heaven-born musician, but he reproached Rachmaninov for not always using his talent justly and lamented his presumed defections to fashion and sensation. Medtner was also jealous of Rachmaninov's professional success. As Swan put it, however, "One can state with certainty that no contemporary artist came as close to Medtner's ideal as Rachmaninov did."[3]

Swan narrates a revealing scene between the two composers dating from Medtner's stay with the Rachmaninovs in Switzerland:

> Medtner always longed to talk to him about music, especially composition, but Rachmaninov invariably evaded the issue. There they stood, the two great friends and musicians: Rachmaninov—the world-acclaimed artist, tired after his concert tours, wanting simply to enjoy himself with his family and friends, evidently not inclined to indulge in serious conversation—and Medtner, who is little known to the world at large, who leads a secluded life and looks upon his art as a well-nigh religious calling, and to preserve its purity, is ready to face an empty pocket. For Medtner it was a rare chance to commune with another great artist. But he is so vital and insatiable in his talks about music, art, and the world in general, that he is apt to exhaust his listener. There was perhaps a deeper cause than this for Rachmaninov's reluctance: philosophical talks about music were alien to him, because his creative mind was of the spontaneous, intuitive type.[4]

Medtner believed the artist's role is to create lasting beauty. He held the act of musical creation to be sacred and considered it one of the highest forms of human activity. He loved discussing it and spoke of his disappointment at being unable to have with his friend the serious conversations about music in which he was so quick to engage with others:

> I have known Rachmaninov from my early years. All my life has passed parallel to his, but with no one have I talked so little about music as with him. Once I even told him how I wanted to discuss the subject of harmony. Immediately his face became very distant and he said: "Yes, yes, we must sometime," but he never broached the subject again.[5]

Rachmaninov's avoidance of the matter did not prevent him from admiring Medtner and programming his music. (Despite their close personal ties, Medtner did not feel similar admiration for Rachmaninov's work beyond a few specific pieces, such as the B Minor *Étude-Tableau*.) Rachmaninov wrote fondly of Medtner:

> I love him very much and I admire him, and speaking frankly, I consider him one of the most talented among the contemporary composers. He is one of those rare people—as a musician and a human being—who grows in stature as one knows him better. This is the fate of few and I wish him all the best. Yes, this is Medtner—young, healthy, strong, and energetic, armed with a lyre in his hands!

Rachmaninov continued, in a vein of the depression he suffered for a good part of his adult life, "And I? I am mentally sick . . . and consider myself unarmed and already fairly old. If I have anything good, it is hardly in my future."[6]

Greatly troubled by the political and social effects of the Bolshevik Revolution, Rachmaninov left Russia for good in 1917; Medtner followed four years later. A serious lack of money plagued them both. Although after several years Rachmaninov succeeded in establishing himself, Medtner never achieved any meaningful material security. Outwardly, Rachmaninov had everything: fame, acclaim, financial freedom, and a happy family life with his wife and children. Medtner's marriage was solid, but otherwise his life had none of the accoutrements Rachmaninov possessed in such abundance. Medtner, however, remained unambiguously certain of his life's direction and value, without a hint of the inward doubts that plagued his friend. This security in both his ego and genius created enormous hardships later in life, yet at the beginning of his career, Medtner remained heartily unaware that he was, in the poet Mikhail Lermontov's words, "a young soul, destined for the world of sorrow and tears."[7]

Early Promise and Uncompromising Personality

As a boy, Medtner knew nothing about music theory, but he covered every piece of paper with music and chose the piano for expressing his thoughts. Medtner's father, a factory manager, brought to his children a wide-ranging, cultured background, with special affinities for music, Goethe, and Italian painting. Six-year-old Kolia received his first piano lessons from his mother, who in her youth had been a singer. She possessed a deep knowledge of music, which suited her son's demands to play the best of Bach, Scarlatti, Mozart, and Beethoven instead of those pieces normally given to children. At age ten, when Medtner began composing in earnest, he became a student of his maternal uncle, the well-regarded composer-pianist Fyodor Goedicke. One day Kolia came home from school, threw his books in a corner, and announced with firm determination that from then on he wished to devote himself entirely to music.[8] With the conviction and stubbornness that would later hinder him personally and professionally, the twelve-year-old Medtner announced to his family that he would be going to the Moscow Conservatory. With the help of his brother, Emil, and over the protests of his family, that is exactly what he did.

Medtner entered the Moscow Conservatory on the cusp of his teenage years, in 1892. He studied piano under Vasily Safonov, the teacher of Rachmaninov and Scriabin, both of whom had just graduated. The three musicians benefited from meetings with the influential professor Sergei Taneyev, who became their composition teacher. The close counterpoint, rigorous compositional technique, and well-wrought textures in their music are the direct result of Taneyev's influence, although that widely cultured musical artisan remained untouched by the creative genius of his soon-to-be-celebrated students.

Medtner was no pedantic young man. In fact, he ended up quitting his free composition class because he felt that his own freedom of expression was being held back. He did receive a gold medal upon graduating, and in awarding it to him Safonov said the recognition should ideally have been in the form of a diamond medal, had such an honor existed.[9] Safonov took his student to the third Anton Rubinstein Competition, where Medtner was recognized with first honorable mention. He gave a perfect performance of Rubinstein's Fifth Concerto, and Safonov urged him to play this work many times subsequently. But Medtner disliked the piece and soon refused to play it again. Safonov had planned a glittering tour for the young virtuoso that would have launched his career on the most secure footing. Medtner would have none of it. Out of ambition, stubbornness, and ego, he refused to go along with the plans laid before him, instead devoting his time to composition. Emil—again over the family's objections—supported his brother's decision to forgo the upcoming tours, but this time Taneyev lent his endorsement and encouraged the young musician's budding efforts at composition. As a pianist, Medtner rarely ventured beyond his own music and the occasional nod to Beethoven, although in his youth, under Safonov's influence, he reluctantly played a wide repertoire. Medtner's performances of Tchaikovsky's First Concerto and of bravura Liszt were by all accounts astonishing. Tellingly, after one such occasion playing Liszt's immensely challenging *Feux follets,* Medtner almost apologized, saying "I did not wish, but they did ask."[10] He soon eliminated such virtuoso displays by performing—as had Scriabin before him—mostly and then exclusively his own compositions. Medtner's unwillingness to play others' music caused endless career problems but reflected an antiquated Russian trait: latching onto an idea and stubbornly seeing it through, whatever the consequences.

In Russia Medtner was a beloved figure, viewed on a par with Scriabin and Rachmaninov. His First Sonata, Op. 5, was played and widely discussed, and students at the Moscow Conservatory pored over his works. But although such artists as Vladimir Horowitz and Emil Gilels enjoyed tremendous success playing Medtner in Russia, in the West they were to find a public generally unresponsive to his music, for Medtner's were not immediately accessible works. At the beginning of the twentieth century, the intimate Russian musical soul was apparently best experienced on home soil.

The newly graduated Medtner became part of several musical societies while still living in Russia, including the Circle of Russian Music Lovers and the Free Aesthetics Society. He further ingratiated himself into Moscow's musical life as a member of the board of the Russian Musical Publishing House. Despite his focus on composition, Medtner also frequently performed in Russia's musical capitals.

Nomadic Years and Impulsive Ambition

In 1909 Medtner took the post of professor of piano at the Moscow Conservatory. After a year, growing tired of his obligations and wishing to resume composition, he

Nikolai Medtner, c. 1910.

moved to Weimar, Germany. While he was there, his wife carefully recopied his pencil notes in ink, beginning a lifelong habit. Medtner's compositions were eventually published from her calligraphic copies. In Anna, Medtner had the most sympathetic companion and one who always selflessly concerned herself with his comfort and happiness. She saw her role as facilitating the spiritual work of her husband. She also helped to enable Medtner's sense of divine right—unfortunately, for that aspect of his character ultimately turned out to be a detriment to him in his dealings with others.

An incident in 1911 foreshadowed future difficulties. Sergei Koussevitzky invited Medtner to play Beethoven's Fourth Concerto with the conductor Willem Mengelberg in Moscow and St. Petersburg. Only one rehearsal was planned, and as it happened, in matters of tempo soloist and conductor were in complete disagreement. Medtner asserted that Mengelberg took the first movement too fast, while extending the finale too long. Insisting on his privilege as soloist, he interrupted Mengelberg and drew the conductor's attention to the fact that the accompaniment should follow the soloist's tempo; otherwise there would be total confusion. But Mengelberg said to him with a condescending smile, "You just play, young man, and it will work out somehow," upon which Medtner loudly slammed the grand piano's lid shut and left the hall. Koussevitzky desperately tried to reconcile the parties, but Medtner was adamant, and the Beethoven concerto had to be eliminated from the program. Similarly undiplomatic, if understandable, differences foretold hardships for the composer during his later years as an emigrant traveling the world, since he could not control situations outside the safety of his Moscow home. Only the music mattered to him, and when he found it in danger he cast all politeness aside.[11] Medtner took the concept of personal responsibility very seriously. His spirituality caused him to feel moral accountability, not only for his compositions, but in all aspects of musical life.

Medtner's blatant ambition and subsequent jealousy of other composers' successes contradicted his belief that "an artist is not given his talent to be used for self-assertion, self-expression, and the pleasures of fame; he should receive his gift as an obligation towards God and the art he serves."[12] He was certainly aware of this dichotomy in his own character, and it made him bitter. He could be vain, egotistical, myopic, and self-centered. Clearly Medtner struggled with the demands of living in a society where fame and money were the means of spreading one's compositional gospel. He expected the world to come to him, and it did not.

Upon the outbreak of World War I, Medtner returned to teach at the conservatory. His classes became avenues not only for his students' musical education, but also for schooling in life itself, mirroring their teacher's ideals in service of art, life, religion, self-discipline, and hard work. The shy master, the dead-serious composer, the uncompromising personality: despite the fanciful nature of his *Tales,* humor is not the first quality that comes to mind when one thinks of Medtner, even for those

Medtner, Moscow. He signed the photograph:
"To the Museum of A. N. Skriabin—N. Medtner. May 12, 1927."
Courtesy of the Scriabin Museum, Moscow.

who know the story of his musical life and career. E. T. A. Hoffmann captured a
part of the psyche that may be applied perfectly to Medtner: "True humor in music,
as in general, arises only from profound gravity, from the alert, active recognition of
a higher order."[13] Among friends, Medtner reveled in vitality and fun, with a native
sense of humor as light and whimsical as his music is profound and serious. His
anecdotes—inane and clever, trivial and rich—were legion. However, when the
subject turned to music, he stiffened as if on cue, resuming a seriousness that knew
no light. When the pianist Arthur Alexander—who contributed a sterling article to
Richard Holt's book of recollections about Medtner—suggested improvements to

the orchestration of the Third Concerto, Medtner became piqued. "Who is this person, who is he to dare criticize my work?"[14]

Medtner drifted through Russia following the Bolshevik Revolution before he finally accepted the course taken by many of his compatriots and sought a life elsewhere: Rachmaninov, Horowitz, and Koussevitzky; the violinists Jascha Heifetz, Nathan Milstein, and Leopold Auer; the cellist Gregor Piatigorsky; the singer Fyodor Chaliapin; the painters Vasily Kandinsky and Marc Chagall; and many other members of Russia's artistic and cultural communities emigrated after the October Revolution. In 1921 Medtner left for Europe to further his career, leading to an unforeseen struggle for recognition and money.

A peripatetic existence followed. He and Anna again attempted to settle in Germany, but he made little professional headway there. In the spring of 1924 Medtner traveled to Italy, where he finally had the opportunity to enjoy the Italian art and culture he had loved since his boyhood. It was also the site of a warm reunion with Rachmaninov, and they spoke nostalgically of the country they had left behind. Desperately missing his homeland, Medtner waited before returning and reluctantly toured the United States later that autumn. Medtner's New York debut occurred in November 1924 with the Philadelphia Orchestra and Leopold Stokowski, then at the height of their mutual fame. The concert received much publicity, with the composer performing his C Minor Concerto. It must be acknowledged, however, that the reception was immediately brighter for Rachmaninov when he performed and recorded his own C Minor Concerto with the same conductor and orchestra. While in America, Medtner played his own works as well as representative pieces of the standard repertoire, including those by Rachmaninov. This was to be one of the last periods when Medtner was willing to program works other than his own. (In a fascinating coincidence, Medtner's general unwillingness to play others' works occurred in his forty-fifth year. At just the same age, Rachmaninov began to develop the large repertoire needed to make a good part of his living as a concert pianist. At that stage in their lives, Rachmaninov was the more popular, yet he never possessed the hubris to think that he could make his way solely by playing his own compositions, even though he may have been able to do so.)

Medtner was always complaining that he had very little money and Rachmaninov, dear friend though he was, took the stand, "Let him work like the rest of us."[15] Rachmaninov wanted Medtner to concertize, but the latter saw his difficult compositional work as being more important than his concerns about money. In turn, he said of Rachmaninov, "He prostituted himself for the dollar."[16]

Medtner's move to a Paris suburb in April 1925 proved inconsequential, as the focus was then on Les Six, Ravel, and other contemporary artists not overly concerned with classical music's past. There were, however, a few encouraging events. Not only was Medtner acclaimed as a musical icon at concerts during his 1927 Russian visit, but he again toured America three years later, making his Carnegie Hall

Medtner. Courtesy of the State Music Publishing House, Moscow.

recital debut playing his own music with extraordinary success. But it was the beginning of the Great Depression, and these successes were not the hoped-for breakthrough, nor could they mask later adversity. Finally, in 1936, Medtner, who adored the English culture and language, found himself in London. Before that time, because of his years of traveling, he had failed to establish a base in any one country. The Second World War, which cut off music royalties and performance opportunities, deepened his distress, which was worsened by health problems. Had he at least played others' music along with his own, Medtner would be far better known today, and he likely would have made more recordings.

Medtner suffered from the same sort of burnout that affects many traveling pianists and musicians, but in addition, his internal *minacciosa* (translated "menacing," it describes a large part of Medtner's psyche) possessed him. He frequently used that word in his works, insisting, "Have I not been threatened by life?"[17] Medtner found himself isolated, and with his limited opportunities and uncompromising output, his small group of staunch supporters held out little hope that his fortunes would change for the better.

Medtner became a resolute critic. His bolts against modernism hardly endeared him to cutting-edge musical thinkers or to their influential institutions. At the very same time Richard Strauss was finding great success with his operas and tone poems, Medtner wrote of him as a musical fakir and decadent. Strauss was explosively popular, and Medtner's diatribe caused many people to see him as a stubborn outsider. His birth on Christmas Eve (according to the old Russian Julian calendar) lent special significance to his religious beliefs: Medtner felt musically chosen from the earliest years and saw it as his birthright to defend his immutable conception of art.

Medtner hated exaggerations and clichés, was repulsed by pretentiousness and reserved in crowds, and detested the business of music. There can be no question that he was as ambitious for recognition and performances as were any of his peers, and he hungered after public success as a composer. When it came to his art, however, Medtner's scorched-earth proselytizing and stubbornness threw up enormous obstacles. His difficult personality, coupled with his refusal to play works other than his own, constantly impeded his success, creating that hardship that found full expression through his music. His frequent referrals to tragedy, as in his "Tragedy Fragments" and *Sonata tragica*, further played on the *minacciosa* theme. Although more outwardly successful, Busoni described a common theme of the creator—whether in art, literature, or music—that was perfectly applicable to Medtner: "It would be psychologically interesting to know why during peaceful periods I have fewest ideas, and become unpeaceful myself."[18] Though frustrated, Medtner had every opportunity to emerge from obscurity into the fame and comfort enjoyed by Busoni and Rachmaninov, but he instinctively—if unknowingly—kept himself back. The substantial body of music he produced began to find its true place in the repertoire only in the late twentieth century.

Medtner's Musical Speech

Medtner's music is starkly realistic; the lyrical and the psychological coexist comfortably. His art finds literary parallels in the tragedy and irony of such writers as Tolstoy and Dostoevsky, in the spiritual weight of Pushkin and Goethe, and in the hardships of life found in much of Maxim Gorky's writings. Medtner's early pieces derive from German traditions (coincident with his family's German ancestry), not only in the use of classic musical forms, but also in his love of the poets Goethe and Heine and of the philosophers Kant and Nietzsche. Medtner also embraced the great Russian poets—his beloved Pushkin and also Tyutchev, Lermontov, Afanasy Fyet, and others. His innate ability to set their words to music put Medtner on a plane with Schubert and Rachmaninov as a songwriter. Sorabji felt that Medtner's songs "are among the greatest that exist—for beauty of vocal line, for brilliance, richness, imaginativeness of treatment in the piano parts, they have no superiors in any song literature, but their technical difficulties are great."[19] Describing Medtner as an accompanist and composer, the singer Tatiana Makushina wrote, "Deep tragedy, mysticism, glimpses of another world, and sometimes expression of tender, youthful love were all to be found in his music."[20]

Medtner borrowed for his songs just three poems from Nietzsche's vast output, and a letter to his brother Emil reveals much about Medtner's creative impulse:

> The form is as good as Goethe, yet at the same time it is incredibly typical of Nietzsche [in its pessimism]. But can a person really live with such a mood? This is why I especially love Pushkin and Goethe: with all their genius and spirituality they still always justify life.[21]

The lyricist in Medtner felt an immediate affinity with nineteenth-century Russian poets, who grappled with the most profound issues of life, philosophy, and the eternal questions of existence. Their perfect craft, ageless wisdom, and conservative idiom found a soul mate in Medtner. His works conjure the voice, with a *cantabile* and sense of narrative that have been hallmarks of the vaunted Russian school since Anton Rubinstein's day.

Medtner's fascination with language leads to a stimulating analogy. Does an author need to recreate grammar and vocabulary to be considered new or revolutionary? Notwithstanding the radical innovations of the celebrated masterpiece *Ulysses,* published by Medtner's contemporary James Joyce in 1922, great works of literature continue to be created in traditional forms. Busoni's paraphrase of Schopenhauer well applies to Medtner: "Uncommon things . . . should be expressed with common words and not vice versa. Hence: Mozart and Goethe."[22]

Even without words, sound still conveys song. In Medtner's works for solo piano, and in his performances of the classical repertoire, this facet of his art predominated. According to Swan,

Medtner. Courtesy of the State Music Publishing House.

whoever has heard him play the first movement of the "Waldstein" Sonata of Beethoven will have noticed how, gradually, the whole form of the movement acquired the breath of melody, how every arpeggio, needed to complete the form, became a most inspired song.[23]

Medtner's works, through their psychological weight, suffering, and nostalgia, exemplify the Russian soul. His lifelong love of poetry reflected his questing desire to decipher the essence of philosophy and spirituality. And in both poetry and music, the best material is often found between the lines.

Like Bach, Beethoven, Schumann, and Brahms, Medtner placed more emphasis on harmony and rhythm than on the purely sensuous aspects of sound itself, and his concerts were models of probity and seriousness. He appreciated the genius of Tchaikovsky and Musorgsky but did not share their vivid sense of color. He mistrusted the impressionists, whose timbral baths, he felt, covered up a lack of solid grounding and craft. His evaluation of their technique was erroneous—the music of Debussy and Ravel, for example, is extremely well crafted—but Medtner could not see beyond their emphasis on sound: "Modern musicians, whose work, intentionally or unintentionally, is lacking in subjective content have made a fetish of timbre. . . . They have made sound, as such, the theme of music."[24]

Medtner was never considered a futurist like Busoni, although both composers learned from and felt true kinship with the musical past. Medtner preached, literally, a return to the classical use of harmony and notation. He was behind the times in his unwillingness to embrace the early twentieth century's biting dissonance. But he was ahead of his time given the general return to more conventional tonality decades after he died. He was stuck in the harmonic hinterlands of his own era, perhaps unsurprising given that he considered himself Beethoven's musical scion.

Nonetheless, Medtner's works are—harmonically speaking—inspired, and demonstrate an overriding interest in structure, form, and rhythm. Sorabji took note of Medtner's conservatism, writing of his music's

> entirely personal and individual use of superficially simple proceedings, that ends by having an expressive scope far wider and deeper than the handful of remorselessly exploited, harmonically neologistic tricks wherewith the "experimental" seekers after a cloak for the platitudes of their musical thinking endeavor to conceal them. . . . The whole of Medtner's work is a most remarkable object-lesson of the way in which it is possible to convey, musically, the most intensely personal and individual thinking without any recourse to the fashionable tricks of the "linear" this or the other, the tom-tom drummings of another, or the fiddling about with one or two harmonies or "funny chords" in various permutations and inversions.[25]

Medtner's contemporaries went off into radical experimentation with new sonic languages—witness the revolutionary challenges thrown across the world by such composers as Schoenberg, Stravinsky, and Debussy, who found their public with atonality, modernism, and impressionism. True, Medtner upheld tradition by writing sonatas and concertos, but he used these structures from strength of conviction rather than from weakness of inspiration. In praising Medtner, Sorabji pointedly criticized others who used traditional forms to try to conceal their tepid creativity, calling this strategy "a straight-jacket to give a jellyfish a backbone."[26] Medtner possessed a musical mind given to very few, and his passion, sensitivity, and sharp, playful sense of humor—as displayed to his friends—ensured equal roles for emotion and intellect in his music. His characteristic independence strengthened his resolve to stay true to his musical vision, but his avoidance, in Sorabji's words, of "all the various modish cliques of neo-this, poly- or atonal that, twelve-tone something or other, has deprived him of the organized press-gangs and professional claques of any of these."[27] The result was, during much of Medtner's lifetime, a generally lonely, unpopular musical existence.

His core group of influential defenders included Swan, who suggested that

those who approach a work of art in an exterior and modish frame of mind, looking merely for exciting novelty, nerve-racking stimulants, and a dose of flattery to prevailing fashions, will be completely disappointed. But to those who are ready to shake off all accretion and look straight for the infallible principles of all great art, Medtner will be a revelation.[28]

Medtner's narrow focus on the piano found a parallel in the mid-nineteenth-century work of Alkan and Chopin. In his own time, however, this attribute was seen as a deficiency in his abilities. Medtner wrote no grand symphonies à la Prokofiev and Shostakovich, nor stunning orchestral fantasies on the order of Scriabin's *Poem of Ecstasy* and Rachmaninov's *Isle of the Dead*. Nor did he ever produce a novelty piece with orchestra—in the nature of Rachmaninov's *Rhapsody on a Theme of Paganini* or the composer-pianist Ernő Dohnányi's *Nursery Variations*—that would have given him instant entrée to subscription symphony audiences the world over. And Medtner did not write an overwhelming Third Concerto, comparable to those by Prokofiev or Rachmaninov; Medtner's music cannot be said to bring down the house. His seemingly uncompromising works resonate with more intimate rewards and require pianists of the highest accomplishment, technique, stamina, and intellectual probity. Those instrumentalists who recognized Medtner's genius but were ill equipped to see it through were another of Sorabji's targets:

By a perverse stroke of irony, by that utter incapacity to realize when they are hopelessly miscast . . . [they] have been the ones to take it upon themselves to give occasional public malperformances of some of the great piano works of Medtner with results utterly deplorable and caricatural, travestying them out of recognition.[29]

Although his style is firmly rooted in traditional harmonic language, Medtner's modern use of rhythmic constructions, syncopation, and contrapuntal diversity cast him as a twentieth-century pioneer. His music's extraordinarily detailed, complex rhythmic patterns may remind listeners of the Stravinsky of *The Rite of Spring*, minus that work's bombast and clashing harmonies. Yet where Stravinsky's music explodes, Medtner's implodes: he preferred to challenge his listeners with unimpeachable craft and harmonic form.

Like that of Beethoven, Schubert, Prokofiev, Scriabin, and Feinberg, Medtner's legacy includes a rich and substantial body of piano sonatas, justifying Taneyev's observation that Medtner was born with sonata form. His music falls into five broad categories, all involving the piano: shorter solo pieces, sonatas, piano concertos, songs, and chamber works. He is one of the most important composers in small forms, yet labeling him a miniaturist would be to call Georges Seurat a painter of dots. Even these brief compositions are intensely concentrated.

Most composers' earliest efforts are derivative, but Medtner's style, developed through much work, study, and experimentation, was apparent from the outset, and his Op. 1 is thoroughly mature. Rachmaninov noted, "Only Medtner has, from the beginning, published works that it would be hard for him to equal in later life. He stands alone in this."[30] Medtner's first published works, the eight short *Stimmungsbilder*, present a series of extraordinary mood pictures. The dense layout of the achingly beautiful Prolog remains hidden among the complex cross-rhythms, contrapuntal devices, and fragmentary motifs that characterized his music for the rest of his life. Medtner's joyous epigraph with Lermontov's words, "Over the midnight sky an angel was flying, and gently he sang," fulfills a prologue's classical definition as a play's introductory speech and marks Medtner's boundless fascination with language and poetry as they interact with music. This superb beginning of a lifetime's work, in the key (E major) Chopin and others adopted to express elevated beauty, is truly idyllic.

The first of the *Three Arabesques* (Op. 7) is called "Idyll," a favorite expression describing the composer's own personal goals. The second, "Tragedy Fragment"— a name that harks back to Medtner's beloved Goethe—follows the title in its grave sentiment. Bernard Pinsonneault, in his book *Nicolas Medtner*, relates that Rachmaninov cried while listening to this work and professed, "Write one such piece and one can die."[31]

Of an entirely different nature are the *Three Hymns in Praise of Work*, Op. 49. These pieces reveal Medtner's attitude toward his life and art. He created these hymns to honor labor, paying tribute to the value and satisfaction of hard work— whether within or outside of artistic realms. Medtner wrote that creative individuals "must earn our works of art by hard labor, like miners, and not attempt to pluck them like the flowers of the fields, as we saunter through them."[32] Rachmaninov, who loved these pieces, performed them during the 1929–30 season, sending a

Medtner. Courtesy of the State Music Publishing House.

one-word telegram to Medtner: "Superb."[33] With devotional themes embedded throughout, they evoke the clarity of Medtner's faith, set in what he considered the pure key of C major. Sorabji specifically singled them out in his review of a Rachmaninov recital in London.

In addition to fourteen piano sonatas, Medtner's output also includes two major sets of works: *Tales* and *Forgotten Melodies*. At the age of twenty-five, he wrote the first of his *Tales* (an irrelevant sobriquet, *Fairy Tales,* was appended only as a commercial expedient), a collection comprising nearly three dozen pieces written throughout his career. Reminiscent of the whimsical, poetic side of Schumann, with a strong rhythmic component, they represent an entirely new genre that fuses literary and folk sources with equal parts dark fantasy and theater. Even more than that, they describe their composer's reaction to "life's grim substance."[34] In their sweeping exploration of human conflicts, drives, disappointments, and happiness, they transcend simple folklore. The *Tale,* Op. 8, No. 2, employs the vivid terms *minaccioso, soffocando,* and *haotico* (in Medtner's often wayward Italian). One of Prokofiev's first introductions to Medtner's music came through a recommendation by the composer Nikolai Miaskovsky, who suggested these *Tales*. Prokofiev greatly enjoyed them, especially the second of the set, but it was hard to play, although everything was pianistic. . . . In general, it was very typical of Medtner's piano technique that all the notes should be right there under your fingers. I hoped that someone would play me this . . . Tale in the right tempo, but there was no such person, so I had to work at it quite a lot in my spare time. It wasn't until many years later that I finally mastered and played it at a concert somewhere in America.[35]

"Ophelia's Song," Op. 14, No. 1, was derived from Shakespeare's *Hamlet,* and a scene from *King Lear* inspired the dramatic *Tale,* Op. 35, No. 4. Both reflect Medtner's lifelong love of Shakespeare. The turbulent "March of the Paladin," Op. 14, No. 2, cunningly weaves contrapuntal devices that give rise to a graphic depiction of knights riding to battle. Rachmaninov called it a miracle. The Op. 20 *Tales* are among Medtner's best-known compositions; the second, "Campanella"—marked "minaccioso"—is far more potent than Liszt's famous piece of the same name. One hears the tolling of Russian bells, foreshadowing Medtner's sense of fervor and foreboding. The two-piano "Russian Round Dance," a thoroughly engaging work and a lighthearted contrast to its weightier companion, the "Knight-Errant" (Op. 58, Nos. 1 and 2), was recorded by Medtner with his friend Benno Moiseiwitsch.

The nineteen pieces of Opp. 38–40 are known as *Forgotten Melodies.* More properly termed "Forgotten Motifs" in light of their recurring themes and ideas, they draw upon previously undeveloped sketches and were given Italian titles in tribute to the Renaissance art, painting, and sculpture Medtner cherished. Composed during the three years before Medtner's fortieth birthday, they contain some of his most heartfelt works. The critic Henry Gerstle offered a cursory statement about them, asserting, "One thing is certain: they point backwards rather than forwards, and possess no more individuality than his Op. 1. Perhaps they were published through necessity."[36] His words appeared right after the release of these pieces, today acknowledged as some of Medtner's finest music. Had Gerstle had the opportunity to live longer with them, he may well have felt the same as he did with other Medtner works: "Some of the pieces which at first made little impression on the writer are now among the most treasured in his possession."[37]

The *Sonata reminiscenza,* the first piece of Op. 38, highlights the importance of sonata form in the composer's life. A matrix for the drama and experiences of a rich, long life, this work's soul mate is Pushkin's affecting poem "Remembrance." The *Reminiscenza* was written in the countryside during the harsh Russian winter of 1920, as Medtner contemplated leaving his homeland. In it, one already hears the nostalgia that was to haunt him for the rest of his life, and it expresses the uncertainty and stoicism with which he faced the future. Medtner's predisposition to musical unity may best be heard in these pieces. The theme of reminiscence that opens Op. 38 frequently recurs during other pieces of the set.

The *Lyric Motifs,* Op. 39, include "Primavera" (No. 3), whose exhilarating coda is reminiscent of an overdue spring's radiant blossoming. Like Rachmaninov, Medtner reveled in nature, a trait appearing often in his works. Medtner found the laws of music and nature inseparable. The order of the stars, the trees, the mystery of life itself lent strength to his ideology. The cycle of *Dancing Motifs,* Op. 40, is perhaps less compelling. Stronger examples of dance forms may be found in the high-spirited "Dance" *Tale,* Op. 48, or the bracing "Danza festiva," Op. 38, No. 3, both of which display a surefooted athleticism not often acknowledged in Medtner's music.

The *Forgotten Melodies* demonstrate Sorabji's point that Medtner "is constantly reminding one of Busoni in the way in which he gives to a quite ordinary passage of harmony an entirely individual flavor by an ingenious and unexpected twist."[38] Medtner possessed Beethoven's skill in creating intricate and moving works using triads, arpeggios, and scale patterns; indeed, he told Richard Holt that "the greatest originality is to create a new atmosphere by familiar materials."[39] For example, the "Night Wind" Sonata (Op. 25, No. 2), a peak in Medtner's output, projects a restless maelstrom of energy, its themes aswirl with lyric streaks of melancholy. Sorabji's first exposure to Medtner came through this piece, and he ranked it alongside Busoni's *Fantasia contrappuntistica* as one of the greatest piano works ever written. It drew immediate admiration from Prokofiev, Feinberg, and Rachmaninov, to whom it was dedicated. Although Rachmaninov never performed it publicly, Feinberg and Horowitz considered it among their favorites and programmed it in Russia. At the inaugural meeting of the Medtner Society in October 1984 in Kentucky, Sorabji's close friend Norman Gentieu said, "Very darkly and somberly colored, [the "Night Wind"] is charged from first to last with the intense, infinite, and inhuman sadness of vast, cold, lonely expanses—a true elegiac nature poem."[40] It contains a poetic epigraph from Tyutchev (also used in the last song of Op. 37, "Winter Storm") revealing both Medtner's sensibilities and the psyche of this particular work, beginning, "What are you howling about, night wind." Sorabji wrote of how good this sonata felt under the fingers, "like the pile of some richly and somberly colored silk Persian rug."[41]

The troubling undercurrents of the *Sonata romantica* are amplified in its intense companion, *Sonata minacciosa,* Op. 53, Nos. 1 and 2. Translated as the "Tempest" Sonata in his given Russian and French titles, it may have expressed homage to Beethoven's own "Tempest" Sonata. After becoming acquainted with these works, Sorabji wrote that Medtner's musical speech owed little to then-current modernistic fashions, and that "he does not so much flout contemporary prejudices, as merely ignore them. Of the absolute individuality of this music . . . there can be no two opinions."[42] The *Sonata idillica,* Op. 56—last among the fourteen and completed in 1937—reverts to a hard-won simplicity of expression, which dovetails beautifully with less complicated pianistic writing. (Ironically, Medtner had for years been pressured by his publisher to write in a more accessible way.)

Conceived three years later at the outset of World War II, the Two Elegies, Op. 59, are a crest of Medtner's creative achievement and plangently represent his last testament for the piano. Similarly to Chopin's "Revolutionary" Étude, which more than a century earlier had heralded the Polish uprising of 1830, these pieces became Medtner's personal artistic statement on the war and reflected deep concern for his distant country. His pained letters of the period expressed the hope that Russia would be able to survive with her spirit and culture intact.

The elegies mine intimate, personal depths and resonate with the same fatefulness as the *Sonata reminiscenza*, though with heightened urgency and brevity. The second elegy (reminiscent of Rachmaninov's Elegy, Op. 3, and the third of his *Moments musicaux*, Op. 16, a lifelong favorite of Medtner's) employs a tango rhythm with a poignancy unseen until John Corigliano's Symphony No. 1, which recalls—through its central use of an offstage piano work, the Albéniz-Godowsky *Tango*—a close friend lost to AIDS.

Rounding out Medtner's oeuvre are pieces in which the piano shares the stage. The three great piano concertos stem from the composer's early, middle, and late periods. Describing the broad canvas Medtner employed in these works, Sorabji wrote:

> Nothing is more remote from the true Medtner musical impulse than the short-windedness that advertises itself under the trade-name of concision, attributing to itself, as a quality, what in reality springs only from poverty of spirit, musically speaking, anemia of invention, and, to put it bluntly, gutlessness.[43]

Unlike Rachmaninov, Medtner never had the opportunity to work closely with orchestras, but given his personality, it is hard to imagine his tolerating the many differing viewpoints they comprise. The *solo* piano remained his. Of Medtner's First Concerto, Sorabji wrote that it was

> stripped bare of all the commoner frills and furbelows so beloved of exhibitionist pianists and voyeur audiences—it is what is usually called "ungrateful" to play, since none but the finest artistry and musicianship can release the secrets of this strange, intensely reticent, and reserved music.[44]

He also called it "a noble, austere, and lofty conception."[45] The famed conductor Arthur Nikisch thought highly of this concerto and intended to perform it with Medtner as soloist. (Nikisch died before the concert could be scheduled.) Then, as now, advocacy by influential conductors is essential to success on the concert stage. Few others had the courage to program these works, requiring as they did the most careful and time-consuming rehearsals. Sorabji favorably compared the mastery of Medtner's last piano concerto to Busoni's concerto. Sorabji responded to the Third Concerto's

> glowing warmth and richness, a lofty, serene beauty . . . a depth and intensity of feeling that made the hearing of the wonderful first performance, under the

composer's own incomparable hands . . . one of the most moving experiences of the present writer's long experience of concert-going. The great work is a glorious climax to a superb life's work, a life too short, ended by suffering and illness, doubtless intensified by sorrow for his native country in its tragic tribulations.[46]

Medtner's music reveals a distinct connection with Schubert, he of the sublime song and expressiveness. Schubert is essentially a twentieth-century rediscovery. And only many years after Medtner's death has wide attention focused on his indelibly inspiring body of music. In Sorabji's beautiful, succinct observation, Medtner "has made for himself, by the sheer strength of his own personality, that impregnable inner shrine and retreat that only the finest spirits either dare or can inhabit."[47]

Public, Peer, and Critical Reception

Although the minute hand of daily existence turned much more slowly in Medtner's day than it does in our own, audiences were already generally unwilling to commit the time and attention his music seeks. Certainly the pace of the modern world leaves performers and audiences even less time for such pursuits. Listening to Medtner requires effort. Above all, this characteristic element has prevented his being embraced widely, as other great writers for the piano have been. The pianist must not only cope with the music's intellectual and structural demands but also possess a technique equal to the purely pianistic challenges regularly put forth by the best composer-pianists. The audience must listen closely, attentive to melodic fragments and harmonic incident as appealing as anything by Rachmaninov, yet hidden from passive ears. Often Medtner's richness can be perceived only after repeated listenings.

Though unequaled as a performer of his own music, Medtner never had a pianistic titan to spread his name, as Rachmaninov did in Horowitz, with his incendiary interpretation of the Third Concerto. Nor did Medtner compose his own "Für Elise," Minuet, or Prelude in C-sharp Minor to engender the worldwide fame that Beethoven, Paderewski, and Rachmaninov experienced. At Horowitz's first meeting with Rachmaninov, both played Medtner, whose music—along with Rachmaninov's own—initially revealed their similar affinities. As Horowitz related: "We both liked Medtner's music very much, though I had not played it in public for a long time."[48] Audiences responded warmly to Medtner's Op. 22 Sonata, although critical reaction to the music was mixed. Horowitz, ever sensitive to negative reviews, gave up programming Medtner after the 1942–43 season.

Although Rachmaninov called Medtner the greatest living composer, others were less convinced. Scriabin dismissed him out of hand, saying, "Medtner has too many notes."[49] Such a remark, however, is akin to claiming that a highly wrought mosaic has too many tiles. Critics, including Scriabin and Prokofiev, often complained about how complicated Medtner's pianistic writing could be. Medtner's classicism depressed Scriabin, who found in the music a bewildering lack of the radical: "I do not understand how one can in our time write 'just music.' This is so uninteresting."[50] Although Prokofiev was an admirer of Medtner, when he heard the *Sonata minacciosa* he wrote, "It was dreadfully boring and unnecessary." Upon hearing Medtner play another of his sonatas, Prokofiev noted, "That is more suited for domestic use."[51] In the same letter he wrote, "Rachmaninov performed some long Variations on a Theme of Corelli, written with the proper ordinariness."[52] Rachmaninov later indignantly said that Prokofiev "divided sonatas into ordinary sonatas and those for domestic use."[53]

One must live with the music for some time to realize how perfectly Medtner wrote for the instrument—an ideal to which Rachmaninov aspired. Medtner was more successful than Rachmaninov in paring down every texture to its absolute, elemental form. He pored over his works for a prolonged time, while Rachmaninov was content to publish and then constantly revise.

Rachmaninov felt that perhaps Medtner's "Night Wind" Sonata could be abridged (to which Hamelin responds, "Would you want to cut off a loved one's limb?"). Rachmaninov dedicated his Fourth Concerto to Medtner and wrote in a letter to him, "I recalled my conversations with you on the theme of length and the need to cut down, compress, and not to be so long-winded, and I was ashamed!"[54]

Medtner's music has not been widely embraced by professional pianists, who more often than not are prisoners of current fashion. Theirs is a competitive lot, with little free time and few opportunities for experimentation; simply trying to attract an audience can be difficult. Hamelin has furthered the Medtner revival with his performances and recordings. In 1997, at Canada's Lanaudière Festival, Hamelin was given the opportunity to play any work; he chose Medtner's Second Concerto. Despite the prolonged ovation given his performance, Hamelin wistfully acknowledged that he would not likely be playing the work again for some time, since presenters perceive Medtner as a programming risk. Sorabji, though, wrote of Medtner and that concerto's virtuosity and substance: "Almost alone among contemporary composers now that Rachmaninov is no longer with us, he has the piano in his blood in a remarkable way." Sorabji called its big first-movement cadenza "a world away from the empty cavortings of the conventional cadenza to which the average concert virtuoso settles down with such self-satisfied unction."[55]

In describing Medtner's piano music, the eminent English critic Ernest Newman offered a fascinating analogy: though music may be considered "dry," that is "no more a drawback in music than it is in champagne."[56] An acquired taste is often sweeter than the obvious confections. According to Stephen Hough,

> Medtner had been very underrated. Although there are times when I listen
> to the music and it doesn't speak to me, at other times I find it absolutely

fascinating and touching in its emotional understatement. I find the G Minor Sonata endlessly absorbing to work on. He writes gorgeously for the instrument. Medtner's music is always beautifully polished, if difficult, but he never overwrote for the instrument and knew exactly what he was doing.

Richard Holt, who later became one of Medtner's most ardent supporters, was initially cold to Medtner when asked to write the album notes for the Medtner Society's recordings. His reaction was typical of those uninitiated to Medtner's world:

> I was not very enthusiastic because, for one thing, studying the work of a replica of another composer, Brahms, made little appeal to me, and for another, influenced by criticisms I had read throughout the years, I imagined Medtner to be a rather dry and academic composer, mainly absorbed in abstruse contrapuntal studies, in fact, the Russian Reger![57]

After studying the Medtner canon, Holt—who considered Beethoven to be the greatest mind in music—came to agree with Newman's assessment and drew the same conclusion that many pianists and wider audiences have come to realize: Medtner ranks among the foremost writers for the piano. Holt had heard nearly every prominent pianist during the half century before Medtner's death and recalled:

> None . . . had a greater power of articulate scale playing and passage work than Medtner, nor a more dynamic and subtle sense of rhythm. His playing bubbled over with energy, tumultuous in its onrush, yet ever under command, and it was sensitively plastic, to a rare degree, in the control and shaping of phrases.[58]

Holt's compilation of essays on Medtner by prominent writers and musicians is filled with comments about Medtner's humility and modesty, a one-sided view of his character. The book, which holds Medtner up as a saint, has the unintended effect of making him seem sanctimonious and ultimately does him no favors. Holt completed his book under Anna's persistent influence and editing; she saw it as a final gesture to her husband's memory. Although a forceful and eloquent advocate of Medtner, Sorabji was not afraid to point out Medtner's failings as he saw them. In discussing the Second Violin Sonata, Sorabji wrote that it possesses "a freedom of style and movement that Medtner seemed to have lost for a time . . . and has less of the contracted, constricted quality that occasionally crops up in his work."[59]

There is consensus among Medtner's advocates that he must be presented in the best possible light—as human being, as composer, and as pianist—and that somehow his normal failings should be kept from readers. Let it be said without doubt or provocation: Medtner was an exceptionally self-disciplined and striving person whose flawed character served art flawlessly.

Inspiration

Russian composers took poetry as inspiration, as their country's poets drew on vast and richly descriptive sources of human drama. Medtner turned Russia's poetic legacy into songs of lasting beauty and meaning. Rachmaninov, whose ideology involved love, tragedy, realism, and nature, also felt a deep connection between music and poetry: "Our Pushkin I find admirable. Shakespeare and Byron I read constantly in the Russian. I always have books of poetry around me. Poetry inspires music—for there is so much music in poetry. They are like twin sisters."[60]

Medtner complained that although the mechanics of music are always stressed during the learning process, the higher creative spark could not always be counted upon to fall unbidden from the imagination. He noted ironically, "What a good thing that in conservatories where they have classes in harmony, fugue, and counterpoint, they haven't yet started a class in *inspiration*! It should be a kind of consecratory discipline, and ought to treat of spiritual experience."[61]

Rachmaninov, who realized that inspiration is hardly self-contained, once said of his friend:

Medtner's whole mode of life in Montmorency [the Paris suburb where Medtner lived] is so monotonous. An artist cannot give everything from within. There must be outward impressions. I told him once: "You should go and spend the night in some den, get thoroughly drunk. An artist cannot be a moralizer."[62]

Medtner pushed himself as composer even when he felt little inspiration, and although he experienced no great fulfillment in public performances to keep him going during dry creative periods, he acknowledged, "An artist cannot perform or create for himself, he has to have a public."[63]

Medtner viewed hard work as the portal to inspiration. Highly disciplined and ascetic, he wrote at age sixty, "Constancy in work is just as important as in love, as in prayer."[64] By communing daily with his craft and stretching his abilities in the service of an internal moral guidance, he fostered the means for inspired creativity.

Rachmaninov could not begin to compose without the fires of inspiration; he came to seek artistic satisfaction through his concerts. He stoically endured strenuous daily work at the piano:

The greatest art is that which is done unconsciously. Of course, there must be years of grinding labor to produce any great end or reach any high goal. One does not soar to the heights of art like an angel. The work, the climb is there. But the difference is that the great artist usually forgets that he is working, so completely does his love and enthusiasm for what he is doing camouflage drudgery.[65]

Rachmaninov at Medtner's London House, 1938.

In a disturbing presentiment of his later debilitating difficulties with the creative process, Rachmaninov frankly admitted:

Real inspiration must come from within. If there is nothing within, nothing from outside can help. The best of poetry, the greatest of painting, the sublimest of nature cannot produce any worthwhile result if the divine spark of creative faculty is lacking within the artist.[66]

Like many composers, Rachmaninov found it difficult to pinpoint the sources of his own inspiration. He spoke of love, beauty, and the grandeur of nature as powerful creative stimulants. His Villa Senar (an acronym taken from the first letters of Sergei and Natalya Rachmaninov) on Lake Lucerne became a summer sanctuary, at which his commune with nature restored mind and body for his grueling seasonal tours. Rachmaninov also loved his hobby of speedboating and took pleasure in showing others around the lake.

Rachmaninov as Composer and Pianist

The creative part of Rachmaninov's life largely ended when he left Russia; only the last six of his opus numbers were written outside his native country. He suffered from a stultifying homesickness and depression. Although he found it much easier to compose when he was young, a fact that was to cause him endless despair, the incessant self-critic in Rachmaninov admitted, "I look at my early works and see how much there is that is superfluous. . . . It is incredible how many stupid things I did at the age of nineteen." Of the C-sharp Minor Prelude that first earned him world fame at that age, Rachmaninov said, "It came with such force that I could not shake it off even though I tried hard to do so." He added, "I received only twenty dollars for it. The piece was printed and sold in large quantities throughout the world but I never received any further compensation. The recognition which the piece brought me, however, was worth considerable."[67]

Rachmaninov's later self-doubts found dubious validation in much published criticism and in the excoriating opinion of Eric Blom, who in 1954 wrote in the fifth edition of *Grove's Dictionary* that he lacked the

> individuality of Taneyev or Medtner. Technically he was highly gifted, but also severely limited. His music is well constructed and effective, but monotonous in texture, which consists in essence mainly of artificial and gushing tunes. . . . The enormous popular success some few of Rachmaninov's works had in his lifetime is not likely to last, and musicians never regarded it with much favor. The Third Pianoforte Concerto was on the whole liked by the public only because of its close resemblance to the Second.[68]

But years earlier Godowsky, who knew considerably more about Rachmaninov and the piano, had written:

> Not only is he a very remarkable composer, but a great pianist as well. His third concerto for piano and orchestra . . . is ideal for the musician. It has all the salient characteristics necessary in the work of a perfect pianist. I know of no modern work that is more beautiful from the standpoint of the artist.[69]

Sorabji wrote a number of letters and articles decrying the posthumous denigration of Rachmaninov. During the mid-twentieth century, Rachmaninov was the subject of harsh critical opinion that generally saw his music as syrupy, showy, and saccharine, though it remained highly popular with audiences. Rachmaninov's great melodies and obvious romanticism have at times masked the inspired craft, the finely spun counterpoint, and the structural cohesion indicative of the greatest composers. His stature continues into the twenty-first century, with many of his orchestral works and concertos being heard by sellout crowds.

Rachmaninov as a student at the Moscow Conservatory.

A withering disappointment occurred after Rachmaninov premiered the Fourth Concerto in 1927 with his beloved Philadelphia Orchestra, conducted by Stokowski. As described by Richard Anthony Leonard in *A History of Russian Music*, "Those who were present at that event, or its repetition four days later in New York, remember the chill of disappointment. This concerto seemed like a pale ghost of its clanging and colorful predecessors."[70] Rachmaninov knew the work had problems, and in an echo of a previous musical disaster—the premiere of his First Symphony under a drunken Glazunov—Rachmaninov's creativity went largely dry until seven years later, when his *Rhapsody on a Theme of Paganini* found immediate success under the same conductor and orchestra. This work and another masterpiece written two years earlier, the Variations on a Theme of Corelli, demonstrate Rachmaninov's brilliant exploration of variation form. But, significantly, these works are based on themes by other composers; Rachmaninov continued to have trouble writing new music. Liszt and Brahms had made Paganini's theme famous; Rachmaninov brought it into the twentieth century. Sorabji saw in the rhapsody "a profoundly original and independent mind at work, a mind that stands as aloof and apart in its way as does that of Medtner . . . from the fashionable monkey-tricks of Paris, Berlin, Vienna, and Moscow."[71]

A charming story has come to be associated with the Paganini rhapsody. A few days before Rachmaninov gave its world premiere, he confessed to his close friend Benno Moiseiwitsch at a New York dinner party that overall he was very pleased with it, but he was having real trouble with the high-wire jumps in the twenty-fourth variation. As Moiseiwitsch related:

> A butler entered the room with a tray full of liqueurs. Rachmaninov, a teetotaler, refused. "Why Sergei Vasilievich," I urged, "you *must* have a glass of Crème de Menthe. It is the best thing in the world for jumps." "Do you mean it?" he asked seriously. "Definitely," I assured. Whereupon he called the butler back and helped himself to a generous quaff of the emerald cordial. Afterwards, in the drawing room, he gave a faultlessly executed preview of his new composition. Eyewitnesses testify that before the performance in Philadelphia, Rachmaninov downed another large Crème de Menthe and that, following the spectacular success of the Rhapsody on that occasion, he never failed to have a Crème de Menthe in the greenroom before playing the work publicly. On the score of the Paganini Rhapsody inscribed to me, the twenty-fourth variation is plainly marked in the composer's hand: "The Crème de Menthe Variation."[72]

Rachmaninov achieved great success as a pianist, but he continued to conduct his own works and those of others, developing a substantial reputation with that branch of his art. He declined an offer to be permanent conductor of the Boston Symphony Orchestra in 1917, in part on the advice of his friend Josef Hofmann, who warned

Rachmaninov against the power politics he was likely to encounter. Hofmann's own proclivities led him to urge his friend to pursue a pianistic career.

It became one of the most storied careers in all of music. Sorabji felt that Rachmaninov's "strongly magnetic and compelling personality, and its most attractive combination of restraint and dignity" placed him in the highest echelon of pianists.[73] Sorabji colorfully described Rachmaninov's Chopin interpretations as "pure and clean of all weak sentiment, filtered of the dirty muddy dregs of emotional slush that are industriously stirred up in it by so many others, and yet full of fine imaginativeness and poetry."[74]

Observers spoke of Rachmaninov's sound above all else. His lifelong friend, the great bass Fyodor Chaliapin, gratefully acknowledged, "When he plays for me I can truly say, not that 'I'm singing,' but 'we are singing.'"[75] This sense of song, of beautiful sound, was a hallmark of Rachmaninov's playing from the beginning. Harold C. Schonberg speaks of Rachmaninov's "incredible bronze sound; I can't remember hearing anything like it. It was a sound capable of all kinds of nuance. After all, he was one of the two greatest pianists of my time [Hofmann was the other]."[76] Arthur Rubinstein called Rachmaninov "the most fascinating pianist of them all since Busoni. He had the secret of the golden, living tone which comes from the heart and which is inimitable."[77] The pianist Earl Wild recalls:

> His sound was so beautiful, something never captured on his recordings and the most intoxicating I have ever heard. It distinguished him from everyone else. He never played like some pianists today, looking up at the sky, pouncing on the pedals. . . . The presentation was always direct and simple. There was no sense of ego. My first exposure to Medtner, in fact, came when I heard Rachmaninov in the First Improvisation. It was marvelous, the most beautiful music, and that led me to more Medtner.[78]

Medtner himself wrote about Rachmaninov and his sound in larger terms:

> It is precisely because of his fame that it is difficult to speak of Rachmaninov. This fame is more than his: it is the glory of our art. This unbroken contact of his entire being with art itself can be sensed each time his touch produces sound. This sound, in score or keyboard, is never neutral, impersonal, empty. It is as distinct from other sounds as a bell is different from street noises; it is the result of incomparable intensity, flame, and the saturation of beauty.[79]

The Rachmaninov sense of rhythm was always an essential component of his artistry as well. Alfred and Katherine Swan wrote, "His rhythm, like his sound, is always included in his musical soul—it is, as it were, the beating of his living pulse."[80]

He initially played his own works almost exclusively, but when Scriabin died Rachmaninov swore at the graveside to honor his former classmate's memory with a series of concerts devoted to his music. "After the death of Scriabin I toured all

Rachmaninov, Kiev. Photograph by V. Meczynski.
Courtesy of the Scriabin Museum.

over Russia playing his compositions as my humble homage to that great master of music," he said.[81] With his large hands and analytical composer's mind, Rachmaninov interpreted Scriabin's oeuvre in a manner that angered many of Scriabin's admirers; they felt the mystery, if not the sensuousness, had been drained out of the music. Indeed, Scriabin himself had reacted against Rachmaninov's deep, bronze sound, observing, "Though he plays with a beautiful tone, everything . . . has that same lyric quality as his own music. In his 'sound' there is so much of materialism, so much meat . . . almost some kind of boiled ham."[82] It must be noted, however, that Scriabin considered Rachmaninov's playing of his own music incomparable: "Take the notes of something by Rachmaninov. Listen to it with your eyes and then hear Rachmaninov play it on the piano. The same notes, yes, but the quality is entirely different. Unquestionably beautiful, no argument, convincing, everything sings."[83]

Rachmaninov met Prokofiev the year Scriabin died. Their friendship began well, but at one of Rachmaninov's memorial Scriabin concerts where he played the Fifth Sonata, Prokofiev said, "When Scriabin played this sonata everything seemed to be flying upward; with Rachmaninov all the notes stood firmly planted on earth." Everyone was used to the composer's way, and Rachmaninov's created no small amount of conflict among the Scriabinists. Prokofiev (who actually was receptive to this sort of interpretation) said to Rachmaninov after the concert, "After all, Sergei Vasilievich, I think you played it very well," whereupon Rachmaninov shot back with a wry smile before turning away, "Did you think I would play it badly?"[84] This exchange promptly cut off their short friendship, already rather shaky because Rachmaninov did not generally like Prokofiev's modernist music.

After playing many of Scriabin's works publicly, Rachmaninov gradually began to perform a wide repertoire by other composers, although he was still criticized for playing his own music too much. Barbed comments came mostly from critics, however; audiences could not get enough of Rachmaninov playing Rachmaninov. Basanta Koomar Roy, writing in the *Musical Observer* in 1927, presciently observed, "In the course of the next hundred years or so the excellence of his piano playing will no doubt have become mythical."[85] Sorabji concurred:

> Now that Busoni is no more (one can never utter *that* supreme name without emotion) there is no greater pianist. He has, too, certain qualities that remind one strongly of Busoni. To a stupendous technique is added a musical intellect of magnificent power, and that quality of haughty imperious mastery that is the mark of only the very highest. It is piano playing of the grand manner, which gets less and less as time goes on, with its serene dignity and great but quiet-voiced emotional power.[86]

A review in the *New York Times* in 1924 noted Rachmaninov's presence in recital at Carnegie Hall: "In appearance and in performance he is singularly unadorned.

His personality is one that suggests thought and much reserve power, but it is not romantic or picturesque."[87] Rachmaninov's stage manner sharply contrasted with his actual playing, which was invariably charismatic, grand, and emotional. In a London concert review, Sorabji wrote:

> This very great artist comes again to show us that he is one of the few remaining exponents of the grand manner of piano playing. To a power and fire the equal of Paderewski at his best he has a subtlety, a finesse, and, on occasion and when he wants it, a grace, elegance, and urbanity of style. . . . His platform manner . . . is a model, dignified, grave, and reserved, never overstepping the bounds between artist and public, who are quietly and gently but very firmly kept in their place.[88]

Rachmaninov took much longer to develop as a pianist than as a composer. He described the process in simple terms: "A technique must be built, just as a house must be built. There are no real short cuts. The muscles grow in power and dexterity, through a course of years of daily hard work."[89] Naturally taking a composer's approach, he was exceptionally thorough and systematic in learning new music, which undoubtedly gave his interpretations their solidity and definitive cast. On the other hand, the alchemy of a great performer extends well beyond the process of acquiring a repertoire and playing it properly. According to Rachmaninov,

> the personality of a musician has a great deal to do with it. If personality does not count, then why not listen to the phonograph or radio? Why go to concerts at all? Take one concrete example. Mr. Kreisler [Fritz Kreisler, the celebrated violinist and close friend of Rachmaninov] has a tremendous personality. He comes on the stage, he plays and conquers. Now suppose at one of his concerts he played from behind a curtain. Do you think the audience would enthuse as much as is usually the custom? The personality of a musician influences the audience, consciously or unconsciously, in the appreciation of music. In the enjoyment of music human hearts play a more important part than human brains.[90]

Although more interested in composing than in performing, as was Medtner, Rachmaninov was far more practical and had a family to support (Medtner never had children). When compositional ideas failed him, Rachmaninov turned to his performing career for comfort and validation, even well after he achieved financial security. Toward the end of his life, he was a very wealthy man, yet he literally worked himself to death. This tendency was already there in his thirties:

> On the whole I have an awful lot of work piled up. . . . I am offering two thousand rubles as reward to anyone who will release me from my job at the theater. I would like to put an ad in the paper: "Lost last spring my peace of mind because of signing a contract. Will reward the one who will deliver it to the following address."[91]

Even before his career as a pianist took precedence, Rachmaninov plainly admitted that "to be a father, composer, and a conductor all at the same time is very difficult and very painful."[92]

Nostalgia and Melancholy

As a young man, Rachmaninov was both typical and exceptional. His biographer Victor Seroff made it clear that

> Rachmaninov in his youth was very different from the portrait that has been painted of him. He was a young man with a very passionate nature, easily carried away, sentimental, spoiled by early success, flattery, and fame, and with none of the strength of will and equilibrium which he fully developed later.[93]

The composer himself acknowledged, "I was silly and stuck-up on myself in those days."[94] Things quickly changed:

> I had my full share of sorrows, sufferings, and privations. Though born in a wealthy family I soon discovered that I had to support and educate myself. Something went wrong with our family fortunes. So trouble began. As a boy I made good progress in music, and began giving lessons in piano when I was only sixteen years old. It was necessary for me to earn money by this means in order to continue my musical education. . . . In order to be able to teach conscientiously, I had to know much more than my pupils and I learned how to solve many problems of technique. My forced pedagogy was certainly a blessing in disguise in my development. For I am proud to say that I am a self-made musician. So after much trial and tribulation, when appreciation came I was happy.[95]

Rachmaninov's nostalgia may be traced to his departure from Russia, which he was never to see again. His melancholia appears to have had its roots in a serious early illness. This brush with mortality, combined with a natural sensitivity, gave rise to his increasing preoccupation with death and became fodder for a burst of creativity. The Dies Irae theme may be heard in many of his works.

In keeping with his willingness to live with and draw creative strength from a preoccupation with death, Rachmaninov worked unapologetically with pure emotionalism, dressed in the finest craft. He also came under the influence of a famous compatriot: Tchaikovsky. To Russians he was an icon, and Rachmaninov had adored him ever since meeting the great composer at the house of Nikolai Zverev, who taught piano at the Moscow Conservatory. One of Rachmaninov's first works was a piano arrangement of Tchaikovsky's "Manfred" Symphony, intended as both homage and educational exercise. Rachmaninov's connection with his mentor found full expression after Tchaikovsky died—in a work for piano, violin, and cello.

The resulting *Trio élégiaque* was dedicated "to the memory of a great artist." (Rachmaninov's trio took its precedent from Tchaikovsky's own trio, Op. 50, written in memory of Nikolai Rubinstein.) Rachmaninov empathized with Tchaikovsky's dark, tormented view of life, but, as he explained, their history went deeper:

> Whenever I think of my career as a musician I cannot forget the patronage of Tchaikovsky. He thought I had talent; so he encouraged me and helped my development. At the premiere of my first opera, *Aleko,* he desired that his one-act opera, *Iolanthe,* might be produced along with my first attempt. *Aleko* was a one-act opera taken from Pushkin's dramatic poem, *The Gypsies.* I was indeed proud of the compliment thus bestowed. You really cannot realize what it meant to me then. The great Tchaikovsky, our national musical hero, wished that his opera might be produced with mine. I was simply intoxicated with joy. . . . Patronage from such a great musical figure certainly did help me in carving out a career for myself. Tchaikovsky was a dynamic personality, even as Chekhov.[96]

Chekhov, Dostoevsky, Tolstoy: surely the wistful melancholy and dramatic line of indigenous Russian literature played its part in influencing Medtner and Rachmaninov, among many other composers. The first words that Anton Chekhov said to the youthful Rachmaninov were, "Young man, I see a brilliant future written on your face."[97] Nearly half a century later, a month before he died, Rachmaninov recalled the compliment in a conversation with his biographer Seroff, saying that it was the greatest he ever received. He was devoted to the theater and had always admired Chekhov. The composer's experience with Leo Tolstoy proved less opportune. When Rachmaninov was in the middle of a severe depression, brought about by the failure of his First Symphony, friends arranged for him to meet the celebrated writer with the idea of lifting his spirits. He was received indifferently. Rachmaninov and Chaliapin went to see Tolstoy in January 1900. Rachmaninov felt his hands becoming cold (he later always wore gloves and used a hand warmer before concerts). "If they ask me to play I don't honestly know if I'll be able to. My hands are like ice." Tolstoy did ask, and after Rachmaninov complied, Tolstoy looked him straight in the eye and questioned, "Tell me, does anyone want this type of music?"[98] (Tolstoy's favorites were Haydn, Mozart, and Chopin.) This devastating event led to Rachmaninov's meetings with Dr. Nikolai Dahl—remembered as the dedicatee of the Second Concerto—whose early experiments in psychotherapy brought about Rachmaninov's brilliant reemergence with that work. Medtner wrote of this seminal concerto:

> The theme of his magnificently inspired second concerto is not only the theme of his life, but it always produces an impression of one of the most vivid Russian themes . . . each time from the very first bell stroke, you can feel how Russia is rising in all its glory.[99]

Rachmaninov's first American tour in 1909, for which he wrote his next concerto, the Third, only deepened his homesickness and melancholy. He was excited neither by America nor with the tour in general. His letters written the year before were filled with unhappiness at having to make the trip, notwithstanding what he knew would be a large material gain. During the tour itself, he wrote to friends in Moscow how weary he was of America, despite great success playing his own compositions. Perhaps this had to do with his performing almost every day during the three-month tour, and his susceptibility to fatigue. His letters make repeated reference to his having no time and to being constantly tired.

Rachmaninov became introverted and more modest as he grew older. To the larger world he could seem aloof. Swan observed that

Rachmaninov, as a rule, spoke very little, especially among strangers. Having reached the top, he probably realized that a man in his position is much less independent than an obscure person. He must also have seen much flattery, envy, vanity around him, and so he shut himself up. It was easier and wiser to do so. This way he placed himself above gossip, squabbles, and rivalries.[100]

Stravinsky agreed: "As I think about him, his silence looms as a noble contrast to the self-approbations which are the only conversation of all performing and most other musicians."[101] A friend wrote, "Like all truly great men, he was absolutely simple and sincere."[102] An interview Rachmaninov granted at age fifty-seven gave a glimpse into his simple life and tastes:

He shuns luxury and costly habits in every shape and form. He is absorbed in his art and devotes much time to reading, playing, and gardening in the summer time. He is seldom seen at concerts. But when his old friend Chaliapin sings, or when Medtner plays, it is hard to keep him away.[103]

In quiet, intimate moments, Rachmaninov often turned to nostalgic Russian works, such as the first movement of Scriabin's *Sonata-Fantasy* (Sonata No. 2 in G-sharp Minor). Many artists were vulnerable to Rachmaninov and his often elegiac music. For years Moiseiwitsch gave annual Rachmaninov concerts in London, one of which was scheduled in late March 1943. Just before the concert, which was to feature the Second Concerto—a work pivotal in Rachmaninov's own life—Moiseiwitsch read that the composer, his great friend and colleague, had died. His reaction became a heartfelt tribute:

Stunned and sorrowed, I felt that I could not possibly go ahead with the afternoon's concert and pleaded with the management to find a replacement. No other pianist could be found on such short notice, so at noon, I finally decided not to let the orchestra and public down—but with three stipulations: I would go through with the concert on condition that there would be no rehearsal beforehand; that I should not be obliged to dress; and that there would be no applause as I walked on stage or when I finished. Promptly at 2:30, still in traveling clothes, I played the Second Rachmaninov Piano Concerto. Then, as 2500 people stood in silence, I played the Funeral March from Chopin's Sonata in B-flat Minor, walked off the stage without a word to anyone, and went directly home.[104]

Depression and Perfectionism

The two works Moiseiwitsch played that afternoon held central themes for Rachmaninov. Chopin's sonata represented the striving for compositional economy, and its funeral march held special significance for Rachmaninov, given his preoccupation with death. The Second Concerto's conception and success had delivered him from a debilitating depression. When Medtner asked Rachmaninov why he had stopped composing, the reply was pointed: "The melody has gone, I can no longer compose. If it returns, then I shall write again."[105] The acknowledgment of a dry creative spring ultimately crystallized Rachmaninov's darker tendencies and caused a more lasting depression, assuaged only by the constant touring that took his mind off what he considered his failings as a composer. Swan observed, "In spite of a deeply affectionate family, in spite of his great success all over the world and the devotion of his audiences, Rachmaninov lived shut up within himself, alone in spirit and everlastingly homesick for his Russia."[106] Here was a man anesthetized only by feverish professional activity. Despite fame, wealth, and family, Rachmaninov's innate self-awareness kept him from self-delusion:

> The artist tries, and tries again to achieve the impossible. Sometimes he is lucky and gets a little nearer to his goal. But all of the time he is forced way out someplace, way out where no one can comfort him, nothing can help him.[107]

Medtner's prescription for his friend Rachmaninov borrowed a tenet from his own life:

> A creator must be a ne'er-do-well, to a certain extent. If Rachmaninov could only become a ne'er-do-well, if only for a short time, then he would again begin to compose. But he is tied hand and foot by his obligations; everything with him is measured by the hour.[108]

For all of Medtner's own troubles, his self-doubt never became paralyzing. He made it clear that

> an artist's mistrust can be twofold: of himself and of his art. The former is inevitable, the latter pernicious. We cannot avoid being swayed by doubts as to how we compose, how we serve music; this is self-criticism, a testing of ourselves that only increases our watchfulness in serving art.[109]

Rachmaninov delivered a crushing self-assessment: "If I ever had faith in myself, that was a long time ago, a very long time ago—in my youth!"[110] Dr. Dahl worked with Rachmaninov to strengthen his courage and faith, but with mixed long-term results:

> Sometimes I succeed in doing it. But my sickness sits in me so firmly, and with the years has developed even deeper. It will be understandable if eventually I will decide to give up composing and will become either a pianist, a conductor, or a country squire—perhaps, even an automobile racer.[111]

Rachmaninov and Medtner shared an almost pathological perfectionism in their music and public performances, a trait common to The Eight and of course to many other figures of creative bent. Despite his fantastic successes, Rachmaninov simply could not tolerate anything less than perfection. His friend Marietta Shaginian observed:

> Once during an intermission such a storm of wild enthusiasm reigned in the hall that it was almost impossible to get through the crowd. When we entered the green room, we found Rachmaninov in a terrible state. Before we had a chance to congratulate him, Rachmaninov, angrily biting his lip, began to complain that he was getting old, losing his mind, that he belonged to the scrap heap, that one should prepare an obituary for him telling everyone that there had been a musician, but now nothing was left of him, that he could not forgive himself. . . . He said, "Didn't you notice that I missed the point? The point came down, do you understand?"[112]

Rachmaninov was referring to the climactic point that he found in every piece of music, the result of the most careful and exact preparation. This applied to music he both created and performed. The point could come at the middle or the end, it could be loud or soft, but without it the whole work would collapse and lose shape.

His compositional perfectionism clearly spilled over to his pianistic activities as well. Rachmaninov made a famous recording of Chopin's Second Sonata, and although he played the Third in 1918, his interpretation of that piece remains unknown to us—for a reason. After a Hofmann performance of that work at Carnegie Hall, Rachmaninov sat silently for a few moments and then said:

> Well, there goes one more composition out of my repertoire. Not since Anton Rubinstein have I heard anything like this. There's no use. It is the music itself and the only way to play it, and nobody else can do it.[113]

Rachmaninov's life, despite its dark and melancholy streaks, did include humor. In 1907, from Dresden, he wrote about Franz Lehár's operetta *The Merry Widow*: "I laughed like a fool. Absolutely wonderful."[114] Rachmaninov could evince an almost childlike simplicity. He was "observed to chuckle in childish glee over the *primo* part of [Godowsky's] Toccatina—a tricky little *moto perpetuo* of interlacing passage work—playing it again and again as though he could not hear it often enough."[115] Gina Bachauer, his student and a famed pianist in her own right, commented:

> Among all the illuminating words on the music itself, Rachmaninov took the time to make little drawings in the scores—a smiling face when he wanted me to sing out a phrase happily, a little angel when he wanted . . . a heavenly tone.[116]

Once, at a dinner gathering with friends including Medtner, Rachmaninov's daughter Irina

> stealthily crawled to Medtner's feet and pinned big yellow bows to his shoes. There was an outburst of laughter when everybody got up and Medtner proceeded to the drawing-room unconscious of his strange footwear. Rachmaninov laughed in his peculiar, silent way, but inwardly he was rocking with glee, so that he had to wipe the tears from his eyes. He was touchingly fond of his children to the point of being proud even of their pranks.[117]

Rachmaninov often began letters to his good friends the Swans, "Dear goosi-lebedi," an endearment he took from a call in a popular Russian children's game.[118] One such letter read, "The tennis court is being lengthened and widened. The surface is being rolled and improved. I have bought new rackets. New balls. I am bankrupt. When will you come?"[119]

Rachmaninov's warmth toward his friends and compatriots was genuine and constant. Chasins wrote:

> He was as thrilled as a child at the circus when the Moscow Art Theater came to New York in 1923. Each performance found Rachmaninov there, tears of happiness streaming from his eyes while those gigantic hands wiped them from his face.[120]

He and Medtner—such uncompromising personalities—found release in good company, where they could be themselves without the enormous weight of responsibility that each felt toward his art. Although he made fun of Medtner's peculiarities now and then, Rachmaninov demonstrated unfailing generosity and magnanimity to his friend in word and deed. Medtner was once cheated by an American promoter who bounced a check. This would have created terrible hardship for the Medtners, but through Anna's complicity, and making sure that Medtner never knew about it, Rachmaninov bought the note and later dropped the matter altogether.

Rachmaninov presented contrasting public and private personae. On the concert stage, though he could perform Godowsky's *Künstlerleben* paraphrase with wit and insouciance to wildly enthusiastic audiences, he famously never smiled. He frequently appeared gaunt and sad and was hardly approachable by the general public. But among peers and friends, he was gentle, humorous, unstintingly generous, and genuinely interested in the society around him. Early in his career, Earl Wild met

Rachmaninov; they talked for a long time at their first meeting—the budding young pianist to the great master. Wild recalls, "Rachmaninov was the exact opposite of the public image he projected. He was a very kind person, patient and congenial."

Rachmaninov's friend, the great violinist Kreisler, related in a now-famous story that at one of their joint New York recitals, he had a memory lapse and whispered to Rachmaninov, "Where are we?" Rachmaninov's quick reply: "In Carnegie Hall!"[121] Another time, in London, Rachmaninov and Moiseiwitsch compared notes on other prominent pianists over lunch. They managed to find some fault with each. "Thank you, thank you very much, my dear friend," said Rachmaninov. "You have run down all the finest pianists in the world, except me." Moiseiwitsch replied with a smile, "Ah, but I am having lunch next week with Josef Hofmann and you may be sure that we'll get around to your name!"[122] Much like Medtner, Rachmaninov was able to be the carefree raconteur only in close company.

Rachmaninov rarely prevailed upon any of his colleagues to perform his music, although he did ask Moiseiwitsch to play his transcription of the blistering Scherzo from Mendelssohn's *A Midsummer Night's Dream*. The two shared a good-natured rivalry concerning the Rachmaninov repertoire. Once in New York, Rachmaninov asked the Steinway representative, Alexander Greiner, "Tell me, how is it, Sasha, that Moiseiwitsch's recordings of Rachmaninov outsell my own two-to-one? Can it be that he is a better Rachmaninov pianist than I am?"[123] Greiner then happily pulled out a record catalog to show the relieved composer that Moiseiwitsch's discs, made in England, retailed for half the price of Rachmaninov's American-made ones.

But Rachmaninov's professional attitude was absolutely uncompromising. He insisted:

> The performer must give the best that is in him, even if he is playing in the smallest town in the most terrible theater, even if the audience is only one person—the doorman, holding the keys, waiting for the concert to finish as soon as possible, so he can lock the doors.[124]

Of course, Rachmaninov never had to contend with sparse audiences. As he grew older, his fame increased dramatically, and he was incessantly cheered. He could well have rested on his achievements, yet he continued to push himself relentlessly. According to Seroff, "He would burn himself out performing and then, white, looking like a squeezed lemon, exhausted from the work, he would lie half dead during the intermission."[125] But Rachmaninov told his doctor, who advised him to perform less often:

> This is my only joy—the concerts. If you deprive me of them, I shall wither away. If I have a pain, it stops when I am playing. Sometimes this neuralgia in the left side of my face and head torments me for twenty-four hours, but before a concert it disappears as if by magic. . . . No, I cannot play less. . . . It is best to die on the concert platform.[126]

Rachmaninov. Photograph by Eric Schaal, published in *Life*, 1943.

Rachmaninov fulfilled his tours and engagements without cancellations or compromise, even toward the end of his life, when he was severely afflicted with a bad back, arthritis, exhaustion, and breathing difficulties. He told Swan:

> The blood-vessels on my fingertips have begun to burst, bruises are forming. I don't say much about it at home. But it can happen at any concert. Then I can't play with that spot for about two minutes, I have to strum some chords. It is probably old age, and yet take away from me these concerts and it will be the end of me.[127]

Rachmaninov's concerns about his health deepened with age. His creativity waned, and he found artistic solace primarily in performing. Rachmaninov publicly announced his intention to retire from the concert stage nearly three years before his death, but he continued performing nonetheless. His health problems were capped by terminal cancer; he died eight years before heart disease claimed Medtner.

Medtner suffered a series of strokes that ended his performing career, though at least he was able to make a final series of recordings. He looked increasingly to composition as a palliative, whereas Rachmaninov turned to concertizing. Their work both saved them and hastened their deaths.

Medtner and Rachmaninov: The Muse and Fashion

Medtner and Rachmaninov have come to occupy secure positions in music history. Neither man had any burning desire to radically alter the musical landscape of the era; Sorabji called them "violently unfashionable composers."[128] He also observed that Rachmaninov was "far aloof, as a creative artist, from the fads, fashions, and follies of contemporary music festivals."[129] Reviewing a Medtner concert in London, Sorabji noted the presence of a large audience,

> attracted to listen to one of the most distinguished and interesting figures in modern music, whose aloofness from the fashionable musical circles of Berlin and Paris (Russian and French) is one of the by no means least attractive things about him.[130]

Medtner viewed as a sham much of the new music born in the early part of the century, believing that traditional means of musical expression were becoming subsumed by an inferiority that passed for innovation. He called modernism "the tacit accord of a whole generation to expel the Muse, the former inspirer and teacher of poets and musicians, and install Fashion in her place, as autocratic ruler and supreme judge."[131]

Medtner retrospectively set the foundation of his life with a personal artistic treatise, *The Muse and Fashion*. A mid-twentieth-century equivalent of Busoni's *Outline of a New Aesthetic of Music*, it articulates his reaction to his own era and codifies his longstanding beliefs. Subtitled "Being a Defence of the Foundations of the Art of Music," the book cloaks its idealism in pedantry. Medtner attempts to defend not only the "sacred laws of art" but also to lay down a twentieth-century response to the principles of classical music traditions that were being uprooted during his lifetime. It is important to note, however, that Schoenberg, Stravinsky, Hindemith, and others also wrote persuasively and extensively—much more so than Medtner—in defense of their own beliefs and philosophies.

Rachmaninov's Tair (derived from his daughters' names, Tatyana and Irina) Publishing House released *The Muse and Fashion* in Paris in 1935, in its original Russian (the English translation, by Swan, was published in 1951). Despite his love of languages, the widely read Medtner never achieved the same succinctness with words as he did in his music. *The Muse and Fashion* takes 146 pages to say what could have been conveyed in no more than 100. His need to be absolutely precise results in the opposite effect, his stream-of-consciousness style tending to obscure larger issues. Even to the sympathetic reader, passages such as the following (in Swan's translation) are bewildering: "Action which has not been preceded by contemplation is the most manifest absurdity and lawlessness in art. It is not even a manifestation of individuality, but an instinct of the will that has isolated itself, i.e. wantonness."[132] An uncompromising manifesto of his belief in the fundamentals of hard work, discipline, inspiration, and song, the book—with parenthetical observations and words capitalized for emphasis scattered all throughout its pages— nonetheless emerges as obtuse and awkward. If it were condensed and well edited, it would likely be on every musician's bookshelf.

Sorabji saw past the book's drawbacks and was drawn to Medtner's courage in facing down the establishment:

> Medtner has committed the unforgivable sin of expressing himself forcibly and powerfully against many of the fashionable musical tricks of the time; has shown his complete indifference to and aloofness from them, as to all passing winds of musical *coiffure* and *couture*.[133]

Goethe's poem "The Mirror of the Muse" adorns part two of Medtner's book. The poem describes the muse as she searches for a calm section of a rolling stream in order to see her reflection, but her image is never clear in the rushing water. She is mocked by the current, which Medtner viewed as the changing tides of fashion. Rachmaninov distilled a prime tenet of *The Muse and Fashion*: "Let us have all the new music that the greatest genius of the world can produce; let it be rich and original; but, above all things, let it be based upon the time-old principles of real beauty and not false art."[134]

If harmony was Medtner's driving force, melody was Rachmaninov's: "Melody is music and the foundation of all music. . . . I do not appreciate composers who abandon melody and harmony for an orgy of noises and dissonances as an end in itself."[135] Rachmaninov shared Medtner's disdain for atonality and various aspects of modernism and was not at all reticent to express himself on the subject:

> Audiences learn that it is fashionable to admire certain phases of what is termed futurism. They like the pose of being "modern," "up-to-date," and they affect to like the works that no human being with a rational mind could possibly enjoy. Such a public rarely thinks for itself; it is much more comfortable for them to accept a fashion that others applaud, even if that fashion is altogether hideous. Human nature is odd in this respect. Time, however, decides between the permanent and the artificial, and inevitably preserves the good, the true, and the beautiful.[136]

While Medtner followed the precepts of Beethoven into the twentieth century, Rachmaninov—who said of Beethoven's Ninth, "Nobody will ever write anything better than this symphony"[137]—made one of the German composer's prime objectives his own: "The element of contrast is one of the most powerful in art. There must be light and shade. Discord emphasizes beauty, but incessant cacophony, carried to pitiless extremes, is never art and never can be."[138] Such remarks confirm Rachmaninov's instinct for positive public reaction. But his loyal constituency made it much easier for him to challenge the prevailing state of affairs than it was for Medtner. Sorabji wrote of new music in the context of Medtner's relative lack of success: "How stale, futile, and utterly boring are all the antics of the 'advanced ones,' the avant-garde quacks, and all such canaille."[139] Medtner desperately wanted to see *The Muse and Fashion* translated and published before his death, so that history would not misjudge him based on what he saw as ignorant polemics.

Rachmaninov and his friend Chaliapin were often joined by the writers Maxim Gorky and Ivan Bunin—along with other influential artistic figures—in trying to preserve nineteenth-century traditions in the wake of symbolism and futurism in literature, cubism in art, and modernism and atonality in music. Their feelings on beauty in art versus ugliness coincided with trends then developing in art and architecture. Those in the vanguard of radical artistic change rarely took the traditionalists seriously, but Rachmaninov's great popular success shielded him in a way unavailable to Medtner.

The two artists railed against modernism. Rachmaninov complained, "Europe is suffering from a kind of a contagious mania for cacophony, as represented in the works of the ultra-modern composers."[140] And Medtner abhorred, for example, what he regarded as Arnold Schoenberg's disregard for harmony. The early twentieth century was an age of egos and frontiers. Schoenberg, however, as well as Stravinsky, Hindemith, Reger, Bartók, Strauss, and others—in short, the coterie of twentieth-century musical thought—venerated tradition, viewing it as something to be studied, respected, and then departed from. Medtner insisted on developing traditional means through his own voice, without having the radical avant-garde affront his sensibilities. Describing one of Strauss's tone poems, Medtner became shaken and depressed over what he saw as an insult to his craft. In the new musical freedoms then being promulgated, as Swan put it,

> Medtner saw a loose discipline that seemed like any counterfeit which, temporarily at least, might pass for the genuine thing among the commonality. Essentially, he felt that there was an abandonment of all strict criteria, an assumption that an inferior quality would do just as well, and that a basic dishonesty was involved in the difference between what had been before and was currently being presented.[141]

Intransigent and vocal in his distaste for much contemporary music, Medtner did not help his cause. He was often dismissed as reactionary, closed-minded, and—along with Rachmaninov—behind the times. Prokofiev said in disgust, "Only Rachmaninov and Medtner with extraordinary unanimity turned down everything that had the slightest suspicion of novelty."[142] (Prokofiev had attempted to get several works published by Koussevitzky's new firm in 1910 but was stonewalled by the advisory board, which included Scriabin, Medtner, and Rachmaninov.)

Medtner died in 1951, quietly maintaining—as did a fervent group of supporters—that his life's work would eventually survive the changing forces of fashion. Half a century later his conviction has become reality, which he would have accepted with a wry Russian sense of *ironiya*. Will Medtner ever become as popular as Rachmaninov? Though Medtner may have wished so either during or after his lifetime, the relevance of that question remains buried under the incontestable quality of the two men's music.

Rachmaninov and especially Medtner viewed art as a religion. Although Medtner possessed personal vanity in good measure—something Rachmaninov completely discarded as an adult—anything that hinted at insincerity in their music became anathema. Direct as ever, Rachmaninov suggested that

> music should speak from the heart. . . . My desire to compose is actually the urge within me to give musical expression to my feelings—just as I speak to give utterance to my thoughts. I have little sympathy with the composer who produces works according to pre-conceived formulas or theories; or with the composer who writes in a certain style because it is the fashion to do so. Great music has never been produced in that way, and it seems to me it never will.[143]

Medtner essentially put forth the same thoughts, brilliantly reflected in his own music. He remained deeply agitated by what he saw as the hypocrisy and pretense of much new music created during his lifetime. He saw himself as a lonely beacon of trust and spirituality. Unimpeachably principled, Medtner and Rachmaninov readily capitulated to their muse, closely aware of and repelled by the pull of fashion.

5 FROM ALKAN TO HAMELIN

Lincoln Center, New York, nearing the end of the year 2000. Heightened anticipation from the audience, many of whom have heard the pianist solely through his celebrated recordings. As Marc-André Hamelin emerges from stage left and walks briskly to the piano, the applause erupts, continuing unabated as he bows, seats himself, and adjusts the bench. He cannot begin the concert until he rises to acknowledge the ovation once again—itself a highly unusual deviation from normal concert etiquette and an indication of the stature he has achieved. As the concert begins, the strength and determination inherent in Busoni's transcription of Bach's solo violin chaconne come to the fore, abetted by the pianist's searching intellectual probity and legendary technique. From the very first notes, it is patently clear that here is a pianist capable of realizing—through his chosen instrument and repertoire—anything his restless imagination demands. Later, Schubert's last sonata lingers in the air, aching and otherworldly in expression, modern sounding in the pianist's unapologetic adherence to the composer's vast silences and striking accents. The formal part of the concert—that night Hamelin would be called back for five encores—concludes with exceptionally difficult, rarely performed works by Medtner and Scriabin, presented with breathtaking refinement and passion to an audience rapt and eerily silent—the usual coughing and other ambient distractions are absent. Throughout the evening, the effects the triumvirate of pianist, piano, and composer produces are alternately volcanic and volatile, heady and heartfelt. Yet the music is uncolored by narcissism. Hamelin's noticeable perspiration and his alchemical ability to generate musical heat appear at odds with his undemonstrative performing profile and stage presence.

Marc-André Hamelin (born in 1961) has come to live a life unburdened by the fetters of artistic convention. He is a pianistic iconoclast, following his own path and instincts, wary of easy success and self-promotion. The archetypal Hamelin concert—anything but typical—embraces music by The Eight and others, and encompasses a repertoire involving intense physical demands and seductive fancy. "Hamelin's legend will grow," wrote the influential critic Alex Ross in a *New Yorker*

Marc-André Hamelin at the Grammy Awards ceremony, live televised performance,
Los Angeles, 2001. Photo by Scott Gries, Image Direct. Courtesy of
The National Academy of Recording Arts & Sciences.

review of the concert described at this chapter's opening (30 November 2000), for "right now there is no one like him."[1]

As described by his student Heinrich Neuhaus, Godowsky in performance bore an uncanny resemblance to Hamelin:

> The main impression was that everything is terribly simple, natural, beautiful, and completely effortless. But turn your gaze from his hands to his face and you see the incredible concentration: eyes with lids lowered, the shape of the eyebrows, the forehead, reflect thought, enormous concentration—and nothing else! Then you see immediately what this apparent lightness, this ease, costs; what enormous spiritual energy is required to create it. This is where real technique comes from![2]

Clearly, much of the music Hamelin plays is athletic and requires stamina, but the brain plays the predominant part in the physical act of performing. He betrays remarkably little sense of obvious physical barriers and is relatively still in concert;

the presentation has been pared to eliminate excesses that may distort the composer's conception. Hamelin's performances give the kinesthetic impression of complete ease, but he is quick to correct this perception:

> Even with the conscious relaxation that I always cultivate, some of the works I play make me abnormally tense, which is some measure of how difficult they actually are. I am amazed when I watch myself on video; there seems to be no effort involved. I can perhaps understand people who say that I do not *look* emotionally involved, but one goes to a concert to have an immediate acoustic experience, certainly more present than on records. Watching is secondary.

A review of an all-Liszt London concert colorfully bears out a fascinating dichotomy unique to this pianist:

> Hamelin does not conform to the stereotype of the flamboyant Liszt pianists. He is content to let his technique do the talking, and his phenomenal control and articulation, his ability to keep a cool head while all hell is breaking loose underneath his fingers, give his performances a crystalline clarity.[3]

There are those who miss the flamboyance. Ross noted that Hamelin "has the mien of a lab technician engaged in unholy experiments."[4] But then, why do some prefer a Klimt over a Kandinsky, a Cabernet over a Chardonnay? In considering and evaluating Hamelin the pianist, the age-old questions remain.

In sovereign keyboard command, speed, and control, Hamelin is a Horowitz sans neuroses. In his ultrasensitive awareness of keyboard color and the three pedals, he is a Gieseking sans ego.[5] Born with intellect, imagination, mercurial reflexes, and a perfect ear, Hamelin demonstrates a secure grasp of complexity of the sort that The Eight idealized. Yet he severely disdains virtuosity as an end in itself and has no time for those who see his musical achievements as one endurance test after another. Ross also wrote (in a review titled "Extreme Piano: Playing the Unplayable") that Hamelin's hands "are among the wonders of the musical world. No living pianist is as capable of playing more notes more clearly in a shorter span of time."[6] While it may be true, Hamelin responds, "That kind of statement has been done to death, and it is the farthest thing from what I'm about as a musician and as a performer."

And yet, Hamelin admits to some dissatisfaction with his playing in the past, performances that squarely contradicted his musical aspirations. Although he is largely unafflicted with nerves before or during a concert, they nonetheless have their effect:

> Nerves have never daunted me. As far back as I can remember, at age nine in a local competition that was my first public performance, I cannot remember being scared of the public. It was perhaps a blissful unawareness of what the possibilities were. Nerves manifest themselves most significantly in the

sometimes considerable pumping of adrenaline. Very often I will not feel nervous during a live performance, but a listening of the recording afterward will offer evidence that the adrenaline was positively flowing unabated.

Hearing the tape of his 1996 London recital, Hamelin recoiled at the *precipitato* final movement of Prokofiev's Seventh Sonata. Getting through the notes accurately at such a scorching tempo (which he did) was only a Pyrrhic victory; a pianist should leave more than smoldering ashes on stage, and Hamelin knows this better than anyone. Recounting an all-Liszt recital in New York, also in 1996, he describes the last half of the *Norma* Fantasy as

> absolutely, ridiculously fast. I heard this and cringed. While playing, musically and technically I thought it was going well. That very evening while listening to the tape I was startled. This allowed me to make changes. The next day in Boston, I gave a much more convincing performance, musically truer at that point in the score.

Such incidents have become much less common as Hamelin has grown as a musician. His unassailable technique is ratified by a warmth and humanity uncommon in this era's competitive, stainless-steel society.

The Pedals and Performance Style

True technique, transcendental technique, requires so much more than finger speed and control. Godowsky revealed one of the secrets to his art: "In my Chopin studies or in my Symphonic Metamorphoses the pedal actually takes the place of a *third* and sometimes even a *fourth* hand."[7] Hamelin embraces Godowsky's view and discusses the art of singing at the piano, making it clear that the pedals are elemental:

> They are the *lungs* of the piano! They provide connective tissue to everything. If one does not use the pedals creatively, textures are simply not going to come to life. By now all the pedaling I do is completely subconscious and is governed by my ear. If someone gave me the score of a work I play and asked me to notate pedaling, I would be dumbstruck. The notation would be highly complex because the pedal is not a cut-and-dried process. There are infinitely gradual shadings involved and, importantly, those will change on every piano. Pedaling happens spontaneously at every performance because often there is not much time to spend with an instrument before the concert; several hours are not enough. The true arbiter for pedaling is the ear and that *must* be nurtured. It is not cultivated in schools. Very few teachers directly sensitize young pianists to the intricacies of pedaling. Harvey Wedeen caused me to think and listen to what subtle things the pedals can actually produce, indispensable in singing at the piano. It is getting to be a lost art, this hyperfine awareness of pedal shading. Otherwise, one might as well be playing the drums or any other percussion instrument.

Such refined exploration of the pedals is emblematic of the efficient and economical technique Hamelin stresses in his entire approach to the piano. This economy of means has its roots in ideas and ideals first explored in depth by Busoni and Godowsky, who sought the greatest effects and projection with the most efficient possible effort. Their extensive experiments with the pedal were the foundation of radical and modern pedal techniques, employed by Hamelin and others but still lacking in many virtuosos. The pedals are also the key to developing a sophisticated inner ear, which is directly responsible for a physical technique acquired much more by ear and thought—as with most great pianists—than through incessant practice. Indeed, Hamelin confesses to being lazy by nature (although one may question the standard he applies in making this self-judgment).

On Alkan and Sorabji

Even though he is drawn to repertoire that reaches particularly far in expressing thoughts and emotions, Hamelin's nature guards against pushing excessively, thus preventing his performances from moving beyond those realms he views as unintended by the composer. Hamelin's sense of boundaries prohibits banging or any sort of harshness in his approach or his sound. "My interpretation will convey only the extremes within the piece itself. Alkan's Concerto for Solo Piano [Études 8, 9, and 10, Op. 39] is a prime example." Although Hamelin does not see this Alkan work as overwhelmingly complex compositionally, he reflects on the subject of complexity and why he gravitates toward music of this kind:

> It is difficult to fully grasp this instinct just as I cannot know why I like the color green rather than gray. I appreciate simplicity just as much, but complexity has its attractions. There is richness in music of this kind, combined with the desire to make it accessible to the listener.

Hamelin's psyche and instincts, as well as his preference for the repertoire's larger forms, have drawn him close to Alkan's music, the increasing popularity of which is due in no small part to Hamelin's ardent advocacy. "Alkan's music is becoming better known," he observes,

> but ideally there could be still more awareness. There are not many blank stares anymore when his name is mentioned to pianists, although they also hear about the fact that his music is difficult and generally they do not want to bother. Many pianists seek instant success with that which does not require much effort.

Hamelin's perfect pitch makes him ever aware of key relationships, an essential asset in performing music of such extended dimensions. He believes that Alkan's music is structurally rather simple:

I have never considered it complicated from a compositional point of view. There are harmonic innovations galore, and though difficult to play, the music is not forbidding to read and is not overly polyphonic. The first movement of Alkan's concerto, for example, is a reasonably normal sonata-allegro with a proper orchestral introduction. However, it is so distended in time that initially the listener may have trouble untangling the form. It has been said that within this movement one could end in at least three different places. Considering the structure, though, it is absolutely impossible for it to end at any other place than it actually does. The form is obvious to me, like a scroll unraveling.

Reclusive, diffident, hypochondriacal, secretive—how can one possibly reconcile Alkan's cloistered personal lifestyle and character with the heroic nature of music so far beyond the reach of so many that the composer never dreamed it would be played? Do composers not write for performance? What good is music whose impact is limited to manuscript paper? Hamelin proffers a few answers:

> We can safely say that Alkan did not envisage performance of many pieces. He never performed the big works, Op. 39 for example, which were completed well after he became a recluse. He likely felt freer to let the demons loose without the restraints of performance practicality.

Those few pianists capable of reproducing music of such virtuosic and emotional writing are bringing the impractical to life. Hamelin elaborates on a few of the difficulties:

> It is interesting that Holst, when he wrote *The Planets,* had no hope of ever having it performed because the large orchestra needed was too costly. Significantly, this is the same with Sorabji's major works. He did not expect performance. Practicality in performing Sorabji is an enormous obstacle for pianists. To illustrate the point—in *Gulistān,* which I edited for publication, one requires an *extremely* sensitive instrument to make any sense of the texture in separating all the polyphonic strands. Getting something like that in one's fingers is understandably a very gradual and time-consuming process. It feels almost like two or three *Ondines* piled on top of each other! The proper dynamic projection must be considered; a special kind of technique is required in which one must get across many notes in an aerial, delicate way. There is never an indication louder than mezzo forte, and that is an extreme. Very fast repeated chords must be projected dolcissimo. Such an effect is not something that is achieved easily, especially when the right piano is not at hand. I would *never* play this piece without knowing the piano in advance. It requires the most extraordinary sensitivity.

Sir Michael Tippett, the distinguished British composer and conductor, has called some of Sorabji's music impenetrable and beyond the pale of complexity. Hamelin resists such an attitude:

Hamelin at Alkan's tombstone, Montparnasse, France, October 1999.
Photograph by Jody Karin Applebaum.

I find it a rash judgment in this case, because I do not feel that Sorabji's music has been adequately presented yet, at least his mature works such as the *Opus clavicembalisticum*. It is pointless, then, to make that kind of statement. I can understand why it would provide a kind of sensory overload; it is so distended in time that one can be lost without listening carefully. If his music is well presented it can be a fascinating experience.

Sorabji's First Sonata is an earlier, less dense work; Hamelin calls it

> a thrilling magic-carpet ride, hurtling from splendor to splendor within a virtually unprecedented breadth of tonal and instrumental audacity. It should prove an exhilarating and rejuvenating aural experience for those still caring to attune themselves to the joys of youthful excess.[8]

Sorabji was heavily under Scriabin's influence while composing this work, and its writing is redolent with Scriabin-like harmonies and textures. The breathtaking coda, with its torrent of repeated chords, is saturated with the ecstasy and liberation of Scriabin's climaxes in his Fourth Sonata. The darker side of Scriabin's personality was to find expression in his later works, primarily after that sonata's completion.

On Scriabin

Hamelin adores the Fourth Sonata and relates equally well to the dark mysticism of the later compositions.

> Extremes of darkness go in tandem with extremes of complexity and pianistic expression. I have a very dark streak, which is perhaps reflected in my taste for subversive and underground literature. Extremes of thought and action lead directly to Scriabin. These are not the only criteria, but in looking at new music I often look at what is going to jump at me from the page.

The composer in Hamelin has not been able to answer questions raised by the wild, almost neurotic elements in Scriabin's music:

> There is a very puzzling dichotomy in that his highly intense emotions and surrealistic preoccupations are expressed within the confines of what are basically rather strict sonata-allegro conventions, especially in the later sonatas. Why would Scriabin confine himself to a recognizable form? If he were merely pouring out feelings, the conscious classical thought would be absent. While translating these incredible emotions on paper, Scriabin was apparently being considerate of his listeners, so they would find something with which to anchor themselves. Using a sort of free-form fantasy without the confines of classical norms would have been a more obvious way to express the intensity of his feelings. The stream-of-consciousness kind of improvisational writing is clearly missing. In his last works, even the key relationships between tonal centers are often correct. He thus lends legitimacy and tradition to his thoughts.

Faubion Bowers has described one of Scriabin's late works, *Vers la flamme* (Op. 72), as

> composed essentially of two notes . . . which crackle like lashing flames, sputtering and sparkling . . . [it] is like a Roman candle of increasing, magnifying blazes, until it becomes consumed in its own flames. Trills no longer suffice for Scriabin's frenetic pianism. He now writes spasms of eight clustered, shaking, and quivering notes.[9]

This is just the sort of mystical, colorful musical expression that Hamelin would normally gravitate toward, but here an anomaly presents itself. "I am not partial to *Vers la flamme*. I enjoy the music but do not wish to play it. To perceptibly give it the growing intensity that it needs is a relentless endurance act." Can the five minutes of *Vers la flamme* really daunt the same pianist who frequently performs Alkan's fifty-minute Concerto for Solo Piano?

> That is an entirely different animal. In Alkan, the textures change. Here, Scriabin focuses on the same obstinate figures. There are two pages of left-

hand tremolos that must become *singed*; such passages are in decreasing proportion to the readiness of the hand to carry them out.

Such extreme piano writing is often reflected in Scriabin's letters. They are filled with copious references linking sex and inspiration, revealing a central aspect of his creativity. Although Hamelin responds to erotic and sexual expression in books and the cinema, he offers a personal viewpoint on several of Scriabin's sonatas:

> I do not think of these works as necessarily sexual, though intensely mystical and physical. In the late piano works in particular, I respond above all to sound; other associations are secondary. I consider harmony the driving force of music, even before melody, timbre, or rhythm, because harmony determines form. The harmonic world of Scriabin is incredibly inspiring.

Hamelin smiles when asked whether he would be disappointed if his listeners did not experience a sense of the sexual—as conceived by the composer—while he played Scriabin, and he coyly acknowledges the benefits of such a reaction. However, "the music itself is so powerful. If one is able to realize the interior drama between the lines, a darkly convincing and sensuous performance becomes inevitable." Many critics agree. Paul Griffiths, writing in the *New York Times,* described Hamelin's performance of two Scriabin sonatas as "brilliantly spun, with an exact control of their palpitations and frenzy."[10] Hamelin reveals a deep thirst for the emotional needs of this music, whatever its psychological and sexual tangents. "I get as much song, as much soul, as much *juice* out of the piano as I possibly can. Scriabin demands nothing less."

On Medtner and Rachmaninov

The search for music laced with such layered sound and emotion is an ongoing preoccupation in Hamelin's work. Nostalgia is a subject that many magnificent works address; Rachmaninov's Second Sonata and Medtner's *Sonata reminiscenza*—both central to Hamelin's repertoire—reflect a desperate homesickness, perhaps even defiance. The uniquely Russian sense of looking back is best expressed through Pushkin's poem "Remembrance," which vulnerably recalls remorse and the anguish of sorrowful memories, themes blanketed over vast amounts of Russian prose and poetry. Hamelin (who owns the original manuscript) deflects the issue of nostalgia as a motivating factor for his looking into the *Reminiscenza* but acknowledges its importance:

> Even if the title itself did not indicate reminiscence, there is definitely that feeling of looking back. I do not expect this sonata to lose the hold it has over me at any time in the future. There is nothing like the *Reminiscenza* in the literature. It is one of the most personal statements that I have known any

composer to share. If it had been written later in Medtner's life, it could well have served as a summation of life experiences: looking back with fondness over the good things one remembers and with regret at the negative events or those one is not proud of. It contains the richest concentration of conflicting emotions I have ever witnessed. Its sixteen minutes are a microcosm of life.

Hamelin is more inclined to look ahead in his own life, so the ideas of nostalgia and looking back are not particularly relevant to him. (Busoni felt even more strongly: "Digging into the past is repulsive to me."[11]) Hamelin has tapes of his earlier performances and with a few exceptions does not care to listen to them. He continues to develop musically as he becomes older and feels a stronger ability to listen intently to himself. "My goal is to be as true as possible to what the composer has intended and to convey all that is exciting, challenging, and *vital*." Hamelin's progress makes what he has done before rather obsolete. He feels considerably more resolute with himself, both personally and professionally.

The pianist and conductor Daniel Barenboim has described a path of wisdom and fortitude that few young instrumentalists are willing or able to follow:

> The greatest privilege as an artist is not to be well known and not to make a lot of money, but to achieve total independence. The more you grow as an artist, the more independent you can become, and the less you have to try to adjust to public taste. Indeed, you are able, in your independence, and with your knowledge and talent, to influence public taste.[12]

This is the route taken by Hamelin, who is one of only a few pianists to have influenced public acceptance of Alkan, Godowsky, and Medtner. Hamelin quietly recalls his struggle to reach a level of personal security in life. Before his ascent to international prominence, he experienced years of relative obscurity, doubts about the vicissitudes of a musical career, and financial insecurities, but also he was able to devote the time needed for self-mastery. Medtner's bitter career and financial problems, on the other hand, continued throughout his life, and he never achieved a meaningful level of security. Hamelin senses a close affinity with Medtner's sound world and reveals the highest respect for his compositional abilities:

> True, I am not the kind of person he was, for example he was very religious and I am not. But my ongoing discovery of his music has been one wonder after another. Pianists often have the idea that Medtner's music is uninteresting and therefore feel that he is a great risk in concert because of this. They question why they should bother with Medtner when they have Rachmaninov. What a terribly shortsighted attitude! When Medtner is described as a second-rate Rachmaninov, I want to *scream*.

Hamelin continues, "No other composer has been able to realize such an amazing marriage between instrumental craft and musical thought. Medtner went to

incredible lengths in making his music comfortable to play without sacrificing anything he aimed to address." This effort behind the notes is an acutely apparent characteristic of Medtner's muse. As far as purely pianistic writing is concerned, his is the
best that Hamelin has ever seen:

> Working on the Second Concerto, I understood how wonderfully considerate
> Medtner is to the pianist. In every small detail he strove to make very
> difficult-sounding music as physically harmonious as possible. It cost him
> great effort to do so.

On Godowsky

According to Hamelin,

> In many ways Godowsky was similar, although I would not rate him as a
> composer in the same way because Medtner was clearly superior. Godowsky's
> musical expression is much more polyphonic and dense. Remarkably,
> Medtner achieves largely the same feeling with fewer notes and contrapuntal
> lines, by striving for maximum effect with minimum pianistic means.
> Godowsky did have the same kind of craft, but he expressed it differently and
> more through transcriptions. It is true that Godowsky's music can be more
> immediately appealing than Medtner's, but not everything he wrote is worthy
> of consideration. A number of his pieces are outmoded, with indulgent
> sentimentality, especially when he gets into waltz mode. Some of his music is
> difficult to reconcile today with what we consider to be genuine sentiment.

Hamelin also finds many performances of Godowsky's music emotionally wanting. Speed, strength, and stamina by themselves cannot shape Godowsky's emotional requirements any more than a machete can sculpt the human figure. Many
pianists simply do not have the capacity to get beyond the notes and into the realm
of the music itself.

Alexander Dreyschock, an obscure nineteenth-century pianist, is said to have
spent up to twelve hours a day practicing Chopin's "Revolutionary" Étude with left-
hand octaves in place of the single notes in Chopin's original. Such a vacuous exercise, however astonishing its effect, is worlds away from the Godowsky credo. Left-
hand-challenged pianists generally scorn the idea of a composer writing for that
hand alone out of anything but necessity. Mirroring Godowsky's own abilities and
seriousness of intent, Hamelin has achieved sovereign control of the left hand; his
layered performances of Godowsky's left-hand études may even spark the illusion
of three hands at work. And as always in Hamelin's playing, the pedals are operated
with such guile and transparency that the fierce technical challenges generally
remain hidden. The effect is utterly musical.

Personalities

And what if Hamelin had been able to communicate directly with Godowsky and the others? He muses on the possibilities:

> I would very much have enjoyed spending time with Godowsky because the study of his works has occupied me almost since childhood. I hope that he would have approved of my way of playing his music. Alkan—a very interesting figure to think about speaking with: brilliant, reclusive, mysterious. Busoni would also have been fascinating in conversation, despite some unpleasant personal characteristics. He was quite vain and felt threatened by competition. Scriabin's was a volatile sort of personality, extreme in many ways, nervous and sinewy. Medtner apparently was not an easy man. He had every reason to be bitter about his career, but generally he was a good soul. I certainly regret not having met Sorabji. In 1977 I ordered the *Opus clavicembalisticum* from England. I would have had every opportunity to meet Sorabji, but it was rather late. In fact, my first letter to the Sorabji Archive reached the curator Alistair Hinton three weeks after the composer's death. I don't know if I could have coped with his intellectuality, but Alistair felt that Sorabji would have enjoyed meeting me.

Busoni strongly influenced Sorabji personally. Feinberg felt a similar pull toward Scriabin. Medtner and Rachmaninov learned much from one another. Personal musical mentors have been essential in the development of so many pianists and composers, but Hamelin, by choice, flatly denies the notion:

> I have no heroes. My father was very close to my development at almost all times, though I would not say that I looked up to him. It was more collaborative. I consider myself rather abnormal in that there is no figure that I have ever wanted to emulate. I have always been able to see the positive and negative sides of just about everything or everyone I have come across.

Godowsky felt much the same way. "Close contact is detrimental to hero-worship," he wrote, "and when you realize that the others are not 'Mont Blancs,' you begin to think you are more than a mere mole hill."[13]

The Conscious and the Subconscious

This kind of discriminating nature does not suggest that Hamelin is overly analytical in his life or work:

> There are many things I do which if consistently analyzed would lose their charm. Often something subconscious will surface and it works. There are conscious avenues walked, of course, but I do not try to analyze the subconscious. One's instincts should be trusted and embraced.

Learning and memorizing, however, cannot always be left to instinct. Hamelin expresses an element of frustration when learning a new piece of music:

> If I read a passage, it gets in my fingers very quickly, but this does not imply retention. It means that while looking at the music I can do it motorically and there's no problem. But if I come back in half an hour I will have lost all of it. It is only after a few times, frequently after many times and after careful analytical study, that my brain will retain. In my case, aural memory lags behind tactile memory. There is a general pattern in what I do as far as the learning process goes. I find that I must work on music often enough so that I can start dreaming and thinking about it in wakeful as well as sleeping moments. Sleeping memory is a reality. I have tried to memorize music while practicing at night and nothing happens. When I awake in the morning it is suddenly there. The process is often subconscious.

Repertoire

Hamelin has, of course, learned and performed the more traditional monuments of classical music, such as Schubert's last, great Sonata in B-flat and Beethoven's vast "Hammerklavier" Sonata. In fact, there is quite a bit of Beethoven in Hamelin's repertoire, including three of the five concertos and the Choral Fantasy. He describes the first time he publicly performed the Sonata, Op. 10, No. 3:

> I was apprehensive and had every reason to fear this, because I am not known as a Beethoven pianist. As it turned out, each of the movements was sharply characterized and I was happy with the clarity of projection. The impact of the slow movement was never more apparent than when I performed it for the first time with an audience present.

Hamelin would love to play Beethoven's *Diabelli Variations* publicly, but such a work demands time and repeated performances. One of the late masterworks, the *Diabelli*'s fifty minutes of parody, profundity, and thematic transformations are ideally suited to Hamelin's temperament. However, the differing demands of concert presenters make the possibility of including this work on a long tour remote.

As to favored concerto repertoire, Hamelin is quite conventional. "If I had three concertos to name as particularly close to my affections, I would be most willing and able to play the Mozart Concerto in E-flat Major, K. 271, the Brahms Second, and Tchaikovsky First." This reference to three safely dead composers may be surprising coming from such an inquisitive pianist who has the more contemporary repertoire entirely at his disposal, let alone concertos by Alkan, Busoni, and Medtner. Is it contradictory in a pianist who can no longer listen to Beethoven's "Appassionata" Sonata because it has been so overplayed?

The originality and genuineness of Tchaikovsky's creation strike me substantially more than the "Appassionata." I feel closer to it. The entire introduction to the first movement, which comes from nowhere and does not get used again, is wonderful, and then the work progresses elsewhere. That is novel and extremely attractive.

Hamelin continually emphasizes that if he cannot present overplayed repertoire in a freshly authentic way, he has little interest in playing it. A typical program is one performed in 1997 at the Queen Elizabeth Hall in London: Busoni's transcription of Bach's Prelude and Fugue in D Major, Reger's Variations and Fugue on a Theme of J. S. Bach, and Ives's "Concord" Sonata.

It still remains difficult repertoire and I imagine this was not a concert for everyone. Occasionally, I do not enjoy program building because it can be difficult to satisfy the needs of the presenter, especially when we disagree on what is a good program. There should be none of these restrictions. Overall, however, I do not conform to the same safe set of secure repertoire (to paraphrase Glenn Gould) that people seem to want to hear. I do have a taste for density and complexity, and gravitate toward this aspect of composition whether in my own works or others. Yet I will be just as happy playing Janáček's "Overgrown Path" pieces, which are emotionally complex but texturally simple. I never take up music just for the sake of the challenge.

Hamelin's taste for emotionally and pianistically complicated music informs his preferences in the modern repertoire. He believes that Frederic Rzewski's *The People United Will Never Be Defeated!* and Ronn Yedidia's Third Sonata are miracles of contemporary writing. "At one point, as a mid-to-late teenager, most of what I focused on was Boulez, Cage, Stockhausen, Xenakis, and that sort of music, which over time has touched me less. I have since become distanced from that and am very selective now. One naturally gravitates toward music that provides the strongest personal connection." Hamelin's quest for emotional and artistic fulfillment has led him to The Eight and to other areas of the repertoire.

Hamelin's selectivity has cost him engagements in the past. He describes an occasion when he was offered the opportunity to play Bartók's First Piano Concerto with a major European radio orchestra, but he declined simply because the work holds no real emotional attraction for him. Many pianists seize these chances anyway. Barenboim has described just such an opportunity with Boulez and the Berlin Philharmonic for the same concerto; he immediately agreed to play it without ever having heard the music.[14]

Hamelin needs to feel innately receptive to the music he chooses to play. The fact that Alkan was French has no bearing on the French-Canadian Hamelin's choice of this music. He feels close to the Russians: Scriabin, Rachmaninov, and

Medtner, among others, are integral to his repertoire, but he does no continental warehousing in his selection of music.

> It has to do strictly with the quality of the writing and emotional expression, not with any national characteristics. For instance, I find the same engaging qualities in most good German music. Fundamentally, geographical boundaries should not exist. They are too prevalent, especially when one is concerned with concert and CD programming. That kind of thinking has no bearing and when I am a more active composer, I will especially take that to heart.

Recordings

Hamelin's large and increasing discography knows no boundaries. His discs have often brooked territory previously uncharted and have earned phenomenal critical response across the board. He is also an avid record collector.

> There is so much to be gleaned from recordings. In Medtner's case, however, his own are not always satisfactory. One has to remember that he made many recordings when he was older and ailing from heart problems. He had to rest for several days between movements of his concertos. I do not find the recordings consistently involving on an emotional level. His performance of the "Campanella" [*Tale* in B Minor, Op. 20, No. 2] gives little impression of gigantism. The feeling of accumulation that can be imparted to this piece can be tremendous. Medtner does not make enough of the climaxes. In general, many recordings of his works do not come off because of the performances themselves, rather than weakness in the music. It is my firm belief that if one gives Medtner everything, he will come alive on first hearing. I have had enough positive reaction to my own performances to be able to assert this.

Upon listening to Feinberg's recordings of Bach for the first time, Hamelin knew that he was hearing a born composer. Several of Feinberg's recordings were made in the last years of his life, but they betray no concessions to age. Hamelin concurs with many of those who have discovered these discs and also points out a problem that inhibits wider awareness of this composer:

> I love Feinberg's recordings of Bach. They are extremely fresh and vital— individualistic, but without harm to the music. I am hopeful that Feinberg is someone who becomes better known as a composer, but his music and that of many others has suffered because of its lack of availability. Alkan, Godowsky, Medtner, Sorabji, and to some extent Busoni have all been affected. When or if the music is finally found, it can be prohibitively expensive.

Horowitz has called recordings mere postcards; live concerts are much more immediate. Hamelin, recalling a Berlin broadcast of Boulez's Second Sonata performed by Maurizio Pollini, echoes an opinion held by many others: "He threw all caution to the wind and it was amazing. I was quite disappointed with the commercial recording. It is somewhat slower, cautious, cold, and calculated. The piece came alive in concert."

Hamelin's own recordings give as good an indication of his playing as possible, yet there is no substitute for the immediacy of performer, audience, and concert hall. His live performances and recordings provoke different reactions:

> Although I approach them with the same musically forthright attitude, the difference lies in the adrenaline, how my body processes emotions. I do not feel differently in a recording studio and certainly there is the same degree of commitment. People tell me that my live performances of Alkan's concerto are better than the recording, yet I remember playing it with as much dedication and enthusiasm as at the concert the previous night. It is likely that the live concert provides more of a nervous excitement, but I was recording among friends and it was a love offering just as much as at any public concert. Live recording, though, is generally not necessary for me. I find my live performances of Alkan's Sonatine, for example, difficult to control and the music frequently comes out too fast, but the recording is exemplary of what I want to accomplish with this piece. I am serious about accuracy, and sometimes the live concerts are not always perfectly accurate. My primary impetus is to present repertoire that I feel deserves to be heard. If the repertoire is known, I want to play it in a way that is particularly revelatory. I am much more interested in breaking a kind of logjam as far as many of these pieces are concerned.

Hamelin's Scriabin recordings are presented with strict observance of the composer's careful notations:

> Perhaps the second movement of Scriabin's Third Sonata is not as tempestuous on the CD as I would have liked, but otherwise I am very happy with the Scriabin recordings. Although the text has been scrupulously observed, I feel that the fantasy element is especially well reproduced. Apart from the fact that I appreciate and have always loved the music, I wanted to make these sonatas *clear*, as I have heard so many unsatisfactory performances in that regard. Presently, I feel that I have done enough for Scriabin . . . perhaps *to* Scriabin!

Hamelin learns from his recordings and loves the process of making them, although it can be grueling. When he recorded Medtner's *Sonata minacciosa*, the fugue became a rank ordeal.

> I was more exhausted at the end of that day than I care to remember, but at the same time felt very good about what I achieved. The feeling that I am going to contribute a legacy which will help people better appreciate unknown repertoire is always in the back of my mind. It is a wonderful pursuit.

Composers, Conductors, and Concertos

As for live music making, sharing insights on a mutual basis is what Hamelin ideally looks for in conductors and other musicians. He feels that playing concertos should be like chamber music: they are collaborations between orchestra, soloist, and conductor.

> I react well to communication on a personal level. It should not be a dictatorship, but an exchange of ideas with mutual respect. This does not always happen. I will often defer to the conductor's wishes because he or she ostensibly knows the score better than I do, as well as the possibilities of the orchestra they are dealing with. If I am told that a particular tempo is too fast, of course I will concur. A certain woodwind figure, for example, may not come out with the greatest clarity. This is the reason why I would never conduct Mozart's concertos from the keyboard. It can be a vain activity to attempt, and, more importantly, I do not pretend to be a conductor. I possess neither the experience nor the rehearsal techniques to be able to shape a performance in the way I would want. Doing it myself is presumptuous, yet I know the orchestral parts as much as possible. Though not always aware of every single line, I am well attuned to the harmonic and rhythmic flow. I rarely look at the conductor when performing concertos because I rely primarily on my ear and not on anything visual, which introduces a third element. Working with conductors and composers is not altogether dissimilar. It would have been so interesting to work with Olivier Messiaen, although he left such precise indications in his music that I feel close to what he intended. His *Turangalîla* Symphony, for example, is now terrific to play, but not at first and only when the learning process brought a full understanding of Messiaen's vast, unusual harmonic language.

Sorabji, on the other hand, did not leave detailed directions to the performer; as a result, any kind of meaningful collaboration with him would have been fortuitous. Hamelin's experience with modern composers has given him much satisfaction. He has had stimulating contact with them. "It is important for younger instrumentalists to work side by side with composers," Hamelin insists. "How many times have we wished we could ask something of Mozart or Beethoven? With living composers the opportunity is there, yet musicians take little advantage of it."

Hamelin as Composer

Whatever the future may hold, Hamelin himself cannot at the beginning of the twenty-first century be called one of the great composers. He is the last person to argue the point, for he has thus far produced no considerable body of work, nor has he composed a single piece worthy to be placed alongside the classical, roman-

Hamelin rehearsing Leon Kirchner's Second Piano Concerto with the
Philadelphia Orchestra and Erich Leinsdorf as page turner.
Academy of Music, Philadelphia, 10 March 1988. Photograph by Robert Dias.

tic, or modern masterpieces. Even had he produced such a work at this point, a single gem does not necessarily a composer make. Chopin's "Funeral March" Sonata would be infrequently performed if that were all he wrote; it might have suffered the same fate as the rewarding sonata by Paul Dukas (widely known as a musical one-trick pony for his marvelous orchestral scherzo *The Sorcerer's Apprentice*).

Fiercely protective of the composer's craft, Hamelin is possessed of the unstinting attitude of a Medtner, without yet achieving the Russian composer's fully developed compositional sense. Hamelin views Medtner's achievements as the exemplar in his own works. "He went out of his way to make his music pianistic. The result was the truest possible kind of compositional craft. One feels no compromise at all with Medtner because his musical voice is so closely allied to its physical expression." The distillation of musical ideas into their purest form remains a difficult pursuit. One famous example of a composer's search for this virtue is Rachmaninov's dissatisfaction with his Sonata in B-flat Minor, later revised and shortened. Upon playing Chopin's sonata in the same key, he said of his own, "I look at my early works and see how much there is that is superfluous. . . . Chopin's Sonata lasts nineteen minutes and all has been said."[15]

What Hamelin thus far brings to bear on composition are the analytical tools of a great composer, strengthened by inspired pianistic skills. His works to date reveal a contrapuntal awareness descended from—if dissimilar to—that of Bach and Chopin, often combined with a devilish sense of fun and dark humor. Hamelin's music is remarkably similar to his conversation: colorful, typically spontaneous but well considered, and liberally doused with emphasis and humor. In person, these qualities are conveyed by the animated and unusually expressive way he uses his facial features; musically, such signal traits are easily recognized in his compositions and have produced a number of remarkable works. His Prelude and Fugue of 1985–86 is infused with unbridled directions to the pianist such as *velocissimo, grottesco, en avalanche,* and *criard* (screaming). "The composer must con the performer into providing extremes," Hamelin contends, "because he or she will not provide them otherwise. Composers are often too conservative in notating their music." There is slight risk that Hamelin could be called conservative. His *Homage to Kaikhosru Shapurji Sorabji: Preambulum to an Imaginary Piano Symphony,* written the year after Sorabji's death, would make any pianist blanch at its dense, if elegant, visual layout. The work is a delicious meal for pianists, if barely digestible by any but the hungriest.

Hamelin was initially quite reluctant to share his completed works with anyone, and even more so to actually play them. He has a trunk full of music, since disowned and dismissed, largely written under the influence of atonality ("but what a great trip it was!"). He says pragmatically, "As with a novelist or poet, one learns how to write music by writing. A learning period must be lived through, putting thoughts to paper at least mechanically if not emotionally. Advanced composition is an acquired skill."

Hamelin does not simply start with a blank piece of manuscript paper in front of him; a specific idea must already be in mind. He generally does not compose at the piano and finds that inspiration develops more freely away from the instrument. He thus does not have the physicality of a piano at his disposal to verify that what he writes is possible. The Prelude and Fugue (Étude 12) is a case in point:

I wrote the prelude largely at one sitting. I was at a New Year's Eve party and found myself on the second floor writing intently, almost oblivious to anything else. The fugue, however, consumed much time—nine months, normal gestation period!

Hamelin's attitude toward his études is surprising. "Am I satisfied with them? Musically yes, pianistically no." Despite his outwardly relaxed appearance, he speaks of an inherent physical tension when playing the Prelude and Fugue. It is a maze of digital duress, but once the piece was completed he elected not to change anything because it felt *musically* right.

Hamelin acknowledges the fugue's similarities with the last movement of Samuel Barber's magnificent sonata, premiered by Horowitz in 1949 to universal acclaim. Hamelin's Prelude and Fugue is written in A-flat minor, a first cousin to Barber's in E-flat minor. Both are written in a tough, virtuosic style of cumulative energy and have similar closing ideas. Hamelin concedes:

> It is true that I wanted my own type of Barber fugue, but I did not know then and was quite appalled to discover later that the fugue has some alarming similarities with the Taneyev prelude and fugue, Op. 29. They share a 12/16 time signature and the key of G-sharp minor, which is enharmonic with the A-flat minor I used. These connections give both works a similar aura.

Writing of his four-part fugue, Hamelin explains in a preface to the published edition:

> It seems to me that the fugue in particular has quite a lot in common with the tarantella-like fourth movement of Busoni's piano concerto, which I was learning at the time. The work was never meant to become such a monstrous agglomeration of cruel virtuosic devices; I simply wanted to explore some of the developmental and expansional possibilities of the rather silly and banal fugue subject.[16]

The fugue was sown by Barber and Busoni; other influences point to a still-developing style. Hamelin refers to his Sixth Étude, a delightful homage to Scarlatti, as a pastiche, in an indirect nod to those by Sorabji. Its cartooned sections can be hilarious if manipulated properly, and it even includes a performance direction referring to Spike Jones.

Hamelin has, however, become used to the idea that being recognized as a composer is secondary. Although he often feels that he has more to offer as a pianist, he views composing as a vital necessity. Despite his restless compositional imagination, the impulse to act upon it is inversely proportionate to how busy he is as a pianist. Blocks of uninterrupted time are scarce. He gives some indication that he will follow the same path as Busoni, who at age twenty-six wrote, "I have great successes as a pianist; the composer I conceal for the present."[17] Indeed, Hamelin might not have achieved pianistic prominence had he spent much more time composing. The requirements of adding to and maintaining a world-class repertoire, as well as the constant toll of international travel, can preclude the focused time requisite for a serious composer. Rachmaninov told Alfred Swan, "With all my travels . . . I really have no time to compose, and when I now sit down to write, it does not come to me very easily. Not as in former years."[18] Today's society places great financial strains on the creative artist,[19] and as six of The Eight—the exceptions are the reclusive Alkan and Sorabji—came to realize, the demands of an international concert career can play havoc with a composer's life. Having passed his fortieth birthday, Hamelin has begun to carve out more time for composition.

The music he has produced centers around the piano, which is a characteristic thread woven throughout the careers of The Eight. Rachmaninov and Busoni were the most diverse in the types and genres of music they explored; however, the primary output of these composers is focused on solo piano works, and secondarily on the piano in other forms—such as voice and piano, chamber music, and concertos. Hamelin provides a ready explanation:

> I write largely for my own instrument. I do not hear the blending of orchestral timbres very well in my mind. It is wise to write for what you know and stick with it. Medtner wrote for the piano almost exclusively and he disliked the task of orchestration. The main reason he wrote for the voice and violin so much was that his wife sang and played the violin, and was therefore able to work with him.

Hamelin is married to the American soprano Jody Karin Applebaum. Their partnership revolves closely around music. Cabaret songs have been a particular preoccupation: Applebaum has done extensive research into German and French cabaret as it was originally conceived. Such music is classically oriented and covers an enormous range of emotions. The songs of William Bolcom, Arnold Schoenberg, Benjamin Britten, Friedrich Holländer, and others have been performed by Applebaum and Hamelin on recordings and in concert, often for the first time since the 1920s. With the exception of an unaccompanied Ave Maria, Hamelin has not composed for the voice, as he has always found it difficult to discover the proper text and pacing of expression.

Sources of Inspiration

Where does Hamelin the composer and pianist find inspiration? His knowledge of art and painting is selective ("It's quite possible to play Debussy beautifully if one is not moved by Monet"), and it is fairly safe to posit that he does not pine for the landscapes of an inaccessible motherland. Hamelin explains what comes naturally:

> Sources for elements of interpretation are not always the obvious ones. Sometimes a turn of phrase will be inspired by the way I saw someone smile, an inflection may be directly influenced by the way someone spoke. I draw from the oral, tactile, or any of the hidden senses.

Classical music presents a long history of composers' using visual stimuli to provide musical inspiration. Liszt painted beautiful tone poems in the great series *Années de pèlerinage,* in which his sensory reactions to Italy and Switzerland powerfully dovetailed with his compositional style. Musorgsky practically defined the brooding nature of Russian pianism with his piano suite *Pictures at an Exhibition.* Written in 1874, it portrays a walking gallery tour of drawings and watercolors by the Russian

Hamelin and his wife, Jody Karin Applebaum, at their joint birthday party, September 1997.

painter and architect Viktor Hartmann. Rachmaninov created his orchestral tone poem *Isle of the Dead* after seeing Arnold Böcklin's striking work of the same name.

Alkan took the aspect of visual stimulation directly to his manuscript paper. He went to great lengths to make his music curiously interesting to look at by employing unconventional notation and layout. Hamelin's own music is similarly well designed. A jaunt through his cadenza to Liszt's Second Hungarian Rhapsody reveals a style of writing heavily dusted with wit and virtuosity. "Music should be visually appealing to look at." Hamelin insists:

> It has always been my belief that if a score is printed with the same number of measures per page or system, it ends up looking like a kind of boring graph. Measures should be shortened or lengthened based on inherent requirements. Music must engage the eyes as well as the hands.

He warms to the subject. "As far as compositional inspiration, I am not visually reliant. Sound is so beguiling and such a wonderful stimulus in itself that I do not normally need the pictorial connection, but rather a distinct emotional image." Given Hamelin's thoughts on the visual aspects of music, it is natural that he relates individual keys more with emotions, as did Medtner, Rachmaninov, and others. Scriabin, by contrast, literally saw the different keys as vibrant colors. (Some research has been done on synesthesia, one aspect of which involves the association of certain pitches or keys with specific colors. It is a real, if rare, psychological phenomenon; Scriabin was apparently a synesthete.)

Humor in Music

Humor is one of Hamelin's primary colors and an abundant inspirational source. In his own compositions, he expresses humor overtly and is not above using deliberate wrong notes to obtain *l'effet juste*. In his transcription of Rossini's *La danza*, Hamelin's sly parody of compositional technique readily brings laughter from the audience. He freely acknowledges:

> Many passages in this piece are deliberately cartoonish and off center. Everything is inverted and upside down. There is a crude shift to the major key and with the melody a third too high. I will grant that it is nothing radically profound, but . . .

Hamelin is capable of producing a connoisseur's soliloquy on the relative merits of Tom and Jerry, Bugs Bunny, Rocky and Bullwinkle, and other animated stars, and he is well aware of these cartoons' adult puns and often sophisticated comedy. (So, apparently, are other artists, including the tenor Luciano Pavarotti, who watches cartoons with relish. "Really, they are masterpieces," he declares.[20])

Hamelin's own musical sense of humor is something that comes out naturally; he

Hamelin with Abigail, winter 1992–93.

tries neither to control nor to hide it. His study based on Chopin's étude for the black keys (Op. 10, No. 5) is devilishly subtitled "Pour les idées noires" (For Dark Thoughts). In this way, Hamelin finds himself somewhat akin to Alkan, who "certainly hid nothing; his music ran the gamut of emotions. The humor in Alkan's music is subversive, often tinged with black and never quite overt. Whenever humor is present it is not without uneasiness."

When Sorabji decided to be humorous he succeeded quite well, primarily in pieces such as the *Carmen* and *Sadko* pastiches. Listening to Sorabji's pianistic take on *Sadko*, Hamelin slouches, coolly takes a drag from an imaginary *cigarette spéciale*, and blows smoke at Rimsky-Korsakov's fabled characters. Hamelin inherited his own taste for satire from his father:

> He had a great fondness for literary and musical pastiches, and loved anyone making fun of others. I likely have more respect than he did for those who have been satirized, but there is an element in me of what he had.

Father and Youth, Curiosity and Fantasy

Hamelin's musical life was nurtured during his boyhood in Montreal. His father, a skilled amateur pianist, strongly influenced his son's direction.

> My father was very desirous for one of his children to accomplish what he was not able to do himself. He did not have the necessary musical equipment for a career and decided very early on to go into something more lucrative. He did have considerable natural gifts, including perfect pitch, which many professional musicians do not. Unlike me, he definitely had a taste in virtuosity for its own sake. This meant that he was short on patience for composers such as Schubert, who bored him, particularly in the longer sonatas. Horowitz was my father's idol in the 1950s and 1960s.

The first four years of Hamelin's piano study were with a private instructor. He does, however, consider his father to be one of his teachers. In fact, the senior Hamelin expressed the wish that his son attribute this role to him.

> I was close to my father, but not necessarily emotionally, as he was rather undemonstrative. He gave me a great deal of guidance yet was sometimes at odds with what teachers were telling me. If he did not like what I was being told or taught, he would say so. He did not think ahead far enough that it might confuse me and without hesitation offered rational constructive criticism. He had an authoritative manner, even a bit scary at times. My father barely had to raise his voice before becoming a menacing presence. When he became angry, it was not pleasant.

Nonetheless, Hamelin recalls his father, who died in 1995, with love, respect, and a certain wistfulness for a youth that is permanently bound with his present life and work.

The recollection of his early years moves Hamelin to reveal that he still feels like a child in some respects, especially relating to those elements of fantasy and curiosity in his psyche that were fostered at an early age. He leans toward cultural stimulations that are comfortably down-to-earth; emotionally uncluttered, informal, and easygoing, here is a devotee not only of cartoons, but also of underground comics and cult horror movies. He is more likely to pick up a magazine than classic literature. Among Hamelin's first musical impressions were the Tchaikovsky ballet suites, recorded by Eugene Ormandy with the Philadelphia Orchestra. "I also had various children's records such as Prokofiev's *Peter and the Wolf* and Saint-Saëns's *Carnival of the Animals.* I'm so glad I was introduced to *Peter* at the time, because what a fantastic offering to children that is!" As a boy, Hamelin wrote out the entire text of *Carnival,* picking it up from the recording he used to listen to. (If asked, he will recount it with innocent humor and a mock-deepened voice.) Writing an Album for the Young would seem natural for him, almost inevitable, and Hamelin has at various times desired to follow in the footsteps of Schumann, Tchaikovsky, and Busoni (*An die Jugend*):

> I would like my own Album for the Young to be a true musical challenge and not necessarily for young people alone. It could be for beginning adults who would like to have some musical meat to chew on and with it a strong sense of fantasy. Experience has shown that I am perfectly capable of scaling down my notation—not writing down to people, but making it more accessible. As opposed to Sorabji, I would like my music to be performed.

Early musical impressions play a crucial role in an artist's subsequent development. Hamelin equates his response to Godowsky's difficult, multilayered musical language with the ease of learning another spoken language early in life:

> Through my father, to whom I dedicated my recording of the Chopin-Godowsky studies, Godowsky's music has been with me from the earliest age. We had many of his scores at home, and I well remember a recording of Earl Wild playing the *Künstlerleben* paraphrase when I was still very young. The music has been part of my consciousness as much as anything by Chopin. Because of this, I find playing Godowsky to be entirely natural.

From childhood, Hamelin has always displayed a hunger for new musical discoveries. At thirteen he won his first prize of $500 at a competition and began collecting scores. "My first great interest was Charles Ives, who came to my attention through a special issue of *Clavier* magazine commemorating his one-hundredth anniversary. It contained intriguing articles and one of the works mentioned repeatedly was the 'Concord' Sonata." Hamelin's early fascination with Ives has produced a classic CD of this masterwork, regularly cited as its finest recording. Next to inspire Hamelin was Scriabin:

> His Fourth Sonata was the first one to capture my attention at the age of sixteen. While listening to Roberto Szidon's recording of Sonatas 4 through 10, I became entranced with what I was hearing. It was an area wide open to explore.

Hamelin believes that Scriabin's close contemporary, Maurice Ravel, has written one of the twentieth century's greatest masterpieces—*Gaspard de la nuit*. Beyond its bravura piano writing and richness of inspiration is the fantasy tale that the French poet and author Aloysius Bertrand (1807–1841) created with such relish. *Gaspard* is a collection of prose poems that describe Gaspard the dreamer and wanderer, with his otherworldly visions. The first movement of this three-part suite, titled "Ondine," describes Gaspard's meeting with an irresistible mermaid: Ravel's musical siren.

Hamelin feels that "Ondine" is the most emotionally and technically difficult of the set. "It has always been, for me, the greatest musical love poem ever written,

Hamelin, 1999. Photograph by Malcolm Crowthers. Courtesy of Hyperion Records Ltd.

even though it presents a very twisted kind of love." Schumann's Fantasy, a pure expression of love for his wife-to-be, Clara, and a work of palpable beauty, is predictably less immediate to someone so fascinated with extremes. "Though a wonderful masterpiece," Hamelin acknowledges, "it does not touch me quite as much. 'Ondine' is the more fantastic, passionate work."

Extremes in Music and in Life

Hamelin possesses a measure of reticence that recalls Godowsky, who wrote before his Berlin debut, "I was greatly astonished to find that I was well known among Berlin pianists and teachers."[21] For his part, upon meeting the celebrated pianist Martha Argerich backstage after her 1998 concert with the Philadelphia Orchestra, Hamelin was surprised that she even knew of him, while she expressed her genuine admiration in their mutual language of French. Further, when Hamelin read *Classic CD* magazine's list of the world's one hundred top instrumentalists, he was "astonished" to find his name among them and gratified to discover the standing he holds in the musical world. In life and in music, though, Hamelin explains,

> I do respond to extremes. The music of Conlon Nancarrow, for one, changed my life. I was particularly attracted to his concentrated exploration of rhythmic complexity, textural density, and tempo that meld into something rather stupendous. I had never heard anything remotely like it before. It greatly expanded my perception and way of listening to music.

Nancarrow (1912–1997) broke new ground in his use of abstrusely irregular and complex metrical relationships. His incredible series *Player Piano Studies,* composed over a period of forty years, continues to attract wide interest. Similarly original is György Ligeti (b. 1923), one of Hungary's leading compositional voices, who also counts Nancarrow among his influences. Hamelin finds Ligeti's music fascinating:

> I attempted to learn his first étude, but I could not divide my brain. To play it properly almost requires two brains, because the hands do such completely different things. It would not be enough simply to read the notes and play the two hands as cross accents. I would have to think of both hands as two separate strands of music that concur or conflict with each other, not as one texture. This is a very important distinction. Ligeti goes the distance in pushing tempo and rhythmic frontiers. The syncopation is increasingly intense, and physically the piece becomes extremely demanding. I may just take this music up again one day.

Hamelin has always had a natural desire to see how far people are willing to go, not only in music, but also in language, sexual provocativeness, or violence. He is open to movie directors who exceed convention in terms of graphic expressions of violence, saying simply, "I would assume it to be a harmless outlet for a possibly more violent side of my personality." Motion pictures have long been a vehicle for expressing extremes and exploring the darkness within. Hamelin finds natural stimulation in movies of this kind, especially the brilliant work of such directors as David Lynch and Brian de Palma. Lynch's movie *Wild at Heart* displays ruthless violence and intense sexuality. Conversely, it is also an altogether outrageous romp, full of very funny one-liners. Hamelin loves de Palma's fierce *Phantom of the Paradise,* an entertaining mix of *Faust* and *Phantom of the Opera.*

On the surface, these cultural influences may seem to be absurdly far from the concert stage and classical music, but composers have always explored the violence that has been with us from earliest times. Before the advent of movies, audiences thrilled to no less savage behavior in opera. Hamelin finds a distinct place for savagery in music, and one of the works in his repertoire is Leo Ornstein's brutal *Danse sauvage* (Wild Men's Dance), twenty-one pages of carefully written chord clusters that strike a stark mood of aggression. Visually and aurally foreboding, the music is dense, with an air of primitive ritual about it. Hamelin believes there is a place for this: "Violence and anger in music can be very beautiful."

Outside of movies and music, Hamelin feels a particular kinship with the cult author Richard Matheson, whose subtly imaginative science fiction and horror stories have captivated the pianist for years:

> The extent to which he is willing to go to create as realistic a narrative as he can with an improbable situation is fine art. I enjoy his explorations of the psyche and see this as evidence of my basic curiosity, which often leads me to unknown repertoire and extremes in the music I choose.

Music as Craft and Career

All of the music Hamelin plays, whether obscure or well known, is presented with scrupulous adherence to the composer's notation. He is impatient to the point of severity with those in his profession, past or present, who do not live up to his own ethics. This attitude would be gratuitous pretension were it not for his uncompromising practice. Vladimir Sofronitsky (1901–1961), the famous Scriabin interpreter and son-in-law of the composer, made a series of controversial recordings of Scriabin's works. "True, the quality of his emotional projection and conjured images can be immediate," Hamelin concedes, "but this is coupled with frequent disregard for textual accuracy. The rhythms are wrong, lines are missing, and there are crude misreadings of notes." When reminded that Sofronitsky had physical and alcohol problems, Hamelin insists, "I am not ready to make concessions. Are we supposed to make allowances for this? Music is music." He recalls a recital at which he heard a famous elderly pianist. "She was playing the Mozart Sonata K. 330. It was dry, uneven, and practically unpedaled. The given impression was of a bad seventeen-year-old conservatory student, and people were applauding this like genius." When it is suggested that people were applauding the legend and career, he is firmly unwilling to settle.

Furthermore, Hamelin shares the active disgust each of The Eight felt for unprofessional attitudes among musicians. Although they accepted different religious beliefs and diversity in people, they were steadfastly intolerant of any performer or composer who was musically lacking or less than completely honest. Hamelin observes:

> Sadly, it is not necessarily the most talented who rise to the top. Those who promote themselves the best often do. With so many pianists, the competition aspect becomes frustrating. I do not like to see the craft mutilated; there are many people who get away with very little professional attitude. They catch the public's attention or eye because they are physically attractive or have an interesting publicity angle or sponsor. Perhaps pianists think the cachet of a certain school gives them a leg up on the competition. The great mistake young people are making nowadays is to go for the institution rather than the teacher. They are blinded by the idea of Curtis or Juilliard. Harvey Wedeen was a guest teacher at the Vincent d'Indy School where I studied in Canada. He was influential enough to provide me with a full scholarship to Temple University in Philadelphia.

Music's novelty acts and misplaced institutional cachet may be fleeting, but they reflect the need impresarios have to fill seats. Hamelin is well aware of this.

> People are always looking for a hook in trying to stem the decline in audiences. This has to do with several reasons, one of which is financial. Ticket prices are far too high and the repertoire is limited. On the one hand, presenters complain about the lack of audiences, and on the other, they repeatedly present the same things. As we say in French, they do not know on which foot to dance.

Hamelin and a group of Canadian pianists have attracted wide attention in Canada for their work as "Piano Six," which has captured audiences who would not otherwise have access to live classical piano music. Hamelin elaborates:

> It was conceived in 1993 as the brainchild of Canadian pianist Janina Fialkowska and developed with the help of Jon Kimura Parker. They thought it unfortunate that small Canadian towns never got to hear music making of our caliber, so the idea was to do concert tours and have an association of pianists. Six was good because the word is the same in English as in French; it is a good number and offers diversity. We aim for both the French- and English-speaking markets. We lower our fees and arrange concerts in tours, and if we can connect them to engagements in the larger cities, so much the better. We've found tremendous enthusiasm presenting classical music to communities that often have never before experienced it. That makes those

audiences quite attentive listeners; it is completely new for them. I think of it as giving something to the people of Canada. We set aside a ten-day block each season. To bring media attention to the project we have performed six-piano galas, in Toronto, Quebec City, and Winnipeg. The public should be aware that we tour as individual pianists, not as a group.

The project is rewarding and communal in a profession widely known as scathingly competitive, and it is indicative of Hamelin's approach and ambivalence toward most aspects of competition:

> I do not have much contact with the competitiveness, except what I read in record reviews or whenever I have the bad idea to pick up the *Musical America* directory and realize that a lot of these people aren't working, despite their glitzy advertisements. I rarely ask for advice, nor do many people influence me. That may be an advantage. I am musically true to whatever my concerts bring and proceed independently as much as possible.

Whether Hamelin's compositions will occupy a place in the rarefied pantheon of those lasting, those performed, and those beloved remains to be seen. Brahms produced his First Symphony after the age of forty. The great American eclectic Charles Ives completed the landmark "Concord" Sonata in his late thirties. Alkan, Busoni, Godowsky, and Medtner all evolved as established composers well into their thirties and beyond. Feinberg's name as a composer experienced wider recognition forty years after his death. Unquestioned is Marc-André Hamelin's generous, consummate pianism. He has garnered a permanent and venerated place in our musical culture.

6 THE PITFALLS OF MUSIC CRITICISM

Sorabji distinguished himself as a critic of individual performances and as a highly entertaining guide to the larger issues facing music, framing his words around the foibles of human behavior. His books and many articles provide a full statement of his artistic and societal beliefs. Just as Alkan has come to be known as the Berlioz of the piano, so may Sorabji be viewed as the Berlioz of music criticism, a sobriquet that reflects Sorabji's colorful use of language, earthy manipulation of ideas, and larger-than-life balancing of phrase and fanaticism. Less well known is that Busoni, Feinberg, and Medtner were also serious writers and critics whose words provide invaluable commentary on the state of their art and times. One reason their writings are not more widely disseminated is that the sporadic absence of their works from the world's concert stages has kept their written thoughts in obscurity. The books of Schumann and Stravinsky, by contrast, have no trouble staying in print, thanks to their authors' "name" status. The constant presence of a composer's works before the public often determines his or her commercial viability as a writer. Sorabji's two out-of-print books, *Around Music* and *Mi Contra Fa*, not only feature most of The Eight, but are endlessly entertaining musical guides. Medtner's *The Muse and Fashion*, Busoni's *Outline of a New Aesthetic of Music*, and Feinberg's *Pianism as Art* also provide us with enlightening windows into the art of criticism.

Of all the higher disciplines concerned with study and practice, however, music is the least susceptible to objective criticism. Science, medicine, and law have the benefits of fact, logic, and precedent. Architecture and the visual arts involve easily verified physical forms. Prose and poetry are judged on the interplay of concrete words. Music—whether abstract or programmatic, classical or romantic, sonata or symphony—stands alone. The philosopher Arthur Schopenhauer concluded: "Far from being a mere aid to poetry, music is certainly an independent art; in fact, it is the most powerful of all the arts, and therefore attains its ends entirely from its own resources."[1] One can argue about the accuracy of this pianist's technique or that violinist's intonation, but the objectification of emotional states remains an improbable pursuit.

Sorabji's simple credo on the written judgment of music provides insight into his modus operandi and may instructively guide critic and reader alike: "It is my office, as I see it, to set down without any *arrière-pensée* of . . . idiot or ideological prejudice, of classical or modern prepossessions . . . certain observations, and to set them down as completely and uncompromisingly as possible, so far as my own faculties of expression and observation will enable me to do so." However, Sorabji then abandoned all restraint, insisting that "in the course of doing all this, I shall be—I do not doubt—on occasion, coarse, vulgar, crude, venomous, spiteful, and a number of other things that no one who tries to get round a critics' circle ought to be."[2] One of Sorabji's idols, Oscar Wilde, clearly felt the same way when he wrote, "Indiscretion is the greater part of valor."[3] The English writer John Steane perceptively observed that Sorabji's "critical skirmishes . . . had nothing in them of that superior boredom which is the real deadliness of criticism, and his hatred of mediocrity was the necessary obverse of his love of excellence."[4]

Sorabji was among the most educated and erudite critics of his day. His mordant wit joined a sensibility intolerant of hypocrisy or fakery; it was impossible for him not to call it as he saw it. But however poorly he suffered the slack attitudes of those within and outside his multiple professions, Sorabji's voluminous written criticism never descended to malice. As a result, his ever-increasing readership grew to trust the colorful outpourings of his prolific pen. The relationship between critic and reader is comparable to that between artist and audience, in which the former must, over time, earn the latter's trust. The critic must be creative without becoming self-serving. He or she must be able to stimulate a readership much larger than the audience of any single concert, as a musician does through recordings.

Critics would not exist without the artists they write about—a beholden, uneasy relationship. Subjectivity rules when reason fails. *Comparative* criticism is often the most useful and objective. Is pianist X's technique up to the standards demonstrated by pianist Y? Has pianist Z moved the audience? Within these bounds, the critic occupies an integral place in concert life. Sorabji surely had the gift of persuasion, despite his ambivalence about any kind of self-promotion or politico-musical quarrels. His writing was independent and held to a strong moral line. Clinton Gray-Fiske, chief critic of the influential periodical *Musical Opinion,* called Sorabji one of England's foremost music critics, a sentiment echoed by many readers. And Harold C. Schonberg, the doyen of American music critics and longtime chief music reviewer for the *New York Times,* recalls the lasting impression Sorabji's strong, no-nonsense books made on him as a young man.

The Music Critic

Hamelin addresses a complicated issue:

> I believe that Sorabji as a critic often went too far. His writing is vastly entertaining, but if you were the object of his negativity, you'd want to crawl

into a hole and die. I can only guess, but this kind of attitude may have stemmed at least partly from his being homosexual, which was much less accepted in his time. It's difficult enough today, vis-à-vis being at ease with society. He considered himself in a class apart and may not have been entirely comfortable with that. It's a very involved subject. The bottom line is that good or bad reviews should be constructive.

The fleeting nature of live music makes a pretense of permanent pronouncements. The harried reporter rushes to a concert, usually flees before any encores, pieces together a few paragraphs under deadline, and offers the product of all this hectic activity as definitive. Once a concert is over, the music critic who wishes to provide more careful analysis or thoughtful consideration cannot revisit it—he or she must take instantaneous aural snapshots. With recordings or other art forms, their critics can mull over this poem or that painting by having the object comfortably at hand.

Critics of long standing who have survived and thrived in the profession inevitably acquire a huge storehouse of knowledge and experience that performing artists rarely match. Freed from the obligations of incessant practice and travel, the established critic can focus attention on a wide range of concerts and repertoire. Sorabji saw himself as eminently qualified to write, with the necessary breadth of experience, but he railed against the lesser lights in his profession who had the temerity to overreach their station:

> The idea that the average concert-goer or the average critic has either the musical or intellectual qualifications to pass judgment on the views of such a master as Busoni would be grotesquely ridiculous were it not so immeasurably indecent and impudent.[5]

Hamelin—the recipient of a broad range of published criticism from a broad range of practicing critics—offers another viewpoint:

> Critics come from widely differing backgrounds. There is one reviewer from a major music magazine who is a very respectable writer, but people might not tend to take him seriously because by trade he's a janitor. He is one of the most eloquent and learned people who write for this magazine. A janitor is certainly a respectable profession, but many people wouldn't think so.

Experience, knowledge, a discerning ear, a skilled pen: to these essential critical qualities must be added the constitution of a soldier. The successful critic can count on all manner of reproach from disagreeing and disagreeable readers. Those critics unwilling or unable to earn their independence fall into a convenient, incestuous circle, what Sorabji dubbed

> a series of interlocking concentric rings, movement of one wheel being automatically followed by the movement of others. These rings center

generally upon some composer, or executant, and one of the wheels is as often as not a critic. The thing is a little clockwork mechanism. Thus A (a composer or player) is the spring of a mechanism of which D (a critic) is one of the wheels. Movement on his part sets D going, dealing out praise, or, if he happens to belong to an opposing mechanism, blame; and no defect or merit on the part of A will alter the working of D.

Sorabji went on to outline a labyrinthine "who's on first" routine of critical interlocking causes, effects, and events. He offered a few concrete, if idealistic, suggestions for defeating the various forces working against the critic:

First, by making the conditions of his work such that a self-respecting writer can work under them; making it obligatory on him only to mention concerts of the first interest, giving him plenty of time in which to write his notices, and allowing him as much latitude as is consistent with immunity from the action of scandalous libel laws carefully framed, like most laws, in the interests of rogues, to denounce with severity that which he thinks deserves it. Further, he shall be a man chosen for wide general culture, knowledge of music and musicianship, and as far as possible free from entangling connections with academies and colleges, those hotbeds of cliques, rings, and toadies. Last, and most important of all, at a maximum he should not be expected to do more than half a dozen concerts a week (really far too many), and should be allowed at least two or three days before his notices are required to appear.[6]

Music criticism during the nineteenth century often consisted of equal parts quackery and bribery. Sorabji wasted no time denouncing a practice relatively common during the late 1800s and early 1900s, wishing that some means could be found to immunize the critic

to the blandishments of seductive and unscrupulous females who, in default of claims to attention as artists, seek to gain it—differently. Mature years are no guarantee, as many melancholy examples show us—the extraordinary success of Miss —, whose voice and musicianship are as null as her technique, glares upon us. The sexual red-herring again?[7]

In defending those he felt were unfairly placed out of fashion, Sorabji was not above pricking the particularly airy bubbles in his writing. Describing Busoni and his piano concerto, Sorabji wrote, "It is music that is not inhuman, but unhuman. It exists in a spiritual world outside the gamut of the ordinary emotional experience of the world, of *this* world that is. . . . *In* the world he was, but *of* it, a thousand times no." In his next sentence, Sorabji admitted, "Coming down from transcendental poppy-cock, as all this of necessity is."[8] Critics, at least the good ones, realize they have their limits. "One can slip all too easily into artificial, over-subtle language, drunk with nuances," wrote the renowned German critic Joachim Kaiser, "if one tries to devise a fresh vocabulary for every situation."[9]

Medtner, through his writings and the force of sometimes unpopular opinions, could give the impression of being out of touch, reactionary, and old-fashioned. Writers such as Medtner and Sorabji had the benefit of the widest knowledge and experience, yet when they went against the trend or prevailing tide, they risked the possibility of severe backlash from critics often ignorant or ill-experienced. Above all, critics must maintain their burden of credibility. Sorabji would say that to stress such a basic truth is "flood-lighting the obvious,"[10] but higher moral qualities are not to be taken for granted. He once critiqued a particularly galling review that he felt was a caricature of responsible criticism:

> As for critics and writers on music who produce these horrors of transper-version, they would need to be almost superhumanly honest to admit the wholly detestable nature of the activity in which they are engaged and out of which some of them make quite a lot of money. It's like expecting a Bank Manager to condemn the Banking system.[11]

Disdain versus Fairness

Condemnation and disdain are the buckshot of a critic's arsenal, and as long as such sallies refrain from hidden agendas, ignorance, or malice, they have their place. Honest opinions from the well-educated and cultured critic serve to foster debate and provoke thought, but critics are often at a loss to characterize a creator who breaks new ground or fits into no established critical glove. Sorabji became impatient with those who complained of such terrific difficulties in his works that no one but the best pianists could play them. He responded by asking why music should not in fact be created only for the best instrumentalists, or even further, why should it not be created for its composer above all? He was not alone in this opinion. When the violinist Ignaz Schuppanzigh once complained to Beethoven about the difficulty of some of his music, the composer replied, "Do you really believe that I think of your wretched fiddle when the Spirit speaks to me?"[12]

Sorabji pointed out that as in Beethoven's case, the Busonis of the world wear no easy labels. In describing the latter's Toccata and his *Carmen* and *Indian* fantasies, Sorabji noted that Busoni's works can be hard to pigeonhole, "hence the puzzled dislike they have aroused amongst the more ignorant of the critics."[13] Sorabji carried this theme to his chapter on Busoni in *Around Music*:

> The popular mind hates and fears nothing so much as that which it cannot classify, whether in men, manners, or morals; it also hates thought—hence the offence which the highly intellectualized qualities of Busoni's work so often give those who resent being called upon to perform intellectual effort

in terms of music—or indeed, of anything at all. People have for so long been accustomed to have their music labeled, to accept it as a sort of sonorous powder concealed within the jam of an anecdotal program, that they have lost the faculty of listening to pure music, music which does not pretend to be or say this or that.[14]

Throughout his life, Busoni remained musically independent, refusing to be swayed by any manner of public or critical opinion—an attitude that, though often denigrated, the critic could at least respect. Sorabji, like many of his peers, had little patience for Busoni's opposite: the pianist more inclined to play for the crowd than for the music. "[The audience] would have the wallow of their lives," Sorabji opined, "especially if Miss — could be secured to give her unique act of combined gymnastics, acrobatics, calisthenics, eurhythmics, and choreographics at the keyboard."[15]

How does a critic judge Sorabji's own music upon first hearing? Performance traditions have been used as critical benchmarks by most critics and represent a valid approach. However, a critic who is neither familiar with such a tradition nor has the benefit of intensive study is more likely to come up with something less than compelling. Paul Bechert, in a review titled "Persian composer-pianist baffles," freely admitted as much:

Mr. Sorabji . . . played his two piano sonatas, and frankness compels the statement that, at least on first hearing, they are absolutely beyond the grasp of ever so modern a hearer, who still expects from a composition such ancient things as form, rhythm, and thematic or harmonic treatment of any kind. There seem to be some interesting oriental colorings in these sonatas, and a few of their passages "sound" beautifully, but the feeling one derives from them is, in short, that compared to Mr. Sorabji, Arnold Schoenberg must be a tame reactionary. Withal, the impression Mr. Sorabji creates is that of a fully sincere personality, in whose madness there must be some sort of method. Just what that method implies, future generations may perhaps be able to discover.[16]

As it turns out, subsequent generations have indeed begun to discover the visionary nature of the work by Sorabji and others of The Eight. Pianists who perform their music engender and perpetuate living traditions through which critics and audiences come to appreciate what were once the repertorial byways.

Superficiality

Critics are at times unequipped to write about music outside the mainstream, or they may be uninterested in anything more than a superficial gloss over it, a situation that has contributed to a general lack of awareness of much music by The Eight.

The English critic Ernest Newman wrote of the evasive guesswork that occurs when a new work is given its premiere. Even time and study often have little effect on cursorily formed attitudes and in any case are no guarantee of *depth* perception. At the beginning of the nineteenth century, E. T. A. Hoffmann wrote that "no art, and music least of all, suffers pedantry, and a certain latitude of mind is sometimes precisely what makes a great genius."[17]

To hear John Runciman describe it in the *Musical Quarterly* in 1915, "[Scriabin's] novel harmonies lose their novelty when one looks carefully at them. They are very ordinary harmonies with accidentals thrown in arbitrarily to make them sound extraordinary."[18] A meaningful understanding of Scriabin's meticulous logic and craftsmanship would have revealed this emphatically not to be the case. The reviewer also ought to have been aware of the reams of material contemporary writers and musicologists were then turning out about Scriabin's special harmonic vocabulary. In another example of critical folly, the writer Boris Schwarz insisted that "there is a streak of mysticism and decadence in Scriabin's music that, to us, appears more representative of the effete preciousness of pre-Revolutionary days than of the harsh realities of post-October."[19] This is akin to calling Chopin a dreamy sentimentalist, discounting the harsh realities of that composer's Poland expressed in the "Revolutionary" Étude, the "Heroic" Polonaise, and other works born of strength and defiance. Scriabin's virile and striving later works express the power of a composer constantly seeking to extract from life its very essence. "Effete preciousness" may be found in a few of the smaller works, but the epithet is far from representative.

In addition to lackluster technical analysis and the whims of fashion, another pit into which critics can fall is ignorance or incomprehension of deeper emotional content. Sorabji pointed out that those who cannot understand Busoni's expressive world think that his music lacks emotion altogether, "a fatuity thoroughly typical of those with no imagination of anything that is not represented to them in the form of a cinema film or an illuminated sign."[20] Although he praised Alkan's Études, Op. 39, Henry Bellamann wrote in the *Musical Quarterly* that "too often his expansion of the technical means at the expense of the idea results in a peculiar hollowness that verges dangerously near bombast." He then asserted that Alkan's "execution was so sure, his designs so superb, and his structure so solid that the lack of content was never before, nor ever again, so little apparent."[21] At first glance, agree or disagree, this would appear to be a fair enough critical appraisal. But Bellamann was just barely able to run through these works by himself at the piano, and he had never heard them performed by a real virtuoso; what remained under his hands and in his ears was only a vague notion of Alkan's musical worth. Such perfunctory printed judgments often dissuade pianists from taking the requisite time to learn Alkan and discourage audiences from listening even if pianists do so. The same review also indicted the Études, Op. 76: "the left-hand study is of extreme paucity of content," and the right-hand study, though more original, is "not especially useful." Again, as the music is practically unapproachable by all but the most imaginative and physically gifted virtuosos, such pronouncements may generously be called uninformed and irresponsible.

What makes these examples worse is that the *Musical Quarterly* positioned itself as a beacon of careful musical journalism and probity, in contrast to the sometimes ridiculous commentary prevalent in the nonspecialist press. Hamelin has carefully considered the balancing act many critics must grapple with on a regular basis:

> It's such a complex subject. There's the question of the reviewer not having performed these pieces. How is the critic supposed to give an accurate assessment if he is not as educated as the performer? It's very difficult. They do it because it's expected. People want to know what someone thought of the event. They may find comfort in knowing that an "expert" matches their opinions, but ostensibly the critic may have been in the same position as the audience. There may not be anything to compare with. One of the great problems with unfamiliar works is that if the performance of a little-known piece doesn't appear to come off, the performer is never going to be blamed. It is assumed that the performer will have done his job in getting the most out of the piece. As far as unknown or contemporary music is concerned, most of the time that is not the case. It's usually much easier to blame the composer, because there's just no frame of reference performance-wise.

Lax and Loose

As a composer of fundamentally complex and groundbreaking music, Godowsky experienced his share of reprobation. "Unfortunately," he complained, "every opinion announced by any innovator immediately leads to all sorts of fallacious statements, contradictions, and misunderstandings, by those who jump at conclusions without comprehending the fundamental principles."[22] This was true in Godowsky's case even though he had the inestimable advantage of his own understanding and playing as pianist, which provided authentic guidance to his aims and principles. Many critics would have us believe that the era's modernist music, such as that created by Arnold Schoenberg or Igor Stravinsky, represented what Nietzsche called necessary nihilism in a reaction against the past. Busoni was called a futurist. And yet all of these composers studied and venerated tradition, using it as a means of departure, not repudiation.

Falling several stories below elevated debate, however, are the outright lies. Sorabji described an incident in which a well-known critic devoted seven of twelve lines of his review to a singer's performance of a famous Strauss song. The only problem? The singer had announced from the stage that that particular song would be omitted, since she had left the music behind.[23] The reviewer wrote a detailed critique of what he had never heard. Wilde noted the mordant absurdity of such a situation: "To give an accurate description of what has never occurred is not merely the proper occupation of the historian, but the inalienable privilege of any man of parts and culture."[24]

Sorabji found that if critics were inclined to write in detail about nonexistent performances, they certainly had no qualms about excoriating those performers not on their "A" list:

> If you can hear a work that was never played, or hear it long after you have left the Hall, you can, if you try hard enough, find all the things you look for in the works of Rachmaninov; indeed, it would be remarkable if you did not, having set out with the fixed intention of finding or forging a fault.

Sorabji wrote that the critics probably never forgave Rachmaninov

> for their exhibition of their own ignorance on the occasion of one of his 1938 recitals in this country, when, instead of the usual form of the Bach *Weinen Klagen* variations, he played an earlier shorter and unfamiliar composition on the same motive. We were told "he stopped half-way through the work," and again, "No one but he would have dared to do such a thing." Observe the eager malice in the assumption that he *had* dared to do "such a thing," and the implication of contemptuous behavior to the audience that lurks behind the words; it sets the tone of the attitude of these creatures to Rachmaninov.[25]

Sorabji also described incidents when he and a friend sat at concerts near a well-known London critic; on several occasions the very same words his friend had used about a work or performance were reproduced the next morning in the critic's reviews. Once, Sorabji's friend "gleefully warned me beforehand what he was going to do, and deliberately said something entirely idiotic, which was duly reproduced the following morning by the critic in question!"[26] Hamelin recounts a slip that was perhaps inadvertent, though with results just as foolish:

> The event was funny and also a bit sad, considering where it happened. I was on tour in November of 1987 with the Montreal Symphony in Europe. The last stop was the Leipzig Gewandhaus for two consecutive concerts. On the first night I was asked not to give encores, because it's really the orchestra's show and they didn't want to go over the time limit with the union. The second night the audience was particularly insistent after the Rachmaninov *Rhapsody* so I sat down and played my Prelude and Fugue. Big enthusiasm. I walked off the stage and the orchestra's personnel manager, who had been in the wings out of earshot and didn't hear what I had played, asked what the encore was. I said prelude and fugue. "Bach?" he asked. Thinking of course that he had heard it and knowing that he is musically educated, I replied, "Sure, sure." The very next day the Leipzig paper wrote that Mr. Hamelin played a prelude and fugue by Bach! And of course my piece sounds *nothing*

like Bach! There I was, a thousand feet or less from Bach's Thomaskirche, and who knows what the old master himself would have thought of such absurdity!

Something like the reverse happened to Busoni. Once, in Berlin, he played Beethoven's Fourth Concerto with the composer's cadenzas, which the critic Leopold Schmidt attributed to Busoni and duly tore to shreds. The next day,

> Schmidt was called to the telephone. To his question, "Who's speaking?" a sepulchral voice replied, "This is Ludwig van Beethoven." "My dear Schmidt," it continued, "it is not very kind of you to tear my cadenzas to pieces. However, next time I'm born, I promise I'll try harder." Whereupon Busoni put down the receiver.[27]

Accurate hearing, of course, is part ability and part perception. In remarks he gave just before a New York performance in 1996 of Nikolai Roslavets's three études, Hamelin noted that the pieces quite possibly were being given their première, as he was not aware of anyone with the "perseverance-slash-craziness" to attempt them.[28] Jack Sullivan, reviewing the concert in the *American Record Guide,* wrote that Hamelin said no one had been "perverse" enough to play them in public.[29] In this instance, the reviewer may simply have heard incorrectly or chose to hear something more provocative, but "perverse" is quite different from "perseverance" and does justice neither to Roslavets nor to Hamelin.

Reviewing the same concert, in a more serious case of critical reaching, Alex Ross in the *New York Times* wrote that Hamelin had grown bored with the standard literature.[30] The pianist counters, "That's the kind of gratuitous assumption and cavalier nonsense that reviewers write because they only have twenty minutes to come up with a review. He could have picked up a phone and *asked.*"

Busoni reacted with equal disgust to a similar diatribe thrown by the composer Hans Pfitzner, who wrote a pamphlet—"The Danger of Futurism"—primarily directed against Busoni's *Outline of a New Aesthetic of Music.* Busoni's public response: "You proclaim me openly as a disowner and despiser of all great composers of the past without quoting any of my sentences as proof of such a monstrous accusation."[31] Hamelin describes a common no-win situation: "Some people will complain that the standard fare is always presented to them, and when they get a concert of unusual works, they'll find other things to complain about, that there's nothing familiar in the concert."

Sorabji vociferously decried those numerous critics who demonstrated blatant ignorance:

> My frequent strictures upon the incompetence of the usual music criticism to which we are treated in England may sometimes have appeared excessively severe, but the example which I am about to produce will more than justify me. In . . . one of the leading monthly periodicals devoted to music appear

some remarks upon Busoni as a composer, of such grotesque impudence
that they would be almost incredible in the more ignorantly conducted daily
sheets; in a periodical devoted . . . exclusively to music, one has a right to
expect that such an outrage should be an impossibility. The writer first shows
his complete ignorance of Busoni's work as a whole by remarking on the
smallness of Busoni's creative output . . . the solo piano works of which *alone*
fill *nearly* four pages of the new Teichmüller catalog of modern piano music.
There are numbers of other very big works, three stage works, five operas,
three large works for piano and orchestra, including the titanic Concerto,
to mention some only. The writer proceeds to sum up the creator of all these
things, a musical mind that is recognized by those who know, even if they
do not like his work, as of the most commanding technical accomplishment,
with a unique mastery of architectonic and of counterpoint, all of which is
undeniable by anyone who has studied Busoni's work with intelligence . . . as
an amateur.[32]

The author of the critical sally about which Sorabji wrote had had ample time for
evaluation and reflection: he was writing four years after Busoni's death.

A critic may vacillate in his opinions as proficiently as the smoothest politician.
Sorabji once described a critic who, on the occasion of Godowsky's last visit to England when he introduced some of his most mature works,

fell upon [Godowsky] with ferocity. It was piquant to see this very person
later, upon the foundation of the Godowsky Society, saying that "Godowsky's
eminence as a composer has long been recognized by the critics," when in
point of fact at that time there were, so far as I am aware, not more than three
people in this country who were publicly paying Godowsky's work its due
tribute.[33]

Sorabji did, however, note the uptick in Godowsky's critical fortunes: "One does
not nowadays hear quite so often the desolating asininities about Godowsky and his
work that used to be the small change of English musical critics' chit-chat during his
lifetime."[34]

And So the Story Goes . . .

Desolating asininities. Sorabji's purple prose, perhaps, but one cannot argue with
the sentiment it expressed. Flaccid musical gossip falls under the same category.
The cliché tells us that by the time a story has been passed down a dozen times, it is
no longer recognizable. A critic wrote nearly thirty years after Busoni's death:

There is a story that once during a concert he was particularly peeved by a
cold audience, whereupon he played Bach's Chromatic Fugue with one pedal,
from beginning to end, and then turned and grinned broadly at the audience
which was shocked into confusion by the perverse trick.[35]

Maybe a shade of something similar happened once at a Busoni concert, maybe not. But Busoni held Bach as a musical god; it is highly unlikely that he ever would have painted such musical graffiti on Bach's masterwork.

Nor would Rachmaninov ever give less to each composer than his due. Especially in England, however, critics severely denounced him, a fashionable folly after the influential *Grove's Dictionary of Music* took the lead (later retracted) in doing so. About the criticism that Rachmaninov received, Sorabji lamented that "every performance, every recording of a work by this great and powerful Master is the signal for a chorus of sneers, cheap gibes, contemptuous disparagement."[36]

Rachmaninov could not escape such invective even in the country of his birth. It happened that he was fond of Scriabin's music, although the Russian press conjured a storm around their supposed differences and tried to spin their relationship as some sort of feud. When Rachmaninov engaged Scriabin to perform his own piano concerto under Rachmaninov's direction at a Moscow Philharmonic concert, the press then argued about all of their musical conflicts, despite their rather harmonious interaction.

As for Rachmaninov's Fourth Concerto and the supposed presence in it of the tune "Three Blind Mice," Sorabji wrote of the "orgy of imbecility" on the part of critics who pointed this out repeatedly. In such cases, less is truly more. A judicious editor is often the reader's best friend. After a lengthy debate in its pages about great pianists in general and Godowsky and Busoni in particular, the editor of *Gramophone* deliciously ended an unending subject with, "This interesting and spacious topic must now be guillotined."[37]

Sorabji the critic realized that often the fewest words carry the most weight. In describing a performance of Rachmaninov's Third Concerto with the composer at the piano, Sorabji wrote of "playing which can only be described as magnificent, one of those few performances so complete, so consummate, that it is the hardest thing in the world to talk about them afterwards."[38]

The Pianist as Composer

In Mozart's or Beethoven's day, musicians were often ridiculed if they did not both compose *and* perform. The twentieth century saw an era of specialization; those who did several things very well, including the great virtuoso composer-pianists, tended to be distrusted, especially by critics. The notion that a person could never excel in more than one field has held sway since the death of Chopin. Sorabji ridiculed those who refused to acknowledge Rachmaninov's multiple talents, writing sarcastically:

> In the *best* musical circles today, to play as superbly as the great Russian master and also to compose fine music is simply NOT DONE—and that if

anyone is so utterly lost to ALL sense of the DONE THING as to be as Busoni was, a transcendent pianist and a master of composition, or like Rachmaninov is, at all costs (and truth is the first thing naturally to pay the price), it must be denied, and one or other or both aspects of the Master belittled.[39]

Sorabji further wrote of

the sort of *reportage* rubbish that it is the flattering custom to call music criticism, in the form of hostility to an artist who practices—and with distinction—more than one branch of his art. . . . Excellence along one single track is much more likely to receive admission—even if insincere and grudging—from those who in no imaginable circumstances could function along any but a single track themselves. . . . Sergei Vasilievich Rachmaninov, whose death a few days short of his seventieth birthday in 1943 deprived the art of music of one of its greatest ornaments both as creator and performer, was just such a one whose combination of gifts and qualities were almost perfectly calculated to make him *persona ingratissima* among such people.[40]

There have been exceptions. Busoni once received a letter from George Bernard Shaw suggesting that he would have done well to compose under an assumed name:

It is incredible that one man could do more than one thing well; and when I heard you play, I said, "It is impossible that he should compose: there is not room enough in a single life for more than one supreme excellence."[41]

Can a musician do more than one thing extraordinarily well? Should he or she be judged by those who cannot? Sorabji noted a commonplace among critics of a lesser grasp and intellect than those they write about, pointing to "the inevitable abuse from the circles in which Busoni, precisely because of his intellectual immensity, was hated and feared."[42] Busoni was fully aware of the uphill battle he faced to be taken seriously as a composer, simply because he happened to play the piano so well. Constitutionally, he could do no less. In a barely veiled musing directed at himself, Busoni acknowledged that the fame enjoyed by Liszt and Saint-Saëns as pianists obscured their reputations as composers.

Busoni, Godowsky, and Rachmaninov each demonstrated his distaste to be seen as any kind of "specialist" musician. Rachmaninov countered with no mean irony:

The musicians and critics were always waiting to devour me. One would say: "Rachmaninov is not a composer, but a pianist." And another: "He is primarily a conductor." But the public . . . I love it. Everywhere and at all times it has treated me wonderfully.[43]

Rachmaninov remained stoic and held himself above all the criticism directed his way. "If the critics are not satisfied there is nothing to be done," he flatly observed. "A composer must write as he feels: he cannot change his style and remain sincere."[44] Rachmaninov's close friend Godowsky—like Sorabji and a host of other artists—firmly believed that practicing musicians had much more to say of value than critics not active in the profession: "The experience of the artist and the teacher is always more reliable, more susceptible to finer appreciations of artistic values than that of the pure theorist, who views his problems through material rather than spiritual eyes."[45] Put another way, the doctor is generally better qualified to judge procedure than is the hospital administrator. Many writers and musicians recognized Sorabji's qualifications to write from a practitioner's perspective about other composers and pianists. Hugh MacDiarmid wrote of Sorabji's "unmatched authority, derived from the fact that the writer understands the creative process from inside, and has himself made great contributions to the art or arts he writes about and is on a level with the greatest of those he criticizes."[46]

Views from the Stage

The triad of artist, audience, and critic remains intertwined, although each comes from a different perspective. Ernest Newman wrote, "The composer and the performer regard the critic as a mere fault-finder who earns a dishonest and precarious livelihood by picking holes in other men's work—better men's work, as they would say in their modest fashion."[47] Godowsky complained (before his widespread recognition and success), "All the critics are prejudiced in favor of one artist or another. There is much chauvinism here. Pedantry is in full force."[48] Many of Godowsky's articles, interviews, and written commentaries were directed at explaining his reasoning and motivations. He sounded a common theme among artists:

> I have now an entirely different idea of what the attitude of the artist should be towards critics and criticism. I feel now that whatever I do now no critic can destroy! Who are they that criticize the work of a specialist in his art? Do they know or understand the intricacies, details, the purely pianistic fine points, the mental and musical, the psychical and external workings of a superior pianist? If they did they would not be critics.[49]

Busoni looked to history to guide him through the critical shoals:

> For his contemporaries, Beethoven was chiefly an amazing curiosity—a concert at which the fifth and sixth Symphonies and the G major Pianoforte Concerto were performed for the first time left the public quite unmoved. *Fidelio* was a fiasco twice, the Violin Concerto was described as being unmelodious and forced.[50]

Busoni's awareness of the past added strength to conviction. His piano concerto was almost uniformly trashed at its premiere; it would take many years to find its audience, although the composer was rather philosophical about the situation. Even though critics would have none of it at the time, Busoni took responsibility for his creation and well realized its value:

Criticism, it seems to me, is like a breaking wave: it can knock a man down, but the water is dashed on the rocks and the man picks himself up again. . . . I have created a work for every note of which I can answer, and which will endure, inasmuch as human achievements are at all durable.[51]

Busoni was always his own man, whether composing and playing his concerto, performing Alkan to hostile German audiences, or remaining aloof from outside influences. Sorabji noted that Busoni "never allowed himself to be deflected from his artistic path half a hair's width by critical clamor, indeed showed every sign that it was, as far as he was concerned, non-existent."[52]

Rachmaninov was devastated by initial reaction to his first symphony, but he was young, and it was his first major effort. When national politics enters the picture, however, the results can be oppressive. After Rachmaninov's departure from Russia, he fell victim to "the insensate venom—the dancing dervish fury—of the Bolshevik press."[53]

Hamelin maintains that "if you hold to the rule that criticism indicates something has to be improved, you're going to go absolutely crazy." As someone whose repertoire includes many very fine works to which the audience may be unaccustomed, he offers this evaluation:

It is becoming apparent with the proliferation of CD releases and the unfamiliarity reviewers face with unknown repertoire, they often don't know what they're talking about. Frequently, there just isn't time to become more familiar with the music. There are many factors that contribute to a given review that might cause a far-from-true assessment of the worth of a concert or recording.

Performers have rarely felt that critics devote enough time or care to their profession. Liszt often retold one of his favorite aphorisms, that when he did not practice one day, he noticed it; when he did not practice two days, his friends noticed it; and when he did not practice three days, his public noticed it. Godowsky would repeat this, but add at the end, "And when I don't practice four days, the critics notice it."[54] Witticisms of this sort, naturally, failed to endear him to the critics. Godowsky's son observed, "The really good ones didn't mind, but some of the second-stringers got quite angry with him and let him have it in their reviews."[55] Throughout his career, Godowsky had an uneasy relationship with those who misunderstood his artistic credo. In a larger sense, despite all his personal and pianistic gifts, he found the entire business of music offensive, a distaste often shared by the others of The Eight:

One has to live here for a while and learn to know the machinery employed to make or ruin reputations. The partiality of almost all the critics in Europe; the wire pulling in favor of certain artists; the baseness of most agents; the organization of social cliques to further the interests of certain artists at the expense of others; all these matters do anything but make the life of the serious and honest artist pleasant.[56]

Pleasant or not, the bringing together of musicians and listeners, abetted by influential critics, has always been one aspect of music. Sorabji protested:

> Masters of real individuality and independence, such as . . . Busoni . . . or Medtner, stand absolutely no chance of recognition in Paris, where it is damnation for you if you cannot be tacked on to the fashionable "école" of the moment. Indeed, it is not being unjust to say that the particular school of French criticism of which I am speaking . . . is not in the least interested in music itself . . . but in fashions in music.[57]

Among The Eight, only Feinberg appears generally to have escaped critical negativity. The fact that his elevated and remote music remained beyond wide recognition outside Russia had everything to do with his being spared the critical bullets received by his colleagues. Had Feinberg dared compose and then stage his own "Busoni Concerto"; had he, like Godowsky, had the temerity to explore and rework Chopin; had he, like Medtner and Rachmaninov, spoken out against many of the newest trends in music—the name Feinberg would have firmly entered the debate. Hamelin strikes a conciliatory note:

> I will have all the time in the world to read an unfavorable review of a concert if I feel the reviewer to be analytical and perceptive, but if it's just an opportunity to get fancy images in print and to strut his literary stuff, then it's bad form. Even great performers have off days and I don't think there's anything wrong in pointing that out, provided it's not mean-spirited. The pool of critical talent is not large, and very often a critic's lack of musical education will show. That's less of a problem in Europe, but there are not that many people who want to write criticism professionally after they find out what's involved. People may think it to be easy . . . but writing consistent, perceptive criticism at the highest level is, after all, a very difficult job.

The Direction of Music Criticism

At the onset of the twenty-first century, many performers are digging deeper into the repertoire pool to present more varied recitals to receptive audiences. Hamelin has become a favorite among critics in many countries, in part because they can look forward to hearing works of The Eight, for example, side by side with a major Schubert sonata or other concert staples. Sorabji and several other leading critics were among the first major advocates for Busoni and Godowsky, and they emboldened perhaps less adventurous writers to give meaningful attention to music outside the mainstream. Devoted critics have a vested interest in expanding coverage and attention to the full breadth of the concert repertoire. As audiences and record buyers continue to become more discerning about this Mozart concerto or that Beethoven symphony, there is less need for critics to regurgitate well-worn truisms about such pervasive music. In many newspaper reviews, critics devote more space to a new or neglected work than to the various warhorses of the repertoire. As a result, music by The Eight continues to gain awareness and momentum within our musical consciousness.

7 THE LIABILITY OF VIRTUOSITY

The Eight considered absurd the notion of virtuosity (and by extension, complexity) for its own sake. Each of them—especially Feinberg and Godowsky—sought to redress widespread misconceptions and put forth eloquent views on the scope of virtuosity which represent a sine qua non for pianists, critics, and audiences often captivated by its superficial aspects. Awareness of true virtuosity helps to put lingering myths to rest.

Technique: The word fills the public imagination with images of blinding speed in scales, double notes, and octaves. Some people go to concerts looking for the equivalent of an ice skater's final spin, so fast that the eyes disbelieve what they actually see. Word gets around, and audiences come to see a young firebrand turn eighty-eight keys into shards of flamed ivory. Such spectators fidget through the rest of the obligatory program. They come to be thrown, not transported. But those stunning gifts quickly tire, applied as they are even to miniatures of the repertoire more suited to a gentler approach. Pianists who rely on such pyrotechnics frequently attempt to sustain a torrid technique in the wake of more temperate scores.

Virtuosity: Despite the word's origins (it has the same root as "virtuous"), the legends of Liszt and Horowitz still define the concept's more sinister associations. However, high-level development of pianistic ideas involves high-level technique, and the greatest musical thoughts would evaporate without the proper means to realize them.

In no other sphere of human activity is the necessity for extraordinary physical prowess so closely aligned with the greatest intellectual and emotional capacities. The virtuoso must possess a memory capable of maintaining thousands of pages of music in the mind and fingers, under the stress and distractions of public performance; the virtuoso must be cultured and self-aware, musically able to convey the great range of meaning embodied within a chosen repertoire; the virtuoso must project both physical excitement and emotional communication; and the virtuoso must experience life to the fullest while remaining cloistered with an instrument in a relentless quest to maintain his or her craft at its highest pitch.

The Virtuoso Myth

Virtuosity has become narrowly defined as the ability to play with great speed and dexterity. All of The Eight, however, were repelled by music's high-wire exhibitionists. Sorabji observed that

> the adulation of the public for the virtuoso is essentially an interest and enthusiasm for acrobatism, not differing in kind from that of a music-hall audience's delicious frisson as they watch the daring trapeze act of "The Four Fridolinis." The half-expectation-cum-dread of an accident . . . in the case of the trapeze "artistes" is strictly analogous with the mingled excited anticipation and terror of a wrong note or other disaster . . . as the pianist rattles on his way just a bit faster and just a bit louder than anyone has ever done before in the same work.[1]

Sorabji worried about practitioners of the piano's art who denigrated its soul through empty virtuosic display; conversely, he sympathized with musicians such as Liszt, who, seen as the most perfect pianist of his time, was vulnerable to scathing criticism when virtuosity permeated his compositions. Those performers who achieve the highest command over their instrument and who also choose to compose are easy critical targets of those who view extroversion in music—either played or created—as empty surface virtuosity. However, as Feinberg asks:

> Does the composer not have to overcome the most complicated difficulties on the artistic path? Is the relentless and consistent logic of thematic development not one of the most difficult tasks, the solution of which requires some form of virtuosity?[2]

Inspired composition is a skill requiring perhaps even more painstaking effort than playing, yet the physical form of virtuosity—performance—is more often reproached. Feinberg initially found Liszt's music coarse; it was only after studying the latter's sonata that Feinberg came to realize Liszt's true value as a composer. It has been Godowsky's and Alkan's misfortune to become known for several of their virtuoso pieces, and some critics have largely ignored the complicated, substantial works that make up much of their oeuvre. Once the epithet of "virtuoso" is taken up by the critics, it becomes a stain extremely difficult to remove. Sorabji noted a truth overlooked by those determined to see otherwise:

> The current delusion of the half-baked and quarter-witted, that Liszt is a flamboyant vulgarian and exhibitionist, [is] a charge that could with equal justice be applied to many other great Masters, if you concentrated your attention solely on the handful of works in their output that exhibit these characteristics.[3]

Most critics and audiences do realize that rare physical ability with an instrument is no guarantee of artistic maturity. Sorabji was happy to recognize that a fellow critic, Ernest Newman,

> has been engaged upon one of his delightfully spirited, ironical, and devastating debunkings of the virtuoso myth: this time the supposition that a freakish anatomical and muscular constitution which goes ninety-nine hundredths of the way towards making the average virtuoso of the violin or piano, makes a sort of higher human being *d'élite* automatically, without the possession of the other intellectual and artistic qualities that would make him so . . . in which case he becomes a Toscanini, a Busoni, a Casals, and indeed, a creature set apart.[4]

The Interpreter

The performer, together with the composer and the audience, is a crucial part of the triangle needed for the full expression of music. Feinberg noted that creators in other arts—such as painters, sculptors, and architects—do not require an interpreter in order to complete their art. An architect, for instance, may have assistance in consummating a finished work, but such help is of a mechanical rather than a creative nature: the builder simply uses the architect's plans to erect a structure. The case is different in music:

> The composer needs a mediator-performer, a creative interpreter of his composition. The word "performer" does not express the essence of the artistically significant and actively creative process of musical interpretation. The more perfect, polished, and brilliant the artist's playing is, the more first and foremost his creative personality becomes. He is not an "executant" of someone else's will, but the composer's intent should become the interpreter's own, merged with the individual features of his talent and artistic aspirations. In this confluence the performer gains the strength and courage necessary for a concrete completion of ideas and images contained in the composition through sound.[5]

According to Feinberg, this is the ideal balance between interpreter and composer; in practice, that balance remains elusive. Busoni described the conflict between the creative and the recreative artist: "Where the performer has, after all, to reach a compromise between his own originality and that of his program, the composer is free of such binding agreements."[6] The narcissists among pianists may choose to impose far more of their will on a composition than the work can reasonably sustain. On the other hand, slavish adherence to the printed note *without* the necessary addition of artistic personality usually results in a bland, mechanical performance.

Feinberg took these ideas to their logical conclusion, insisting that the balance between performer and listener is often as elusive as that between performer and composer:

> The listener finds an answer in music only within reasonable limits of his or her spiritual needs. The purest source can suffuse only a thirsty person. The force of musical influence is divided between the performer and listener, and depends—to the same extent—on both participants of an artistic act. . . . Having lost the right course, the forces of musical influence can rush in an undesirable direction. The conditions in which performance proceeds, either in a close circle or performance in a concert hall, can therefore be both favorable and unproductive. Falseness appears not only through sound, but also in perception. The performer goes through special schooling and receives high musical training. But both of them—the performer and the listener— are trained by life and its social conditioning. . . . The artist himself is a bearer of the feelings and ideas contained in a composition. For the listener the artist-interpreter's personality merges with the images and ideas arising from the music. The performer, like an actor, assumes the joy and grief, love and hatred, meditation or exultation—all the vital content of music. He concretizes it and makes it real through sound.[7]

Virtuous or Virtuoso?

The supreme physicality of playing the piano—especially in Liszt's and Alkan's heyday during the nineteenth century—came to be seen as being beneath higher mental and spiritual aspirations. The standard-bearer of this line of reasoning was Clara Schumann, who saw herself as an antiheroine of acrobatics-seeking audiences, and the antithesis of Liszt. To this day each camp continues to be suspicious of the other. Newman offered an analogy reflecting this dichotomy:

> In all ages there has been an inability on the part of the Aristotelian and Platonian, the cat and the dog, the Brahmsian and the Wagnerian, the slow coach and the fast coach, to see things from the other's point of view. The virtuoso has once more been cold-shouldered by the virtuous.[8]

Clara Schumann's message—musicianship over virtuosity—continues to hover, ghostlike, over critical perception of The Eight. But these two aspects of the pianist's art are by no means mutually exclusive. It is true that one must be a card-carrying virtuoso just to be admitted to the concert stage. The proliferation and wide availability of recordings, however, have conditioned audiences to (often artificial) flawlessness: musicians are expected to be perfect. An insensitive and unrealistic expectation, perhaps, but if the equivalent of medical malpractice existed for pianists, we would doubtless be subjected to reams of litigious ticket holders incensed at having to tolerate this inaccurate note or that imprecise jump.

Feinberg questioned the type of musician who does not take the pure craft of playing the piano as seriously as the more elusive artistic goals. He ironically described the performer who "demonstrates lightmindedness in totally waving aside this sphere of performing art as a purely outward side, which does not deserve the attention of a great connoisseur of music":

> Is it really possible to occupy a high level in the hierarchy of performing arts without having exceptional achievements in the sphere of pure pianism? Can a gifted musician really achieve high performing mastery by skipping the work on technical perfection, instead relying only on the penetration into a composer's intention, and a comprehension of the inward image and content of music, or simply depending upon his or her knowledge and general artistic culture?[9]

Those pianists who possess the full measure of music's transcendent qualities must still work very hard to hone their skills. The question then becomes, "Is the work ethic not virtuous in itself?" In the realm of ice-skating competition, for example, scores are explicitly broken down for technical and artistic merit. Music, however, carries no such demarcation. Feinberg reminded us that physical prowess is a virtue that can enable higher aspirations: "The notion of virtuosity can be associated with the root word *virtus,* meaning not only valor, but also virtue. In folk fairy tales a favorite hero accomplishes moral feats by means of his physical strength and deftness."[10] The pianist Earl Wild achieved his technique's true potential through painstaking practice; however, as with each of The Eight, he has little patience for those not willing or able to see his artistic message beyond its technical gift wrap:

> Technique comes from labor. Comments from people who criticize an abundance of technical ability usually come from people with little technique, those who dramatize (or should I say *traumatize*?) every note, or from some critics who can't play a note themselves.

Too Much of a Good Thing?

How, in any artistic endeavor, so long as the underlying emotional heft is present, could one possibly be too good at one's craft? Rachmaninov stated the obvious: "One hears a great deal about the danger of too much technique in America, which seems absurd. To my mind, the first thing a pupil should seek is to acquire as much technique as he can possibly comprehend."[11] Stephen Hough agrees with Rachmaninov but believes that young pianists often go too far:

> There's no question that excess virtuosity is a danger, especially at the student stage, among those who can play very fast and therefore . . . do! While behind the wheel of a Ferrari, the temptation is to drive it at 120 miles an hour, when one can drive it very well at 70—certainly more safely and appropriately,

enjoying all the scenery when going past. On the whole, though, the better one plays an instrument, the clearer one is able to convey the composer's message.

A technically less skilled pianist may have nothing more interesting to convey than a headstrong virtuoso would, but that simply means that the performer is deficient on either the emotional or the physical side of the art. The notion that most great virtuosos bide their time in slow music—waiting for the arousal of its display sections—is outdated, outmoded, and out-and-out dismissable. Radu Lupu sees beyond the superficial aspects of virtuosity:

> I'm no *Klaviertiger,* but many of the Russians are. If only some of them knew what to do with their fingers. . . . I wish I had some of their powers! Velocity is only a very small part of a virtuoso technique, which is a much higher concept that Neuhaus and Feinberg taught. It deals with touch, dynamics, and control of sound: all the means necessary for *musical* expression. There can never be too much virtuosity. It's what's done with it that counts.

In performance, tension and emotional pitch can cause the body to react faster than desired. Rachmaninov fought against playing too fast on stage, especially when he was younger. Given his own megawatt virtuosity, Hamelin has had similar experiences. Bryce Morrison, reviewing Hamelin's Scriabin recordings, described his reflexes as "rapier." "Perhaps too rapier," the pianist responds. "That's always been one of my problems. Although I can certainly keep it in check now, the adrenaline really speeds up my performances. It's better than when I was younger because I listen to myself much more critically."

Careful listening, the spur of the moment, flights of inspiration—so many factors combine to cause a successful performance, but if the pianist lacks the requisite technical ability, those intangibles have little chance to move an audience. Why limit possibilities with insufficient technique? True virtuosity remains the undercurrent of inspiration. Busoni wrote, "The more means the artist has at his disposal the more use will be found for them."[12] And he emphatically meant *musical* use: the pianist searching for ways merely to show off abdicates his or her artistic responsibility.

Visceral Pianism

A frequent criticism leveled at the most accomplished virtuosos concerns the relative ease with which they traverse the repertoire's highest peaks. How can an audience viscerally share in Rachmaninov's monumental Third Concerto if the pianist dispatches it with no more effort than that needed to operate a car's power steering and power windows? Feinberg distilled the issue:

If you imagine a full absence of effort from the performer's side; if you equate the spent physical energy of the heavy chordal moves in Rachmaninov's Third Concerto with Mozart's light passages; if you exclude any resistance to technical difficulties—the musical fabric loses its tension, necessary for the artistic impression. Music ceases to be materially sensible: it loses its weight, volume, and density.[13]

Busoni posed an important related question:

If it is true that "the power of expression is increased when a singer has to take trouble to sing a high note," how does the matter stand in the case where the greatest difficulties are to be found in artistically subordinate places? These will then be brought into undue prominence in consequence of the effort.[14]

Hamelin has been criticized for his apparent ease in performance, although he argues:

Some people feel a sense of visceral struggle missing in my playing, that a given work may not sound difficult enough. To me, it's an element that does not enter into the equation. The important factor is the presentation of music with as few blocks as possible. Nothing should impair the original. I don't feel that people should be listening to me—they should be listening to the music itself. I am only the channel.

In most creative pursuits, pure craft is not an artist's perquisite, but a prerequisite. Any manner of sloppiness precludes viewers or listeners from taking an artist's poetic aims seriously. Feinberg, frustrated with those who refuse to acknowledge the importance of pure pianism, stated the case plainly:

Virtuosity and all the perfections of mastery are needed only for attainment of goals set by the musician and artist. However, high creative tasks are rarely fulfilled in the line of least resistance. They require a summoning—even strain—of all the spiritual, intellectual, and physical strength of playing, as though the gates to the world of high aesthetic values were well guarded and an exploit were needed to penetrate into this sphere. Thus, technical perfection and virtuosity are necessary for a performer. But virtuosity is a means and should not turn into a tasteless end in itself—bravura. Indeed, are there any great musical compositions that do not require effort and labor?[15]

Repudiation

Each of The Eight mastered elevated techniques in performance and composition, reacting strongly against any suggestion of gifts flaunted or misdirected. As Godowsky told it:

Virtuosity is a fault, not a virtue and I, who detest virtuosity as such, have been branded a virtuoso, though entirely innocent. Ostentatious mastery of technique, a mastery intended merely to dazzle, I loathe. In the really great player his mastery attracts no attention. In fact, virtuosity is a parvenu and genuine mastery is "to the manner born." I can honestly say that in my compositions my aim has never been virtuoso display, but rich and beautiful development of the musical idea. Because in my Chopin studies I have joined two studies in one and the same composition, I have been regarded as a kind of keyboard acrobat and my playing of the studies as a bit of theatrical legerdemain. This is really unfair, as what I have accomplished is, in fact, a free musical development along modern polyphonic lines.[16]

Of his Suite for the Left Hand Alone, Godowsky continued,

I wish to avoid the preconceived notion that because they are for the left hand they are therefore of an acrobatic nature—a virtuoso tour de force. The works are as far removed from that as a fugue of Bach or an étude of Chopin.[17]

For participants in disciplines outside of music that require physical craft— sports, medicine, any of the other arts—to disdain virtuosity is unheard of. Has any athlete railed against the media for calling him or her either too fast or too coordinated? Has any surgeon campaigned against the medical journals for being branded too steady of hand? Has any artist ever complained of being criticized for painting with excessive technical accomplishment? Those not able to see beyond a pianist's veneer of virtuosity are quick to attack the musical premise of an interpretation. Jack Sullivan in the *American Record Guide* asserted:

When Hamelin plays traditional romantic material where his hyper-virtuosity isn't severely challenged, he can be cool and detached. Chopin's Barcarolle in F-sharp was note-perfect but soulless. Hamelin is a genuine virtuoso for whom technical difficulty is the gateway to the soul.[18]

Many people would disagree with this assessment, although to be fair, a listener's perception of music is the paramount concern. If an educated reviewer is receptive and has no ax to grind, such comments represent valid criticism. As to the presumption of a virtuoso's psyche, however, Hamelin replies with an amalgam of impatience and disgust:

Having recourse to the idea of virtuosity for its own sake is a very easy conclusion to draw and shows a lack of thinking. I would guess that what I do is unusual enough that some people don't know how to react to it. I don't expect everyone to understand, ever, that I'm not at all interested in pure virtuosity. Whether I want it or not, I am considered a virtuoso performer. There are some people who think of me only as a finger merchant, but that is too easy a conclusion to draw and shows unfamiliarity with my work. A concert is not an Olympic presentation or event; if people realize this, they may be better able to enjoy the performance. Virtuosity as an end in itself has no place at all. I'm just sorry that many people don't seem to be able to see beyond it. Somehow virtuosity robs them of the ability to listen. If people are truly engaged in a performance, they will realize that my only aim is to communicate the incredible range of emotions inherent to the music I perform and the love that I have for it.

It can be a lonely path to convince others—even when one is fully justified—that abundant intellectual, emotional, and virtuosic qualities appear in the same person. Intellectuality and virtuosity are not mutually exclusive. This school of thought regarding technique came to the fore with Godowsky and Busoni, who wrote in the preface to a collection of exercises:

Technique is not, and never will be, the alpha and the omega of piano playing. . . . A great pianist has to be a great technician. But technique, being only one part of the art of a pianist, lies not only in the fingers and in the wrists, or in the force or endurance; the even more important technique lies in the brain.[19]

Busoni took every opportunity to expound his philosophy, as it contradicted prevailing attitudes:

During the lifelong course of his pianistic studies the editor has always endeavored to simplify the mechanism of piano playing and to reduce it to what is absolutely indispensable in movement and expenditure of strength. His mature opinion is that the acquirement of a technique is nothing else than fitting a given difficulty to one's own capacities. That this will be furthered to a lesser extent through physical practicing and to a greater extent through keeping an eye on the task mentally is a truth which perhaps has not been obvious to every pianoforte pedagogue, but surely it is obvious to every player who attains his aim through self-education and reflection.[20]

Godowsky elaborated further, offering a key explanation not necessarily in conformity with popular thought:

Technique is something entirely different from virtuosity. It embraces everything that makes for artistic piano playing—good fingering, phrasing, pedaling, dynamics, agogics, time, and rhythm—in a word, the art of musical expression distinct from the mechanics. Some critics think they are abusing me when they call me a technician but they don't know that they couldn't pay me a higher compliment. I consider it an insult to be called a virtuoso. Any fool can learn the mechanics of piano playing.[21]

Godowsky further ascribed to "mechanics" those skills that could become subconscious or automatic. According to him, that which requires conscious thought belongs in the realm of technique. This is an important distinction. Self-awareness and the capacity for detailed study are the pianist-musician's intrinsic companions.

Busoni found it similarly distasteful to be called a virtuoso. After arranging one of Arnold Schoenberg's piano works (Op. 11, No. 2) with the intent of making it more pianistic, Busoni reacted against its composer's first negative impressions:

> When you speak of a "tonal palate *[sic]* in the customary sense," you have in mind—in me—the so-called virtuoso pianist. Here *I* must defend myself, for I am very conscious of having particularly devised pure, unspecified, refined ideas for the piano, *sound without technique.*[22]

Feinberg took this concept a step further, writing of imagined sounds as part of the artist's technique. He felt that a great interpretation should be so thought through and layered with ideas that its meaning, achieved through an awareness of the emotions lying between the lines, transcends the piano's actual sound.

Transparent Virtuosity

The advanced concepts put forth by Godowsky, Busoni, and Feinberg involve a transparent technique: the performer must strive to remove all imaginable barriers between composer and listener. As Busoni once observed, "Merely to master the difficulties does not count, they must be surmounted with grace; and they must not be put on show at all."[23]

Many factors go into the making of a technique prepared not to draw attention to itself. Hamelin's philosophy could well have been voiced by any of The Eight:

> I happen to be able to do certain things. My technical ability developed very early, and I stress that because it must happen at a young age. I also cultivated an independence of the fingers and hands (some very proficient pianists still have trouble with their left hand). I was fortunate to gain a strong analytical footing early as well. Not only does the ability to analyze music help one to better understand what one does, it provides the means to get out of tight spots, as in a memory lapse. Unfortunately, one hears countless examples of a lack of such skills in competitions and in recitals. All of these factors are simply prerequisites. I'm mainly interested in sharing with an audience what I love, and guiding them through the amazing treasure cache of music. Especially with works they may be hearing for the first time, there's nothing more that I want than to say, "Listen to how beautiful this is!" That's already such a payoff. Virtuosity allows me—as an instrument or tool—to untangle thorny analytical problems and to present music clearly. The key is clarity of emotional, textural, and structural projection.

Even in the more sensuous or ephemeral scores, clarity is an important element of all great interpretations. Feinberg the teacher employed the same clear-sightedness as Feinberg the virtuoso:

Naive is the division of musical compositions into difficult and easy, depending on tempo or some special rank of technique. Beyond excessive rapidity and exaggerated force of sound, significant shortcomings of playing are often hidden. They reveal themselves when the performer switches to a more moderate tempo. In slow movements . . . as much mastery and technical skill can be shown as in the fast passages. Knowledge of the instrument is displayed through subtle pedalization, graphic phrasing, and variety of colors as much with a slow tempo as in extremely quick episodes. It would be wrong to take only the surface brilliance of playing for virtuosity. In this case, virtuosity implies overcoming difficulties in ways that draw the audience's attention and are visually impressive. Most often these difficulties are far from being the largest. On the contrary, many of the greatest problems remain unnoticed; successfully overcoming them can be appreciated only by a specialist. A piece can possess exceptional technical difficulties, but it is called masterly only if the performer's effort and deftness are noticeable enough and do not remain a secret to the general audience. Thus, on one hand, some very difficult compositions are not "masterly" and, on the other hand, those not too difficult may in fact be referred to as such. The greatest level of a performer's mastery turns all compositions into "non-masterly" ones, as it makes the encountered difficulties almost imperceptible.

Feinberg insisted that once a work's technical problems are overcome, virtuosity becomes an expressive device:

How distinctly our aesthetic consciousness perceives the increasing distances of octaves at the beginning of Liszt's E-flat Major Concerto! How expressive the movement of light, falling passages as in Chopin's Third Scherzo, or the sudden, impassioned changes in the first movement of Beethoven's Op. 111 Sonata! . . . Impression by virtuosity is not always outward: it is connected with musical images and activates the perception of music. There are concertgoers who strive to obtain seats in the left side of the hall. Such listeners are not satisfied just with the sound, but want to see the pianist's hand movements. By doing so, they do not give away—as it is sometimes thought—their "unmusicality," but they simply want to receive a more complete impression of all components that go into the performing process. Even a person otherwise indifferent to the display of physical dexterity, quickness, and accuracy can admiringly watch a virtuoso's playing. The aesthetic delight of music, then, partially rests upon the performer's technical perfection.[24]

Sorabji felt that the greatest pianists have the ability to eschew all outward considerations of technique by virtue of that very technique. He wrote that Busoni was one of the few pianists capable of virtuosity without ostentation:

To speak of technical considerations is almost an insult in connection with such a transcendent Master, but it may well be asked if any one in Busoni's audiences had ever dreamt that such astonishingly varied qualities of tone could be drawn, coaxed, or compelled from one very indifferent piano.[25]

Many works by The Eight contain complex difficulties—often barely apparent to the audience—that must be performed quietly and without ostentation. To knowledgeable musicians and others with sensitive hearing, these facets of composition and execution feed into the legendary cult status of The Eight. The pianist who must put tremendous effort into mastering the contrapuntal lines, pedaling, and musical intent of a Godowsky or a Busoni is left without the bravura double octaves or soaring themes of a Tchaikovsky or a Liszt. Sorabji wrote of Busoni's mesmeric *Indian Fantasy*:

Although of great complexity there is no uproar—the dynamic level as a whole is decidedly low, but the subdued richness and sumptuousness of effect has not its equal in modern music. One thinks of the rich dark glow of colors on some rare old silk rug from Khorasan.[26]

Sorabji's words apply equally well to many of his own works, such as *Gulistān* and *Le jardin parfumé*. These intriguing pieces, which display the utmost delicacy and intricacy, are musical balm for the initiated. Sorabji's music can project ineffable beauty and peace, the kind of affect a Chopin nocturne may convey to the general public, though at a much cheaper price to the performer. (Pianists once kept to tried-and-true works in a bid for surefire success, but in a welcome about-face, they have realized what record companies have known for years: programs with fascinating, unusual repertoire are given much more attention than yet another recital of warhorses.)

Busoni insisted that "touch also belongs to true technique as does very particularly the use of the pedals."[27] His playing of Liszt rose far above the vulgar display of those pianists whose complete focus on virtuosity allowed them nothing more. "Before everything there must be technique," Busoni explained. "The difficulties must be hidden, in order that the musical thread, of which the player holds one end and the listener the other, may remain taut."[28] In performance, all of The Eight demonstrated just such a hidden, unshowy technique. Hamelin's interpretations of the Chopin-Godowsky studies, the Medtner and Scriabin sonatas, and other complex works continue this tradition.

Technique and Truth

A pianist chooses repertoire based upon personal affinity, ability, desire, and a host of intangibles. For one seeking fidelity to the message of music, Feinberg suggested, "the high goal elevates the means leading to its attainment. The special—in a word, moral—side of virtuosity consists in the attainment of spiritual values through physical effort." He made no apologies for the requirement of virtuosity as a step-ping-stone to greater truths:

> One cannot conclude even an approximate review of different performers' principles, stylistic peculiarities, and various approaches to interpreting a musical composition without mentioning virtuosity and technical brilliance, which makes such an impression in the concert hall and sometimes forms the primary foundation upon which an artist's popularity is based.[29]

Godowsky's motives were questioned and misunderstood at every step of his career. From his early years, however, he chose musical substance over any other consideration. No matter how prodigious he was as a pianist, he refused to pander to audiences with easy successes:

> Every concert is a test of the artist's sincerity, not merely an exhibition of his prowess, or his acrobatic accomplishments on the keyboard. He must have some vital message to convey to his audience or else his entire performance will prove meaningless, soulless, worthless. . . . If we depend upon artifice or what might be called in vulgar parlance "tricks of the trade," pianism will inevitably descend to a vastly lower level.[30]

Medtner was also among the first to rail against virtuosity for its own sake. Given the complexity in much of his music, this may seem contradictory, but Medtner's compositional virtuosity can be like distant flowers: fragrant yet unseen. Although his music requires intense physical effort, it is entirely shorn of excess. Technique always took second place to his search for musical truth.

Busoni described a musical person as someone receptive to the subtleties of the technical aspects of the art, which he referred to as rhythm, harmony, intonation, voice-leading, and thematic treatment:

> In view of the great importance attached to these elements of the art, this "musical" temperament has naturally become of the highest consequence. And so an artist who plays with perfect technical finish should be deemed the most musical player. But as we mean by "technique" only the mechanical mastery of the instrument, the terms "technical" and "musical" have been turned into opposites. The matter has been carried so far as to call a composition itself "musical" or even to assert of a great composer like Berlioz that he was not sufficiently musical. "Unmusical" conveys the strongest reproach; branded thus, its object becomes an outlaw.[31]

In a display of the irony each of The Eight possessed, Busoni inserted the fol-lowing footnote after the above quote: "'My dog is *very* musical,' I have heard said in all seriousness. Should the dog take precedence of Berlioz?" Busoni recognized that his own fate came to this in the opinion of many, but he perceived it differently: "While the virtuoso in me still abides by older habits, I believe that I have, as composer, stripped myself of all superficiality and 'inevitability' in the practice of my profession."[32]

The original works and transcriptions of The Eight—first-rate musical thinkers and technicians—are filled with all the means of true masters. Their goal, however, was not to use technique as an end in itself, but to further the musical tableaux. What appears to the critic as gratuitous or lavish pianism (especially when he or she has not heard an exemplary performance by either the composer or another artist, but has merely examined the score) may actually involve musical construction designed to subordinate technique in service of the idea. Hamelin's paraphrase based on Rossini's *La danza* makes for some hilarious moments. But for those not able to see beyond its fearsome virtuosity—how can they laugh?

Provided the technical ability is in place, an artist's personal integrity and sincerity remain powerful stimulants in the search for musical meaning. Feinberg wrote that if the performer "misinterpreted the composer's idea or if he substituted the pure service to art for the vain decision to make a brilliant display of his outward technical bravura . . . his playing would sound insincere and artificial."[33] These words crystallize the debate over virtuosity. The issue is intent. Sitting at the altar of either empty display or depth of expression, *how* does the pianist deploy technique? Is a search for musical truth the prime consideration? The sincere, relentless quest for universal meaning guided the souls of The Eight. Their subordination of virtuosity—for its own sake—to music's loftier goals may emphatically be taken for granted.

8   THE EROTIC MUSE

The linkage of love, sex, and inspiration was at various times indispensable to five of The Eight. Scriabin played most often on this theme, and not just in the obvious example of *The Poem of Ecstasy*. As he explained in his letters and diaries, his later sonatas attempt parallels to orgasm and its subsequent relaxation. Sorabji devoted an entire chapter to music and sex in *Around Music*. Rachmaninov, Busoni, and Medtner, though perhaps outwardly more chaste, found their creative muse strengthened and renewed by strong, loving women.

Although several musicologists have ventured into this area, the topic of sexuality in classical music has generally remained beyond the purview of mainstream publications and wider public discussion. Opera may have been music's original medium for erotic expression, but abstract music also reflects these powerful impulses and stimulates visceral responses including joy, ecstasy, and calm.

Why do so many of us make love to music, and, increasingly, to classical music? The creation of music itself thrives upon imagination and planning, skill and technique, and artfulness without artifice. While not absolute requirements for fulfilling lovemaking, such qualities greatly enhance the experience. Music and sex draw upon intuition and instinct, evincing beauty, love, passion, playfulness, warmth, and human communication on the most basic level.

Higher sexual and musical awareness, while challenging and complicated, offers a sense of renewal. The labyrinthine nature of music by The Eight seizes upon these issues. As one listens repeatedly to their works, over days, months, and years, something new—perhaps a previously unnoticed inflection or sensual pleasure—reveals itself. Innate curiosity and a willingness to be open to new experiences are powerful qualities in both musicians and lovers.

Music often possesses an appealing innocence, tentative and virginal, recapturing feelings of youth and first experiences. Alkan's "Le premier billet doux" (The First Love Letter); Medtner's first published work, the Prolog from his Op. 1 *Stimmungsbilder*, and any number of early Scriabin preludes all evoke fundamental wonders. With music and sex alike, we must be receptive and in the mood. We may crave the sensuality of Rachmaninov's inspiration one day and find it too strong the next. Medtner may provide the perfect balm one moment and more passion at another. We can feel lust from Scriabin's openly erotic scores or choose Godowsky's more temperate pleasures. The length, challenge, and complexity of Sorabji's works may be stimulating now and overwhelming later. The type of music we desire and the frequency with which we choose to experience it often parallel the choices we make in our sexual lives. Both can be ever beautiful in all their forms, whether emotional or intellectual, passive or aggressive, fast or slow, loud or soft.

Love and Inspiration

When asked for a definition of music, Rachmaninov questioned, "How can one define it? Music is a calm, moonlit night . . . a rustling of summer foliage. Music is born only in the heart and it appeals only to the heart. Music is love."[1] He continually returned to the subject: "Love is certainly a never failing source of inspiration. Love inspires as nothing else does. To love is to gain happiness and strength of mind. It is the unfoldment of a new vista of intellectual energy."[2]

For his part, Hamelin feels that every performance is a "love offering." Over time, a sense of intimacy develops between artist and listener; mutual trust builds and, as with any lasting love, becomes part of the relationship.

Medtner placed much significance on the importance of love. Many of his more than one hundred songs are set to romantic love lyrics and to other poetry dealing with nature, fantasy, and philosophy. He believed that the human experience is instinctively receptive to love and affection.

Scriabin drew great inspiration from his second wife, Tatyana; his letters to her are filled with his need for love and work, and often demonstrate the impatience all lovers feel at being separated. Scriabin clearly needed her to be tender, supportive, and available. His passions and love were irrepressible, although his concern for Tatyana's health was often directed to ensuring that she was healthy for him:

> My little wings, be strong. I need you! Oh how I need you! Soon I will be taking care of you in person! . . . May our mad rapture come soon. Until I arrive, do not do anything foolish. Do not go near an open window or any such thing. How happy I would be to find you well. Sleep deep . . . Tanya, do you understand what I want?[3]

Scriabin's burning words contrast starkly with his down-to-earth admonition about the window. But this letter precisely mirrors both his creative and his physical life, mixing long-held sensations of infinite fire and ecstasy with more earthly concerns. Scriabin remained the center of his own world, and though he clearly loved Tatyana, much of both his love for her and his occasional displeasure with her involved how she could help him and his work. Just the thought of being away from Tatyana—

without the requisite stimulation of sensuality and sex—often left Scriabin wanting for inspiration and unable to concentrate, and the frustration exacerbated his loneliness: "Tunya, my joy, my dear, my little star, I am lonely without you, and am dying to see you. Six more days and then . . . TOGETHER! What bliss!"[4]

Busoni's letters are also filled with poetic love for his wife, Gerda, the source of much inspiration: "I kiss you in my inmost thoughts, for in this medley you alone stand firm."[5] Busoni could have written "I think of you" or "I miss you," but instead he chose the word "kiss"; the ardency of their correspondence over many years suggests a highly passionate relationship. Busoni recognized and cherished the love *in* his life as well as the love *of* his life, writing, "Dear Gerda, for few is it so beautiful as it is for us. Let us be thankful and happy."[6] A few years before his death, Busoni's passion remained undimmed: "I think of you as the only woman."[7] When they were apart, he could be morose and unproductive: "A deaf and dumb emptiness seems to surround me since you left."[8] Busoni not only drew strength and inspiration from her but also felt the same kind of bliss that Scriabin wrote about: "I feel so youthfully indeterminate today. . . . You were so very dear, you are so good!"[9] Here Busoni was likely thinking of a night of shared love. The happiness their life together brought him fed his inner muse during the periods that his touring caused them to spend apart.

By all accounts, Rachmaninov's wife Natalya played an equally important and supportive role in his life, and he freely acknowledged her part in his success. Although every bit the sensualist in his approach to music, Rachmaninov took a more reserved stance than did Scriabin. He acknowledged with the beginnings of a smile:

Everything of beauty helps. A beautiful woman is certainly a source of perpetual inspiration. But you must run away from her and seek seclusion, otherwise you will compose nothing—you will accomplish nothing. Carry the inspiration in your heart and mind; think of her, but be all by yourself for creative work.[10]

The pull of passion versus work can be enormous. Musicians are no different in this respect than those in any other profession requiring mental or physical acumen combined with high levels of creativity. Scriabin's efforts were constantly directed toward fusing those elements of life. He would virtually shout in his notebooks:

I want to enthrall the world by my creative work, by its wondrous beauty. I want to be the brightest imaginable light, the largest sun. I want to illumine the universe by my light. I want to engulf everything in my individuality. I want to give delight to the world. I want to take the world as one takes a woman. I need the world. I am what my senses feel.[11]

Sensuality and Spirituality

Scriabin's instinct for combining the divine with the sensual marked much of his later music, as he ingeniously mixed the worldly with the otherworldly. He called his third symphony *The Divine Poem* and used the word "poem" in many of his piano pieces. Its second movement, an erotic play of sound, is marked "Voluptés" (Sensual Pleasures).

If less overtly erotic than Scriabin's music, Rachmaninov's is more often than not sensuous and suggestive. Many of his works offer the pianist—and, vicariously, the audience—a physicality demanding the highest response from artist and keyboard alike. Such music instinctively seeks resolution through resourceful and often athletic forays. Rachmaninov's *Rhapsody on a Theme of Paganini* illustrates a musical duality, where the recurring presence of the Dies Irae—associated with musical themes of death or damnation—represents evil spirits, while its eleventh through eighteenth variations evoke sensual love. The eighteenth is written in D-flat major, a key used by Chopin in some of his most tender music. (There is a lively corollary to Chopin's use of this key. In *Chopin* [New York: Harper and Row, 1978], by George Marek and Maria Gordon-Smith, letters show the composer engaged in a sexual affair with Countess Delfina Potocka; he referred to her vagina as "your little D-flat Major." These writings have been exhaustively but inconclusively analyzed; if authentic, they suggest that this key was Chopin's private erotic inspiration.) The use of specific keys to convey particular sentiments is a common compositional device. Scriabin wrote in F-sharp major to explore feelings of ecstasy and human freedom, and most composers have turned to minor keys to evoke darker moods.

The emotions maintain their sovereign control over musical expression. For the pianist, however, music without the physical element of playing and touching the keyboard carries a faint notion of celibacy. How long can a musician go without contact with the instrument? The purely sensuous aspects of fingers on ivory and wood—combined with the amazing aural satisfaction the piano so readily provides—can be compared to a lover's touch on flesh: smooth and warm, with the promise of deeply pleasurable response. The greater the exertion, the more powerful the answer. Musicians often feel unsatisfied unless they are physically connected—merged—with an instrument. Pianists often speak of the sheer physical pleasure of playing, and of the keys as extensions of their arms and fingers—just as, during sex, we perceive another's body as an extension of our own. Scriabin wrote that his Ninth Sonata needed a fondling touch, as if making love to the piano. He also called that work's conclusion—where soft trills evoke the peace and calm after sex—"non-existence after the act of love."[12]

Scriabin conceived the final ecstasy in his *Mysterium* as a "grandiose sexual act."[13] He also planned for caresses and tastes to be included, with the sensual aspects of using the mouth and tongue as part of the experience. This ultimate work came to him as a vast musical apparition that he continued to refine until his death. The logistics of such an undertaking, the performance of which the composer intended to last for perhaps a week or more, remain speculative. Scriabin's ideal centered on his quest for spiritual elevation through sensuality. "Ecstasy" has a dual meaning here. Faubion Bowers explained that Scriabin, in his Seventh Sonata,

> expresses his philosophy in sound—the contrast, interplay, and interrelation of the poles of subject and object, spirit and matter, male (active) and female (passive) principles. The seventh sonata is a purification, because it describes the process of opposite poles touching, merging, fusing. The world (object) is transformed by the artist-creator (subject) who leads us through ecstasy into dematerialization. In the course of this ideological journey, the Seventh produces . . . a variety of effects—chords of perfume, mystic bells of sanctification, fountains of spraying fires, vortexes of wind, a final dance of ecstasy.[14]

The composer-pianist seeks higher emotional meaning as well as pleasure in the act of performance. Music or sex without spiritual fulfillment evaporates into the purely physical; in either case, the result is simply the satisfaction of the body or the ear. Hamelin has described getting to a crucial point with Medtner's *Sonata reminiscenza*: "It wasn't more than a week into knowing the piece that I needed it every day." Such a basic imperative for music parallels our need for love, intimacy, and sexual union.

Eroticism

Many of Scriabin's works progress in a strong line from affection to eroticism. His *Poem*, Op. 32, No. 1, is marked "con affetto," a phrase he often used. Its mood is evanescent, sensuous, and glowing. Leonid Sabaneyev called it "an erotic kiss . . . a kind of sexual dissolving in waves of sensation."[15] Sensuousness and eroticism lay at Scriabin's core: many of his printed directions to the performer use such words as "voluptuously," "ravishingly," and "orgiastic." But he was never coarse or vulgar, and the elegance and poetry of the titles he gave his works bespeak his refinement: he called the last of Opp. 51 and 52 "Dance of Languor" and "Poem of Languor," and the two pieces of Op. 57 "Desire" and "Danced Caress."

Aiding our erotic perception of music is the pianist, who is complicit in the twin roles of fantasy and desire. Hamelin's description of every concert and recording as a love offering is not meant sexually, but people sense his openness in performance and are drawn to him. The performer has the power to move the soul and stir the sexual response.

Sorabji minced no words in describing the opposite sort of pianist,

> of the writhing, intense type, the kind that plays with every part of her body, naturally except the part most concerned, her fingers. Her success, I am

convinced, is chiefly due to her sinuosities, our audiences being far too much concerned with the sinful lusts of the eye to enable properly to attend with their ears.[16]

Foreplay

Music often draws liberating climaxes from intricate and well-planned musical foreplay. Lengthy minor-key works will often end in the affirmation of the major key: witness Rachmaninov's Third Concerto and his Second Sonata, or Medtner's *Sonata minacciosa*. How neatly a short musical work fills our need for pleasure! But time and complexity add depth to music and to lovemaking, so that they may be enjoyed as journey rather than as destination. Sorabji's *Opus clavicembalisticum* and Alkan's Concerto for Solo Piano are not for everyday listening. But neither, perhaps, are the miniatures of the repertoire. Alkan's *Esquisses* or Medtner's *Tales* may not be enough to satisfy if the mood requires more. Our sexual desire may encompass a short expression and resolution before sleep, or it may take the form of extended satisfactions—made more pleasurable or complicated with the addition of food, flowers, flame, or ice—analogous to the extended development of complex musical works. Scriabin felt that incense, candles, and touches all had roles to play. Intended to be a kind of cosmic prelude to the finality of the *Mysterium*, his "Prefatory Action"—performed with colored lights, flavors, and scents—created the mood for musical love:

> The tender delight
> Of touching for the first time
> The mysterious sweetness
> Of moist lips kissing
> The sweet moaning . . . by amorous lights.[17]

The progression of Scriabin's life's work was a kind of extended foreplay; each new piece led into the next, in a search for ever-greater pleasure and aspiration. Delving into the body of his music—as in the Second, Fourth, Ninth, and Tenth Sonatas—one hears an unbroken line from the softly expectant introduction, full of anticipation, to vigorous movement and then breathtaking climax. Successfully building toward the climactic moments of a Scriabin or a Rachmaninov work requires tremendous stamina from the performer. The pianist's sheer athleticism in attempting to harness such music makes the concert stage a potent forum.

The Eight referred frequently to the elusive goal of balancing music's physical, mental, and emotional requirements. Focusing on one aspect to the exclusion of the others can make the musical projection less than completely satisfying. Any kind of performance, musical or sexual, that focuses on aggressive physicality can be an amazing experience, but lacking emotional or spiritual commitment, it can be manipulative, empty, even painful.

Pain and Pleasure

Scriabin confided in one of his notebooks:

Whatever may be my activity in a given moment (whether I am composing, or whether I am making love . . .), I feel pleasure if there is an obstacle placed in my path but one not greater than my ability to overcome. If circumstances paralyze my energy, I suffer. From this point of view, pleasure and pain accompany every moment of our life, even if we try to disregard them.[18]

His relationship with Tatyana was volatile, openly reflecting the dichotomy between pain and pleasure in life and in music. "I am infinite desiring! There will come that day of rejoicing!" Scriabin wrote; then, in a line at once beautiful and raw: "We will suffocate. We will be consumed in flames. The world will burn with us in our bliss."[19] Scriabin felt the same way toward much of his music. He wrote of the climactic section (marked "puissant, radieux") of his Tenth Sonata: "Here is blinding light as if the sun has come close. Here is the suffocation one feels in the moment of ecstasy."[20] Scriabin was forever impatient to slake his desires, and commentators were quick to perceive Scriabin's intrepid broaching of the pain-pleasure principle. Sorabji described a live performance of Scriabin's *Prometheus*: "It was so sublime to me, as to be almost painful; the ecstasy and gloriousness of it!"[21]

One of Scriabin's last piano works, *Vers la flamme* (Op. 72), boldly plays on the beauty and destructiveness of searing flames. Through dissonance, satanic trills, and burning climaxes, the music illuminates the affects of both pain and pleasure.

The Climax

Each of The Eight seized upon Beethoven's concept of the coda; the last pages of Rachmaninov's Second Sonata, Sorabji's First, and many of Scriabin's sonatas seek to intensify and conclude preceding musical material. In the natural order of both music and sex, climax occurs near the end. Radiant performances of such electrifying works as Alkan's Concerto for Solo Piano, Busoni's Piano Concerto, or a Scriabin sonata can lead to a calm satiety.

The effects of music are not only emotional and intellectual. The most physical, vertiginous passages of music by The Eight can induce in the listener the increased pulse and breathing, and the single-minded focus, that intense sexual experiences bring. From what may be called the "first kiss" of the quiet opening of Rachmaninov's Third Concerto, for example, the intense climax of the first-movement cadenza builds inexorably through waves of increasing tension. Many pianists choose the quicksilver cadenza to this concerto that Rachmaninov himself played, as opposed to his longer, more physical *ossia* (alternative), feeling that such a heavy climax coming so soon into the work takes it out of balance. Orgasm, after all, does not precede foreplay. Climaxes were a prime consideration in the formation of Rachmaninov's music and were not necessarily reached through huge sounds. If placed properly, they could also come about through the stillest *pianissimo*. Rachmaninov set up his climactic moments carefully, whether in a four- or a forty-minute work. Everything, he said, must be geared toward reaching that climactic moment in inevitable sequence.

Busoni spoke of Wagner's tendency to build in his music a carefully graded rush of emotion:

> With and after Wagner, voluptuous sensuality came to the fore; the form of *intensification of passion* is still insurmounted by contemporary composers. On every tranquil beginning followed a swift upward surge. Wagner, in this point insatiable, but not inexhaustible, turned from sheer necessity to the expedient, after reaching a climax, of starting afresh softly, to soar to a sudden new intensification.[22]

Feelings of ecstasy may not automatically accompany even an overwhelming sexual experience, nor may such feelings be taken for granted after a monumental musical experience. In fact, Scriabin, in his notebooks, described feeling sadness just after he made love, sensing a letdown that the experience was at least temporarily over. To this common response is attributed the proverb *Post coitum omne animal triste est.*

Sex was a necessary, vital part of Scriabin's creative process. In his grandiloquent way, he wrote:

> I am forever
> Negation
> Again and
> Ever anew!
> More powerful
> Tenderer
> New torture,
> Fresh beatitude.
> Delighting in this dance,
> Choking in its vortex.
> Unmindful of goals
> Beloved aspirations
> Spirit surrenders to playful drunkenness.
> On powerful wings It speeds
> Into realms of new discovery
> Of Ecstasy.[23]

Such writing is not merely erotic, but also points to a melodramatic ego that craves the power to give life.

Second Opinions

Although Busoni was an ardent admirer of Scriabin's later works, he felt that descriptive elements of life are better omitted from a composer's work:

> The measurements of what is artistic do not refer only to proportions, to the boundaries of what is beautiful and the preservation of taste, they mean above all not assigning to art tasks which lie outside its nature. Description in music, for instance.[24]

(Nonetheless, about his own piano concerto, Busoni wrote to Gerda, several years before its premiere, "There is a night of love, with a Serenade, in the *Tarantelle* [fourth movement], and a Vesuvius eruption too."[25]) Scriabin's works, however, though erotic and sexual in nature, still fall comfortably into the category of what is called abstract music. Busoni—who classified music as either chaste or sensuous—reacted specifically against open eroticism onstage. "In the last fifty years," he wrote, "music has had to be *erotic*. . . . Wagner's music is sexual, inactively erotic, thus: *lascivious*. This also explains why his inordinate duration is tolerated. *Potency acts swiftly*. Eroticism is protracted."[26] But it is equally true that the swift act may *lack* potency, and eroticism may take fleeting forms.

Busoni believed that music imitated neither life nor nature; rather, he conceived it as a stylized expression of mood and emotion.[27] Here another point of debate enters: Is the erotic feeling not an emotion? Is it not spiritual, not mythical? Busoni felt that music "repeats the emotions of life."[28] Yet how can the emotions of life exclude eroticism and sexuality? Busoni's contradictory position reflected his own conflict of sensibilities on the subject. With regard to opera, however, and the overt display of an onstage love duet, Busoni insisted:

> Eroticism is no subject for art but a concern of life. Those who feel the inclination should experience it; but not represent it or read a representation of it and least of all set it to music. Anyone who has made a third in the company of lovers will have felt this to be painful.[29]

In his music—including the four operas—he was disinclined to go the way of Wagner. Busoni was attracted to the nocturnes of John Field for their chaste qualities; he found those by Chopin too obviously sensual. In Sorabji's words, Busoni attempted the

> casting off of what is "sensuous" and the renunciation of subjectivity (the road to objectivity, which means the author standing back from his work, a purifying road, a hard way, a trial of fire and water) and the re-conquest of serenity . . . the smile of wisdom, of divinity, and absolute music. Not profundity and personal feeling and metaphysics, but music which is absolute, distilled.[30]

Sorabji perceived that Busoni's attitudes about eroticism filtered through to his playing, noting in a concert review, "Along comes Busoni who alone, it seems, has the power and courage to dissipate those languishing erotico-sentimental miasmata that have hung stagnantly about the music of [Chopin]."[31]

Sorabji generally agreed with Busoni's views on the relationship of music to eroticism and sex:

> It may be foolish prejudice on my part, but when I hear of music spoken of . . . as an outlet for sexual energy, via what I believe is "sublimation," I am moved to indignant protest. I absolutely refuse to regard the very deliberate, very intellectual, and . . . very cold-blooded processes of music-making as a sort of substitutional self-abuse, a mystical masturbation, a psycho-sexual whoremongering. Such a view of art seems to be definitely obscene. . . . I do not wish to be misunderstood nor for it to be imagined that my attitude springs from any puritanistic prejudices against the sex-function as such nor its exercise. Art, still less the musical department thereof, is *not* . . . an aphrodisiac—there are others far more effectual.

Yet at the same time, Sorabji recognized the benefits of sexuality to the creative process:

> So far from the practice of art being a diversion of sexual energy it enhances and stimulates it. No virgin, male or female, has ever been known to produce a great work of art, but again let me not be misunderstood, this time in the opposite direction. Unbridled lecherousness is no more indication of artistic gifts . . . than its absence. On the other hand, that the modish arty Blooms-bohemian, damply libidinous type of human who revolves on the fringes of "Society" and "Art" and used to haunt the performances of the Russian Ballet, does derive specifically sexual exciting sensations from music cannot . . . be denied.

Sorabji noted that music and art have been regarded as a "happy hunting ground for sexual titillation" in the homosexual community, although again he hedged:

> That the now defunct Russian Ballet or any organization whose success depends largely upon the display of the more spectacular portions of the human body should especially appeal to this type is understandable enough, but that music in and by itself should do so . . . is to a serious musician almost incomprehensible. Perhaps the subterranean process at work might best be described as a sort of psychological metathesis whereby there is transferred to the music the sexual appeal of the performer, and once this has been done, it is perhaps not too fantastic to assume that by a process of association, the same music may thereafter produce the same erotic emotions apart from the original performer.

Sorabji wrote of critics becoming swayed by the sexual favors, implied or otherwise, proffered by performers, and expressed frustration at seeing his craft suborned to the wiles of those less musically endowed.

> But although in certain cases, quite unconsciously and involuntarily on his part, an artist's success may be due in some degree to his sexual attractiveness, there are other cases in which he or she . . . trails the sexual red-herring deliberately and unscrupulously. On the stage this practice is carried to extreme lengths by all the sexes equally, and astonishing and diverting are the forms it will take. . . . But by none is this red-herring trailing more shamelessly practiced than by the female practitioners of the baser sort in music. The object is plain, to produce that condition of half-hysterical, suppressed erotic excitement in the more stupid male members of the audience, so that a wretched performance may seem to go down satisfactorily in the welter of applause wherein these suppressed feelings have a sort of vent. Those corybantic, maenadic, terpsichorean, bacchic, acrobatic sinuosities of certain young ladies at the piano, whose convolutions reach to the ultimate limit of the decent, and often a good way beyond, the large, comprehensively amorous gestures of those . . . whose demeanor suggests none too finely but quite unambiguously that music is a mere side-line—the carefully practiced girlish timidities, the moppings and mowings of those young ladies who acknowledge the applause that greets some shapeless piece of jelly that it is an abuse of language to call a composition, all those things have one object in view—an appeal to what politeness calls the hearts of the audience, and truth something considerably less delicate.

Like Busoni, Sorabji refused to be drawn publicly into the very real issues of eroticism in music as demonstrated by Scriabin (whom they both respected). Sorabji instead fell back on his gifts of wit and observation:

> And lastly, on the question of the erotically exciting effect of music as music pure and simple? I confess I have hardly any opinion to offer. As I have already said, to me and to many other musicians the notion is fantastic, grotesque. Of course, we have all heard about those strange people to whom such funny things happen when they listen to Tristan—some of them, we are told, even have to go home and change between the acts, so embarrassing are the effects. They are of a piece, I feel, with that worst type of sentimental amateur who pumps up emotions of moonlight (whatever they may be) when they hear a certain sonata of Beethoven, or who feel they are suffocating when they hear that one equally notorious composition of Rachmaninov—people who must stick music on as a false caudal appendage to anything else on earth rather than accept it as just music first and last. Psychological metathesis again. There are transferred to the music—in the case of Tristan—the erotic or supposedly erotic qualities of the story, and I am perfectly convinced that had the music been originally presented to them without its dramatico-

literary context they would listen to it quite unmoved. Possibly the too stimulating proximities engendered by those crowded galleries whence such excessively susceptible people are wont to listen to this opera may also have something to do with it, but let us not pursue these indelicate investigations any further![32]

Music, Sex, and Life

Music and sex may be among the last domains of wonder in the modern era of instant information, although their expressive power is often demeaned by our fast-moving, market-oriented culture. And life is full of many elements, let alone the other arts, capable of inspiring awe. However, the liminal qualities of music and sex join the emotional, mental, and physical worlds as do few experiences.

To succumb to the body is to lose oneself in life's music. We frequently seek the freshness of new musical experiences. Novelty in sex is just as important to many people. If not seeking new partners, we may be exploring new positions or sensations. (One of the names Scriabin ascribed to his unusual harmonic vocabulary is the Russian word for "sensations," as he continually strove for physical and musical stimulation.) As great as a given Scriabin sonata is, we cannot survive on it alone. Mixing the familiar with the unknown—in our musical or sexual repertoires—fosters exciting experiences that speak of renewal and can hold our interest for a lifetime. Although tension and anxiety may well hinder the performance of either the pianist or the lover, sex and music can insulate us from the responsibilities and complications of daily lives or may relieve loneliness and emptiness. Making love after a profound personal loss can be a warm, deeply comforting experience. In their most basic forms, music and sex provide a sense of hope and rejuvenation, as well as their own special healing powers. They transport us back to nature. Our dreams often include music and sex, in a kind of inner musical theater. Making love in the water or on the grass, among the trees, in the rain, or under the sun or moon is inseparable from the scheme of life. The Eight and many other composers have been inspired to incorporate nature's aural and visual stimulants to great effect in their music.

The acts of sexual and musical creation often lend a sense of immortality to their participants. Just as parents hope that the child that emerges from their sexual union will survive them, composers wish for their creations to outlast them. Each of The Eight, with the exception of Sorabji, wished to be known primarily for his musical children—his compositions. Their careers as solo pianists—however satisfying or lucrative—took second place to their desire to leave strong, compelling legacies surviving well beyond their lives and our own.

9 THE ART OF TRANSCRIPTION

A transcription may be narrowly defined as the transfer of music from one medium to another, although the term has metamorphosed into all manner of freely conceived arrangements and paraphrases. What purpose do they serve? To musical purists, transcriptions possess the element of artifice. Why not write original music? Why have so many great composers felt compelled to transfer or expand the thoughts of others to the piano? Are the originals thus improved? Why do we need piano reductions of Bach and Schubert when we have an abundance of organists, violinists, and singers—and their recordings—to give us this repertoire unretouched? Does transcription represent an homage—a communion—from one musical thinker to another? Or is the transcribed work a narcissistic vehicle for coupling one's own name to that of a celebrated composer of the past?

At the heart of the argument lies the question of whether anyone—no matter how gifted and sincere—has the right to tamper with established masterpieces. The debate is not limited to music. The restoration or modernization of great architecture and works of art is fraught with similar questions. In some of these cases, however, the original does not survive intact. The outcry over colorizing classic black-and-white films is more closely analogous to musical transcription: the originals remain for anyone who wishes to see the movie or to read or hear the music.

Composers of all types have transcribed music for the piano. The fear that transcriptions will supplant the originals is unfounded: such works exist on their own terms and expand the repertoire, often opening new windows into the study of technique, sonority, and musical possibilities. Busoni well understood the nature of transcriptions:

> A transcription does not destroy the original; so there can be no question
> of loss arising from it. The performance of a work is also a transcription and
> this too—however free the performance may be—can never do away with
> the original. For the musical work of art exists whole and intact before it has
> sounded and after the sound has finished.[1]

When two ingenious musical thinkers meet through transcriptions, whether on manuscript paper, at the piano, or in the concert hall, the results can be enormously satisfying, akin to two distinct chemicals combining to create an entirely new substance. A prime criterion is to write idiomatically for the keyboard. With the exceptions of Scriabin and Medtner—who rarely looked beyond their own music and thus felt no real desire to rework that of others—each of The Eight significantly contributed to the piano repertoire through transcriptions. Those who choose to transcribe for the piano are invariably accomplished pianists, who know their instrument and its capabilities intimately, and who want to experience the pleasure of playing the great works not originally created for piano.

The art of transcription has made it possible for the piano—with its capacity for reproducing many voices simultaneously and its wide range of tonal possibilities—to take possession of the entire literature of music. The propensity for transcription prevalent in the nineteenth century was renewed by the efforts of Godowsky and Busoni. Others also produced eloquent written and musical justification for transcriptions.

Alkan and Liszt

These two great pianists elevated the art of transcription to an altogether higher level from the vacuous virtuoso fare of the early nineteenth century, turning to the best of Bach, Handel, Haydn, Mozart, and Beethoven, among other composers. Liszt is generally credited with initiating the real art of transcribing for the piano. He had the imagination and technique to carry it off, bringing orchestral scores, operas, and songs to an eager public. In Liszt's case, the impetus grew out of his passion to introduce great masterworks to his public in an age before recordings and widely accessible concerts, rather than out of any virtuosic desire to set the keys afire. (Later and lesser virtuosos—such as Sigismund Thalberg, whose music is now largely forgotten but who at one time enjoyed a certain vogue with the public—misdirected these admirable aims to produce shallow display pieces.) Liszt's reputation as an original composer has suffered in part because of his association with transcriptions; however, his reworkings of Hector Berlioz's *Symphonie fantastique* and of the Beethoven symphonies demonstrate a keen orchestral awareness, faithfully recasting the composers' inspiration in the piano's voice.

In close parallel to Liszt, Alkan systematically raised the standard in both deed and word:

> The number of excerpts from operas or symphonies capable of being arranged for a single piano in a manner both clear and complete, yet within the limits of difficulty, must be quite small. Furthermore they require a perfect knowledge of those effects, timbres, and "illusions" of voices and instruments in their innumerable combinations that are made possible by the

peculiar sonorities of the modern piano; for these sonorities are wide-ranging if one knows how to obtain them through various methods of attack, through the intelligent use of certain fingerings, hand-crossing, etc. The selection of these pieces and the talent to adapt them forms an art on its own, one which demands above all long, hard work, extreme delicacy, sensibility, fine instinct, and the appropriation of all available means.[2]

Liszt was less rigorous than Alkan in conveying all of the music's details. He instinctively worked around treacherous technical difficulties with his inimitable pianistic guile, and as a result, virtuosos have continued to perform Liszt's transcriptions, difficult as they may be on their own terms. Alkan had the large hands and technique to negotiate practically anything. But his painstaking attention to detail and his uncompromising style generally led to complex results that have hindered his acceptance (and even awareness of him) as a transcriber. Prime examples of this aspect of Alkan's art are found in piano concertos; his reductions of Mozart's D Minor and the first movement of Beethoven's C Minor Concertos brilliantly re-enact the orchestra's role. Mozart provided no cadenzas to his frequently performed D Minor Concerto; those that Beethoven composed for it are often played by less adventurous pianists who by tradition should attempt their own. Alkan made no effort to stay within true Mozart style, even summoning that composer's "Jupiter" Symphony at one point. Alkan's contrapuntally audacious final cadenza recalls themes from all three of the concerto's movements.

The outlandish cadenza that Alkan wrote for the Beethoven concerto has gained notoriety ever since Busoni conducted the work at one of his Berlin Philharmonic concerts in 1906, with Rudolph Ganz as soloist. Critics excoriated all participants for such blasphemy against Beethoven. Hamelin has resuscitated the entire transcription in his solo recitals, although he performed its cadenza only once in the context of the original concerto. "It may be inappropriate at a serious concert with orchestra," Hamelin demurs, noting the keen humor Alkan brought to it. This colossal cadenza explores every detail of Beethoven's thought, climaxing with a combination in C major of the concerto's main theme with the glorious music that begins the finale of the Fifth Symphony. This musical merger foreshadowed Godowsky's ingenious contrapuntal combinations of several of the Chopin études into one piece, as well as Busoni's own similar treatment of Bach's music. The vivid arrangements of Godowsky and Busoni, rising from the brilliant groundwork laid by Alkan and Liszt, at once follow and depart from those of their predecessors.

Bach, Busoni, and the Idea

The most significant musicians have in common a devotion to the best music, whether choosing it for performance or transcription. Busoni in particular devoted a substantial portion of his activities to deciphering the universality of Bach, who brilliantly justified the transfer of music to different instruments. Bach himself transcribed not only the music of other baroque composers, but also his own works, giving his ideas new life through different instrumentation. Bach's compositional style—stressing counterpoint and an often motoric sense of rhythm—lends itself particularly well to complexity and rigorous intellectual probity. It is thus no coincidence that Bach himself is transcribed more than any other composer, and the titles of many works by The Eight and others imply tradition and respect for him, if not similarity. For example, Alkan's preludes; Sorabji's Prelude, Interlude, and Fugue; Rachmaninov's preludes; and Hamelin's Prelude and Fugue impart the spirit of Bach through counterpoint and the classic triumvirate of harmony, rhythm, and melody.

Many in the original-instrument movement find it the height of heresy to perform Bach on a modern concert grand, much less in any kind of arrangement. The forward-thinking Busoni would have none of that kind of pedantry:

> Like his successors, Mozart and Beethoven, Bach committed some of his most valuable thoughts to the keyboard, that discredited, indispensable, and most comprehensive of all instruments. Modern times have taken possession of the instrument as well as the master with increasing interests and understanding; both become more alive the further and more deeply one penetrates into them.[3]

Busoni ardently defended the validity and originality of transcriptions, for which "Bach-Busoni" became a byword. Bach felt that the medium employed was entirely secondary to the musical idea it served. The piano remained Busoni's preferred means of expression, but the idea remained paramount for him as well. He therefore would not hesitate to alter scores to obtain what he considered the optimal effect. He believed the printed note and its subsequent performance often represented an incomplete expression of material sound; it was the spiritual essence behind the concept that was of surpassing significance.

Busoni based his *Fantasia contrappuntistica* on the final, unfinished fugue of Bach's *Art of Fugue*. The result has been criticized for its stylistic unfaithfulness to Bach's methods, but Busoni insisted on the universality of great music, however it is clothed:

> The spirit of an art-work, the measure of emotion, of humanity, that is in it— these remain unchanged in value through changing years; the form which these three assumed, the manner of their expression, and the flavor of the epoch which gave them birth, are transient and age rapidly.[4]

Notwithstanding his well-known transcription of Bach's Chaconne, Busoni is best known for his transcriptions of Bach's ageless organ masterpieces, ingeniously imitating their characteristic textures and effects through changes in color, register, and the use of room-filling chords. Many transcriptions, including those by Liszt, choose to arpeggiate (break) chords, extending their range but robbing the texture of its solidity; Busoni avoided them. He considered the process of transcription akin to translating words from one language to another, where the conception takes precedence, even if the words (instruments) are different. Following in the tradition of Busoni as a world-class pianist, conductor, composer, writer, and critic, Zoltán Kocsis concurs with Busoni that

> the essence of music is much more important than the final form in which it emerges. I am in the camp that says that if Bach knew the modern piano, he would certainly use it. I do much historical work on original instruments, but if Bach had the possibilities of the pedals, for instance, he would definitely use them. They greatly extend the range of sonority, especially in recalling orchestral colors and illusions.[5]

Busoni's extensive study of the pedals proved enormously helpful in his transcriptions, manifested in a widespread use of the piano's middle pedal, used to sustain bass notes without the overtones of the middle and upper keyboard registers. He also built monumental, organlike climaxes through careful placement of *forte* and *piano* notations, making full use of the instrument's dynamic capabilities.

Busoni viewed the art of composition as "descended in a straight line from that of Bach (in so far as it strives more and more consciously through polyphony to become feeling in sound)."[6] He came honestly by his knowledge of Bach, whose music is a wellspring of the classic disciplines of counterpoint and voice leading: Busoni analyzed and dissected the *Well-Tempered Clavier*'s forty-eight preludes and fugues as no other musician had ever previously attempted. He also attributed apt, colorful concepts to the set, calling the first four preludes, for example, "the four elements—water, fire, earth, and air."[7]

Bach provided Busoni with an unimpeachable rationale for transcriptions:

> In the virtuoso sense transcriptions are suiting another's ideas to the personality of the transcriber. With weak personalities such transcriptions become weak pictures of stronger originals and mediocrity, which is always in the majority, brought forth during the virtuosi period a great number of mediocre and even tasteless and distorted transcriptions. Music like this gave transcriptions a bad name and forced them into an altogether subordinate position. It is only necessary to mention J. S. Bach in order, with one decisive blow, to raise the rank of the transcription to artistic honor in the reader's estimation. He was one of the most prolific arrangers of his own and other pieces, especially as organist. From him I learnt to recognize the truth that Good and Great Universal Music remains the same through whatever medium it is sounded.[8]

Writing of Busoni's classic Bach transcriptions, Sorabji flatly stated: "As always in Art, the end justifies the means, for what else matters but the end? . . . and not merely justifies but glorifies it."[9] Busoni knew that the art of transcription was misunderstood and almost discredited. He concisely and eloquently pleaded for its wider understanding and acceptance:

> The frequent antagonism which I have excited with "transcriptions," and the opposition to which an ofttimes irrational criticism has provoked me, caused me to seek a clear understanding of this point. My final conclusion concerning it is this: Every notation is, in itself, the transcription of an abstract idea. The instant the pen seizes it, the idea loses its original form. The very intention to write down the idea compels a choice of measure and key. The form and the musical agency, which the composer must decide upon, still more closely define the way and the limits.[10]

Busoni's liberal philosophy even extended to performance:

> Transcription occupies an important place in the literature of the piano; and looked at from a right point of view, every important piano piece is the reduction of a big thought to a practical instrument. But transcription has become an independent art; no matter whether the starting-point of a composition is original or unoriginal. Bach, Beethoven, Liszt, and Brahms were evidently all of the opinion that there is artistic value concealed in a pure transcription, for they all cultivated the art themselves, seriously and lovingly. In fact, the art of transcription has made it possible for the piano to take possession of the entire literature of music. Much that is inartistic, however, has got mixed up with this branch of the art and it was because of the cheap, superficial estimation of it made by certain men, who had to hide their nakedness with a mantle of "being serious," that it sank down to what was considered a low level.[11]

Beyond Bach

The composer who works in various musical forms may be viewed as the equivalent of medicine's general practitioner and not as a specialist in one particular area. Although known mainly for his Bach transcriptions, Busoni also transcribed orchestral works by Mozart, Mendelssohn, Schubert, and others. Busoni pointed out other great composers' way with transcriptions:

> Vivaldi's concertos, Schubert's songs, Weber's "Invitation to the Waltz" are still there in each case, when changed over to Bach's organ, Liszt's pianoforte, Berlioz's orchestra. But where does the transcription begin? A second Liszt setting of his Spanish Rhapsody exists which bears the title *Great Fantasy on Spanish Airs*. It is another piece; there are, in part, the same themes. Which of them is the transcription? The one which was written later? But is not the first one already an arrangement of a Spanish folk-song? That Spanish Fantasy commences with a theme which tallies with the dance motive in Mozart's

Figaro and Mozart took this from someone else too. It is not his, it is transcribed. Moreover the same theme appears again in Gluck's ballet *Don Juan*.[12]

Busoni elevated the concept of transcription to a new level of scholarship in his published edition of Liszt's "Paganini" Étude No. 6, based upon the famous melody also used by Brahms, Rachmaninov, and others. Paganini's original, Liszt's two versions, and Busoni's own are presented together, so that the pianist may compare all four in detail.

In addition to transcriptions, Busoni wrote a number of pieces in variation form, in which a theme is continually modified while retaining its basic elements—his variations on a Chopin prelude are a classic example—but he questioned why variations attracted none of the derision heaped upon transcriptions:

> This is odd, because if the variation form is built up on a borrowed theme, it produces a whole series of transcriptions, and the more regardless of the theme they are, the more ingenious is the type of variation. Thus, *arrangements* are not permitted because they change the original whereas the *variation* is permitted although it *does change* the original.[13]

Brahms was never derided for bastardizing Paganini's theme in his masterful variations, nor was Rachmaninov in the *Rhapsody on a Theme of Paganini*. And when have we heard Anton Diabelli's partisans derisively scorning Beethoven's *Diabelli Variations*?

Godowsky: Exceeding Boundaries

Busoni and Godowsky were pilloried in many quarters for tampering with the genius of Bach and Chopin. The reasons for the critical contempt of Godowsky's Chopin studies are superficial. Somehow, during his time, writing in variation form and calling the resulting work "variations" was considered more acceptable than transcription. Taking melodies from works not originally conceived for the piano was also accepted. The Chopin études, on the other hand, were acknowledged from their inception as untouchably great jewels of the piano repertoire. Had Rachmaninov produced his own set of Chopin-Rachmaninov studies, he would likely have received the same kind of contempt accorded Godowsky. But few on either side of the argument really took the time to absorb the essence of Godowsky's motivations and intentions. Had they done so, the transcription debate could have evolved more thoughtfully and less caustically.

The notoriety of Godowsky's Chopin studies has tended to overshadow his achievements in the realm of Bach transcription. Like Busoni, Godowsky turned to Bach for some of his most inspired work, recreating six of the solo violin and solo cello works. Sorabji was among the first to recognize the greatness of Godowsky's Bach transcriptions, calling them a really astounding feat of creative re-interpretation equal to, and even in some respects surpassing, Busoni's own work along the same lines. These grinning, grimacing skeletons of compositions are transformed by Godowsky into magnificent piano works, miraculously endowed with the greatness and grandeur of Bach at his greatest, yet all the time being plainly Godowsky.[14]

As Busoni had with the Paganini-Liszt étude, Godowsky took the unusual step of appending Bach's originals to what he called his free elaborations. He did so out of respect for the music as well as for educational purposes: Godowsky wished for his students, other pianists, and the public to learn from his efforts. He was particularly proud of his Bach transcriptions, but they never found anywhere near the favor or recognition that Busoni's had, a fact that bred in Godowsky real feelings of hopelessness. Busoni, however, took mostly from the organ works; those originally composed for solo strings—despite the unsurpassed mastery, respect, and brilliance Godowsky achieved—may sound overblown on the piano. Organ music, as opposed to that written for the violin or cello, is generally better suited for transcription to another pedaled keyboard.

Godowsky remains a supreme figure in the province of recreative musical transcription. Sorabji went so far as to assert that this aspect of Godowsky's genius overshadowed his achievements as a pianist. Godowsky's most famous transcriptions are of works by Albéniz: the Tango in D Major and "Triana" from the *Suite Iberia.* Also well known are Godowsky's three *Symphonic Metamorphoses* on waltzes by Johann Strauss, which travel well beyond routes normally taken by transcriptions. Their tightly woven harmonic complexity, free thematic association, and contrapuntal combination of Strauss's themes make the designation "metamorphoses" particularly apt. Despite their obvious virtuoso requirements, Godowsky felt their musical virtues to be substantial. Closely following his three transformations of Strauss waltzes, Godowsky's sixteen pieces grouped under the name *Renaissance* provided another, if less overtly demonstrative, outlet for his creative mind. Subtitled *Free Adaptations of Old Piano Masterworks,* this suite gives rebirth to harpsichord pieces by Rameau, Corelli, Lully, Scarlatti, and others through the modern grand piano's voice. All received the ingenious Godowsky treatment.

As did Liszt in the nineteenth century, Godowsky also transcribed Schubert lieder. Both composers brilliantly overcame the challenges of incorporating the vocal line into the pianistic texture. Above all, they were drawn to Schubert's vocal inspiration. Godowsky's transcriptions—again, the works are described as "freely transcribed for the piano"—are magnificent realizations, although they tend to be weighed down by contrapuntal complications that make them more inaccessible than Liszt's.

Godowsky also spent much time with Chopin's music. His studies on the Chopin études followed and greatly expanded the concept of Busoni's variations based on a Chopin prelude as material for fascinating musical development. Godowsky's

Chopin studies resemble the most exquisite oriental rugs: years in the making, they are neither showy nor obvious, and their value depends upon a connoisseur's appreciation. Sorabji immediately recognized their beauty and ingenuity, which "only blind bigotry or insensate obscurantism can deny." He accurately pointed to them as "the principal cause of the Niagaras of abuse which have been poured on his head."[15]Although Godowsky's aim was the development and extension of piano technique to evolutionary levels, as was Chopin's goal little over half a century earlier, both considered any loss of musical expression an inexcusable failing. Godowsky could have lapsed into technical reveries at the expense of purely musical values, but he chose the higher ground. Of course, without a pianist of Godowsky's accomplishment (and few such have ever existed), the études can degenerate into mechanical coarseness, which is precisely what the critics have latched onto. Hamelin stresses that the primary focus in his Chopin-Godowsky recordings was to maintain the musical intent of the originals, with no compromise to the technical "Niagaras of abuse" that Godowsky heaps upon the ordinary pianist. In his written commentary, Hamelin pointedly asks:

> But wait! What's this? *Dolce, dolcissimo, molto espressivo* markings by the dozen? Here a nocturne, a polonaise, there a mazurka? Beautifully involved harmony in velvety rich textures? Anyone who has taken the trouble to spend more than a short amount of time with these pieces finds that Godowsky's fervent wish to revolutionize pianistic writing carried with it only the loftiest aesthetic aims, and each of the Studies, while perhaps not all being equally successful musically, adheres unquestionably to this dual purpose. Despite their formidable reputation, many of them are serene in character, hardly ever exploiting the forceful, percussive side of piano writing.[16]

Many listeners, upon hearing Godowsky's transcriptions, simply refused to take him seriously. Completely missing the point, they asked what he was doing spending so much time on that subterranean aspect of the art, one they saw as a step below original creation. One such critic, Carl Engel—musicologist, writer, editor, and one-time president of the publishing company G. Schirmer—wrote in the *Musical Quarterly* (after describing how many people cannot use the phone without needing something to write or draw with):

> Go into any public telephone booth. The walls of these lethal chambers will afford the excavators of New York, in a couple of thousand years, a precious opportunity to study the mental state of our cliff dwellers. . . . This mania for telephonic polygons . . . takes the form of transcriptural obsessions in some musicians. One of the worst cases, undoubtedly, is that of Mr. Leopold Godowsky. He can not pick up a sheet of music, without wanting to trace over it convolutions of octave runs and double trills, rhomboids of countermelodies, and all very cleverly, at that. No doubt, whenever his telephone

rings, instead of wasting the time with defacing the walls or spoiling clean paper, he quickly makes a lucrative little transcription. It all depends on the length of the conversation. Nothing from Weber's "Invitation to the Dance," which he elaborates contrapuntally for three pianos, to Carl Bohm's "Calm as the Night," is safe from Mr. Godowsky's hands.[17]

(Hamelin, it turns out, has gone Godowsky three better by transcribing Scott Joplin's "Maple Leaf Rag" for six pianos.)

Godowsky the transcriber has always had his supporters as well. Sorabji, for one, observed, "As a creative transcriber and arranger Godowsky occupies quite a unique place, the scope and range of his work in this respect sometimes surpassing even that of Busoni himself."[18] The eminent former chief critic of the *New York Times,* Harold C. Schonberg, said of Godowsky's Chopin studies: "I'm mad about them. They throw a different aspect on Chopin, taking technique just about to its limits."

Those limits extend, significantly, to making the left hand a full partner in the pianist's musical dialogue, rather than just allowing it to play a supporting role; indeed, the knowledgeable critic James Huneker called Godowsky "The Apostle of the Left Hand." Godowsky himself explained:

> The left hand is favored by nature in having the stronger part of the hand for the upper voice of all double notes and chords and also by generally having the strongest fingers for the strongest parts of a melody. . . . [C]ommanding as it does the lower half of the keyboard, [the left hand] has the incontestable advantage of enabling the player to produce with less effort and more elasticity a fuller and mellower tone, superior in quantity and quality to that of the right hand. . . . If it is possible to assign to the left hand alone the work done usually by both hands simultaneously, what vistas are opened to future composers, were this attainment to be extended to both hands![19]

Not only did Godowsky transform a number of the Chopin études for the left hand alone, he also combined several of them into one grand study, such as Chopin's "Black Key" and "Butterfly" études (Op. 10, No. 5, with Op. 25, No. 9—both in the key of G-flat Major). He called this study "Badinage," meaning a playful banter between the hands.

At a New York concert in June 1996, Hamelin offered his own étude à la Godowsky as an encore. His prefatory remarks to the audience?

> I'll have you know that I'm about to commit suicide, by the way, with this next piece. It requires some explanation. There were some fifty-four published Chopin-Godowsky studies, and a further ten or eleven never published. The manuscripts were most likely lost during World War II. Among these was to have been a contrapuntal combination of all three A minor studies: Op. 10, No. 2; Op. 25, No. 4; and Op. 25, No. 11. No one knows what Godowsky did with this . . . but a friend of mine . . . *dared* me to

reproduce that stunt, and I'm afraid I took him up on it. Enough said. It's called, of course, *Triple Étude*.[20]

At that, Hamelin crossed himself and began two minutes of legerdemain that eerily echoed what Godowsky himself must have sounded like. Each line was clearly drawn with tightly controlled polyphonic virtuosity, while the piece's wrenching difficulties remained practically transparent to all but the experienced pianists in the audience. Is it merely an elaborate stunt or an extension of creativity? Hamelin insists that his motivations were entirely lyrical and intellectual, as did Godowsky; these tenets, however, often remain abusively misunderstood within the musical establishment.

Naturally, the performer's integrity and ability play a key role in the potential of any transcription. Godowsky summed up his reasoning:

> To justify himself in the controversy which exists regarding the aesthetic and ethic[al] rights of one composer to use another composer's works, themes or ideas, in order to freely build upon them new musical creations, such as arrangements, transcriptions, paraphrases, and variations . . . the author desires to say that it entirely depends upon the intentions, nature, and quality of the work of the so-called transgressors. As the Chopin studies are, as compositions in étude form, universally acknowledged to be the highest attainment in the realm of beautiful pianoforte music combined with indispensable mechanical and technical usefulness, the author thought it wisest to build upon their solid and invulnerable foundation, for the purpose of furthering the art of pianoforte playing. Being adverse to any alterations in the original texts of any master works when played in their original form, the author would strongly condemn any artists for tampering ever so little with such works as those of Chopin.[21]

Feinberg and Rachmaninov

Like Godowsky, Feinberg is better known for his brilliant transcriptions than for his substantial body of original work. He rarely felt the same freedom in transcribing as did Godowsky, although neither composer would have considered altering the score while performing original music. They reserved their alterations purely for transcriptions and arrangements. Although Russian pianists in particular have adopted Feinberg's Bach and Tchaikovsky transcriptions, these works continue to suffer from a problem common to much music outside the most well-traveled mainstream: lack of availability. Row upon row of Liszt and Busoni transcriptions adorn the shelves of every respectable music store around the world, and the Internet brings them all that much closer to home. Even the most determined seeker, however, may find Feinberg's music only in the largest libraries, and many pieces are available only in Russia. Why would a publisher not take up the cause, at least for Feinberg's ingenious

and musically accessible transcriptions? Because original plates must be obtained—
if they still exist; because copyright considerations must somehow be determined
from Russia's murky laws and precedent; and because above even those considerations, any publisher would have to be prepared to make a significant long-term
investment, as Feinberg is not a household name—largely because of his music's
unavailability (music, too, has its chicken-and-egg conundrums).

Nonetheless, those wishing to play or simply to study the work of a master transcriber may begin with Feinberg's Bach-Vivaldi organ concerto and three movements from Tchaikovsky's symphonies; these are among the most beautiful examples of transcription in the literature. They carefully imitate the orchestra's kaleido-
scopic range, making little concession to pianistic difficulty. On a more intimate
level are Feinberg's Bach chorale preludes. Busoni's own versions of a number of the
chorales are still often performed, but Feinberg's are fully equal to Busoni's and just
as finely spun. Radu Lupu recalls a potent influence at the Moscow Conservatory:
"Though Samuel Feinberg died before I arrived, his was a revered name, and Professor Neuhaus spoke of him with the warmest words. His Bach and Tchaikovsky
transcriptions are among the greatest examples of the form."

In 1997 Harris Goldsmith wrote in the liner notes for Arcadi Volodos's recording debut, devoted entirely to transcriptions:

> I have left the biggest surprise for the last. The eminent virtuoso, Samuel
> Feinberg, remained hidden behind the unlamented Iron Curtain and is sadly
> unknown to western ears. A few fine recordings . . . introduced us to an
> obviously major artist with a lyrical style and beautiful singing tone. . . . As
> with Liszt's Beethoven and Berlioz piano reductions, Feinberg's Tchaikovsky
> recasting is deeply respectful of the original, yet infused with genius and
> inspiration. It is really quite remarkable to hear how much of the ravishing
> instrumental detail has been retained by a mere ten fingers: the feathery cross-
> rhythms at the beginning are there; and so are the off-beat violin notes; the
> squealing downward scales for strings and winds in alternation; the thwack of
> the bass drum; and even an approximation of the climactic cymbal crashes.
> No doubt about it: This amazing arrangement . . . is truly golden age
> pianism.[22]

Feinberg also produced transcriptions of seventeenth- and eighteenth-century
Italian composers. Stricter and less intrusive than Godowsky's *Renaissance* pieces,
they give renewed vigor to baroque forms. Feinberg frequently performed his Bach-
Vivaldi transcription, transferring organ textures to the piano and employing the
supreme control of inner voices characteristic of the best transcriptions. Though
pianistically somewhat awkward, the work faithfully recreates its model.

Godowsky and Feinberg are not generally known for the large amount of original music they composed. Ironically, the opposite is the case with Rachmaninov. He
so captured public imagination with his original works that his transcriptions tend

to be overlooked. A few pieces occasionally turn up on recital programs. His transcription of the Scherzo from Mendelssohn's incidental music to Shakespeare's *A Midsummer Night's Dream* remains well known, as does his short encore on "The Flight of the Bumblebee" from Rimsky-Korsakov's *Tale of Tsar Saltan*. Rachmaninov gives two pieces by his good friend Fritz Kreisler—*Liebesleid* and *Liebesfreud*—heavily polyphonic treatment along the lines of what Godowsky might have done with them.

Although Rachmaninov did not go as far as Feinberg in transcribing Tchaikovsky's works, he did complete a four-hand arrangement of the "Manfred" Symphony as well as the lyrical "Lullaby." Rachmaninov also transcribed "Wohin?" from Schubert's song cycle *Die schöne Müllerin*. This was accomplished under the clear influence of Godowsky, who in turn dedicated his own transcription of it to Rachmaninov, "because he transcribed the same piece . . . and which shows very clearly my influence. I thought it a good joke to dedicate my version to him."[23] (Rachmaninov had earlier dedicated his *Polka de V. R.* to Godowsky.) Rachmaninov's songs "Lilacs" and "Daisies" were also later reworked for solo piano by the composer.

Rachmaninov created a suite for piano from three movements of Bach's Partita No. 3 for Solo Violin. Although the original contains nothing like the grandeur of the second partita's chaconne, in which Busoni found such expansive possibilities, Rachmaninov's transcriptions are every bit as ingenious. Among his other transcriptions are the Gopak (a lively Byelorussian dance) from Musorgsky's opera *Sorochintsy Fair* and the minuet from Bizet's *L'Arlésienne* Suite.

Free Adaptations, Arrangements, and Paraphrases

Two of the most striking instances of free adaptation for the piano come from Busoni and Sorabji, both based on material from Bizet's opera *Carmen*. Sorabji eloquently described the effect of Busoni's Sonatina No. 6:

> In the eerily fascinating *Fantasia da Camera* on *Carmen,* one feels that the themes lose all their identity although not perceptibly altered, and that one is witnessing an extraordinary case of "possession" by an enormously powerful intelligence acting on something which is helpless in its grasp.[24]

Mysticism was always part of Sorabji's consciousness. He found much to relate to in this and other works of Busoni, who

> invests the comparatively commonplace Bizet "tunes" . . . with a strange and sinister charm and beauty which certainly has nothing to owe to Bizet! It is this quality of strangeness, hints and suggestions at dangerous powers and forces lurking just within or without reach, "Black Magic," and the fantastic, unreal, eerie beauty of this music that makes its hold over some of us so strong and its fascination so inescapable, so ineluctable.[25]

Busoni's masterly reworking of Bizet's material directly inspired Sorabji's own evocative adaptation of the same subject matter, which sinuously hints at Bizet's themes in a gossamer haze of sound. Sorabji called this adaptation a pastiche. He gave similar treatment to Chopin's "Minute" Waltz and to the "Hindu Merchant's Song" from Rimsky-Korsakov's opera *Sadko*, whose themes are combined and transformed into inspired exoticism. Hamelin has also composed his own free arrangements on themes by Rimsky-Korsakov, Chopin, and Rossini.

Sorabji found the source material for his pastiches quite ordinary but felt they were worth elaboration. Given his mystical and occult leanings, he was particularly interested in the idea of musical transformation—the concept that the original loses its own identity and merges with the transcriber's in an act of possession. On a practical level, Sorabji took care to distinguish between adaptations or paraphrases (the free manipulation of themes), arrangements (the note-for-note transference from one medium to another), and transcriptions (the translation of a work into another medium). "A transcription," he wrote,

> is a radically different thing, and is almost a rewriting of the work in terms of the new medium. Decorative matter may be added, derived harmonically from the original . . . as in the piano transcriptions by Busoni of Bach's organ works, in which the transcriber has sought literally to translate into pianistic equivalent the effect of these works as played by an accomplished organist. Here . . . will be a great deal of additional matter calling for a degree of ingenuity, skill, and artistry of the greatest order.[26]

Busoni's *Fantasia after J. S. Bach* displays just such artistry, incorporating material from three organ pieces that Bach based on chorales. To create his work, Busoni forged equal parts literal transcription, reconstruction of Bach's originals, and his own inventive music—all melded into a deeply moving conception. Busoni placed his Bach transcriptions into the general categories of arrangements, transcriptions, and free transcriptions. Similarly, Godowsky's preface to his Chopin studies instructively divides the field into five general categories:

> *Strict Transcriptions*—studies in which the text of the original is as closely followed as an adaptation for the left hand would allow . . . *Free Transcriptions* —studies in which the text is either a) freely treated, b) inverted, c) combined with another study, d) is being imitated through the medium of another study . . . *Cantus Firmus Versions*—studies in which the text of the original study in the right hand is strictly adhered to in the left hand of the version while the right hand is freely treated in a contrapuntal way . . . *Versions in form of Variations*—studies in which the text of the original étude is used as a basis for free variations . . . *Metamorphoses*—studies in which the character, design, and rhythm of the original text are altered while the architectural structure remains intact although the melodic and harmonic outline is often considerably modified.[27]

Not everyone was as careful and thorough as Godowsky. Feinberg observed that music editors often treat compositions as their own province and playground, willfully changing details to suit self-delusional whims. In such cases, the composer's original itself almost becomes a free adaptation:

> Instead of attentive and careful reading of the composer's text, understanding of his intention and purposes, and carefully preserving the composer's particular style, many editors deem it possible to redo and implicate their personal ideas in all the details of the text, adding duplications, transferring voices into other octaves, and almost in every case changing ligatures and performing directions. The editor condescendingly treats the composer as an enthusiastic madman or a spoilt child who has no time to engage in a precise recording of his intentions.[28]

Against Transcriptions . . .

Scriabin and Medtner carefully edited their own music but devoted no time to arrangements or transcriptions. By contrast, openness to others' ideas and a willingness to deal in quasi-original musical forms are hallmarks of the transcriber. How the results are received by critics, audiences, and musicians is another matter entirely, whatever a work's merit.

Significantly, however, many of the greatest musical thinkers scorn transcriptions, and their opinions must be taken seriously. Most of the time, the composer whose work is being transcribed is not around to offer an opinion. Bach and Chopin, after all, died well before the time of Busoni and Godowsky. When composer does meet composer, the interaction is not always smooth. After Busoni rescored the second of Arnold Schoenberg's Op. 11 piano pieces, the composer felt Busoni did him a true injustice and spent the bulk of a very long letter detailing the ways in which his intentions were not respected. Busoni wanted to publish his transcription side-by-side with Schoenberg's original, following the precedent that he and Godowsky had set with their respective Liszt and Bach transcriptions. Schoenberg responded:

> It is impossible for me to publish my piece together with a transcription which shows how I could have done it *better*. Which thus indicates that my piece is *imperfect*. And it is impossible to try to make the public believe that my piece is *good*, if I simultaneously indicate that it is not *good*. I could not do this—out of my instinct for self-preservation—even if I believed it. In this case I would either have to destroy my piece or *rework it myself*.

He argued succinctly against transcriptions, believing that they amounted to blatant manipulation and would *introduce* what I avoid, either fundamentally or according to my preferences; *add* what I myself . . . would never have devised, thus what is foreign or unattainable to me; *omit* what I would find necessary, or *improve* where I am, and must remain, imperfect. Thus a transcription would be bound to do me violence: whether it helps or hinders my work.[29]

Ironically, though, Schoenberg either sanctioned or prepared a number of transcriptions of his own and other composers' music.

Performers will often take liberties with an original score, as did Busoni, which Feinberg considered to be a low-level form of transcription popular with a self-indulgent musical demimonde:

The practice of concert performances, and—not infrequently—those of famous pianists, demonstrates that even a slight deviation from the composer's notation, either adding an extra note in a chord or changing some other detail, usually leads to a misrepresentation of the composer's intention. Most often such "improvements" prove that the performer does not fully understand the composer's style. . . . It is a pity that many superb musicians and remarkable performers at times do not possess enough tactfulness or artistic sensitivity. They take liberties in changing a composition when they feel disposed to do so, not only on the concert stage which could be explained by a sudden improvisational whim, but also in thought-out and thoroughly developed versions of the classics. Even the greatest performers sin with their excess liberties, Busoni among them. . . . In cases when there are no grounds to question the perfection of a work by a composer possessing impeccable style, the editor's unasked-for intrusion is especially shocking. Therefore, many experienced performers prefer to study compositions with the help of the principal, unedited publications that precisely reproduce the composer's notation.[30]

. . . and in Defense

The debate over transcriptions continues into the twenty-first century, framed with the question, "Does anyone have an ethical right to alter another's work?" Sorabji wasted no time in refuting that premise: "How a question of 'ethics,' the principles of moral conduct . . . can have any imaginable bearing upon the arrangement of a composition written originally for one medium to suit another medium, is not clear to the eye of reason."[31]

Godowsky frequently pointed to great music that was better voiced in transcription, insisting, "There are few things so flawless that they cannot be improved."[32] He used the word "improved" carefully and sparingly, but it was enough—critics continue to seize upon it, accusing him of arrogance. In most cases, however, Godowsky simply aimed to expand and expound upon those works that he considered already in the category of genius. He and Busoni well understood the risks of tampering with such a universal icon as Bach, but both composer-pianists argued their points persuasively. With respect to his Bach transcriptions, Godowsky admitted:

> In venturing to transcribe these works I fully realized the burden of such a responsibility. I likewise took into consideration the possibility of the adverse critical opinion which I was courting by treading on such sacred soil, by trespassing the portals of tradition. In a number of instances Bach himself has shown that he approved of transcriptions, arrangements, adaptations, and diversified versions of the same work. Nor has he limited himself to his own compositions, for he has not hesitated to arrange freely works by other composers of his period for instruments other than those for which they were originally intended. . . . [M]y endeavor has been to develop the polyphony and the harmony in the spirit of the master and his period. . . . I wish to make clear that I have never introduced any themes, motives, or counter-melodies which were not a logical outgrowth of the inherent musical content.[33]

Feinberg also advocated the art of transcription; he was, however, generally more faithful to the composer's original notation and suggested a firmer approach than Godowsky's:

> The only area where the pianist is entitled to make creative alterations to a composer's style is through transcriptions and arrangements. However, one should avoid unnecessary deviation, excessive rhetoric with incompatible passages, and adornments contrary to the composer's aims. The task of transcription is to represent the original's sonic character by other means, while preserving, as far as possible, the composition's style. It cannot be done mechanically. One must have a good knowledge of his instrument's resources, and creatively find sufficient forms and new expressive means to uncover the composer's intent.[34]

One musician with the requisite knowledge and creativity is Kocsis, who provides a twenty-first-century perspective:

> I try to be altogether faithful to the notes of the original, much more so than a Busoni or a Godowsky. It's quite difficult to establish the borderline between paraphrases and transcriptions. What Busoni does is much more on the paraphrase side, and I greatly enjoy his works. My firm opinion about the Chopin-Godowsky studies is that they were conceived and written for technical reasons.

Stephen Hough and many of his peers are inspired by authenticity and motivated to delve into the composer's mind. Must one choose, however, between transcriptions and original music to be considered a serious artist? Thankfully, they are no longer considered mutually exclusive preserves. Hough offers a comparison:

Any great actor would not have a career if he could act only one kind of role. Sir Laurence Olivier, for example, appeared in the most serious theater, but also in comedy, on television, and on film. Actors bring their gifts to any situation and I don't see why it should be any different for a musician. People may have dismissed Busoni for his Bach transcriptions, not realizing that he was an amazing intellectual and a great composer in his own right, and had enormous reverence and erudition toward Bach. The same holds true with Godowsky, who had a deep love for Chopin. Some of the most fascinating examples of romantic counterpoint that we have come from the Chopin-Godowsky studies. They have enormous intellectual and creative virtuosity behind them.

Hough's three "Piano Album" recordings include his own transcriptions, as well as those by Godowsky and others. These discs and others have received little of the criticism leveled at the transcribers among The Eight in their own time. Hough's career essentially began in 1984, by which time the tide of opinion had turned. Even when Wild, Jorge Bolet, and Shura Cherkassky were playing in the 1960s and 1970s, their programming of transcriptions rarely sat well with the critics, and they were often not taken seriously as artists. Hough offers an explanation:

> It likely had to do with postwar modernism that was happening in all of the arts, as well as an exaggerated intellectualism, which comes from lack of self-confidence. People tend to become intellectual snobs when they lack conviction about what they really think and feel, so they retreat into these opinions that make them feel safe and impressive to other people. Another negative factor with transcriptions concerned a reaction against the extremes of the "personality" composer-pianists at the turn of the century. People came to hear de Pachmann or Paderewski rather than the music itself. Such a reaction toward the personality cult was positive on the whole, but as with most such things, it went too far. Then came original-instrument research and *Urtext* editions, and the polemics became absolutely ridiculous.

Feinberg realized that the great composer-pianists bring intellect, education, experience, and insight to the process of transcribing a composer's work—a meeting of minds that may transcend generations or centuries. "An outstanding performer," Feinberg asserted,

> having dedicated his life toward working to fulfill various composers' intentions, having spent many hours devoted to self-training and mastery of technique, having comprehended special sound secrets only he is familiar with—can hardly stay indifferent to flaws or shortcomings in music which can be found even with the greatest composers. It would be wrong always to attribute his amendments and corrections to his immodesty; he often strives to cross borders of the inadequate material presented to him. . . . In the history of music there are examples of great collaborations full of fruitful and

selfless labor. . . . Many transcriptions of Bach's organ compositions made by great masters of pianism—Busoni . . . and others—certainly belong to this category.[35]

With the exceptions of Scriabin and Medtner, each of The Eight significantly enhanced the art of transcription. Alkan filtered works of the classical repertoire through his elfin imagination. Busoni's focus on Bach and the organ led to the formulation of advanced touch and pedaling principles, forever altering his approach to composition and performance. Godowsky's forays into the field brilliantly exceeded previously imagined possibilities. Rachmaninov and Feinberg gave us new ways to experience the classics, from Bach to Tchaikovsky. Sorabji's contributions to the genre cleverly synthesized, in equal measure, Alkan, Busoni, and Godowsky. Above all, their transcriptions—resourceful and provocative, elaborate and vital—recreate the prismatic possibilities of romanticism under the piano's enduring guidance.

10 TOWARD THE FUTURE
The Piano, the Composer-Pianist, and The Eight

Throughout history, the piano has greatly benefited from the quality and depth of its celebrated practitioners. The piano prevails over any other instrument: more concertos have been written for it, more young people begin to learn on it, audiences have consistently favored it, and more pianos and keyboards are being sold than ever before. There have been several composer-violinists, such as Niccolò Paganini and Henryk Wieniawski; but where, for example, are the composer-cellists or the composer-clarinetists? Rachmaninov put it bluntly: "The piano is the most obvious instrument and for that reason will always be the one which has the greatest appeal to the amateur," he said. "It is the door to musical literature, because of its command of bass, treble, and other inner voices. It is simply indispensable in music."[1] Godowsky concurred: "The piano as a medium for expression is a whole world by itself. No other instrument can fill or replace its own say in the world of emotion, sentiment, poetry, imagery, and fancy."[2] He offered an optimistic message for the future:

> The piano will survive, because it is the best vehicle yet devised with which to explore the vast and magnificent realms of music. This, entirely apart from the great literature of the instrument itself, provides man with a means of gratifying his inborn musical curiosity. . . . [I]f one plays the violin, the cello, the flute, the French horn, or any other non-keyboard instrument . . . one is confined, for the most part, to a single melodic line. With the piano, one has both a melodic and harmonic line of expression. Each of the ten digits may be employed.[3]

But few pianists are capable of carrying forward Godowsky's tradition. A perennial question one must ask when hearing little-known music is whether it has been given the best possible performance. Hough offers a generally accepted viewpoint: "This is terribly true of Godowsky, for unless his music is played supremely well, it sounds clumsy and vulgar and does not really make sense. To be effective, it must be played with extraordinary refinement."

252

Rachmaninov and the others of The Eight wrote music for the piano that possessed the breadth of an entire orchestra. Godowsky made clear his own contribution:

The pianoforte, being apart from its strongly individual character in a sense a miniature orchestra, should . . . benefit by the important strides which modern composition and instrumentation have made in the direction of polyphony, harmony, tone coloring, and the use of a vastly extended range in modern counterpoint.[4]

Of course, no instrument can by itself transmit the extreme range of musical expression of which an orchestra is capable. Busoni spoke of limits and possibilities, noting that the piano's disadvantages are

obvious, great, and irremediable: the impossibility of sustaining the sound, and the pitiless, sharp division of the keyboard into unalterable half-tones. But its excellencies and prerogatives are little miracles. With it a single person can command a complete whole, and it surpasses all other instruments by producing the softest and the loudest sound in one single register. Trumpets can blare and not murmur, flutes the reverse. The pianoforte can do both. It admits of the highest and lowest available sounds.[5]

The pianist can alter the quality of individual notes within the same chord by weighting one note louder than the rest, producing, in combination with judicious use of the pedals, the illusion of more than two hands at work. Pianists spend countless hours balancing chords in order to find the most expressive, focused sound possible. Nonpianists often find it hard to believe that different artists can cause the same instrument to sound starkly dissimilar. Sorabji explained:

A piano that sounds vile under one pair of hands will sound ravishing under those of another. *A* produces a hard harsh dry tone, brittle and gritty, *B* a lovely full rich one, from the same piano. Why? How? The variety of *timbre* that a great artist like the fabulous Busoni . . . can draw from this (technically) monochrome instrument is breathtaking. Telepathic suggestion? Busoni often marks his scores of piano works with such things as *quasi trombe* or *quasi flauto*, and he really could make them sound like that. Theoretically and scientifically, he couldn't, but he did![6]

Actually, the rewards of his compositional life gave Busoni the deeper satisfaction. He candidly described the composer-pianist's aesthetic:

It is an effort for me to practice the piano, yet one cannot leave it! It is like an animal, whose head always grows again, however much one cuts off. Composing, by comparison, is like going along a road which is more difficult but beautiful and changeable. One is always folding up long stretches of it, reaching stages further on and leaving them behind, and its final goal is unknown and unattainable.[7]

As the romantic age waned—especially with the deaths of Medtner and Rachmaninov several generations into the twentieth century—the piano generally fell into disfavor as the cutting-edge compositional choice of leading composers. But the fashions of music have reinstated tonal romanticism and the piano, and we are seeing a resurgence of new music composed for it.

The surviving recordings by The Eight (excepting, of course, Alkan, who died just as Edison began his famous experiments), although fraught with technological limitations and inhibitions, remain invaluable guides. The pianist András Schiff notes the importance of learning from the great composer-pianists:

> To me, how a composer plays is almost sacred. Recordings by Medtner, for example, though not perfection, are such important documents. I leave it to others to play the music of Rachmaninov, but I love his piano playing above all and no one can touch him in his own music. The authority that composer-pianists bring to their works is simply incomparable.

Several of The Eight are still generally known for musical ventures outside the realm of solo-piano composition—Busoni for his opera *Doktor Faust* and his Bach transcriptions, Feinberg and Godowsky for their transcriptions, and Sorabji for his two books. In addition to their daunting achievements as composer-pianists, Busoni and Rachmaninov are also remembered as master conductors. Given the complications inherent in performing even one musical activity surpassingly well, their breed of pianist-conductor-composer—equally comfortable in front of piano, podium, and paper—remains exceedingly rare. Zoltán Kocsis and Mikhail Pletnev are two notable figures who have gained recognition and acceptance in these areas of their art.

With romanticism back in vogue at the beginning of the twenty-first century, pianists and audiences have effected a resurgence of interest in music by The Eight. Beyond Hamelin's influential advocacy, other pianists from around the world have been drawn into exploring these avenues of the repertoire. The Italian Francesco Libetta has made something of a specialty performing the Chopin-Godowsky studies, with extraordinary technique and abandon. Another Italian, Carlo Grante, has also played (and recorded) these works, as well as other Godowsky transcriptions, and has explored the music of Busoni and Sorabji. The American Michael Habermann befriended Sorabji and has extensively performed and recorded that composer's music. The Australian Geoffrey Tozer and the British Hamish Milne have persuasively recorded Medtner's complete piano works. Scholars such as Marc-André Roberge, Larry Sitsky, and Donald Manildi have also made important contributions to our understanding of The Eight. Naturally, the Internet has played a considerable role as well (a starting point is *www.88keys.com*). The Alkan, Feinberg, Godowsky, Rachmaninov, and Scriabin Societies; the International Medtner Foundation; and the Sorabji Archive all exist to promulgate The Eight and to provide access to music scores and other related materials. Dover Publications has reprinted significant collections of music by Alkan, Busoni, Medtner, Rachmaninov, and Scriabin. In 2000 the publisher Carl Fischer reprinted a large volume from its extensive Godowsky archives. Boosey and Hawkes, and Zimmermann, continue to make available scores by a number of The Eight. Listeners and readers, amateurs and professionals, are thus exposed to fascinating program choices and magnificent music, while vibrant performing traditions develop and flourish. The piano has once again assumed an elevated position in our emotional, intellectual, and social lives. Rachmaninov's words are still true more than half a century after his death:

> The frontiers of the art of composition for the piano have by no means all been reached. There is much that can be done. It is a fascinating territory; and there will be countless explorers who will see glorious vistas, as did Chopin, and not horrible and loathsome chasms as have some of the modern futurists.[8]

A vital tradition continues, supported by concert pianists and the composers who write for them. Ronald Stevenson—pianist, authority on Busoni, and composer of the *Prelude, Fugue, and Fantasy on Busoni's "Faust"*—has written a work entitled *Le festin d'Alkan* for Hamelin. Lowell Liebermann's *Album for the Young*, Op. 43, also includes a tribute to Alkan. Frederic Rzewski's *The People United Will Never Be Defeated!*, long a mainstay in Hamelin's repertoire, has been called the twentieth century's *Diabelli Variations*. György Ligeti's magnificent études, although without the benefit of a century of performance tradition, have won an assured place in the repertoire. William Bolcom has also composed substantial, idiomatic piano études. Schiff and Kocsis are closely involved with the music of the Hungarian composer-pianist György Kurtág. The Briton Thomas Adès made his mark as a composer-pianist in his twenties, and his recordings are now eagerly anticipated. Are these isolated instances of musical cross-pollination? Opinion is divided. Schiff, for one, laments the state of the art:

> We do not presently have the wonderful wealth of great nineteenth-century composer-pianists—composition and piano playing are too separated. We have this most incredible repertoire, but it's not really growing and not many composers are writing good piano music nowadays. Two notable exceptions are Ligeti and Kurtág, but they are solitary figures.

Schiff's compatriot Kocsis offers a more sanguine assessment:

> I am optimistic going forward. In the recent past, composers generally have not played an instrument properly, nor have instrumentalists been interested

in composing. Sooner or later it will unite again. I would very much like to believe that the future will bring more Busonis and Rachmaninovs. If we specialize too much, then there simply will not be an audience for certain composers. The human attributes in Kurtág's music are extraordinary, of which I would like to see much more among present-day composers.

Time will prove the accuracy of any premature predictions. The pianist Krystian Zimerman believes that the repertoire is growing stronger than ever, even if it is not always immediately recognized:

> One always reads negative things about contemporary music, in whatever century—such as the first reviews of the Brahms D Minor concerto or several articles that Schumann wrote. It's a syndrome that was always there. We just never learned how to cope with it, because it takes the experience of more than one generation—with a long enough historical perspective—to make lasting judgments.[9]

In assessing the future of the composer-pianist's art, Harold C. Schonberg looks back to Mozart's example:

> The best clavier player in his day, and a pretty good composer, so they say. If someone came along with the talent of a Mozart or a Rachmaninov, it's hard to think that they wouldn't be recognized. There are very few today, but the good ones, like Kocsis and Hamelin, are immediately recognized. Of course, I can't speak for other critics. When I go to a concert, I don't care whether the pianist composes or cooks. What matters is what I hear and what my ears tell me.

Even those who do practice this specialized art may be reticent to accept their place in the glorious composer-pianist tradition. Hough acknowledges:

> It's almost not for me to say whether I can be called a composer-pianist. Someone I knew once described himself as a conservative intellectual; whether it's anyone's right to call oneself a conservative intellectual is the sort of qualitative judgment in the same sense as whether my attempts at transcriptions and original pieces make me into a composer.

Busoni's attributes as a creative musician thoroughly reflected his ideology. He set forth his beliefs in a poetic statement of qualities that every enduring composer-pianist must possess:

> The great artist must . . . be widely educated in music and literature and in all matters affecting human existence. The artist must also have character. If one of these requisites is missing, the deficiency will be apparent in every phrase he plays. Then add to this feeling, temperament, imagination, poetry, and finally that personal magnetism which sometimes enables the artist to inspire four thousand people, strangers, whom chance has brought together, with

one and the same state of feeling. . . . Shall one add the feeling for form and style, and the virtue of good taste and originality? How could one ever enumerate all the qualities required? But one requirement comes before all others: *Anyone who will master the language of art must have nurtured his life through the soul.*[10]

As separated as they were in time and location, the rest of The Eight essentially shared Busoni's precepts. But the search for artistic truth and fulfillment comes at a price. It is difficult enough to compose and perform steadily, as Medtner and Scriabin discovered. Busoni, Godowsky, and Rachmaninov, with their many additional activities, suffered from ill health, overwork, stress, and fatigue that shortened their lives. Not coincidentally, the reclusive Alkan and Sorabji lived longer than their brethren in The Eight.

Composer-pianists, who must of course possess the skills and inspiration their related professions require, have always struggled to find meaningful stretches of dedicated compositional time and the energy. Hough admits to a common plight among pianists with the aspiration to compose:

In the early years of a career, there's so little time to do anything except learn the repertoire, travel, and play every concert that comes into the diary. There does come a point when one can begin reducing those commitments. I do have piles and sketches of music that I hope to find time to come back to. I can't say yet that I feel there's something great waiting to come out, although I do feel a burning urge to create in some way rather than just to be a recreative artist. There's surely something there. With all that goes into playing and composing simultaneously, it's a difficult proposition. To treat playing the piano as a craft in itself, the amount of time spent at the instrument is significantly more than it might be under other circumstances. Also, the type of chosen repertoire will often dictate how much time is necessary at the piano. If one's repertoire is mainly the Germanic school of Brahms, Beethoven, and Schubert, this may require less time in developing the pure craft. Playing Godowsky or Alkan, however, requires a level of physical involvement and refinement that goes some measure beyond that. Finding different ways of using the pedals, of voicing, sound, and shading are all stimulating and absorbing, although trying to find the time to do everything is just so difficult. But I am indeed optimistic about the future of the composer-pianist. Marc-André Hamelin has done some wonderful work, and I'm sure he has a lot more to write than he already has. There are others. What I've heard and played of Olli Mustonen's music, for example, is extremely interesting. For all of his wonderful eccentricity, he's someone in whose playing one hears the mind of a true composer.

The future of the composer-pianist's art also appears likely to flower under the influence of jazz, which in a way has allowed composer-pianists to be reborn. Many colleges and conservatories, including the Juilliard School, offer jazz programs. Pianists who demonstrate the kind of spontaneity that comes with improvisation will often notate their music. The Russian composer-pianist Nikolai Kapustin— whose concert music brilliantly fuses jazz with technique in the manner of Liszt— falls into this category.

In the classical realm, students majoring in piano performance ideally should be exposed to composition more than is presently the case. Earl Wild's sights extend beyond the schooling of young pianists. He would like to see a foundation supporting composer-pianists that would remove the burden of having to perform constantly, thus generating essential time for creation. Wild and many forward-thinking educators feel that young people should be encouraged to compose their own music from the time they first start playing the piano. More young people are studying music now than ever before, but Western educational systems would do well to allow a more comprehensive learning approach that includes composition in addition to art, literature, history, languages, and other disciplines. The narrow focus on piano performance may well produce incredible virtuosos, but, as Arthur Rubinstein once said, they are often left with the personality of soda jerks. Hough agrees that the composer-pianist ethic must begin early in the music schools, which generally tend to be one sided:

> So many students go into conservatories unrealistically expecting to come out and have Horowitz-type careers, with a focus on the type of quick material success that surely precludes serious work in composition. Almost every Russian pianist writes music, no matter how slight, but it is nurtured and fostered at a young age. Jacob Lateiner said that everyone who plays an instrument should write down music every day, even if it was someone else's just copied out. The physical pencil against the five staves is an important connection with what we do. So often composers have such a greater grasp of music than someone who's never composed. One turns to the score with a certain kind of reverence, even detective work, in search for what the composer is trying to express.

In all fields of performing activity, especially in modern times, the composer's intention is the interpreter's ultimate destination. Classical composers are looked upon as music's founding fathers, the written scores their legacy and our constitution. The greatest composer-pianists uniquely fuse past traditions and often begin their own. Alkan, Sorabji, Busoni, Godowsky, Feinberg, Scriabin, Medtner, Rachmaninov—any serious composer-pianist of the twenty-first century will return to these names for guidance and inspiration. They represent a living heritage in music's diverse elements. Within the piano's domain, The Eight remain decisive arbiters of the elusive balance between performance and creation.

COMPLETE SOLO PIANO WORKS

For each of The Eight, the solo piano remained the basis of their muse (as it does for Hamelin). Although Busoni and Rachmaninov in particular branched out into other genres, even they saw the piano at the center of their creative activity. Accordingly, the following works lists present their complete oeuvre for solo piano. Individual works within a suite or group of pieces have been listed if their names have descriptive significance. Additionally, although Scriabin and Medtner avoided transcriptions and arrangements, these forms assumed great importance to the others and are therefore included here. Further similarities abound. Godowsky and Rachmaninov wrote contrapuntal arrangements of "The Star-Spangled Banner." Busoni and Rachmaninov both used the same Chopin theme (Prelude No. 20) for significant sets of variations. Hamelin's *Con intimissimo sentimento* is comprised of seven pieces ending with a Berceuse, as with Busoni's elegies. Hamelin and Rachmaninov wrote elaborate cadenzas to Liszt's famous Hungarian Rhapsody No. 2. Alkan, Scriabin, and Rachmaninov composed substantial sets of preludes. Feinberg, Medtner, and Scriabin were among the greatest exponents of sonata form. Readers will notice additional parallels.

Titles are given in their original language, unless they are better known by their English equivalents. Dates given are those of completion (or publication, if dates of composition are unknown). With few exceptions, unpublished works are omitted.

Alkan

Solo Piano

Opus	Title	Date
1	Variations on a Theme by [Daniel] Steibelt [from the Rondo pastoral of the Third Concerto, Orage]	1826
2	Variations: Les omnibus	1829
3	Rondoletto: Il était un petit homme	c. 1833

Opus	Title	Date
5	Rondo based on Largo al factotum, from Rossini's Barber of Seville	c. 1833
8	Six morceaux caractéristiques [published in Leipzig in 1839 as Op. 16, and—c. 1840—included among the twelve pieces of Op. 74] Une nuit d'hiver La pâque Sérénade Une nuit d'été Les moissonneurs L'opéra	1838
12	Rondeau chromatique [The following Opp. 12, 13, 15, and 16 were designated by Alkan as Twelve Caprices in Four Books.]	1833
12	Trois improvisations dans le style brillant	1837
13	Trois andantes romantiques	1837
15	Souvenirs: Trois morceaux dans le genre pathétique Aime-moi Le vent Morte	1837
16	Tre scherzi	1837
16, No. 4	Variations on Ah! Segnata é la mia morte, from Donizetti's Anna Bolena	1834
16, No. 5	Variations on La tremenda ultrice spada, from Bellini's I Capuleti e I Montecchi	1834
16, No. 6	Variations, quasi fantaisie sur une barcarolle napolitaine	1834
17	Concert étude: Le preux	1844
22	Nocturne (No. 1)	1844
23	Saltarelle	1844
24	Gigue et air de ballet, dans le style ancien	1844
25	Alleluia	1844
26	Marche funèbre	1846
27	Marche triomphale	1846
27	Étude: Le chemin de fer	1844
29	Étude: Bourrée d'Auvergne	c. 1846
31	Twenty-Five Preludes in All the Major and Minor Keys, for Piano or Organ, in Three Books	1847
32, No. 1	Premier recueil d'impromptus Vaghezza L'amitié Fantasietta alla morcsca La foi	c. 1848

Opus	Title	Date
32, No. 2	Deuxième recueil d'impromptus	1849
33	Grande sonate: Les quatre ages	1848
34	Scherzo focoso	1848
35	Twelve Études in the Major Keys	1848
37	Trois marches quasi cavalleria	1857
38	Premier recueil de chants	1857
38	Deuxième recueil de chants	1857
39	Twelve Études in the Minor Keys	1857
	Comme le vent	
	En rythme molossique	
	Scherzo diabolico	
	Symphony:	
	Allegro moderato	
	Marche funèbre	
	Minuet	
	Finale	
	Concerto:	
	Allegro assai	
	Adagio	
	Allegretto alla barbaresca	
	Overture	
	Le festin d'Ésope [variations]	
41	Trois petites fantaisies	1857
42	Réconciliation, petit caprice en forme de zorcico	1857
	(danse basque)	
45	Salut, cendre du pauvre!	1856
46	Minuetto alla tedesca	1857
50	Capriccio alla soldatesca	1859
50a.	Esquisse: Le tambour bat aux champs	1859
51	Trois menuets	1859
52	Super flumina Babylonis [paraphase based upon	1859
	Psalm 137]	
53	Caprice: Quasi-caccia	1859
55	Introduction and Impromptu: Une fusée	1859
57	Nocturnes Nos. 2 and 3	1859
60	Deux petites pièces	1859
	Ma chère liberté	
	Ma chère servitude	
60a.	Nocturne No. 4: Le grillon	1859
61	Sonatine	1861

Opus	Title	Date
63	Esquisses: Forty-Eight Motifs	1861
	First Suite:	
	La vision	
	Le staccatissimo	
	Le legatissimo	
	Les cloches	
	Quasi coro	
	Fuguette	
	Le frisson	
	Pseudo-naïveté	
	Confidence	
	Increpatio	
	Les soupirs	
	Barcarollette	
	Second Suite:	
	Ressouvenir	
	Duettino	
	Tutti de concerto dans le genre ancien	
	Fantaisie	
	Petit prélude à trios	
	Liedchen	
	Grâces	
	Petite marche villageoise	
	Morituri te salutant	
	Innocenzia	
	L'homme aux sabots, d'un pas ordinaire	
	Contredanse	
	Third Suite:	
	La poursuite	
	Petit air	
	Rigaudon	
	Inflexibilité	
	Délire	
	Petit air dolent	
	Début de quatuor	
	Minuettino	
	Fais dodo	
	Odi profanum vulgus et arceo: favete linguis	
	Musique militaire	
	Toccatina	
	Fourth Suite:	
	Scherzettino	

Opus	Title	Date
	Le ciel vous soit toujours prospère!	
	Héraclite et Démocrite	
	Attendez-moi sous l'orme	
	Les enharmoniques	
	Petit air à 5 voix	
	Notturnino-innamorato	
	Transports	
	Les diablotins	
	Le premier billet doux	
	Scherzetto	
	En songe	
	Laus Deo [without opus number]	
65	Troisième recueil de chants	c. 1866
67	Quatrième recueil de chants	c. 1868
70	Cinquième recueil de chants	c. 1872
74	Le mois: Douze morceaux caractéristiques [Nos. 1, 4, 5, 7, 8, and 12 were published as Op. 8]	c. 1840
	Suite 1:	
	Une nuit d'hiver	
	Carnaval	
	La retraite	
	Suite 2:	
	La pâque	
	Sérénade	
	Promenade sur l'eau	
	Suite 3:	
	Une nuit d'été	
	Les moissonneurs	
	L'hallali	
	Suite 4:	
	Gros temps	
	Le mourant	
	L'opéra	
75	Toccatina	c. 1872
76	Trois grandes études [for the two hands separately and reunited]	c. 1839
	Fantaisie [left hand alone]	
	Introduction, variations, et finale [right hand alone]	
	Étude à mouvement semblable et perpetual [both hands]	

Opus	Title	Date
WoO	[Arranged alphabetically:]	
	Album-leaf	1863
	Album-leaf: Apassionato [revised and published as Délire, Op. 63, No. 29]	1847
	Fantaisie: Désire	1844
	Caprice or étude	1843
	Fantasticheria	1868
	Deuxième fantasticheria: Chapeau bas!	1872
	Impromptu	1844
	Jean qui pleure et Jean qui rit: Due fughe da camera	c. 1840
	Palpitamento	1855 (unpubl.)
	Petit conte	1859
	Petite mélodie: Les regrets de la Nonnette	1854 (unpubl.)
	Variations on a Theme from Donizetti's Ugo, conte di Parigi	1842
	Zorcico: Danse ibérienne	1869

Transcriptions, Arrangements, and Cadenzas for Solo Piano

Title	Date
Souvenirs des concerts du Conservatoire [in their original order]	1847
Marcello, Benedetto	
Psalm 18: I cieli immensi narrano	
Gluck, Christoph Willibald	
Armide: Jamais dans ces beaux lieux,	
Iphigénie en Tauride: Choeur des scythes	
Haydn, Franz Joseph	
Symphony No. 36: Andante	
Grétry, André-Ernest-Modeste	
Les deux avares: La garde passe, il est minuit	
Mozart, Wolfgang Amadeus	
Symphony No. 40, K. 550: Minuet	
Souvenirs des concerts du Conservatoire [second series]	1861
Handel, George Frideric	
Samson: Choeur des prêtres de Dagon	
Gluck	
Orfeo ed Euridice: Gavotte	

Title	Date
Haydn	
String Quartet Op. 64, No. 5: Finale	
Mozart	
Thamos, König in Ägypten, K. 345/336a: Motet	
Ne pulvis et cinis	
Beethoven, Ludwig van	
Bundeslied, Op.122	
Weber, Carl Maria von	
Oberon: Choeur des filles de la mer	
Souvenirs de musique de chambre	c. 1869
Rigaudons en suite, de la collection des petits	
violons et hautbois de Louis XIV	
Bach, Johann Sebastian	
Flute Sonata BWV 1031: Siciliano	
Haydn	
String Quartet Op. 76, No. 2: Minuet	
Mozart	
String Quartet K. 464: Andante	
Beethoven	
String Quartet Op. 130: Cavatina	
Weber	
Piano Trio: Scherzo	
Beethoven, Ludwig van	1860
Piano Concerto No. 3, Op. 37: Allegro con brio	
[with cadenza]	
Beethoven	unknown
Die Ruinen von Athen: Choeur des derviches	
Meyerbeer, Giacomo	c. 1849
Le prophète: Overture	
Mozart, Wolfgang Amadeus	1861
Piano Concerto No. 20, K. 466 [with cadenzas]	

Busoni

SOLO PIANO

Opus	Title	Date
3	Five Pieces	1877
	Prelude	
	Minuet	
	Gavotte	
	Étude	
	Gigue	
	Three Pieces	1884
4	Scherzo	
5	Prelude and Fugue	
6	Scène de ballet	
8	Scherzo [originally from a sonata]	1877
9	Una festa di villaggio: Sei pezzi caratteristici	1882
	Preparazione alla festa	
	Marcia trionfale	
	In chiesa	
	La fiera	
	Danza	
	Notte	
10	Tre pezzi nello stilo antico	1882
	Minuet	
	Sonatina	
	Gigue	
11	Danze antiche	1833
	Minuet	
	Gavotte	
	Gigue	
	Bourrée	
12	Racconti fantastici (Tre pezzi caratteristici)	1878
	Duello	
	Klein Zaches [after E. T. A. Hoffmann]	
	La caverna di Steenfoll [after Wilhelm Hauff]	
13	Danza notturna	1882
—	Macchiette medievali	1883
	Dama	
	Cavaliere	
	Paggio	
	Guerriero	
	Astrologo	
	Trovatore	

Opus	Title	Date
14	Minuet	1878
16	Six Études	1883
17	Étude en forme de variations	1883
20	Two Ballet Scenes	1885
21	Prelude and Fugue in Free Style	1878
22	Variations and Fugue in Free Form after Chopin's Prelude, Op. 28, No. 20	1884
—	Gavotte	1878
30, No. 1	Contrapuntal Dance Piece	1890
30, No. 2	Little Ballet Scene	1890
30a	Two Dance Pieces	
	Waffentanz	
	Friedenstanz	1914
32	Marcia di paesani e contadine	1883
33	Four Ballet Scenes in the Form of Concert Waltzes	1892
33a	Four Ballet Scenes, Waltz, and Galop	Rev. 1913 (Op. 30)
33b	Six Pieces	
	Schwermut	
	Frohsinn	
	Scherzino	
	Fantasia in modo antico	
	Finnische Ballade	
	Exeunt omnes	1896
36	Prelude and Fugue	1882
37	Twenty-Four Preludes	1879–80
61	Minuetto capriccioso	1879
70	Gavotte	1880
—	Elegies	1907
	Nach der Wendung	
	All'Italia (in modo napoletano)	
	Meine Seele bangt und hofft zu dir (Chorale Prelude)	
	Turandots Frauengemach (Intermezzo)	
	Die Nächtlichen (Waltz)	
	Erscheinung (Nocturne)	
	Berceuse	
—	An die Jugend	1908
	Preludio, fughetta ed esercizio	
	Preludio, fuga e fuga figurate [study after Bach's Well-Tempered Clavier]	

Opus	Title	Date
[—	An die Jugend]	
	Giga, bolero e variazione [study after Mozart]	
	Introduzione, capriccio ed epilogo (Paganinesco)	
—	Esquisse: Nuit de Noël	1908
—	Sonatina No. 1	1910
—	Sonatina No. 2	1912
—	Indianisches Tagebuch	1915
—	Sonatina No. 3 (ad usum infantis)	1916
—	Sonatina No. 4 (in die Nativitatis Christi MCMXVII)	1917
—	Three Albumleaves	
	Zurich	1917
	Rome	1921
	Berlin	1921
—	Sonatina No. 6 (Chamber-Fantasy on Bizet's Carmen)	1920
—	Toccata: Prelude, fantasia, chaconne	1921
—	Prelude et étude en arpèges	—
—	Ten Variations on a Chopin Prelude [revision of Op. 22]	1922
—	Five Short Pieces for the Study of Part-Playing	1923

Transcriptions, Arrangements, and Cadenzas for Solo Piano

Composer and Title	Date
Bach	
Bach-Busoni Edition	
Vol. 1: Arrangements I—Study Works	1914–15
Dedication	
Eighteen Little Preludes and a Fughetta	
Fifteen Two-Part Inventions	
Fifteen Three-Part Inventions	
Four Duets	
Prelude, Fugue, and Allegro	
Vol. 2: Arrangements II—Master Works	
Chromatic Fantasy and Fugue	1911
Piano Concerto in D Minor	
Goldberg Variations	1914
Vol. 3: Transcriptions	
Prelude and Fugue for Organ in D Major	1888
Prelude and Fugue for Organ in E-flat Major	1890
Toccata for Organ in D Minor	1900
Toccata for Organ in C Major	1900
Ten Chorale Preludes	1898

Composer and Title	Date
Partita for Solo Violin No. 2 in D Minor, BWV 1004: Chaconne	1897
Vol. 4: Compositions and Free Transcriptions	1909
Fantasia after J. S. Bach	1909
Preludio, fuga, e fuga figurata	1914
Capriccio on the Departure of a Beloved Brother	1915
Fantasia, adagio e fuga	1912
Chorale Prelude and Fugue on a Fragment by Bach [first version of Fantasia contrappuntistica]	1910
Fantasia contrappuntistica [second version, definitive edition]	1894
	1915
Vol. 5: The Well-Tempered Clavier, Book 1	
Vol. 6: The Well-Tempered Clavier, Book 2	
Vol. 7: Supplements to Vols. 1–4	1920
Arrangements:	
Three Toccatas (E Minor, G Minor, and G Major)	1920
Fantasy and Fugue (A Minor)	
Fantasy, Fugue, Andante, and Scherzo	1916
Compositions and Free Transcriptions:	
Sonatina brevis in Signo Joannis Sebastiani Magni [Sonatina No. 5; free transcription of Bach's Small Fantasia and Fugue in D Minor]	1919
Sarabande con partite	
Aria variata alla maniera italiana	
Two Contrapuntal Studies after J. S. Bach	1907
Fantasia and Fugue	1907
Canonic Variations and Fugue on the Theme of Frederick the Great [from A Musical Offering]	1917
Beethoven	
Ecossaises [concert arrangements]	1889
Two Cadenzas to the Fourth Concerto, Op. 58	1890
Brahms	
Six Chorale Preludes [originally for the organ], Op. 122	1902
Cornelius, Peter	
Fantasia on Themes from The Barber of Baghdad	1886

Composer and Title	Date
Liszt	
Complete Études	1910–24
Three Fantasies	
Fantasy and Fugue on the Chorale Ad nos,	1897
ad salutarem undam, from Meyerbeer's	
Le Prophête [freely transcribed]	
Fantasy on Two Motifs from Mozart's	1918
Le Nozze di Figaro	
Réminiscences de Don Juan [concert fantasy	1905
on themes from Mozart's Don Giovanni]	1920
Heroic March in Hungarian Style	
Hungarian Rhapsody No. 19 [freely arranged]	1904
Scherzo (G Minor)	1909
Mephisto Waltz [transcribed from the orchestral	
score]	
Polonaise in E Major, with final cadenza	
Mozart	
Andantino from the Concerto K. 271, Freely	1914
Arranged with Cadenza	
Cadenzas for Piano Concertos:	1916
No. 9, K. 271	1922
No. 17, K. 453	1920
No. 19, K. 459	1907
No. 20, K. 466	1922
No. 21, K. 467	1919
No. 22, K. 482	1919
No. 23, K. 488	1919
No. 24, K. 491	1922
No. 25, K. 503	
Symphonies [arrangements for piano solo]:	1888
No. 30, K. 202	
No. 32, K. 318	
No. 37, K. 444	
Nováček, Ottokar	
Scherzo from the First String Quartet	1893
Schoenberg, Arnold	
Piano Piece, Op. 11, No. 2 [concert arrangement]	1909
Schubert	
Five German Dances with Coda and Seven Trios,	1888
D. 90	
Five Minuets, with Six Trios and Minuet, D. 89	
Overture in B-flat Major, D. 470	

Composer and Title	Date
Overture in D Major, D. 26	
Overture in D Major, D. 556	
Overture in D Major (in the Italian Style), D. 590	
Overture in C Major (in the Italian Style), D. 591	
Overture in E Minor, D. 648	
Overture to Der Teufel als Hydraulicus, D. 4	
Wagner	
Götterdämmerung: Funeral March for Siegfried's Death	1883

Feinberg

SOLO PIANO

Opus	Title	Date
1	Sonata No. 1	1915
2	Sonata No. 2	1915
3	Sonata No. 3	1917
5	Fantasia No. 1	1917
6	Sonata No. 4	1918
8	Four Preludes	1920
9	Fantasia No. 2	1921
10	Sonata No. 5	1921
11	Suite No. 1	1922
13	Sonata No. 6	1923
15	Three Preludes	1922
19	Humoresque	—
19a	Berceuse	
21	Sonata No. 7	1925
	Sonata No. 8	1928
24a	Two Chuvash Melodies	
25	Suite No. 2	1936
27a	Three Melodies	
	Georgian	
	Tartar	
	Armenian	1938
29	Sonata No. 9	1939
30	Sonata No. 10	
33	Tale	1947
	Procession	1946

Opus	Title	Date
40	Sonata No. 11	1952
48	Sonata No. 12	1962
WoO	Children's Album	1962
	Russian Song	
	Lightly Drizzling (Étude)	
	Aria	
	The Dream Is Coming	
	Morning	
	Unexplored Path	
	The Clouds Are Floating	
	Little Scherzo	
	Greek Song	
	Marcello: Fragment from Cantata, Arrangement in Olden Style	
	Liszt: Margarita, Fragment from the Faust Symphony	
	Mexican Melody	

Transcriptions, Arrangements, and Cadenzas for Solo Piano

Opus	Title	Date
17	Two Cadenzas to Beethoven's Piano Concerto No. 4 [first and third movements]	—
31	Three Arrangements from Tchaikovsky's Symphonies	—
	Andantino marziale (Second Symphony)	
	Waltz (Fifth Symphony)	
	Allegro molto vivace (Sixth Symphony)	
35	Bach-Vivaldi: Concerto	1918
37	Bach: Organ Prelude and Fugue (E Minor)	1956
38	Bach: Largo from Organ Sonata (C Major)	—
41	Four Cadenzas to Mozart's Piano Concerto No. 21, K. 467	—
42	Nocturne from Borodin's String Quartet No. 2	—
43	Arrangements of Tchaikovsky's Three Songs for Children	
	Spring	
	My Little Orchard	
	Children's Song	—
WoO	Bach	
	Thirteen Chorale Preludes	

Opus	Title	Date

Beethoven
  String Quartet Op. 59: Fugue
Borodin, Alexander
  String Quartet No. 2: Scherzo
Corelli, Arcangelo
  Two Sarabandes [from violin sonatas]
Frescobaldi, Girolamo
  Canzone
  Sonata
Locatelli, Pietro
  Fragment of a Concerto
Marcello, Benedetto
  Prelude
  Three Fragments from Cantatas
Musorgsky
  Songs and Dances of Death: Serenade

Godowsky

Title	Date
Moto perpetuo	1888
Grande valse romantique	1888
Valse-scherzo	1888
Märchen [Tale]	1888
Moto perpetuo	1889
Polonaise	1889
Twilight Thoughts: Suite des morceaux	1890
Impressions sur le fleuve de Hudson	
Une nuit de printemps	
Au jardin des fleurs	
Serenade	
Menuet No. 1	1891
Three Concert Studies, Op. 11	1899 (No. 2 unpub.)
Sarabande, Menuet, Courante, Op. 12	1899
Toccata (Perpetual Motion), Op. 13 [revised and transposed from the Moto perpetuo of 1889]	1899

Title	Date
Ein Dämmerungsbild, Valse-idylle, Scherzino, Op. 14	1899
Mélodie meditative, Capriccio, Op. 15	1899
Arabesque, Barcarolle-Valse, Op. 16	1899
Sonata	1911

    Allegro non troppo ma appassionato—Epilogue
      (andante tranquillo)
    Andante cantabile
    Allegretto vivace e scherzando
    Allegretto grazioso e dolce
    Retrospect (lento Fmesto)—Larghetto lamentoso—
      Fuga on Theme B-A-C-H—Dies Irae (maestoso
      lugubre)

Walzermasken	1912

    Book 1:
      Karneval
      Pastell (Schubert)
      Skizze (Brahms)
      Momento capriccioso
      Berceuse
      Kontraste
    Book 2:
      Profil (Chopin)
      Silhouette
      Satire
      Karikatur
      Tyll Ulenspegel
      Legende
    Book 3:
      Humoreske
      Französisch
      Elegie
      Perpetuum mobile
      Menuett
      Schuhplattler
    Book 4:
      Valse macabre
      Abendglocken (Angelus)
      Orientale
      Weinerisch
      Eine sage

Portrait (J. Strauss, Jr.)	1912

Title	Date
Miniatures	1918–20
Humoresque	
Rigaudon	
The Miller's Song	
Processional March	
Arabian Chant (Orientale)	
Triakontameron (Thirty Moods and Scenes in Triple Measure)	1919–20
Vol. 1:	
Nocturnal Tangier	
Sylvan Tyrol	
Paradoxical Moods	
Rendezvous	
Twilight Phantasms	
Vol. 2:	
The Pleading Troubadour	
Yesteryear	
A Watteau Paysage	
Enchanted Glen	
Resignation	
Vol. 3:	
Alt-Wien	
Ethiopian Serenade	
Terpsichorean Vindobona	
Whitecaps	
The Temptress	
Vol. 4:	
An Old Ballade	
An American Idyl	
Anachronisms	
A Little Tango Rag	
Whirling Dervishes	
Vol. 5:	
The Salon	
An Epic	
The Music Box	
Lullaby	
Memories	
Vol. 6:	
The Cuckoo Clock	
Lament	
Quixotic Errantry	

Title	Date
[Triakontameron—Vol. 6:]	
Poème macabre	
Requiem (1914–1918)	
Epilogue [transcription of John Stafford	
Smith's The Star-Spangled Banner]	
Java Suite (Phonoramas: Tonal Journeys for the	1924–25
Pianoforte)	
Part 1:	
Gamelan	
Wayang Purwa [Puppet Shadow Plays]	
Hari Besaar [The Great Day]	
Part 2:	
Chattering Monkeys at the Sacred Lake of	
Wendit	
Boro Budur in Moonlight	
The Bromo Volcano and the Sand Sea at	
Daybreak	
Part 3:	
Three Dances	
The Gardens of Buitenzorg	
In the Streets of Old Batavia	
Part 4:	
In the Kraton	
The Ruined Water Castle at Djokja	
A Court Pageant in Solo	
Poems	
Devotion	1927
Avowal	1927
Adoration	1927
Yearning	1932
Passacaglia (Forty-Four Variations, Cadenza, and	1927
Fugue on the Opening of Schubert's Unfinished	
Symphony)	
Prelude and Fugue for the Left Hand Alone on the	1929
Notes B.A.C.H.	
Suite for the Left Hand Alone	1929
Allemand	
Courante	
Gavotte	
Sarabande	
Bourrée	
Sicilienne	

Title	Date
Menuet	
Gigue	
Capriccio (Patetico) for the Left Hand Alone	1928
Capriccio (Patetico)	1929
Elegy for the Left Hand Alone	1929
Elegy	1929
Étude macabre for the Left Hand Alone	1929
Étude macabre	1929
Impromptu for the Left Hand Alone	1929
Impromptu	1929
Intermezzo (Malinconico) for the Left Hand Alone	1928
Intermezzo (Malinconico)	1928
Meditation for the Left Hand Alone	1929
Meditation	1929
Waltz-Poems, Nos. 1, 2, and 4	1928–29
Six Waltz-Poems for the Left Hand Alone	1929

TRANSCRIPTIONS, ARRANGEMENTS, AND CADENZAS FOR SOLO PIANO

Composer and Title	Date
Albéniz, Isaac	
Tango, Op. 165, No. 2	1921
Iberia, Book 2, No. 3: Triana	1922
Bach	
Sonatas and Suites for Violin Solo and Violoncello	
Solo [very freely transcribed and adapted]	
Sonata No. 1 [violin]	1923
Sonata No. 2 [violin]	1922–23
Sonata No. 3 [violin]	1924
Suite No. 2 [cello]	1923
Suite No. 3 [cello]	1923
Suite No. 5 [cello]	1923
Beethoven	
Cadenza to Piano Concerto No. 4, Op. 58	1909
Bizet, Georges	
L'Arlésienne: Adagietto	1927
Böhm, Carl	
Calm as the Night [Still wie die Nacht]	Publ. 1921
Chopin	
Fifty-Three Studies on Chopin's Études	1894–1914

Composer and Title	Date
[Chopin]	
Concert arrangements:	
Rondo, Op. 16	1899
Waltz, Op. 18	1899
Waltz in D-flat Major, Op. 64, No. 1	1922
Waltz in A-flat Major, Op. 64, No. 3	1927
Waltz in A-flat Major, Op. 69, No. 1	1927
Waltz in F Minor, Op. 70, No. 2	1927
Waltz in D-flat Major, Op. 70, No. 3	1920
Godard, Benjamin	1927
Violin concerto romantique: Canzonetta	
Henselt, Adolph von	
Étude, Si oiseau j'etais, Op. 2, No. 6	
Concert arrangement	1899
Concert arrangement with cadenza	—
Transcription	1931
Kreisler, Fritz	
Rondino on a Theme by Beethoven	1916
Mozart	
Two Cadenzas to the Concerto for Two Pianos,	1920
K. 365	1905
Cadenzas to the Piano Concerto K. 491 [first and	1927
last movements)	
Cadenza to the Piano Concerto K. 488	
Saint-Saëns, Camille	
Carnival of the Animals: The Swan	1927
Schubert	
Rosamunde: Ballet Music [concert arrangement]	1922
Moment musical, Op. 94, No. 3	1922
Twelve Schubert Songs [freely transcribed for the	1926
piano]	
Wohin? D. 795, No. 2	
Das Wandern, D. 795, No. 1	
Heidenröslein, D. 257	
Gute Nacht, D. 911, No. 1	
Morgengrüss, D. 795, No. 8	
Wiegenlied, D. 498	
Die Forelle, D. 550	
Die junge Nonne, D. 828	
Litanei, D. 343	
Liebesbotschaft, D. 957, No. 1	
An Mignon, D. 161	

Composer and Title	Date

Ungeduld, D. 795, No. 7
Schumann
    Du bist wie eine Blume, Op. 25, No. 24 — 1921
Strauss, Johann
    Symphonic Metamorphoses on Themes from — Publ.
    Three Waltzes by Johann Strauss [concert — 1912
    paraphrases]
        Künstlerleben — 1905
        Die Fledermaus — 1907
        Wein, Weib, und Gesang
    Symphonic Metamorphosis of the Schatz-Waltzer — 1928
    [themes from The Gypsy Baron for left hand
    alone]
Strauss, Richard — 1922
    Symphonic Metamorphoses of Richard Strauss's
    Ständchen
Weber, Carl Maria von
    Invitation to the Dance, Op. 65 — 1905
    Momento capriccioso, Op. 12 — 1904
    Perpetuum mobile (Sonata, Op. 24: Rondo) — 1903
Baroque and Renaissance Collections of Arrangements
    and Transcriptions
    Airs of the Eighteenth Century — 1937
        Exaudet's Minuet
        Lisette
        La mère bontemps
        Maman, dites-moi
        Bergère légère
        Pergolesi: Que ne suis-je la fougère
        Venez, agréable printemps
    Renaissance
        Book 1: — 1906
            Jean-Philippe Rameau
            Sarabande
            Rigaudon
            Minuet
            Elegy (on Two Gigues)
            Tambourin
        Book 2: — 1906
            Johann Schobert
            Minuet
            Arcangelo Corelli

Composer and Title	Date
[Baroque and Renaissance Collections—Book 2:]	
Pastorale (Angelus)	
Jean-Baptiste Lully	
Sarabande	
Courante	
François Dandrieu	
Capriccio (Le caquet)	
Jean-Baptiste Loeillet	
Gigue	
Book 3:	1909
Rameau	
Sarabande	
Musette en rondeau	
Gavotte	
Book 4:	1909
Domenico Scarlatti	
Concert allegro	

(The following are straight transcriptions of the
originals, intended more for educational or home
use than for concert presentation, and are thus not
freely arranged for the concert stage as are the
preceding works.)   Publ. 1915

Anonymous
    First French Suite—Bergerettes
      O My Tender Musette
      Phyllis, More Greedy than Kind
      Little Maiden
    First German Suite
      A Joyful Message
      The Fir Tree
      The Ring
      To the Moon
      The Lowlander's Longing
      Three Horsemen
    First Hungarian Suite
      The Departure of the Students
      Twelve, Thirteen, Fourteen
      The Sad Village
      The Foolish Youth
    First Irish Suite

Composer and Title	Date

The Minstrel Boy
The First Swallow
The Faithless Maiden
The Emigrants
Netherland Suite
    Dutch Battle Song
    To a Violet
    Pierlala
On the Alma (Austrian-Tyrol)
On the Bridge of Avignon (France)
First Russian Suite
    The Thistle
    Kamarinskaja
    On the Mountain of Mack
    The Maiden Making Garlands
Second Russian Suite
    In the Green Forest
    The Gypsy
    Blond Locks
    The Dance before the Battle
Ruthenian Melodies (Russia)
Santa Lucia (Barcarolle) (Italy)
First Swedish Suite
    The Judge Dance
    The Dancing Maiden
    There Is Light in Easterland

Beethoven
    Violin Concerto, Op. 61
    Violin Sonata No. 9, Op. 47, Kreutzer

Bellini, Vincenzo
    Norma, Suite No. 1
        Chorus: Norma cometh
        Duet, Norma and Pollione: Do thou guide
            them
        Adalgisa's Pleading
        Chorus: The day of vengeance

Brahms, Johannes
    Wiegenlied, Op. 49, No. 4

Godard, Benjamin
    Florian's Song [France]

Gounod, Charles
    Faust, Suite

Composer and Title	Date

[Gounod, Charles]
    Maiden's Chorus
    Marguerite's Love
    Duet: Faust and Marguerite
    Marguerite's Prayer
Handel, George Friedrich
    Messiah: But who may abide the day
Lassen, Eduard
    Ah! 'Tis a Dream
    Thine Eyes So Blue and Tender
Mozart
    Symphony No. 40, K. 550
Palestrina, Giovanni
    Motet: Adoramus Te
Schubert
    Heidenröslein, Op. 3, No. 3 (D. 257)
    Das Wandern, Op. 25, No. 1 (D. 795, No. 1)
Schumann
    Lied der Braut, Op. 25, No. 12
    Lieb' Liebchen, Op. 24, No. 4
Stradella, Alessandro
    Church Melody: O Salutaris
Thomas, Ambroise
    Mignon: Mignon's Song (Romance)
Verdi, Giuseppe
    Aida: Celeste Aida
    Rigoletto, Suite No. 1
        Ballad
        Minuet
        Perigordino
Operatic Masterpieces   Publ. 1936
    Bizet
        Carmen: Excerpts
    Gounod
        Faust: Excerpts
    Verdi
        Il trovatore: Excerpts
    Wagner
        Tannhäuser: Excerpts
Four Piano Transcriptions of German Lieder   Publ. 1937
    Schubert:
        Schwanengesang, D. 957, No. 12: Am Meer

Composer and Title	Date
Die schöne Müllerin, D. 795, No. 18: Trockne Blumen Schumann: Hochländers Wiegenlied, Op. 25, No. 14 Brahms: Vergebliches Ständchen, Op. 84, No. 4	

Hamelin

SOLO PIANO

Title	Date
Con intimissimo sentimento	2000
Ländler 1	
Ländler 2	
Ländler 3	
Album Leaf	
Music Box	
After Pergolesi	
Berceuse (In tempore belli)	
Homage to Kaikhosru Shapurji Sorabji: Preambulum to an Imaginary Piano Symphony	1989
Prelude	1995
Twelve Études in Minor Keys	
No. 1: Flight of the Bumblebee (after Rimsky-Korsakov)	1987
No. 3: La campanella (after Paganini-Liszt)	1993
No. 6: Homage to Scarlatti	1992
No. 9: After Rossini	1987
No. 10: Pour les idées noires (after Chopin)	1990
No. 12: Prelude and Fugue	1986
Two Short Studies	1979-80

TRANSCRIPTIONS, ARRANGEMENTS, AND CADENZAS FOR SOLO PIANO

Composer and Title	Date
Abreu, Zequinha Tico-tico no fuba	1995
Anonymous Pop Music [transcription of Pop Goes the Weasel]	1998

Composer and Title	Date
Bach, C. P. E.	
Solfegietto a cinque	1999
Chopin, Frédéric	
Triple Étude [based upon Études, Op. 10, No. 2; Op. 25, No. 4; and Op. 25, No. 11]	1992
Glazunov, Alexander	
Petit Adagio [from The Seasons, Op. 67]	2001
Liszt, Franz	
Cadenza to Hungarian Rhapsody No. 2	1995
Mozart, Wolfgang Amadeus	
Cadenzas to piano concertos:	
K. 271: Andantino	1997
K. 453: Two cadenzas for Andante	1994–95
K. 491: Allegro, Allegretto	1994–95

Medtner

SOLO PIANO

Opus	Title	Date
1	Stimmungsbilder	1902
	Prolog	
	Allegro con impeto	
	Maestoso freddo	
	Andante con moto	
	Andante	
	Allegro con umore	
	Allegro con ira	
	Allegro con grazia	
2	Three Improvisations	1902
	Nixie	
	A Ball: Reminiscence	
	Scherzo infernale	
4	Four Pieces	1903
	Étude	
	Caprice	
	Moment musical	
	Prelude	
5	Sonata No. 1	1904

Opus	Title	Date
7	Three Arabesques	1905
	No. 1: Idyll	
	No. 2: Tragedy Fragment	
	No. 3: Tragedy Fragment	
8	Two Tales	1905
9	Three Tales	1906
10	Three Dithyrambs	1906
11	Sonata-Triad	1907
14	Two Tales	1908
	No. 1: Ophelia's Song	
	No. 2: March of the Paladin	
17	Three Novellas	1909
20	Two Tales	1910
22	Sonata	1911
23	Four Lyric Fragments	1912
25	No. 1: Sonata-Tale	1912
	No. 2: Night Wind Sonata	1913
26	Four Tales	1913
27	Sonata-Ballade	1913
30	Sonata	1914
31	Three Pieces	1915
	Improvisation	
	Funeral March	
	Tale	
34	Four Tales	1916
35	Four Tales	1917
38	Forgotten Melodies	1919
	Sonata reminiscenza	
	Danza graziosa	
	Danza festiva	
	Canzona fluviala	
	Danza rustica	
	Canzona serenata	
	Danza silvestra	
	Alla reminiscenza	
39	Forgotten Melodies (Lyric Motifs)	1920
	Meditazione	
	Romanza	
	Primavera	
	Canzona matinata	
	Sonata tragica	

Opus	Title	Date
40	Forgotten Melodies (Dance Motifs)	
	Danza col canto	
	Danza sinfonica	
	Danza fiorata	
	Danza giubilosa	
	Danza ondulata	
	Danza ditirambica	1920
42	Three Tales	1922
47	Improvisation	1926
48	Two Tales	1927
	Dance	
	Elf	
49	Three Hymns in Praise of Work	1928
	Before Work	
	At the Anvil	
	After Work	
51	Six Tales	1920
53	No. 1: Sonata romantica	1930
	No. 2: Sonata minacciosa	1931
54	Romantic Sketches for the Young [in four books]	1933
55	No. 1: Theme and Variations	1934
	No. 2: Cadenzas for Beethoven's Piano Concerto No. 4	
56	Sonata idillica	1935
59	Two Elegies	1945

Rachmaninov

SOLO PIANO

Opus	Title	Date
—	Song without Words	c. 1886
—	Three Nocturnes	c. 1887
—	Four Pieces	c. 1888
	Romance	
	Prelude	
	Mélodie	
	Gavotte	
—	Piece (Canon)	c. 1890
—	Prelude	c. 1891

Opus	Title	Date
3	Five Pieces	1892
	Elegy	
	Prelude	
	Melody	
	Polichinelle	
	Serenade	
10	Seven Pieces	1894
	Nocturne	
	Waltz	
	Barcarolle	
	Melody	
	Humoreske	
	Romance	
	Mazurka	
16	Six moments musicaux	1896
—	Morceau de fantaisie	1899
—	Fughetta	1899
22	Variations on a Theme by Chopin	1903
23	Ten Preludes	1903–04
28	Sonata No. 1	1907
32	Thirteen Preludes	1910
33	Études-Tableaux	1911
36	Sonata No. 2	1913, rev. 1931
39	Études-Tableaux	1916–17
—	Oriental Sketch	1917
—	Piece	1917
—	Fragments	1917
42	Variations on a Theme by Corelli	1932

Transcriptions, Arrangements, and Cadenzas for Solo Piano

Composer and Title	Date
Bach	
Violin Partita No. 3, BWV 1006: Prelude, Gavotte, and Gigue	1933
Behr, Franz	
Polka, Op. 303, La rieuse [published as Polka de V. R.]	1911
Bizet	
L'Arlésienne, Suite No. 1: Minuet	1922

Composer and Title	Date
Kreisler, Fritz	
Liebesfreud	1925
Liebesleid	1921
Liszt	
Cadenza for Hungarian Rhapsody No. 2	1919
Mendelssohn	
A Midsummer Night's Dream: Scherzo	1933
Musorgsky	
Sorochintsy Fair: Gopak	1923
Rachmaninov	
Daisies, Op. 38, No. 3	1922 (rev. 1940)
Lilacs, Op. 21, No. 5	1913
Rimsky-Korsakov, Nikolai	
The Tale of Tsar Saltan: Flight of the Bumblebee	1929
Schubert	
Die schöne Müllerin: Wohin?	1925
Smith	
The Star-Spangled Banner	1918
Tchaikovsky	
Lullaby, Op. 16, No. 1	1941

Scriabin

SOLO PIANO

Opus	Title	Date
1	Waltz	1888
2	Three Pieces	
	Étude	1887
	Prelude	1889
	Impromptu à la Mazur	1889
3	Ten Mazurkas	1888–90
4	Allegro appassionato	1887–93
5	Two Nocturnes	1893
6	Sonata No. 1	1893
7	Two Impromptus à la Mazur	1891
8	Twelve Études	1894–95

Opus	Title	Date
9	Two Pieces for the Left Hand Alone	1894
	Prelude	
	Nocturne	
10	Two Impromptus	1894
11	Twenty-Four Preludes	1888–96
12	Two Impromptus	1895
13	Six Preludes	1895
14	Two Impromptus	1895
15	Five Preludes	1895–96
16	Five Preludes	1894–95
17	Seven Preludes	1895–96
18	Allegro de concert	1895–97
19	Sonata No. 2, Sonata-Fantasy	1892–97
21	Polonaise	1897–98
22	Four Preludes	1897–98
23	Sonata No. 3	1897–98
25	Nine Mazurkas	1899
27	Two Preludes	1900
28	Fantasy	1900–01
30	Sonata No. 4	1901–03
31	Four Preludes	1903
32	Two Poems	1903
33	Four Preludes	1903
34	Tragic Poem	1903
35	Three Preludes	1903
36	Satanic Poem	1903
37	Four Preludes	1903
38	Waltz	1903
39	Four Preludes	1903
40	Two Mazurkas	1903
41	Poem	1903
42	Eight Études	1903
44	Two Poems	1905
45	Three Pieces	1905
46	Scherzo	1905
47	Quasi-Waltz	1905
48	Four Preludes	1905
49	Three Pieces	1905
	Étude	
	Prelude	
	Reverie	

Opus	Title	Date
51	Four Pieces	1906
	Fragilité	
	Prelude	
	Poème ailé	
	Danse languide	
52	Three Pieces	1905–07
	Poem	
	Enigma	
	Poème languide	
53	Sonata No. 5	1907
56	Four Pieces	1908
	Prelude	
	Ironies	
	Nuances	
	Étude	
57	Two Pieces	1908
	Désire	
	Caresse dansée	
58	Album Leaf	1911
59	Two Pieces	1910–11
	Poem	
	Prelude	
61	Poem-Nocturne	1911–12
62	Sonata No. 6	1911-12
63	Two Poems	1912
	Masque	
	Étrangeté	
64	Sonata No. 7, White Mass	1911–12
65	Three Études	1912
66	Sonata No. 8	1913
67	Two Preludes	1912–13
68	Sonata No. 9, Black Mass	1913
69	Two Poems	1913
70	Sonata No. 10	1913
71	Two Poems	1913
	Fantastique	
	En rêvant	
72	Poem: Vers la flamme	1914
73	Two Dances	1914
	Guirlandes	
	Flammes sombres	

Opus	Title	Date
74	Five Preludes	1914
	Douloureux, déchirant	
	Très lent, contemplatif	
	Allegro drammatico	
	Lent, vague, indécis	
	Fier, belliqueux	
Op. posth.		
	Canon	1883
	Mazurkas [two]	1884
		1886
	Nocturne	1884
	Sonata-Fantasy	1886
	Waltz	1886

Sorabji

SOLO PIANO (ARRANGED IN ORDER OF COMPOSITION)

Title	Date
Désir éperdu [fragment]	1917
Quasi habanera	1917
Sonata	1917
Two Piano Pieces	
In the Hothouse	1918
Toccata	1920
Fantaisie espagnole	1919
Sonata No. 1	1919
Prelude, Interlude, and Fugue	1920–22
Sonata No. 2	1920
Sonata No. 3	1922
Three Pastiches	1922
Waltz, from Chopin's Op. 64, No. 1	
Habanera, from Bizet's Carmen	
The Hindu Merchant's Song, from Rimsky-Korsakov's Sadko	
Poem: Le jardin parfumé	1923
Waltz-Fantasy (Homage to Johann Strauss)	1925
Variations and Triple Fugue on Dies Irae	1923–26

Title	Date
Fragment Written for Harold Rutland	1926, rev. 1928
Toccata No. 1	1928
Nocturne: Djâmi	1928
Sonata No. 4	1928–29
Passacaglia [unfinished]	1929
Toccatinetta sopra C. G. F.	1929
Opus clavicembalisticum	1929–30
Fantasia ispanica	1933
Caprice-Pastiche on Chopin's Op. 64, No. 1	1933
Toccata No. 2	1933–34
Sonata No. 5 (Opus archimagicum)	1934–35
Tantrik Symphony (Symphony No. 1 for Piano Solo)	1938–39
Quære reliqua hujus materiei inter secretiora [based upon the story Count Magnus by M. R. James]	1940
Nocturne: Gulistān	1940
St. Bertrand de Comminges: He was Laughing in the Tower [based upon the story Canon Alberic's Scrapbook by M. R. James]	1941
One Hundred Transcendental Studies	1940–44
Concerto per suonare da me solo e senza orchestra, per divertirsi	1946
Sequentia cyclica super Dies Irae ex Missa pro defunctis	1948–49
Un nido di scatole	1954
Symphony No. 2	1954
Rosario d'arabeschi	1956
Symphony No. 3	1959–60
Fantasiettina sul nome illustre dell'egregio poeta Christopher Grieve ossia Hugh McDiarmid	1961
Symphony No. 4	1962–64
Twenty frammenti aforistici	1964
Toccata No. 4	1964–67
104 frammenti aforistici (Sutras)	1962–64, 1972
Symphony No. 5, Symphonia brevis	1973
Symphony No. 6, Symphonia claviensis	1975–76
Four frammenti aforistici	1977
Symphonic Nocturne	1977–78
Villa Tasca: Mezzogiorno siciliano—Evocazione nostalgica	1979–80
Opus secretum	1980–81

Title	Date
Passeggiata variata	1981
Two Sutras sul nome dell'amico Alexis	1981–84

TRANSCRIPTIONS AND ARRANGEMENTS FOR SOLO PIANO

Title	Date
Transcription in the Light of Harpsichord Technique for the Modern Piano of the Chromatic Fantasia of J. S. Bach, followed by a Fugue [transcription with BWV 948, not Bach's original fugue]	1940
Concert Transcription of Maurice Ravel's Rapsodie espagnole	1945
Prelude after J. S. Bach [transcription of the first movement of BWV 815a]	1945
Concert Paraphrase of the Closing Scene from Richard Strauss's Salome	1947
Passeggiata veneziana [based upon the Barcarolle from The Tales of Hoffmann by Jacques Offenbach]	1955–56
Variazione maliziosa e perversa [based upon The Death of Asa, from Grieg's Peer Gynt Suite]	1974
Variations and Fugue on a Theme from Rimsky-Korsakov's Le coq d'Or	1978–79
Passeggiata arlecchinesca sopra [based on material from Busoni's Rondo arlecchinesco]	1981–82

DISCOGRAPHIES

The discographies provided here present the solo-piano recordings of The Eight obtainable as of early 2002. Recording dates are given when available.

The reissue market for older recordings continues to thrive; as a result, much duplication exists among the same recordings released by different labels. Preferred versions are listed here, taking into account the quality of sound and presentation.

Hamelin has made a significant contribution to the recorded music of The Eight. The CD *Marc-André Hamelin Plays the Composer-Pianists* (Hyperion CDA67050) was conceived to provide an aural illustration of their diversity and similarities, collected in this way for the first time. The choice of music, including representative samples of transcription, was rather quickly decided upon. I requested Hamelin's Études 9, 10, and 12 for their wit and diversity; Alkan's "Le premier billet doux" for its personal significance; and Sorabji's *Sadko* Pastiche for its suggestive pianistic delicacy. For Busoni, Hamelin and I immediately thought of the expressive *Fantasia after J. S. Bach*, among our favorite works by the Italian composer. We similarly chose the Scriabin and Rachmaninov pieces. Hamelin suggested Godowsky's Toccata, Alkan's Scherzetto and the Haydn transcription, Feinberg's Berceuse and Bach transcription, and Medtner's First Improvisation. Each work's placement on the disc was carefully considered to create a satisfying whole, with Busoni's *Fantasia* placed precisely in the middle of the seventeen works as the recording's emotional core. Recording sessions were held in January 1998 at London's storied Abbey Road Studio.

Busoni

Composer	Title	Label and Catalog No.	Date recorded
Bach, Johann Sebastian	The Well-Tempered Clavier, Book 1: Prelude and Fugue No. 1, BWV 846	Pearl: 9347	1922

Composer	Title	Label and Catalog No.	Date recorded
Bach-Busoni	Partita for Solo Violin No. 2 in D Minor, BWV 1004: Chaconne	Nimbus: 8810 [piano rolls]	1925
	Chorale Prelude, BWV 734	Pearl: 9347	1922
Beethoven, Ludwig van– Busoni	Ecossaise, WoO 83	Pearl: 9347	1922
Chopin, Frédéric	Étude, Op. 10, No. 5, Black Key	Pearl: 9347	1919
	Étude, Op. 25, No. 5	Pearl: 9347	1922
	Nocturne, Op. 15, No. 2	Pearl: 9347	1922
	Preludes, Op. 28, Nos. 1-7, 9-11, 14–16, 20, 23	Nimbus: 8810	1923
Liszt, Franz	Hungarian Rhapsody No. 13	Pearl: 9347	1922
	Polonaise No. 2	Nimbus: 8810	1915
	Transcendental Étude No. 5, Feux follets	Nimbus: 8810	1915
Paganini, Niccolò– Liszt	Transcendental Études after Paganini:		
	No. 3, La Campanella	Nimbus: 8810	1915
	No. 5, La Chasse	Nimbus: 8810	1915

Feinberg

A number of the following recordings (marked Russia) were made for the Russian label Melodiya or were taped for radio broadcast. They are gradually being released in the West. The numbers provided are from the original Soviet sources.

Bach	Chromatic Fantasy and Fugue, BWV 903	Arbiter: 118	1948
	Fantasia and Fugue, BWV 904	Triton: 24031	1961
	Partita No. 1, BWV 825	Triton: 24031	1948
	Sonata No. 5, BWV 529: Largo	BMG/Melodiya: 74321 25175 2	1962
	Toccata, BWV 911	Triton: 24031	1948
	Toccata, BWV 912	Triton: 24031	1947
	The Well-Tempered Clavier, Book 1: BWV 846–869		

Composer	Title	Label and Catalog No.	Date recorded
[Bach]	The Well-Tempered Clavier, Book 2: BWV 870–893	Russian Disc: 15013	1962
Bach-Feinberg	Chorale Prelude, BWV 647 [two versions]	BMG/Melodiya: 74321 25175 2	1962
	Chorale Prelude, BWV 662	BMG/Melodiya: 74321 25175 2	1952
	Chorale Prelude, BWV 663	BMG/Melodiya: 74321 25175 2	1962
	Chorale Prelude, BWV 711	BMG/Melodiya: 74321 25175 2	1952
	Prelude and Fugue, BWV 548	Triton: 24031	1948
Beethoven	Sonata No. 4, Op. 7	Triton: 24030	1961
	Sonata No. 11, Op. 22	Triton: 24030	1960
	Sonata No. 19, Op. 49, No. 1	Russia: D-2810	
	Sonata No. 20, Op. 49, No. 2	Russia: D-2810	
	Sonata No. 23, Op. 57, Appassionata	Arbiter: 118	c. 1938
	Sonata No. 30, Op. 109	Triton: 24030	1953
Chopin	Three Mazurkas, Op. 59	Russia: C10 20431	
	Tarantelle, Op. 43	Russia: C10 20431	
Feinberg	Suite, Op. 11	Arbiter: 118	1929
Liadov, Anatoly	Idylle, Op. 25	Arbiter: 118	c. 1947
Liszt	Consolations, Nos. 5 and 6	Arbiter: 118	c. 1938
	Mephisto Waltz	Russia: C10 20431	
Mozart, Wolfgang Amadeus	Fantasia and Fugue, K. 394	BMG/Melodiya: 74321 25175 2	1951
	Sonata No. 4, K. 282	BMG/Melodiya: 74321 25175 2	1953
	Sonata No. 17, K. 576	BMG/Melodiya: 74321 25175 2	1952

Composer	Title	Label and Catalog No.	Date recorded
	Twelve Variations on an Allegretto, K. 500	BMG/Melodiya: 74321 25175 2	1951
Schumann, Robert	Allegro, Op. 8	Arlecchino: ARL125	1950
	Humoreske, Op. 20	Arlecchino: ARL125	1953
	Waldszenen, Op. 82	Arlecchino: ARL125	1953
Scriabin	Étude, Op. 42, No. 3	Arbiter: 118	1929
	Fantasy, Op. 28	Russia: C10 20434	
	Mazurkas, Op. 3, Nos. 1–7	Russian Season: 788032	1952
	Mazurkas, Op. 25	Arlecchino:	
	No. 2	ARL50	1951
	No. 3		1947
	No. 8		1951
	No. 9		1951
	Four Pieces, Op. 51	Arlecchino: ARL50	1947
	Sonata No. 2, Op. 19 (Sonata-Fantasy)	Arlecchino: ARL50	
	Sonata No. 4, Op. 30	Arlecchino: ARL50	1947
Stanchinsky, Alexei	Prelude in Canon Form	Arbiter: 118	1929
Tchaikovsky, Piotr	Sonata, Op. 80	Russia: C10 20432	
Vivaldi, Antonio–Feinberg	Concerto in A Minor: Allegro	Arbiter: 118	1929

Godowsky

Albéniz, Isaac	Tango, Op. 165, No. 2	APR: 7011	1920
Beethoven	Sonata No. 26, Op. 81a, Les adieux	APR: 7010	1929
Bishop, Sir Henry–Godowsky	Home, Sweet Home	APR: 7011	1921
Chopin	Berceuse, Op. 57	APR: 7013	1924

Composer	Title	Label and Catalog No.	Date recorded
[Chopin]	Étude, Op. 10, No. 5	Philips: 456 805	1926
	Étude, Op. 25, No. 1	APR: 7011	1924
	Étude, Op. 25, No. 3	APR: 7011	1924
	Étude, Op. 25, No. 9	Philips: 456 805	1926
	Fantaisie-Impromptu, Op. 66	APR: 7011	1921
	Nocturnes, Op. 9, Nos. 1 and 2	Philips: 456 805	1928
	Nocturnes, Op. 15, Nos. 1 and 2	Philips: 456 805	1928
	Nocturnes, Op. 27, Nos. 1 and 2	Philips: 456 805	1928
	Nocturne, Op. 32, No. 1	Philips: 456 805	1928
	Nocturnes, Op. 37, Nos. 1 and 2	Philips: 456 805	1928
	Nocturne, Op. 48, No. 2	Philips: 456 805	1928
	Nocturne, Op. 55, No. 1	Philips: 456 805	1928
	Nocturne, Op. 72, No. 1	Philips: 456 805	1928
	Polonaise, Op. 26, No. 1 (abridged)	APR: 7013	1924
	Scherzo No. 4, Op. 54	Philips: 456 805	1930
	Sonata No. 2, Op. 35, Funeral March	Philips: 456 805	1930
	Waltz, Op. 34, No. 1	APR: 7011	1924
	Waltz, Op. 42	APR: 7011	1924
	Waltz, Op. 64, No. 2	APR: 7011	1913
Chopin-Liszt	Polish Songs		
	No. 1: The Maiden's Wish	APR: 7011	1920
	No. 5: My Joys	APR: 7011	1923
Debussy, Claude	Children's Corner: Golliwog's Cakewalk	APR: 7011	1925
	Preludes, Book 1: Minstrels	APR: 7011	1925
Dohnányi, Ernő	Concert Étude, Op. 28, No. 6, Capriccio	APR: 7011	1922
Godowsky	Java Suite: The Gardens of Buitenzorg	APR: 7011	c. 1935
	Humoresque		
	Miniatures: Hunter's Call and Military March	Apr: 7011	1920 1921
Grieg, Edvard	Ballade, Op. 24	Philips: 456 805	1929
Henselt, Adolph von	Wiegenlied, Op. 45	APR: 7011	1916

Composer	Title	Label and Catalog No.	Date recorded
Lane, Eastwood	American Suite: The Crapshooters	APR: 7011	1925
Liszt	Concert Étude No. 2, Gnomenreigen	APR: 7011	1914
	Concert Étude, La leggierezza	APR: 7011	1924
	Liebestraum, No. 3	APR: 7011	1925
MacDowell, Edward	Hexentanz, Op. 17, No. 2	APR: 7011	1924
Mendelssohn, Felix	Andante and Rondo Capriccioso, Op. 14	APR: 7011	1926
	Songs without Words		
	Op. 62, No. 1	APR: 7011	1913
	Op. 67, No. 4: Spinning Song	APR: 7011	1913
Rubinstein, Anton	Melody, Op. 3, No. 1	APR: 7011	1916
	Kammenoi-Ostrov: Rêve angélique, Op. 10, No. 22	APR: 7011	1924
	Romance, Op. 44, No. 1	APR: 7011	1920
Schubert, Franz– Godowsky	Gute Nacht	Philips: 456 805	1926
	Morgengrüss	Philips: 456 805	1926
Schubert– Carl Tausig	Marche militaire [abridged]	APR: 7011	1924
Schumann	Carnaval, Op. 9	Philips: 456 805	1929
Schütt, Eduard	A la bien-aimée, Op. 59, No. 2	APR: 7011	1920
	Étude mignonne, Op. 16, No. 1	APR: 7011	1920
Sinding, Christian	Frühlingsrauschen, Op. 32, No. 3	APR: 7011	1924
Smith, John Stafford– Godowsky	The Star-Spangled Banner	APR: 7011	1920
Verdi, Giuseppi– Liszt	Paraphrase on Rigoletto [abridged]	Philips: 456 805	1926
Zeckwer, Camille	In a Boat	APR: 7011	1925

Hamelin

Albéniz- Godowsky	Tango, Op. 165, No. 2	CBC/Musica Viva: 1026	1987
Alkan	Alleluia, Op. 25	Hyperion: CDA67218	2000

Composer	Title	Label and Catalog No.	Date recorded
[Alkan]	Esquisses, Op. 63, Fourth Suite:	Hyperion:	1998
	Le premier billet doux	CDA67050	
	Scherzetto		
	Twelve Études in the Minor Keys, Op. 39		
	Nos. 4–7: Symphony	Hyperion: CDA67218	2000
	Nos. 8–10: Concerto	Music & Arts: 724	1992
	No. 12: Le festin d'Ésope	Hyperion: CDA66794	1994
	Trois grandes études, Op. 76	Hyperion: CDA66765	1994
	Grande sonate: Les quatre ages, Op. 33	Hyperion: CDA66794	1994
	Salut, cendre du pauvre!, Op. 45	Hyperion: CDA67218	2000
	Sonatine, Op. 61	Hyperion: CDA66794	1994
	Super flumina Babylonis, Op. 52 [paraphrase based upon Psalm 137]	Hyperion: CDA67218	2000
	Troisième recueil de chants, Op. 65, No. 6: Barcarolle	Hyperion: CDA66794	1994
	Souvenirs: Trois morceaux dans le genre pathétique, Op. 15	Hyperion: CDA67218	2000
Bach-Feinberg	Schübler Chorale No. 6, BWV 650	Hyperion: CDA67050	1998
Beethoven-Alkan	Concerto No. 3, Op. 37: Allegro con brio	Hyperion: CDA66765	1994
Blanchet, Emile-Robert	Au jardin du vieux sérail, Op. 18, No. 3	Hyperion: CDA67275	2001
Blumenfeld, Felix	Étude for the Left Hand	Hyperion: CDA67275	2001
Bolcom, William	Twelve New Études, Books 1–4	New World: 354	1987
Busoni	Fantasia after Johann Sebastian Bach	Hyperion: CDA67050	1998

Composer	Title	Label and Catalog No.	Date recorded
	Sonatina No. 6 (Chamber-Fantasy on Bizet's Carmen)	Hyperion: CDA66765	1994
Casella, Alfredo	Deux Contrastes Grazioso Antigrazioso	Hyperion: CDA67275	2001
Catoire, Georgi	Caprice, Op. 3 Chants du crépuscule, Op. 24 En rêvant Capricciosamente Tranquillo Poco agitato Five Pieces, Op. 10 Prelude Prelude Capriccioso Reverie Legend Four Pieces, Op. 12 Chant du soir Meditation Nocturne Étude fantastique Four Preludes, Op. 17 Intermezzo, Op. 6, No. 5 Poème, Op. 34, No. 2 Prelude, Op. 6, No. 2 Prelude, Op. 34, No. 3 Scherzo, Op. 6, No. 3 Three Pieces, Op. 2 Chant intime Loin du foyer Soirée d'hiver Vision (étude), Op. 8 Waltz, Op. 36	Hyperion: CDA67090	1998
Chopin	Ballade No. 4, Op. 52	Initiativkreis Ruhrgebiet: I	1997
	Sonata No. 2, Op. 35, Funeral March	Port Royal: 5016	1994
Chopin– Mily Balakirev	Concerto No. 1, Op. 11: Romance	Hyperion: CDA66765	1994

Composer	Title	Label and Catalog No.	Date recorded
Chopin-Godowsky	The Complete Études	Hyperion: CDA67411/2	1998, 1999
Chopin–Alexander Michałowski	Étude after the Impromptu, Op. 29	Hyperion: CDA67275	2001
Confrey, Zez	Kitten on the Keys	Danacord: 349	1989
Deshevov, Vladimir	Gleise (Tracks)	Danacord: 399	1992
Eckhardt-Gramatté, Sophie-Carmen	Piano Sonatas No. 1, E 45 No. 2, E 46 No. 3, E 52 No. 4, E 68 No. 5, E 126, Klavierstück No. 6, E 130	Altarus: 9052	1991
Fauré, Gabriel	Barcarolle, Op. 42, No. 3	Initiativkreis Ruhrgebiet: I	1997
Feinberg	Berceuse, Op. 19a	Hyperion: CDA67050	1998
Gieseking, Walter	Schorschi-Batschi [foxtrot]	Danacord: 429	1994
Glazunov, Alexander–Hamelin	The Seasons, Op. 67: Petit adagio	Hyperion: CDA67275	2001
Gnattali, Radames	Three Chôros	Danacord: 479	1997
Godowsky	Triakontameron, Vol. 3: Alt Wien	Hyperion: CDA67275	2001
	Toccata, Op. 13	Hyperion: CDA67050	1998
	Étude macabre Java Suite Wayang Purwa, Part 1, No. 2 The Gardens of Buitenzorg, Part 3, No. 2	CBC/Musica Viva: 1026	1987
	Passacaglia (Forty-Four Variations, Cadenza, and Fugue on the Opening of Schubert's Unfinished Symphony)	Hyperion: CDA67300	2001

Composer	Title	Label and Catalog No.	Date recorded
	Prelude and Fugue for the Left hand on the Notes B.A.C.H.	CBC/Musica Viva: 1026	1987
	Renaissance, Book 2: Gigue [after Loeillet]		
	Rosamunde: Ballet Music		
	Sonata	Hyperion: CDA67300	2001 .
	Symphonic Metamorphoses of Richard Strauss's Ständchen	CBC/Musica Viva: 1026	1987
Grainger, Percy	Colonial Song	Hyperion: CDA66884	1996
	Country Gardens		
	'The Gum-Sucker's' March		
	Handel in the Strand		
	Harvest Hymn		
	The Hunter in his Career		
	In Dahomey		
	Irish Tune from County Derry		
	Jutish Medley		
	A March-Jig		
	Merry King		
	Mock Morris		
	Molly on the Shore		
	Ramble on Love		
	A Reel		
	Scotch Strathspey and Reel		
	Shepherd's Hey		
	Spoon River		
	Walking Tune		
Hamelin	Con intimissimo sentimento	Danacord: 559	2000
	After Pergolesi		
	Music Box		
	Triple Étude	Danacord: 399	1992
	Twelve Études in Minor Keys		
	Étude No. 3: La campanella (after Paganini-Liszt)	Hyperion: CDA67275	2001
	Étude No. 6: Homage to Scarlatti		
	Étude No. 9 (after Rossini)	Hyperion: CDA67050	1998
	Étude No. 10 (after Chopin)		

Composer	Title	Label and Catalog No.	Date recorded
[Hamelin	Twelve Études in Minor Keys] Étude No. 12: Prelude and Fugue		
Haydn, Franz Joseph–Alkan	Symphony No. 94, Surprise: Andante	Hyperion: CDA67050	1998
Hofmann, Josef	Kaleidoscope, Op. 40, No. 4 Nocturne (Complaint)	Hyperion: CDA67275	2001
Ives, Charles	Sonata No. 2, Concord, Mass., 1840–60	New World: 378	1988
Janáček, Leoš	On an Overgrown Path: A blown-away leaf Come with us! Words fail! In tears	Danacord: 559	2001
Kapustin, Nikolai	Toccatina, Op. 36	Hyperion: CDA67275	2001
Liszt	Apparition No. 1	Hyperion: CDA66874	1996
	Bénédiction de Dieu dans la solitude	Music & Arts: 723	1991
	En rêve (Nocturne)	Hyperion: CDA66874	1996
	Hungarian Rhapsodies: Nos. 2, 10, 13	Hyperion: CDA66874	1996
	La leggierezza	Music & Arts: 723	1991
	Nuages gris	Hyperion: CDA66874	1996
	Polonaise No. 2	Music & Arts: 723	1991
	Réminiscences de Don Juan [after Mozart]	Hyperion: CDA66874	1996
	Réminiscences de Norma [after Bellini]	Music & Arts: 723	1991
	Un sospiro	Hyperion: CDA66874	1996
	Waldesrauschen	Hyperion: CDA66874	1996
Lourié, Arthur	Gigue	Hyperion: CDA67275	2001

Composer	Title	Label and Catalog No.	Date recorded
Massenet, Jules	Valse folle	Hyperion: CDA67275	2001
Medtner	Forgotten Melodies, Op. 38	Hyperion: CDA67221/4	1996–98
	Sonata reminiscenza		
	Danza graziosa		
	Danza festiva		
	Canzona fluviala		
	Danza rustica		
	Canzona serenata		
	Danza silvestra		
	Alla reminiscenza		
	Forgotten Melodies, Op. 39		
	Meditazione		
	Romanza		
	Primavera		
	Canzona matinata		
	Sonata tragica		
	Improvisation, Op. 31, No. 1	Hyperion: CDA67050	1998
	Sonata No. 1, Op. 5	Hyperion: CDA67221/4	1996–98
	Sonata-Triad, Op. 11		
	No. 1		
	No. 2, Elegy		
	No. 3		
	Sonata, Op. 22		
	Sonata-Tale, Op. 25, No. 1		
	Night Wind Sonata, Op. 25, No. 2		
	Sonata-Ballade, Op. 27		
	Sonata, Op. 30		
	Sonata romantica, Op. 53, No. 1		
	Sonata minacciosa, Op. 53, No. 2		
	Sonata idillica, Op. 56		
	Two Tales, Op. 8		
Moszkowski, Moritz	Étude, Op. 72, No. 13	Hyperion: CDA67275	2001

Composer	Title	Label and Catalog No.	Date recorded
Offenbach, Jacques– Jakob Gimpel (ed. Hamelin)	Concert Paraphrase of The Song of the Soldiers of the Sea (The Marines' Hymn)	Hyperion: CDA67275	2001
Ornstein, Leo	À la Chinoise Danse Sauvage Impressions of the Thames Nine Arabesques Poems of 1917 Sonata No. 8 Suicide in an Airplane	Hyperion: CDA67320	2001
Poulenc, Francis	Intermezzo	Hyperion: CDA67275	2001
Prokofiev	Sarcasm, Op. 17, No. 1	Danacord: 379	1990
Rachmaninov	Étude-Tableau, Op. 33, No. 7 Moment musical, Op. 16, No. 2	Hyperion: CDA67050	1998
	Polka de V. R.	Hyperion: CDA67275	2001
	Sonata No. 2, Op. 36 (revised 1931)	Port Royal: 5016	1994
Reger, Max	Five Humoresques, Op. 20 Variations and Fugue on a Theme of Johann Sebastian Bach, Op. 81 Variations and Fugue on a Theme of Georg Philipp Telemann, Op. 134	Hyperion: CDA66996	1997, 1998
Roslavets, Nikolai	Five Preludes Prelude Sonata No. 1 Sonata No. 2 Sonata No. 5 Three Compositions Three Études Two Compositions Two Poems	Hyperion: CDA66926	1996
Rzewski, Frederic	North American Ballads No. 3, Down by the Riverside	Hyperion: CDA67077	1998

Composer	Title	Label and Catalog No.	Date recorded
	No. 4, Winnsboro Cotton Mill Blues The People United Will Never be Defeated! (Thirty-Six Variations on ¡El Pueblo Unido Jamás Será Vencido!)		
Schubert-Godowsky	Gute Nacht Litanei	CBC/Musica Viva: 1026	1987
Schumann	Fantasy, Op. 17 Sonata No. 2, Op. 22 Symphonic Études, Op. 13	Hyperion: CDA67166	2000
Scriabin	Two Poems, Op. 71	Hyperion: CDA67050	1998
	Tragic Poem, Op. 34	Hyperion: CDA67050	1998
	Sonatas [complete] No. 1, Op. 6 No. 2, Op. 19, Sonata-Fantasy No. 3, Op. 23 No. 4, Op. 30 No. 5, Op. 53 No. 6, Op. 62 No. 7, Op. 64, White Mass No. 8, Op. 66 No. 9, Op. 68, Black Mass No. 10, Op. 70 Sonata-Fantasy (Op. posth.)	Hyperion: CDA67131/2	1995
Sorabji	Pastiche No. 3, The Hindu Merchant's Song, from Rimsky-Korsakov's Sadko	Hyperion, CDA67050	1998
	Sonata No. 1	Altarus: 9050	1989
Strauss, Johann– Adolph Schulz-Evler	Arabesques on Themes from The Beautiful Blue Danube	Port Royal: 5016	1994
Thalberg, Sigismond	Fantasy on Donizetti's Don Pasquale	Danacord: 429	1994
Vallier, John	Toccatina	Hyperion: CDA67275	2001

Composer	Title	Label and Catalog No.	Date recorded
Villa-Lobos, Heitor	As três Marias	Hyperion: CDA67176	1999
	Rudepoêma Suites Nos. 1, 2: A Prole do Bebê		
Wolpe, Stefan	Battle Piece	New World: 354	1987
Woods, Edna Bentz	Valse phantastique	Hyperion: CDA67275	2001
Wright, Maurice	Sonata	New World: 378	1987
	Sonata No. 2	CRI: 660	1993
	Suite	CRI: 660	1993

Medtner

Beethoven	Sonata No. 23, Op. 57, Appassionata	APR: 5546	1946
Medtner	Three Arabesques, Op. 7:	APR: 5547	
	No. 2, Tragedy Fragment		1947
	No. 3, Tragedy Fragment		1936
	Canzona matinata, Op. 39, No. 4	APR: 5546	1931
	Danza festiva, Op. 38, No. 3	APR: 5546	1931
	Danza jubilosa, Op. 40, No. 4	APR: 5546	1931
	Three Hymns in Praise of Work, Op. 49, No. 1: Before Work	APR: 5546	1931
	Improvisation, Op. 31, No. 1	APR: 5547	
	Novella, Op. 17, No. 1	APR: 5546	1931
	Tale, Op. 8, No. 1	APR: 5546	1931
	Tale, Op. 14, No. 2, March of the Paladin	APR: 5546	1930
	Tales, Op. 20, Nos. 1, 2	APR: 5546	1930
	Tales, Op. 26, Nos. 2, 3	APR: 5546	1931
	Tales, Op. 34, Nos. 2, 3	APR: 5547	1936
	Tale, Op. 51, No. 1	Dante: HPC130	1947
	Tale, Op. 51, No. 2	APR: 5546	1931

Composer	Title	Label and Catalog No.	Date recorded
	Tales, Op. 51, Nos. 3, 5	APR: 5546	1930

Rachmaninov

Composer	Title	Label and Catalog No.	Date recorded
Bach	Partita No. 4, BWV 828: Sarabande	BMG: 09026 61265	1925
Bach-Rachmaninov	Partita for Solo Violin, BWV 1006: Prelude, Gavotte and Gigue		1942
Beethoven	Thirty-Two Variations, WoO 80		1925
Beethoven–Anton Rubinstein	The Ruins of Athens: Turkish March		1925
Bizet, Georges–Rachmaninov	L'Arlésienne, Suite No. 1: Minuet		1922
Borodin, Alexander	Scherzo		1935
Chopin	Ballade, Op. 47		1925
	Mazurka, Op. 63, No. 3		1923
	Mazurka, Op. 68, No. 2		1935
	Nocturne, Op. 9, No. 2		1927
	Nocturne, Op. 15, No. 2		1923
	Scherzo, Op. 39		1924
	Sonata, Op. 35, Funeral March		1930
	Waltz, Op. 18		1921
	Waltz, Op. 34, No. 3		1920, 1922
	Waltz, Op. 42		1919
	Waltzes, Op. 64, Nos. 1–3		1919, 1921, 1923, 1927
	Waltz, Op. 69, No. 2		1923
	Waltz, Op. 70, No. 1		1921
	Waltz (E Minor), Op. posth.		1930
Chopin-Liszt	Polish Songs: The Maiden's Wish The Return Home		1942
Daquin, Louis-Claude	Le coucou		1920

Composer	Title	Label and Catalog No.	Date recorded
Debussy	Children's Corner		1921
	Dr. Gradus ad Parnassum		
	Serenade for the Doll		
	Golliwog's Cakewalk		
Dohnányi	Concert Étude, Op. 28, No. 6:		1921
	Capriccio		
Gluck, Christoph Willibald– Giovanni Sgambati	Orfeo ed Euridice: Mélodie, Dance of the Blessed Spirits		1925
Grieg	Waltz, Op. 12, No. 2		1951
	Elfin Dance, Op. 12, No. 4		
Handel, George Frideric	Keyboard Suite No. 5, The Harmonious Blacksmith		1936
Henselt	Étude caracteristique, Op. 2, No. 6: Si oiseau j'etais		1923
Kreisler, Fritz– Rachmaninov	Liebesfreud		1925, 1942
	Liebesleid		1921
Liszt	Concert Étude No. 2, Gnomenreigen		1925
	Hungarian Rhapsody No. 2		1919
	Polonaise No. 2		1925
Mendelssohn	Songs without Words, Op. 67, No. 4: Spinning Song		1920, 1928
	Études, Op. 104, Nos. 2, 3		1927
Mendelssohn- Rachmaninov	A Midsummer Night's Dream: Scherzo		1935
Moszkowski, Moritz	La jongleuse		1923
Mozart	Sonata No. 11, K. 331		
	Theme and Variations		1919
	Rondo alla turca		1925
Musorgsky, Modest– Rachmaninov	Sorochintsy Fair: Gopak		1925
Paderewski, Ignace	Humoresques de concert, Op. 14, No. 1: Menuet célèbre		1927
Rachmaninov	Daisies, Op. 38, No. 3		1940
	Études-Tableaux, Op. 33, Nos. 2, 7		1940

Composer	Title	Label and Catalog No.	Date recorded
	Étude-Tableau, Op. 39, No. 6		1925
	Five Pieces, Op. 3		
	Prelude		1919, 1921, 1928
	Melody		1940
	Polichinelle		1923
	Serenade		1922, 1936
	Lilacs, Op. 21, No. 5		1923, 1942
	Moment musical, Op. 16, No. 2		1940
	Oriental Sketch		1940
	Polka de V. R.		1919, 1921, 1928
	Ten Preludes, Op. 23		
	No. 5		1920
	No. 10		1940
	Thirteen Preludes, Op. 32		
	No. 3		1940
	No. 5		1920
	No. 6		1940
	No. 7		1940
	No. 12		1921
	Seven Pieces, Op. 10		
	Barcarolle		1919
	Humoreske		1940
Rimsky-Korsakov–Rachmaninov	Tale of Tsar Saltan, Op. 57: The Flight of the Bumblebee		1929
Saint-Saëns, Camille–Alexander Siloti	Carnival of the Animals: The Swan		1924
Scarlatti, Domenico–Carl Tausig	Sonata, L. 413, Pastorale		1919
Schubert	Impromptu, D. 899/Op. 90, No. 4		1925
Schubert-Liszt	Die schöne Müllerin: Das Wandern		
	Schwanengesang: Serenade		

Composer	Title	Label and Catalog No.	Date recorded
Schubert-Rachmaninov	Die schöne Müllerin: Wohin?		
Schumann	Carnaval, Op. 9		1929
Schumann-Tausig	Der Kontrabandiste		1942
Scriabin	Prelude, Op. 11, No. 8		1929
Strauss, Johann Jr.–Tausig	One Lives but Once, Op. 167		1927
Tchaikovsky	Humoresque, Op. 10, No. 2		1923
	The Seasons, Op. 37b, No. 11, November: Troika Drive		1920, 1928
	Waltz, Op. 40, No. 8		1923
Tchaikovsky-Rachmaninov	Lullaby, Op. 16, No. 1		1942

Scriabin

Composer	Title	Label and Catalog No.	Date recorded
Scriabin	Désir, Op. 57, No. 1	Russian Season: 788032	1910
	Étude, Op. 8, No. 12		
	Mazurka, Op. 40, No. 2		
	Poem, Op. 32, No. 1		
	Preludes, Op. 11, Nos. 1, 13, 14		
	Preludes, Op. 22, No. 1		

NOTES

All names, both quoted and incorporated by reference, have been spelled uniformly throughout this book for consistency, even though wide variants are often seen in reference materials. Rachmaninov, for example, spelled his name Rachmaninoff after he came to America; the Russian letter representing a "v" is pronounced as an "f" if it occurs at the end of a name or word. An exception has been made for composers' names in book or article titles, which are reproduced exactly as they appear in print.

All quotes by Lazar Berman, Norman Gentieu, Marc-André Hamelin, Alistair Hinton, Stephen Hough, Zoltán Kocsis, Boris Lvov, Radu Lupu, András Schiff, Harold C. Schonberg, Jane Swan, Earl Wild, and Krystian Zimerman are from interviews with the author, unless otherwise noted.

Notes to Preface

1. The Mighty Handful, a name coined in 1867, were Mily Balakirev, Alexander Borodin, César Cui, Modest Musorgsky, and Nikolai Rimsky-Korsakov. Also known as "The Five," they lobbied for the creation of what is now known as the Russian school. Fifty-three years later, France could boast of Les Six, which comprised a like-minded group of composers—Georges Auric, Louis Durey, Arthur Honegger, Darius Milhaud, Francis Poulenc, and Germaine Tailleferre—dedicated to furthering the aesthetic put forth by Erik Satie.
2. Sorabji 1947, 15.
3. Sorabji 1932a, 99.

Notes to Chapter 1

1. Sorabji 1932a, 215.
2. Sorabji 1957b.
3. Rapoport 1992, 32.
4. Smith 1976, 97.
5. Van Dieren 1935, 17.
6. Léon Kreutzer, *Revue et Gazette*, January 1846; in Smith 1976, 8.
7. Kreutzer, in Smith 1976, 38.

8. Alkan to Ferdinand Hiller; in Smith 1976, 56.
9. Lewenthal 1964b, 8.
10. Hamelin 1998, x.
11. Sorabji 1932a, 216.
12. Sorabji 1932a, 215.
13. Lewenthal 1964a, 44.
14. Schumann 1888, 317.
15. Sorabji 1932a, 216.
16. Schumann 1888, 317.
17. Schumann 1888, 486.
18. Sorabji 1932a, 215.
19. Sitwell 1934, 359.
20. Sorabji 1932a, 219.
21. Huneker 1970, 283.
22. Balthazar Claes, obiturary in *Le ménestrel,* 1 April 1888; in Smith 1976, 13.
23. Brown 1967, 41.
24. Bellamann 1924, 259.
25. Bellamann 1924, 262.
26. Busoni 1909, n.p.
27. Busoni to Emil Hertzka (director of Vienna's Universal Edition), 7 November 1910; in Beaumont 1987, 408.
28. Busoni to Harriet Lanier, 18 August 1915; in Beaumont 1987, 211.
29. Busoni to Harriet Lanier, 18 August 1915; in Beaumont 1987, 212.
30. Sorabji 1921b, 148–149. Though archaic today, Sorabji's use of the term "invert" reflects prevailing research at the time.
31. Whittall 1966b, 129.
32. Rapoport 1992, 259.
33. Sorabji 1930b, 7.
34. Sorabji 1930a, 137.
35. Sorabji 1947, 115.
36. Sorabji 1943c, 7.
37. Whittall 1966a, 216.
38. Busoni, letter of recommendation for Sorabji; in Beaumont 1987, 300.
39. Busoni to Emil Hertzka, Zurich, 5 January 1920; in Beaumont 1987, 303.
40. Busoni to Gerda, 25 November 1919; in Busoni 1938, 289.
41. Rapoport 1992, 40.
42. Sorabji 1955.
43. Sorabji to Philip Heseltine, 8 December 1913, on a performance of Scriabin's *Prometheus;* quoted in Rapoport 1992, 199.
44. Alistair Hinton, interview by the author, Bath, England, November 1999.
45. Stephen Hough, interview by the author, London, March 2000.
46. Williams 1922.
47. Collingwood 1930.
48. Sorabji 1924b.
49. Antcliffe 1951.
50. Gray-Fiske 1934, 190.
51. Blom, 1930, 17.
52. Sorabji 1938, 313.
53. Morrison 1977.
54. Sorabji 1958.
55. Hinton, interview.
56. Sorabji 1932a, 213.
57. Arnold Schoenberg to Emil Hertzka, 31 January 1914; in Stein 1964, 46.

Notes to Chapter 2

1. Busoni to Egon Petri, April 1916; in Dent 1933, 230.
2. Busoni 1957, 53.
3. Busoni to Harriet Lanier, 6 August 1915; in Beaumont 1987, 207.
4. Busoni 1962, 76.
5. Busoni, diary entry, 8 October 1914; in Beaumont 1987, 187.
6. Busoni to Edith Andreae, 23 June 1915; in Beaumont 1987, 203.
7. Pasternak 1972.
8. Busoni to the editor of *Melos,* 17 January 1922; in Busoni 1957, 27.
9. Busoni to Gerda, 20 July 1898; in Busoni 1938, 30.
10. Busoni 1957, 80.
11. Busoni to Egon Petri, 14 September 1912; in Beaumont 1987, 154.
12. Busoni 1962, 102.
13. Cooke 1917, 106.
14. Busoni to Gerda, 5 September 1911; in Busoni 1938, 198.
15. Busoni, in Cooke 1917, 98.
16. Busoni 1957, 19.
17. Saleski 1927, 299.
18. Busoni 1962, 88.
19. Busoni to Gerda, 16 June 1908; in Busoni 1938, 132–133.
20. Busoni 1962, 92.
21. Schonberg 1951.
22. Rattalino 1989, 80.
23. Busoni 1962, 77.
24. Dent 1933, 110.
25. Pasternak 1972.
26. Busoni, *Lokal Anzeiger,* Berlin, 1906; in Busoni 1957, 104. This article was written for the 150th anniversary of Mozart's birth.
27. Busoni 1962, 79.
28. Busoni 1957, 47.
29. Busoni to Gerda, 20 July 1898; in Busoni 1938, 28.
30. Rattalino 1989, 83.
31. Busoni 1957, 53.
32. Busoni 1962, 91.
33. Busoni to Gerda, 10 February 1902; in Busoni 1938, 54.
34. Busoni, in Goodwin 1968.
35. Busoni to Egon Petri, quoting from a St. Petersburg review, 28 November 1913; in Beaumont 1987, 174.
36. Busoni to Robert Freund, 16 November 1904; in Beaumont 1987, 72.
37. Busoni to Egon Petri, 28 November 1913, in Beaumont 1987, 174.
38. Busoni to José Vianna da Motta, 27 September 1916, in Beaumont 1985, 103.
39. Busoni to Scriabin, 1913, in *Alexander Scriabin, 1915–1940: Collection for the Twenty-Fifth Anniversary of the Composer's Death* (Moscow, 1940), 234; reprinted in Rudakova and Kandinsky 1984, 108.
40. Sorabji 1932a, 29.
41. Busoni 1962, 84.
42. Busoni 1957, 47.
43. Busoni 1957, 49.
44. Busoni 1957, 48.
45. Busoni to Hugo Leichtentritt, 25 February 1914; in Beaumont 1987, 177.
46. Busoni to Gerda, 21 March 1910; in Busoni 1938, 163.
47. Sorabji 1934c, 42.

48. Busoni to Egon Petri, 5 July 1917; in Beaumont 1987, 263.
49. Busoni, Berlin, 20 November 1920, in *Von der Einheit der Musik* (1922); in Busoni 1957, 132.
50. Weiss 1975.
51. Kammerer 1955.
52. Sorabji 1924c.
53. Sorabji 1924c.
54. Rubinstein 1973, 31–32.
55. André Watts, in Mach 1991, 187.
56. Godowsky, quoted in Cooke 1953, 62.
57. Godowsky to Maurice Aronson, 15 July 1901; in Nicholas 1989, 56.
58. Flesch 1958, 202–203.
59. Busoni to Gerda, 20 November 1919; in Busoni 1938, 287.
60. Godowsky, letter; in Nicholas 1999.
61. Godowsky to W. S. B. Matthews, 24 December 1900; in Nicholas 1989, 50.
62. Maurice Aronson, "Forty-Two Years with Godowsky," unpublished manuscript; reprinted in Nicholas 1989, 95.
63. Hofmann 1915.
64. Godowsky to Maurice Aronson, 14 November 1927, in Nicholas 1989, 132.
65. Nicholas 1989, 132.
66. Godowsky to Maurice Aronson, 17 November 1923; in Nicholas 1989, 115.
67. Godowsky to Maurice Aronson, 22 January 1924; in Nicholas 1989, 118.
68. Chasins 1967, 29.
69. Wechsberg 1956, 64.
70. Nicholas 1989, 100.
71. Godowsky, in Nicholas 1989, 87.
72. Godowsky, in Nicholas 1989, 97.
73. Godowsky, "Where Technique and Mechanics Differ"; quoted in Brower 1923.
74. Quoted by Busoni in letter to Gerda, 15 March 1911; in Busoni 1938, 191.
75. Godowsky 1933b, 737.
76. Flesch 1958, 201.
77. Chasins 1961, 59.
78. Adler 1953.
79. Huneker 1919.
80. Huneker 1919.
81. Adler 1963, 4.
82. Shaw 1949, 19.
83. Sorabji 1927a.
84. Sorabji 1927a.
85. Saleski 1927, 317.
86. Saleski 1927, 316.
87. Cooke 1953, 26.
88. Saleski 1927, 317.
89. Godowsky, "Foreword to the Miniatures"; in Nicholas 1989, 106.
90. Saleski 1927, 317, 318.
91. Godowsky, in Nicholas 1989, 108.
92. Godowsky 1995, vii.
93. Godowsky to Maurice Aronson, 21 March 1929; in Nicholas 1989, 137.
94. Godowsky to Maurice Aronson, 19 February 1929; in Nicholas 1989, 136.
95. Godowsky 1995, vii.
96. Godowsky, quoted in "Criticizes Music," 1924.
97. Chasins 1961, 35.
98. Godowsky to Paul Howard, May 1933; in Adler 1953.

99. Godowsky 1921, n.p.
100. Godowsky, quoted in Saleski 1927, 317.
101. Busoni to Gerda, 4 March 1906 (while Busoni was visiting his home town of Trieste in the "unchanged surroundings of his childhood"); in Busoni 1938, 95.
102. Busoni to Harriet Lanier, 4 May 1915 (one week after Scriabin's death), in Beaumont 1987, 197.
103. Busoni to H. W. Draber, 21 January 1913; in Beaumont 1987, 158.
104. Busoni to Egon Petri, 20 April 1913, in Beaumont 1987, 163.
105. Godowsky to Maurice Aronson, 22 January 1924; in Nicholas 1989, 115.
106. Busoni 1957, 50.
107. Godowsky to Paul Howard, May 1933; quoted in Adler 1953, 5.
108. Godowsky 1933a, 710.

Notes to Chapter 3

1. Boris Lvov, interview by Anzhela Reno, Moscow, October 1997; transcribed by Reno and the author.
2. Lvov, interview.
3. Merzhanov 1984.
4. Review of Feinberg concert, *Hamburgerfremdenblatt,* 2 September 1927; reprinted in Bunin 1999, 58.
5. Holcman 1961, 55.
6. Feinberg 1969, 63.
7. Feinberg 1999, 19.
8. Feinberg 1969, 534.
9. Belaiev 1925, 327.
10. Lazar Berman, interviews by Anzhela Reno and the author, Italy, October 1997.
11. Feinberg 1969, 59.
12. Radu Lupu, interview by the author, New York, January 2000.
13. Berman, interviews.
14. Holcman 1961, 55.
15. Leonid Feinberg, in Bunin 1999, 37.
16. Belaiev 1925, 328.
17. Feinberg, in Bunin 1999, 22.
18. Letter from Feinberg's mother Anna, 27 March 1913; in Bunin 1999, 26. Feinberg retained neither correspondence nor his invariably positive concert reviews, but he lovingly kept all the letters and postcards he received from his mother.
19. Feinberg 1999, 13.
20. Alexandrov 1924, 131.
21. Feinberg 1999, 14–15.
22. Belaiev 1925, 331.
23. Tatyana Nikolayeva, in Merzhanov 1984, 64.
24. Bunin 1999, 62.
25. Belaiev 1925, 329.
26. Maurice Aronson, "Forty-Two Years with Godowsky"; manuscript excerpt reprinted in Nicholas 1989, 60.
27. Rubinstein 1973, 164.
28. Schloezer 1987, 107.
29. Schloezer 1987, 62.
30. Schloezer 1987, 127.
31. Schloezer 1987, 123.
32. Feinberg 1969, 138.

33. Holmes 1990, 133.
34. Busoni, in Dent 1933, 271.
35. Busoni, 19 November 1912; in Busoni 1938, 215.
36. Somer 1973, 33, 34.
37. Myers 1957, 17–18.
38. Runciman 1915, 151–159 passim.
39. Swan 1973, 154.
40. Feinberg 1969, 107–108.
41. Swan 1973, 148; reprinting Safonov's recollections in Julius Engel's Scriabin biography *Musical Contemporary,* 1916.
42. Pasternak 1972, 1173.
43. Feinberg 1969, 111.
44. Seroff 1950, 169.
45. Grigori Prokofiev, review in the *Russian Musical Gazette,* 1915; quoted in Bowers 1973, 197.
46. Feinberg 1969, 106–112.
47. Quoted from Scriabin's private notebooks in Slonimsky 1949, 115.
48. Leonid Sabaneyev, *Reminiscences of Scriabin* (Moscow, 1925); quoted in Rudakova and Kandinsky 1984, 82.
49. Feinberg 1969, 110.
50. Schloezer 1987, 86.
51. Bowers 1973, 180.
52. Bowers 1973, 181.
53. Bowers 1996, 244–245.
54. Bowers 1996, 337.
55. Schloezer 1987, 132.
56. Sabaneyev, 167.
57. Bowers 1973, 6.
58. Bowers 1973, 180.
59. Sorabji 1914.
60. Sorabji 1957a, 668.
61. Runciman 1915.
62. Busoni, *Lokal Anzeiger,* Berlin, 1906, in Busoni 1957, 104.
63. Alexandrov 1924, 132.

Notes to Chapter 4

1. Frank 1958.
2. Swan 1967, 81.
3. Swan 1967, 81.
4. Swan and Swan 1944a, 7.
5. Swan and Swan 1944a, 7.
6. Rachmaninov to Marietta Shaginian; reprinted in Seroff 1950, 143.
7. Lermontov 1965, 14.
8. Swan 1967, 67.
9. Anna Medtner, "A Short Biography"; in Holt 1955, 18.
10. Arthur Alexander, "Medtner as Pianist"; in Holt 1955, 93.
11. Swan 1967, 75.
12. Eric Prehn, "Medtner and Art"; in Holt 1955, 190.
13. Charlton 1989, 457.
14. Jane Swan, interview by the author, Haverford, Pennsylvania, September 1999.
15. Madeleine LaLiberté (who knew Rachmaninov personally), as told to Hamelin.

16. Private conversation with Wilfrid van Wyck; in Martyn 1990, 26.
17. Swan 1973, 179.
18. Busoni to Gerda, 5 September 1911, in Busoni 1938, 198.
19. Sorabji 1931.
20. Tatiana Makushina, "Memories of Recital Work with Medtner"; in Holt 1955, 116.
21. Vladimir Pohl, "Fragrant Memories—The Last Songs"; in Holt 1955, 215.
22. Busoni to H. W. Draber, 9 April 1919; in Beaumont 1987, 284.
23. Swan, unnumbered note; in Medtner 1951, 17.
24. Konstantin Klimov, "The Last Instrumental Composition"; in Holt 1955, 206.
25. Sorabji 1944b.
26. Sorabji, "The Greatness of Medtner"; reprinted in Holt 1955, 123.
27. Sorabji, "The Greatness of Medtner"; reprinted in Holt 1955, 124.
28. Swan 1927, 54.
29. Sorabji, "The Greatness of Medtner"; reprinted in Holt 1955, 127.
30. Swan and Swan 1944a, 8.
31. Pinsonneault 1956, 29.
32. Medtner 1951, 145.
33. Swan and Swan 1944a, 8.
34. Swan 1973, 172.
35. Prokofiev 1979, 223.
36. Gerstle 1924, 510.
37. Gerstle 1924, 502.
38. Sorabji 1932a, 136.
39. Holt 1951, 150.
40. Gentieu 1990, 105.
41. Sorabji, "The Greatness of Medtner"; reprinted in Holt 1955, 129.
42. Sorabji 1934b.
43. Sorabji, "The Greatness of Medtner"; reprinted in Holt 1955, 129.
44. Gentieu 1990, 108. This quote is from a paper delivered at a Medtner Society Meeting by Gentieu in October 1984, Lexington, Ky. The talk was entitled: "The Art of Nikolai Medtner: An Appreciation by Kaikhosru Sorabji." The words were by Sorabji; their sequence and addenda were by Gentieu, all with Sorabji's enthusiastic permission and encouragement.
45. Sorabji 1932c.
46. Sorabji, "The Greatness of Medtner"; reprinted in Holt 1955, 131.
47. Sorabji 1932a, 137.
48. Schonberg 1992, 104.
49. Swan 1973, 179.
50. Seroff 1950, 168.
51. Prokofiev 1991, 253.
52. Robinson 1998, 126.
53. Prokofiev 1991, 253.
54. Rachmaninov to Medtner, 9 September 1926; in Apetian 1972, 548.
55. Sorabji 1944a.
56. Ernest Newman, "Account of a Medtner Recital in London"; reprinted in Holt 1955, 41.
57. Holt 1951, 149.
58. Holt 1955, 230.
59. Sorabji 1932a, 136.
60. Roy 1927, 16.
61. In Vasiliev 1959, n.p.
62. Swan and Swan 1944a, 7.
63. Swan and Swan 1944b, 183.

64. Medtner to Eric Prehn, December 19, 1941; in Holt 1955, 191.
65. Rachmaninov 1928, 298.
66. Roy 1927, 16.
67. Roy 1927, 16.
68. Blom 1954, 27.
69. Godowsky to Maurice Aronson; in Nicholas 1989, 67.
70. Leonard 1957, 246.
71. Sorabji 1935, 520.
72. Moiseiwitsch 1963.
73. Sorabji 1929b.
74. Sorabji 1924d.
75. Chaliapin 1967, 279.
76. Harold Schonberg, interview by the author, New York, March 1999.
77. Rubinstein 1980, 88.
78. Earl Wild, interview by the author, Columbus, Ohio, September 1999.
79. Medtner; reprinted in Holmes 1990, 115.
80. Swan and Swan 1944b, 174.
81. Swan and Swan 1944b, 174.
82. Quoted in Seroff 1950, 169.
83. Scriabin to Asafiev; in Bowers 1996, 227.
84. Prokofiev 1991, 253.
85. Roy 1927, 16.
86. Sorabji 1924d.
87. *New York Times*, 1 December 1924.
88. Sorabji 1928b.
89. Rachmaninov 1923, 223.
90. Roy 1927, 16.
91. Rachmaninov to Morozov, 2 July 1904; in Seroff 1950, 88.
92. Seroff 1950, 89.
93. Seroff 1950, 65.
94. Swan and Swan 1944b, 177.
95. Roy 1927, 16.
96. Roy 1927, 16.
97. Seroff 1950, 1.
98. Chaliapin 1967, 278.
99. Medtner, in Vasiliev 1959, 5.
100. Swan and Swan 1944a, 18.
101. Stravinsky and Craft 1959, 43.
102. Swan and Swan 1944b, 177.
103. Henderson 1954, 9.
104. Moiseiwitsch 1963.
105. Leonard 1957, 246.
106. Swan and Swan 1944a, 3.
107. Chasins 1961, 41.
108. Medtner, quoted in Swan and Swan 1944a, 7.
109. Medtner 1951, 98.
110. Seroff 1950, 141.
111. Seroff 1950, 142.
112. Marietta Shaginian, article accompanying Rachmaninov's letters; reprinted in Seroff 1950, 153.
113. Chasins 1961, 15.
114. Holmes, *Composers on Composers*, 85; in Bertensson and Leyda 1956, 137.
115. Nicholas 1989, 107.

116. Elder 1973, 13.
117. Swan and Swan 1944a, 2.
118. Swan and Swan 1944b, 176.
119. Swan and Swan 1944a, 5.
120. Chasins 1967, 43.
121. Rachmaninov to Fritz Kreisler; in Chasins 1967, 42.
122. Moiseiwitsch 1963.
123. Moiseiwitch 1963.
124. Elder 1973, 14.
125. Seroff 1950, 154.
126. Swan and Swan 1944b, 186.
127. Swan and Swan 1944a, 9.
128. Sorabji 1961.
129. Sorabji 1943c.
130. Sorabji 1928c.
131. Medtner 1951, 100.
132. Medtner 1951, 14.
133. Sorabji, "The Greatness of Medtner"; in Holt 1955, 131–132.
134. Rachmaninov 1928.
135. Leonard, "A History of Russian-Soviet Music," 253; in Keldysh 1954, 3:352.
136. Rachmaninov 1923.
137. Holmes, *Composers on Composers,* 20; in Bertensson and Leyda 1956, 145.
138. Rachmaninov 1928.
139. Sorabji to Norman Gentieu, 20 June 1984; in Gentieu 1990, 103.
140. Rachmaninov 1928.
141. Swan 1973, 181.
142. Prokofiev 1991, 244–245.
143. Henderson 1954, 14.

Notes to Chapter 5

1. Ross 2000, 104.
2. Neuhaus 1993, 105.
3. Clements 1996.
4. Ross 2000, 102.
5. Walter Gieseking (1895–1956) was famous in his era as an inimitable interpreter of the music of Debussy and Ravel. His ethereal sound and touch remain legendary.
6. Ross 2000, 102.
7. Godowsky, in the *Musical Observer,* May 1920; quoted in Nicholas 1989, 70.
8. Hamelin 1989.
9. Bowers 1996, 255.
10. Griffiths 2000.
11. Busoni 1957, 53.
12. Barenboim 1991, 169–170.
13. Godowsky to Maurice Aronson, 13 March 1902; in Nicholas 1989, 62.
14. Barenboim 1991, 67.
15. Swan and Swan 1944a, 8.
16. Hamelin 1993.
17. Dent 1933, 100.
18. Swan and Swan 1944a, 9.
19. In a late-twentieth-century perspective on money and the arts, Norman Lebrecht, *When the Music Stops* (Great Britain: Simon and Schuster, 1996; published in the

United States as *Who Killed Classical Music* [Secaucus, N.J.: Birch Lane Press, 1997]), presents sharp, controversial arguments on the subject.
20. Pavarotti 1997.
21. Godowsky to W. S. B. Matthews, 24 December 1900; in Nicholas 1989, 50.

Notes to Chapter 6

1. Schopenhauer 1966, 448.
2. Sorabji 1947, 15.
3. Wilde 1997, 12.
4. Steane 1985.
5. Sorabji 1932a, 22–23.
6. Sorabji 1932a, 169.
7. Sorabji 1932a, 171.
8. Sorabji 1934a.
9. Kaiser 1971, 11.
10. Sorabji 1943a, 150.
11. Sorabji 1943b, 200.
12. Antcliffe 1951.
13. Sorabji 1921a.
14. Sorabji 1932a, 24–25.
15. Sorabji 1925a, 564.
16. Bechert 1922.
17. Reprinted in Charlton 1989, 423.
18. Runciman 1915.
19. Schwarz 1972, 72.
20. Sorabji 1921a, 417.
21. Bellamann 1924, 257.
22. Godowsky 1933b, 784.
23. Sorabji 1932b, 124.
24. Wilde 1997, 27–28.
25. Sorabji 1947, 174–176.
26. Sorabji 1932b, 124.
27. Flesch 1958, 234.
28. Hamelin concert, New York City, 9 May 1996.
29. Sullivan 1996, 52.
30. Ross 1996.
31. Busoni, reply originally published in the (Berlin) *Vossische Zeitung* (June 1917); in Busoni 1957, 18.
32. Sorabji 1928a.
33. Sorabji 1947, 64.
34. Sorabji 1947, 70.
35. Paddack 1953, 13.
36. Sorabji 1941.
37. Mackenzie 1930.
38. Sorabji 1924d, 309.
39. Sorabji 1932b, 124–125.
40. Sorabji 1947, 171–172.
41. Busoni (quoting letter from George Bernard Shaw) to Gerda, 28 November 1919; in Busoni 1938, 289.
42. Sorabji 1927b.
43. Swan and Swan 1944b, 175.

44. Sorabji 1947, 177.
45. Cooke 1917, 139–140.
46. MacDiarmid 1966, 66–67.
47. Newman 1925, 95.
48. Godowsky to Maurice Aronson, 30 September 1900, in Nicholas 1989, 46.
49. Godowsky to Maurice Aronson, 19 April 1902, in Nicholas 1989, 61.
50. Busoni 1957, 131
51. Beaumont 1987, 72.
52. Sorabji 1925b.
53. Sorabji 1943c.
54. Wechsberg 1956, 64.
55. Leopold Godowsky, Jr., in Wechsberg 1956, 64.
56. Godowsky to Maurice Aronson, 19 April 1902; in Nicholas 1989, 61.
57. Sorabji 1947, 142–143.

Notes to Chapter 7

1. Sorabji 1943a, 151.
2. Feinberg 1969, 161.
3. Sorabji 1936, 413.
4. Sorabji 1943a, 151.
5. Feinberg 1969, 161.
6. Busoni to Hans Huber, 16 January 1917; in Beaumont 1987, 253.
7. Feinberg 1969, 163–164.
8. Newman 1958, 160.
9. Feinberg 1969, 161.
10. Feinberg 1969, 163.
11. Rachmaninov 1923.
12. Busoni 1957, 180; originally published as "Art and Technique," *Signale* 35 (August 1909).
13. Feinberg 1969, 163.
14. Busoni 1957, 180.
15. Feinberg 1969, 162.
16. Godowsky in Nicholas 1989, 69–70.
17. Godowsky to Maurice Aronson, 21 March 1929; in Nicholas 1989, 137.
18. Sullivan 1996, 52.
19. Busoni, quoted in Goebels n.d., 9.
20. Busoni 1957, 94.
21. Hinderer 1933, 3.
22. Busoni to Arnold Schoenberg, in Beaumont 1987, 386.
23. Busoni 1957, 93.
24. Feinberg 1969, 161–163.
25. Sorabji 1921a, 417.
26. Sorabji 1921a, 418.
27. Busoni 1957, 80.
28. Busoni to Gerda, 21 October 1907; in Busoni 1938, 121.
29. Feinberg 1969, 161–163.
30. Godowsky, in Cooke 1917, 139.
31. Busoni 1962, 87.
32. Busoni to Hans Huber, 16 January 1917; in Beaumont 1987, 253.
33. Feinberg 1969, 164.

Notes to Chapter 8

1. Elder 1973, 14.
2. Roy 1927, 16.
3. Scriabin to Tatyana, 20 January 1905; in Bowers 1996, 30.
4. Scriabin to Tatyana, 8 May 1905; in Bowers 1996, 40.
5. Busoni to Gerda, 3 December 1909; in Busoni 1938, 153.
6. Busoni to Gerda, 9 November 1912; in Busoni 1938, 212.
7. Busoni to Gerda, 15 January 1921; in Busoni 1938, 302.
8. Busoni to Gerda, 20 February 1922; in Busoni 1938, 304.
9. Busoni to Gerda, 18 September 1913; in Busoni 1938, 231.
10. Roy 1927, 16.
11. Scriabin's private notebooks; in Slonimsky 1949, 122.
12. Scriabin, quoted in Nicholls 1996, 17.
13. Schloezer 1987, 17.
14. Bowers 1973, 180.
15. Leonid Sabaneyev, in Bowers 1996, 335.
16. Sorabji 1928d, 215.
17. Bowers 1973, 99.
18. Scriabin, in Bowers 1996, 2:54.
19. Scriabin to Tatyana, 20 January 1905; in Bowers 1996, 2:30.
20. Scriabin to Alexander Goldenweiser; in Bowers 1973, 179–180.
21. Sorabji to Philip Heseltine, 8 December 1913; quoted in Rapoport 1992, 199.
22. Busoni 1962, 99.
23. Quoted in Bowers 1996, 2:133.
24. Busoni 1979, 22.
25. Busoni to Gerda, 22 July 1902; in Busoni 1938, 58.
26. Busoni to Philipp Jarnach, 7 June 1920; in Beaumont 1987, 311.
27. Dmitri Mitropoulos, interview; in Schonberg 1951. The eminent conductor had been a pupil of Busoni's.
28. Busoni 1962, 98.
29. Busoni 1957, 11.
30. Busoni 1957, 21.
31. Sorabji 1921a.
32. Sorabji 1932a, 227–231 passim.

Notes to Chapter 9

1. Busoni 1957, 88.
2. Translation reproduced in Smith 1987, 175.
3. Busoni 1957, 96.
4. Busoni 1962, 75.
5. Zoltán Kocsis, interview by the author, Budapest, Hungary, December 1999.
6. From Busoni's introduction to the Bach edition for Breitkopf und Härtel, October 1915; reprinted in Busoni 1957, 98.
7. Busoni, as told to Dent; in Dent 1933, 39.
8. Busoni 1957, 87.
9. Sorabji 1932a, 163.
10. Busoni 1962, 85.
11. Busoni to Gerda, 22 July 1913, in Busoni 1957, 95.
12. Busoni 1957, 87.
13. Busoni 1957, 88.

14. Sorabji 1940, 109.
15. Sorabji 1947, 69, 68.
16. Hamelin 2000, 11.
17. Engel 1923.
18. Sorabji 1942, 178.
19. Godowsky 1995, vii.
20. Hamelin, spoken remarks before an encore, Merkin Concert Hall, New York, 4 June 1996.
21. Godowsky 1995, iv.
22. Goldsmith 1997, 10–11.
23. Godowsky to Frieda Godowsky, 22 July 1926; in Nicholas 1989, 127.
24. Sorabji 1925a, 563.
25. Sorabji 1924c.
26. Sorabji 1929a.
27. Godowsky 1995, viii.
28. Feinberg 1969, 39–40.
29. Arnold Schoenberg to Busoni, 24 August 1909; in Beaumont 1987, 392–394.
30. Feinberg 1969, 38–39.
31. Sorabji 1947, 62.
32. Godowsky, quoted in Chasins 1967, 58.
33. Godowsky 1924, n.p.
34. Feinberg 1969, 41.
35. Feinberg 1969, 37–38.

Notes to Chapter 10

1. Rachmaninov 1923.
2. Godowsky to Maurice Aronson, 10 July 1931; in Nicholas 1989, xxvii.
3. Godowsky 1933a, 710.
4. Godowsky 1995, vii.
5. Busoni 1957, 79.
6. Sorabji 1955.
7. Busoni to Gerda, 28 July 1907; in Busoni 1938, 114.
8. Rachmaninov 1928.
9. Krystian Zimerman, interview by the author, Basel, Switzerland, May 2000.
10. Busoni 1957, 80.

BIBLIOGRAPHY

Adler, Clarence. 1953. Unusual disciple and his master. *New York Times*, 5 July.

————. 1963. Leopold Godowsky. *Piano Teacher* (July–August): 2–4.

Alexandrov, Anatoly. 1924. S. E. Feinberg. *Sovremennaya Muzika* [Contemporary Music] (November–December): 129–132.

Antcliffe, Herbert. 1951. Music is not esoteric. *Musical Opinion* (March): 271.

Apetian, Z. A. 1972. *N. K. Medtner: Pis'ma* [Letters]. Moscow: Sovyetski Compositor.

Barenboim, Daniel. 1991. *A Life in Music*. New York: Charles Scribner's Sons.

Beaumont, Antony, ed. 1985. *Busoni the Composer*. Bloomington: Indiana University Press.

————. 1987. *Ferruccio Busoni: Selected Letters*. New York: Columbia University Press.

Bechert, Paul. 1922. Persian composer-pianist baffles. *Musical Courier* (2 March): 7.

Belaiev, Victor. 1925. Contemporary Russian composers, chapter two: Samuel Feinberg. *Sackbut* (June): 326–329.

Bellamann, Henry H. 1924. The piano works of C. V. Alkan. *Musical Quarterly* 10 (April): 251–262.

Bertensson, Sergei, and Jay Leyda. 1956. *Sergei Rachmaninoff: A Lifetime in Music*. New York: New York University Press.

Blom, Eric. Music review. *Manchester Guardian*, 17 January 1930, 17.

Blom, Eric, ed. 1954. *Grove's Dictionary of Music and Musicians*. 5th ed. Vol. 7. New York: St. Martin's Press.

Bloom, Peter, ed. 1987. La musique à Paris dans les années mil huit cent trente [Music in Paris in the 1830s]. In *Musical Life in Nineteenth-Century France*, vol. 4. Stuyvesant, N.Y.: Pendragon Press.

Bowers, Faubion. 1973. *The New Scriabin: Enigma and Answers*. New York: St. Martin's Press.

————. 1996. *Scriabin: A Biography*. New York: Dover Publications. (First published 1969. Tokyo and Palo Alto: Kodansha International.)

Brower, Harriette. 1923. Where technique and mechanics differ. *Musician* (September).

Brown, Peter. 1967. Lost cause? *Music and Musicians* (July): 41.

Bunin, Victor. 1999. *Samuel Evgenyevich Feinberg: Life and Creative Work.* Moscow: Muzyka.

Busoni, Ferruccio. 1909. Foreword. *Liszt: Complete Etudes.* Berlin: Breitkopf und Härtel.

———. 1938. *Letters to His Wife.* Translated by Rosamond Ley. London: Edward Arnold.

———. 1957. *The Essence of Music and other Papers.* Translated by Rosamond Ley. New York: Philosophical Library. Reprint: Westport, Conn.: Hyperion Press, 1979.

———. 1962. *Sketch of a New Aesthetic of Music.* New York: Dover. [Author's note: Dover's publication uses this title; however, a more accurate translation replaces the word "Sketch" with "Outline."]

Calvocoressi, Michel-Dmitri. 1974. *A Survey of Russian Music.* Westport, Conn.: Greenwood Press.

Carples, Esther. 1926. An aristocrat. *New Yorker,* 9 January, 15–16.

Chaliapin, Fyodor. 1967. *An Autobiography: As Told to Maxim Gorky.* New York: Stein and Day.

Charlton, David, ed. 1989. *E. T. A. Hoffmann's Musical Writings.* Translated by Martyn Clarke. Cambridge: Cambridge University Press. Reprinted with the permission of Cambridge University Press.

Chasins, Abram. 1967. *Speaking of Pianists.* 2d ed. New York: Alfred A. Knopf.

Clements, Andrew. 1996. Letting his fingers do the talking. *Guardian,* 15 January. Review of Hamelin concert at Wigmore Hall, London, 14 January 1996.

Collingwood, Arthur. 1930. Music in Scotland. *Musical Opinion* (May): 696.

Cooke, James Francis. 1917. *Great Pianists on Piano Playing.* Philadelphia: Theodore Presser.

———. 1953. The genius of Leopold Godowsky. *Etude* (April): 26, 62. © 1953, Theodore Presser Company, Used By Permission.

Cooper, Martin. 1951. *French Music.* New York. Oxford University Press.

"Criticizes Music in Small Cinemas." 1924. *New York Times,* 16 November.

Dawes, Frank. 1965. Alkan. *Musical Times* (August): 620.

Delaborde, E. M., and I. Philipp, eds. [1900?] *Selected Works for Piano by Ch. V. Alkan.* Paris: Costallat.

Dent, Edward J. 1933. *Ferruccio Busoni.* London: Oxford University Press.

Elder, Dean. 1973. Gina Bachauer: My study with Rachmaninoff. *Clavier* (October): 12–16.

Engel, Carl. 1923. Views and reviews. *Musical Quarterly* 9 (April): 299.

Feinberg, Samuel. 1969. *Pianism as Art.* 2d ed. Moscow: State Music Publishing House.

―――. 1999. *Feinberg: First Recordings, 1929–1948.* Arbiter CD 118.

Fere, Victor. 1927. S. E. Feinberg's performances in Germany. *Sovremennaya Muzika* [Contemporary Music] (December): 13–16.

Flesch, Carl. 1958. *The Memoirs of Carl Flesch.* Translated by Hans Keller. New York: Macmillan.

François-Sappey, Brigitte, ed. 1991. *Charles Valentin Alkan.* France: Librarie Arthème Fayard.

Frank, Jonathan. 1958. Rachmaninoff and Medtner: A Comparison. *Musical Opinion* (March): 387.

Garvelmann, Donald. 1969. A talk with Faubion Bowers about Scriabin. *Clavier* (November): 21–23.

Gentieu, Norman P. 1990. *La musique, c'est tout!* Philadelphia: Lowd, Peddle and Keaze.

Gerstle, Henry S. 1924. The piano music of Nicolai Medtner. *Musical Quarterly* 10 (October): 500–510.

Godowsky, Leopold. 1921. Preface. *Cadenzas for Mozart's Concerto in E-flat for 2 Pianos.* New York: Carl Fischer.

―――. 1924. Foreword. *Johann Sebastian Bach: Sonatas and Suites for Violin Solo and Violoncello Solo (Unaccompanied).* New York: Carl Fischer.

―――. 1933a. The best method is eclectic. *Etude,* part 1 (October): 645, 710.

―――. 1933b. The best method is eclectic. *Etude,* part 2 (November): 737, 784.

―――. 1995. Introductory remarks. *Studien über die Etüden von F. Chopin.* Berlin: Robert Lienau Musikverlag.

Goebels, Franzpeter, comp. n.d. The new Busoni: Introductory notes. *The Collected Exercises and Studies for the Piano,* part 1. Wiesbaden: Breitkopf und Härtel.

Goldsmith, Harris. 1997. Container insert notes. *Arcadi Volodos: Piano Transcriptions.* Sony Classical, SL 62691.

Goodwin, Noël. 1968. Busoni's Colossus. *Music and Musicians* (April): 23.

Gray-Fiske, Clinton. 1934. *New Age,* 15 February, 190.

Griffiths, Paul. 2000. Marc-André Hamelin: A sandwich of virtuoso works between ovations. *New York Times,* 5 December.

Grunfeld, Frederic V. 1949. Ferruccio Busoni. *Musical America* 69 (November).

Hamelin, Marc-André. 1989. Container insert notes. *Sorabji: Sonata No. 1.* Altarus AIR-CD9050.

―――. 1993. Introductory notes. *Hamelin: Prélude et fugue.* St. Nicolas, Quebec: Éditions Doberman-Yppan.

―――. 2000. Container insert notes. *Godowsky: The Complete Studies on Chopin's Etudes.* Hyperion CDA67411/12.

―――, comp. 1998. *Charles-Valentin Alkan: "Le festin d'Ésope" and Other Works for Solo Piano.* New York: Dover.

Henderson, A. M. 1954. Rachmaninoff as I knew him. *Etude* (April): 9, 14.

"H. H." 1952. In dual role [review of *Rachmaninoff* by Victor Seroff]. *Musical Opinion* (August): 665.

Hinderer, J. G. 1933. Happens there. *Musician* (July): 3–4.

Hofmann, Josef. 1915. Godowsky and his art. *Vanity Fair,* December, 42.

Holcman, Jan. 1961. The well-tempered Feinberg. *Saturday Review,* 25 November, 55.

Holmes, John L. 1990. *Composers on Composers.* Westport, Conn.: Greenwood Press.

Holt, Richard. 1951. Nicolas Medtner. *Gramophone* (December): 149–150.

———, ed. 1955. *Nicholas Medtner: A Tribute to His Art and Personality.* London: Dennis Dobson.

Hull, A. Eaglefield. 1916. *Scriabin: A Great Russian Tone-Poet.* London: Kegan Paul, Trench, Trubner.

Huneker, James Gibbons. 1919. A Brahma of the keyboard: Leopold Godowsky. *New York Times,* 27 April.

———. 1970 [1904]. *Overtones: A Book of Temperaments.* Freeport, N.Y.: Books for Libraries Press.

Kaiser, Joachim. 1971. *Great Pianists of Our Time.* New York: Herder and Herder.

Kammerer, Rafael. 1955. Philipp compares pianists: Past and Present. *Musical America* 75: 16.

Keldysh, J. 1954. *Istoriya Russkoy Musiki* [History of Russian Music]. Moscow: Muzgiz.

Leichtentritt, Hugo. 1917. Ferruccio Busoni as a composer. *Musical Quarterly* 3 (January): 69–97.

Leonard, Richard Anthony. 1957. *A History of Russian Music.* New York: Macmillan.

Lermontov, Mikhail. 1965. The angel. In *The Demon and Other Poems,* translated by Eugene M. Kayden. Yellow Springs, Ohio: Antioch Press.

Lewenthal, Raymond. 1964a. The Berlioz of the piano. *Musical America* 84 (February): 44.

———. 1964b. Prefatory notes. *The Piano Music of Alkan.* New York: G. Schirmer.

———. 1967. In Search of Alkan. *Music and Musicians* 15. (April): 37.

MacDiarmid, Hugh. 1966. *The Company I've Kept.* London: Hutchinson.

Mach, Elyse. 1991. *Great Contemporary Pianists Speak for Themselves.* New York: Dover.

Mackenzie, Compton. 1930. Reply to letter to the editor. *Gramophone* (August): 164.

Marmontel, Antoine. 1887. *Les pianistes célèbres: Silhouettes et medaillons.* 2d ed. Tours: Imprimerie Paul Bousrez.

Martyn, Barrie. 1990. *Rachmaninoff: Composer, Pianist, Conductor.* London: Scolar Press.

———. 1995. *Nicholas Medtner: His Life and Music.* London: Scolar Press.

Medtner, Nikolai. 1951. *The Muse and the Fashion.* Translated by Alfred J. Swan. Haverford, Pa.: Haverford College Bookstore. [Author's note: The Russian language contains no provision for articles such as "the." A more accurate translation of Medtner's book is *The Muse and Fashion.*]

Merzhanov, Viktor, comp. 1984. *Samuil Evgenyevich Feinberg.* Moscow: Sovyetski Compositor.

Moiseiwitsch, Benno. 1963. Reminiscences of Rachmaninoff. *Music Journal* 21 (January): 68.

Morrison, Bryce. 1974. Alkan the mysterious. *Music and Musicians* 22 (June): 30–32.

———. 1977. Pianists. *Music and Musicians* (September): 62.

———. 1996. [Review of Hamelin's recording of Scriabin sonatas.] *Gramophone* 74 (June): 72.

Myers, Rollo H. 1957. Scriabin: A reassessment. *Musical Times* (January): 17–18.

Neuhaus, Heinrich. 1993. *The Art of Piano Playing.* London: Kahn and Averill.

Newman, Ernest. 1925. *A Musical Motley.* New York: Alfred A. Knopf.

———. 1956. *Essays from the World of Music.* London: John Calder.

———. 1958. *More Essays from the World of Music.* London: John Calder.

Nicholas, Jeremy. 1989. *Godowsky: The Pianists' Pianist.* Northumberland: Appian Publications and Recordings.

———. 1999. Container insert notes. *Godowsky: Great Pianists of the 20th Century.* Vol. 38. Amsterdam: Philips Classics.

Nicholls, Simon. 1996. Container insert notes. Marc-André Hamelin, *Scriabin: The Complete Piano Sonatas.* Hyperion CDA67131/2.

Paddack, Christopher. 1953. The piano art of Ferruccio Busoni. *Etude* (September): 13, 51.

Paperno, Dmitri. 1998. *Notes of a Moscow Pianist.* Portland, Ore.: Amadeus Press.

Pasternak, Alexander. 1972. Skryabin: Summer 1903 and after. *Musical Times* (December): 1173.

Pavarotti, Luciano. 1997. Interview by Ralph Blumenthal. *New York Times,* 21 October.

Pinsonneault, Bernard. 1956. *Nicolas Medtner: Pianiste, compositeur.* Montréal: Editions Beauchemin.

Pirie, Peter J. 1972. The lost generation. *Music and Musicians* (May): 36–41.

Prokofiev, Sergei. 1979. *Prokofiev by Prokofiev: A Composer's Memoir.* Edited by David H. Appel. Translated by Guy Daniels. Garden City, N.Y.: Doubleday.

———. 1991. *Soviet Diary 1927 and Other Writings.* Edited and translated by Oleg Prokofiev. Boston: Northeastern University Press.

Rachmaninov, Sergei. 1923. New lights on the art of the piano. *Etude* (April): 223.

———. 1928. How Russian students work. *Etude* (May): 298.

Rapoport, Paul. 1992. *Sorabji: A Critical Celebration*. Brookfield, Vt.: Ashgate.

Rattalino, Piero. 1989. *Da Clementi a Pollini: Duecento anni con i grandi pianisti* [From Clementi to Pollini: Two Centuries with the Great Pianists]. 3d ed. Milan: Ricordi/Giunti.

Robinson, Harlow. 1998. *Selected Letters of Sergei Prokofiev*. Boston: Northeastern University Press.

Rosenfeld, Paul. 1939. Busoni in his letters. *Musical Quarterly* 25 (April): 226–231.

Ross, Alex. 1996. Marc-André Hamelin [review of a recital by Hamelin at Merkin Concert Hall, 9 May 1996, New York City]. *New York Times,* 14 May.

———. 2000. Extreme piano: Playing the unplayable. *New Yorker,* 18 December, 102–104.

Roy, Basanta Koomar. 1927. Rachmaninoff is reminiscent. *Musical Observer* (May).

Rubinstein, Arthur. 1973. *My Young Years*. New York: Alfred A. Knopf.

———. 1980. *My Many Years*. New York: Alfred A. Knopf.

Rudakova, Y., and A. Kandinsky. 1984. *Scriabin*. Neptune City, N.J.: Paganiniana Publications.

Runciman, John F. 1915. Noises, smells, and colors. *Musical Quarterly* 1 (April): 149–161.

Sabaneyev, Leonid. 1971. *Modern Russian Composers*. Translated by Judah A. Joffe. Freeport, N.Y.: Books for Libraries Press.

Saleski, Gdal. 1927. *Famous Musicians of a Wandering Race: Biographical Sketches of Outstanding Figures of Jewish Origin in the Musical World*. New York: Bloch.

Schloezer, Boris de. 1987. *Scriabin: Artist and Mystic*. Translated by Nicolas Slonimsky. Berkeley and Los Angeles: University of California Press.

Schonberg, Harold C. 1951. Recalling Busoni. *New York Times,* 7 October.

———. 1963. *The Great Pianists*. New York: Simon and Schuster.

———. 1964. Mystery man. *New York Times,* 4 October.

———. 1985. Rachmaninoff, the Russian master. In *The Virtuosi*. New York: Vintage Books.

———. 1992. *Horowitz: His Life and Music*. New York: Simon and Schuster.

Schopenhauer, Arthur. 1966. *The World as Will and Representation*. Vol. 2. Translated by E. F. J. Payne. New York: Dover.

Schumann, Robert. 1888. *Music and Musicians: Essays and Criticisms*. 2d series, 2d ed. Translated and edited by Fanny Raymond Ritter. London: William Reeves.

Schwarz, Boris. 1972. *Music and Musical Life in Soviet Russia*. Bloomington: Indiana University Press.

Seroff, Victor I. 1950. *Rachmaninoff*. New York: Simon and Schuster.

Shaw, Bernard. 1949. *Music in London*. Vol. 1. London: Constable. Used By Permission from England's Society of Authors, on behalf of the Bernard Shaw estate.

Sitsky, Larry. 1974. *Summary Notes for a Study on Alkan*. Studies in Music 8. Crawley, Western Australia: University of Western Australia, Department of Music.

———. 1994. *Music of the Repressed Russian Avant-Garde, 1900–1929.* Westport, Conn.: Greenwood Press.

Sitwell, Sacheverell. 1934. *Liszt.* Boston: Houghton Mifflin.

Slonimsky, Nicholas. 1949. *Music since 1900.* 3d ed. New York: Coleman-Ross.

Smith, Ronald. 1976. The enigma. *Alkan.* Vol. 1. London: Kahn and Averill.

———. 1987. The music. *Alkan.* Vol. 2. London: Kahn and Averill.

Somer, Hilde. 1973. To Alexander Scriabin, the prophet of peace, love and mysticism, my profound gratitude. *Piano Quarterly* 21 (Spring): 32–34.

Sorabji, Kaikhosru. 1914. Scriabin: To the editor. *Musical Standard* 3, no. 58 (7 February): 141.

———. 1921a. Contingencies. *Sackbut* (March): 418.

———. 1921b. Sexual inversion. *Medical Times* (October): 148–149.

———. 1924a. On neglected works. *Musical Times* (1 February): 127–129.

———. 1924b. Music. *New Age,* 12 June, 80.

———. 1924c. The death of Busoni. *New Age,* 14 August, 189.

———. 1924d. Music. *New Age,* 23 October, 308–309.

———. 1925a. The piano concerto in contemporary music. *Musical News and Herald* (13 June): 562–564.

———. 1925b. Music. *New Age,* 8 October, 271.

———. 1927a. Godowsky, Aeolian, February 26. *New Age,* 10 March, 225.

———. 1927b. Mr. Philip Levy, the Court House, November 28. *New Age,* 5 December, 81.

———. 1928a. Current musical criticism. *New Age,* 23 February, 198.

———. 1928b. Rachmaninov, Queen's Hall, May 19. *New Age,* 7 June, 70.

———. 1928c. Medtner Recital, Aeolian, February 16. *New Age,* 15 March, 236.

———. 1928d. *New Age,* 30 August, 215.

———. 1929a. Music. *New Age,* 3 October, 274.

———. 1929b. Rachmaninov, Albert Hall, Nov. 24, 1929. *New Age,* 5 December, 56.

———. 1930a. Music. *New Age,* 23 January, 137.

———. 1930b. *New Age,* 1 May, 7.

———. 1930c. Letter to the editor. *Gramophone* (August): 164.

———. 1931. *New Age,* 22 October, 296.

———. 1932a. *Around Music.* London: Unicorn Press.

———. 1932b. A letter of appreciation. *Musical Mirror and Fanfare* (May–June): 124–125.

———. 1932c. B.B.C. Symphony concerts. *New Age,* 3 March, 214.

———. 1932d. Rachmaninov, Philharmonic Society. *New Age,* 24 March, 250.

———. 1934a. The Busoni concerto, BBC, February 21. *New English Weekly,* 8 March, 495.

———. 1934b. Music. *New Age,* 5 April, 273.

———. 1934c. Concerts. *New English Weekly,* 25 October, 41–42.

———. 1935. New records. *New English Weekly,* 4 April, 520.

———. 1936. New records. *New English Weekly,* 5 March, 412–413.

———. 1937. Music in Italy today: Reflections from Rome. *Musical Times* (June): 501–502.

———. 1938. Alkan. *New English Weekly,* 27 January, 313.

———. 1940. Godowsky. *New English Weekly,* 20 June, 109.

———. 1941. Rachmaninoff and the English Critics. *New English Weekly,* 18 February, 198.

———. 1942. Music. *New English Weekly,* 5 March, 178.

———. 1943a. The way of the virtuoso. *Musical Opinion* (February): 150–151.

———. 1943b. Knob-twiddling. *New English Weekly,* 25 March, 199–200.

———. 1943c. Rachmaninov. *New English Weekly,* 22 April, 7.

———. 1944a. Music. *New English Weekly,* 20 January, 115.

———. 1944b. First performance: Third Piano Concerto, Medtner, R.A.H., February 19th. *New English Weekly,* 2 March, 167–168.

———. 1947. *Mi Contra Fa: The Immoralisings of a Machiavellian Musician.* London: Porcupine Press.

———. 1955. Music: Delusions and pathetic fallacies. *European,* March, 48.

———. 1957a. Broadcast music. *Musical Times* (December): 668.

———. 1957b. Letter to the editor. *Musical Opinion* (March): 333.

———. 1958. Letter to the editor. *Musical Times* (September): 490.

———. 1961. [Obituary of Clinton Gray-Fiske.] *Musical Times* 102 (July): 445.

Steane, John. 1985. English opera criticism in the interwar years: Sorabji of *The New Age. Opera* (June): 631.

Stein, Erwin, ed. 1964. *Arnold Schoenberg: Letters.* English translation by Eithne Wilkins and Ernst Kaiser. London: Faber and Faber.

Stravinsky, Igor, and Robert Craft. 1959. *Conversations with Igor Stravinsky.* Garden City, N.Y.: Doubleday.

Sullivan, Jack. 1996. Music in concert [review of Hamelin recital, 9 May 1996, New York]. *American Record Guide* (September–October): 52.

Swan, Alfred J. 1927. Medtner and the Music of our Time. *Music and Letters* (January): 46–54.

———. 1967. "Das Leben Nicolai Medtners" [The Life of Nikolai Medtner]. From offprint of *Musik des Ostens,* vol. 4, Anthologies of Herder Research Department for the History of Music. Kassel: Bärenreiter.

———. 1973. *Russian Music.* London: John Baker.

Swan, Alfred J., and Katherine Swan. 1944a. Rachmaninoff: Personal reminiscences (Part 1). *Musical Quarterly* 30 (January): 1–19.

———. 1944b. Rachmaninoff: Personal reminiscences (Part 2). *Musical Quarterly* 30 (April): 174–191.

Van Dieren, Bernard. 1935. *Down among the Dead Men.* London: Oxford University Press.

Vasiliev, Panteleymon. 1959. *Introduction to the Twelve-Volume Medtner Complete Works Edition.* Moscow: State Music Publishing House.

Wechsberg, Joseph. 1956. Whistling in the darkroom. *New Yorker,* 10 November, 61–109.

Weiss, Edward. 1975. Busoni: Essence of musical spirituality. *Music Journal* 33 (6 September): 46.

Whittall, Arnold. 1966a. Sorabjiana. *Musical Times* (March): 216–217.

———. 1966b. The isolationists. *Music Review* 27 (May): 122–129.

Widder, Rose Haberman. 1950. Godowsky and his pianistic philosophy. *Musical Courier* 142 (September): 7.

Wigmore, Richard. 2000. The sound and the soul. *Gramophone* (February): 10.

Wilde, Oscar. 1997 [1888]. *The Critic as Artist.* Copenhagen: Green Integer Books.

———. 1908. *Art and Morality: A Defence of "The Picture of Dorian Gray."* Edited by Stuart Mason (pseud.). London: Jacobs.

Williams, C. à Becket. 1922. Random notes on a recent European tour. *Musical Times* (1 May): 319.

Wimbush, Roger. 1966. Busoni. *Gramophone* (April): 486.

Wood, Henry J. 1938. *My Life of Music.* London: Victor Gollancz.

INDEX